THE MASTER

Sri Aurobindo and the Quest for National Education

THE MASTER

Sri Aurobindo and the Quest for National Education

Anirban Ganguly

Aryan Books International New Delhi

THE MASTER
Sri Aurobindo and the Quest for
National Education

ISBN: 978-81-7305-687-1

First Published 2023

Published by
Aryan Books International
Pooja Apartments, 4B, Ansari Road
New Delhi-110002 (India)
Tel.: 23287589, 23255799
Fax: 91-11-23270385
E-mail: aryanbooks@gmail.com
www.aryanbooks.com

Printed in India

Dedicated to

Dr. Syama Prasad Mookerjee

(1901-1953)

Educationist, Statesman, Patriot

Foreword

"

That alone will be a true and living education which helps to bring out to full advantage, makes ready for the full purpose and scope of human life all that is in the individual man, and which at the same time helps him to enter into his right relation with the life, mind, soul of the people to which he belongs and with that great total life, mind and soul of humanity of which he himself is a unit and his people or nation a living, a separate and yet inseparable member.

– **Sri Aurobindo**

Dr Anirban Ganguly ('Gangopadhyay', to give his surname its proper Sanskritised version) represents a comparatively rare breed of political personalities in the country, i.e. people who are by temperament and by training scholars but are at the same time well-grounded in the political realities of the land. I have read with interest the present book authored by him and realised that the research which has gone into its making is of outstanding historical merit.

Many of us have lived under the notion that in the emergent Indian nationalism of the late 19th and early 20th centuries, the primary focus of the nation's mind was on history, leading to a new awareness of its past. The author of the present book demonstrates with unerring accuracy and superb scholarship that the basic intellectual point of the early nationalist scheme was education, a passionate search for the shape it should take in newly resurgent India eager to appreciate the various nuances of national attitudes and feelings. The list of the concerned personalities and the enumeration and analysis of their writings, which have been marshalled by the author, are indeed breathtaking in scope and take our mind way above the relatively mundane world of historical writings.

Here Sri Aurobindo is the principal figure but here we do not have the philosopher Sri Aurobindo but the principal-educationist of the princely state of Baroda (1893-1906) under the rule of the enlightened Sayaji Rao whose name is irrevocably linked with the modern

Maharaja Sayaji Rao University of Baroda (modern Vadodara). The development and multifarious aspects of Sri Aurobindo's ideas and measures related to education have been studied in detail by the author but hardly less interesting is the range of the relevant thoughts of some of his contemporaries, Rabindranath Tagore and Sister Nivedita, for instance. In between we have Bankim Chandra Chattopadhyay (1838-1894), Raj Narayan Bose (1826-1899), Maharshi Dayananda Swami (1824-1883), Swami Shraddhananda (1856-1926), Annie Besant (1847-1933), Guru Das Banerjee (1844-1918), Brahma Bandhav Upadhyay (an associate of Rabindranath in the establishment of *Brahmacharyasram* in Santiniketan), Sarala Devi Ghoshal (1872-1945), Peary Chand Mitra (1814-1883), Bhudev Mukhopadhyay (1827-1894), Akshay Kumar Datta (1820-1886), and a host of other national luminaries of this broad period including Bepin Chandra Pal and Lala Lajpat Rai. Alongside, there are sections on 'western perceptions of Indian education' figuring the influence of George Birdwood, Ananda Coomaraswamy and John Woodroffe. In a sense, the culmination of all these thoughts on what could be considered an ideal base of Indian education was the establishment of the National Council of Education in Bengal in 1906 and its form and functions including the establishment of schools and colleges, of which the modern Jadavpur University is a successor. By putting forward the thoughts of these savants on education in general and Indian education in particular the author has laid open the vast canvas in which the thoughts of Sri Aurobindo assume their rightful place.

In a sense, what the author has done is to put forward a vast panorama of the educational thoughts of some of the true 'makers of modern India', although some modern Indian historians have been reluctant in recent years to accord them this status. It is gratifying to note that Dr Ganguly has not forgotten them and brought them forward along with Sri Aurobindo, the educational philosopher and reformer.

Dilip K Chakrabarti

Padma Shri, Emeritus Professor of South Asian Archaeology

University of Cambridge

Contents

"

The idea of hammering the child into the shape desired by the parent or teacher is a barbarous and ignorant superstition. It is he himself who must be induced to expand in accordance with his own nature. There can be no greater error than for the parent to arrange beforehand that his son shall develop particular qualities, capacities, ideas, virtues, or be prepared for a prearranged career.

– A System of National Education: Some Preliminary Ideas, ***Karmayogin*, 1910**

Acknowledgments

"

We must not take up the nature by the roots from the earth in which it must grow or surround the mind with images and ideas of a life which is alien to that in which it must physically move. If anything has to be brought in from outside, it must be offered, not forced on the mind.

– A System of National Education: Some Preliminary Ideas, ***Karmayogin*, 1910**

In my quest to complete this work on the occasion of Sri Aurobindo's 150th birth anniversary, I am grateful to Professor Indrani Sanyal, founder of the Centre for Sri Aurobindo Studies, Department of Philosophy, Jadavpur University, Kolkata. This work grew out of my thesis which I completed and defended, a decade ago, under her supervision, tutelage, support and encouragement.

I wish to also put on record my indebtedness to Shri Ajit Doval, K.C., National Security Advisor to the Prime Minister of India, who as Director of the premier nationalist think-tank Vivekananda International Foundation in New Delhi, a decade ago, had accorded me the scope, the ambience and the support to do research for this thesis besides my regular work as a research fellow at the Foundation under him.

My gratitude is also due to the Sri Aurobindo Ashram Trust at Puducherry for lending me rare photographs that have been included in this book.

I am grateful to eminent historian Padmashree Professor Dilip Kumar Chakrabarti, Professor Emeritus, South Asian Archaeology, University of Cambridge, for taking note of my thesis and for relentlessly goading me to revise it and get it published and for penning the foreword.

My deep appreciation of Shri Vikas Arya of Aryan Books International, for working with commitment and determination to complete the book and for believing that it has merit and value, especially in the context of the seventy-fifth year of India's independence and Sri Aurobindo's sesquicentennial.

Finally, my deep gratitude to my wife, Smt Anuttama Ganguly, Secretary, Vivekananda International Foundation, New Delhi, without whose unfailing, unwavering and undiminished support and faith, I would not have been able to bring myself around to complete this thesis a decade ago and to revise and rework on it a decade later and to eventually make it see the light of day.

Introduction

"

...Two aspects of Sri Aurobindo's philosophy of 'Revolution' and 'Evolution' are of key importance and should be emphasized. The youth should be encouraged towards the concept of greatness as embodied in the philosophy of Nar to Narayan to create a Maha Manav as propounded by Sri Aurobindo.

– Prime Minister Narendra Modi

I felt the utterance of the ancient Hindu Rishis spoke from him of that equanimity which gives the human soul its freedom of entrance into the All. I said to him, "You have the Word and we are waiting to accept it from you. India will speak through your voice to the world, 'Hearken to me.'"

– Gurudev Rabindranath Tagore

Much has been written on Sri Aurobindo, the revolutionary nationalist and on Sri Aurobindo, the revolutionary philosopher. I have taken a different line of exploration. My approach may be termed as an 'intellectual history' of my subject, Sri Aurobindo, who, during the period I have covered (1893–1910), was still the controversial Aurobindo Ghose – the firebrand political ideologue who had not yet metamorphosed into the unconventional philosopher-seer. I have attempted to explore Sri Aurobindo, or Aurobindo Ghose the educationist, the education activist, the educationist politician and the revolutionary educational seer.

Much has also been written, and commented upon Sri Aurobindo's theory, vision, and philosophy of education; I have tried to revisit and meditate upon his educational activism as it began, immediately after his return from the West (1893), continuing throughout his nationalist phase and ending only with his retirement from active politics. Keeping Sri Aurobindo as the central figure, I have also examined the educational thought and vision of a number of his nationalist and religious contemporaries or near-contemporaries. I have revisited the educational ideas that these thought-leaders presented before the people – then in their first visible stirrings for self-determination – in their quest for attempting to formulate a philosophy and a system of a national education. I have done this through a narrative of their ideas and of the age in which they evolved. This is where I see this approach as that of an 'intellectual history'.

It attempts to draw, through an exploration of ideas, a canvas of the age when Sri Aurobindo actively championed the cause of national education and emerged as one of its advanced thought-leaders and articulators. In that sense, this work has no central thesis; it undertakes, instead, a *tour d'horizon* of the educational thought of some of the nationalist thinkers who were Sri Aurobindo's political collaborators and attempts to define the nationalist education discourse of that period with Sri Aurobindo as the central figure. It examines in some detail Sri Aurobindo's demand for national education, through a study of his early educational writings (as for instance, during the period at Baroda between 1893 and 1906); it examines his political writings on education through a detailed survey of his writings in the popular nationalist daily *Bande Mataram* which he edited; it analyses his speeches on the subject and also looks briefly at his later writings, that is, post-1908, up until 1918, by which time he had retired to the French enclave of Pondicherry.

It does not examine separately, in the sequence of chapters, his educational writings in the *Karmayogin* (1909) which is where most of his educational formulations appeared, but rather weaves the major ideas expressed in its pages within the principal narrative itself. It may appear odd that I have not examined these separately, or that I have not tried to formulate a philosophy of national education through a study of these.

I have not done this, firstly, because such an examination has already been undertaken in the past by many able intellectuals and practitioners of Integral Education and Yoga, like Pavitra (P.B.Saint-Hilaire), Nolini Kanta Gupta, Jugal Kishore Mukherjee, Norman Dowsett, Pranab Kumar Bhattacharya, Madhav Pandit, and Kireet Joshi, all of whom had either direct access to Sri Aurobindo himself, or had been closely involved in assisting his spiritual collaborator, The Mother, in implementing the principles of his educational philosophy at the Centre of Education at Pondicherry, which bears his name. A re-examination of these explorations, therefore, would not be something different but a mere restating of stated positions.

Secondly, I have never been a student of philosophy in the strict sense of the term and therefore found it difficult to attempt to coalesce and synthesise Sri Aurobindo's philosophical perspectives with other formulations and positions. Thirdly, I have undertaken this approach because I realised that the period under discussion (1893–1910) with Sri Aurobindo as the central figure, has never been explored in the past through an examination of his principal educational ideas. Sri Aurobindo's national education activism found place, often a brief one at that, in most works on his life, his politics or even his educational vision. But there has never been an examination of the ideas, of the debate, of the positions on national education at the time when Sri Aurobindo was active as a leader of the nationalist party in Indian politics. Mine is a rather feeble attempt to do what that seminal work *The Origins of the National Education Movement* did, by keeping education reformer Acharya Satish Chandra Mukherjee as the central figure. I have tried to weave the narrative of this quest for a philosophy of national education keeping Sri Aurobindo at the centre, or as a point of reference. Perhaps in doing so, this approach is new and can shed some more light on the period under study.

The narrative also makes a detailed survey of Sri Aurobindo's stated positions on the nationalist educational demand. I have therefore, focused in some detail on his Baroda period in order to show that his educational formulations found first expressions in that clime and period, and have argued that throughout his professional stay in that princely state, Sri Aurobindo was preoccupied with the educational question as much as he was with the political. Such a collection has, to the best of my knowledge, not been made in the past. I have, in a sense, focused mainly on Sri Aurobindo, the politician-educationist rather than Sri Aurobindo, the philosopher-educationist. Politics, like spirituality, formed an integral part of Sri Aurobindo's life and action. He seemed to have never completely given up the former, albeit the forms and manners of his expressions of it kept altering from period to period.

Among Sri Aurobindo's other writings on education that I have attempted to study and analyse, are two of his opuscules, 'The Brain of India' and 'The National Value of Art'. Both were written as a series in the *Karmayogin* around 1909. These texts have never really been taken as part of the exploration of the national education movement. Philosopher and one of Sri Aurobindo's foremost interpreters, Jugal Kishore Mukherjee, discussed the 'Brain of India' to a certain extent in order to widen Sri Aurobindo's education principles,[1] and though excerpts from these articles have been used in the past, they do not seem to have been studied as part of the quest for formulating a philosophy of national education. I have stated separate positions based on these opuscules and have linked them to this quest.

Through both these writings, Sri Aurobindo added different dimensions to the nationalist education debate. In the 'Brain of India', he discusses the classical Indian perception of education – the past conceptions and theories of education in Hindu thought. A study of these enables us to understand Sri Aurobindo's position *vis-à-vis* the classical or ancient Indian educational thought, and to also see at what levels his formulations blend or differ from it. In

1. Jugal Kishore Mukherjee, *Principles and Goals of Integral Education*, 2006.

'Brain of India', he discusses in detail the concept of *Brahmacharya* and its past application and present relevance. This led me to discuss and examine some past concepts of education in India, and a discussion on the thoughts and views of cultural philosopher Ananda Coomaraswamy and Nivedita enhanced the exploration of this facet. I have, for instance, looked at the concept of memory in the past, the understanding of learning, the role of meditation etc. A study of these has revealed that the nationalist thought-leaders made a constant and continuous effort to absorb India's educational past in its spirit, ideas, and essence and tried to inculcate them into the present. They sought to revive the spirit of Indian education – the essence of learning, the method of approaching knowledge, concept of education and of being learned, and a whole gamut of other issues. Acharya Satish Chandra Mukherjee's widely acclaimed *Dawn* magazine regularly carried articles on ancient Indian education thought and principles, demonstrating the urge to re-examine India's past educational experience and to try and look for some direction from it for India's present.

In the 'National Value of Art', Sri Aurobindo essentially makes a case for the democratisation of art education in the country. He discusses why art and aesthetic education is necessary, and dwells on its indispensability in a national scheme of education. I examined in some detail here the nationalist art movement, also called the Swadeshi art movement, and to examine the art in education debate then going on. Some of the central figures in this debate, Nivedita and Coomaraswamy, were already part of my exploration and in order to broaden it, I included E.B.Havell, one of the most vigorous supporters of the Swadeshi art movement, and Abanindranath Tagore, who embodied the expressions of that movement. In this too, I sought to keep Sri Aurobindo as one of the key figures of the debate and have argued that it was through his series on the national value of art that Sri Aurobindo expressed support for the effort of re-discovering and re-stating the techniques of Indian art. I have also argued that in his demand for an aesthetic and art education, Sri Aurobindo did not set limits but called for the training in aesthetics for the entire 'race' – terms such as 'race' were then used frequently mainly to denote the collectivity and obviously not in a pejorative sense – for it was such training alone that could, argued Sri Aurobindo, really restore the sense of harmony and beauty in the nation as a whole. The linking of these articles on art with the broader Swadeshi art movement have not been done, at least in the context of Sri Aurobindo. This is an addition to that study.

Among some of the thinkers that I have covered are those who were once decisive opinion makers in the field of culture and education but who have gone into near oblivion, faced marginalisation, or have been confined to a limited discourse and circle. I have selected them because of their nearness in time to Sri Aurobindo, and at times because of their direct involvement with his nationalist activities. The selection has definitely not been made at random or without method. In this category falls Bipin Chandra Pal, once considered by Sri Aurobindo to be one of the most original thinkers of the Swadeshi age[2]. A study of Pal's educational series in his *New India* weekly makes a fascinating study even today, more than a century after he had first written them. Some of the ideas that Pal articulated through the pages of *New India* are striking for their contemporaneity. As do Sister Nivedita's educational ideas. I have examined them and found striking parallels to Sri Aurobindo's early formulation of a system of national education. This is explained

---

2. Haridas and Uma Mukherjee, *Bipin Chandra Pal and India's Struggle for Swaraj*, 2007.

because of her close collaboration with Sri Aurobindo during the nationalist phase and especially during the period when his last series on education appeared in the *Karmayogin*, which she was entrusted to edit. It was a period when great minds concentrated their energies to further an integral quest for national self-renewal, and in that, the educational question and quest saw one of the keenest and most dynamic focus.

I also chose to include Ananda Coomaraswamy, art historian, critic and philosopher, whose masterly understanding and appreciation of Indian culture and art Sri Aurobindo appears to have greatly admired.[3] Coomaraswamy too was actively involved for a while during the Swadeshi movement and was one of the pillars of the nationalist art movement during that period.[4] Coomaraswamy too, was greatly moved by the educational question and richly contributed to the debate on national education. A contemporary of Sri Aurobindo, Coomaraswamy also visited the National College to address the students.[5]

The other thinker that I have included in my exploration, who had in her own way contributed to metaphysical-philosophical studies in her adopted land of India, is Annie Besant, theosophist, Indian nationalist and educationist. It is perhaps interesting to note that in his political heydays, Sri Aurobindo had taken on Besant when she had publicly presented the idea of forming a national university. Sri Aurobindo had then demanded greater clarity, greater radicalisation, greater originality and innovativeness in the scheme. He had argued that a true proposition for a national

3. *The Complete Works of Sri Aurobindo* (*CWSA*) vol.1, 2003.
4. Partha Mitter, *Art and Nationalism in Colonial India: 1850–1922*, 1995, Ananda Coomaraswamy, *Essays in National Idealism*, 1909.
5. Haridas and Uma Mukherjee, *The Origins of the National Education Movement, 2000.*

university in India must originate from an Indian mind and that a proposed Indian national university would serve no purpose if it chose to merely function as an appendage to a mother-organisation in England.[6] One of Sri Aurobindo's last public messages on national education was given at the behest of Besant in 1918 for a national education week that she had organised nationally.

Satish Chandra Mukherjee, one of the most self-effacing originator and sustainer of the national education movement, has also been included in the narrative. The richness and variety of his educational positions remain strikingly relevant today and his *Dawn* magazine continues to be a repository of educational thoughts and ideas that can still provide direction to the various dimensions of the ongoing educational debates in India. In fact, it was a detailed survey of the educational articles that appeared in the volumes of the *Dawn* magazine, carefully reprinted and preserved for posterity by the National Council of Education in Bengal, that enabled me to form a concrete idea of the educational debate of the period under examination (1893–1910) and also gave me a first-hand insight into the minds of some of the thought-leaders I chose to include. I have also included the Tagore-Brahmabandhab educational experiment. This gives an insight into Tagore's early educational experiment and also an opportunity to revisit and record the educational observations of one of the fieriest rhetoricians of the Swadeshi age, Brahmabandhab Upadhyay. Since Upadhyay played a dynamic role in formulating public opinion during the Swadeshi period, was a nationalist collaborator of Sri Aurobindo, and was himself a scholar and died as a symbol of defiance to colonial rule, a survey of his educational thought appeared to me to be relevant in this study.

---

6. *CWSA* vol.6, 2002.

What prompted me to undertake this exploration is an observation Sri Aurobindo made on his past participation in and future hope for the attempt for a national education system and approach in India. The passage needs to be quoted in its entirety as it forms the basis of my exploration of his quest for a philosophy of national education. In short, it was this passage that urged me to take an alternative approach in exploring national education and Sri Aurobindo:

National education was another item [in the nationalist scheme of revolution and national regeneration] to which Sri Aurobindo attached much importance. He had been disgusted with the education given by the British system in the schools and colleges and universities, a system of which, as a professor in the Baroda College, he had full experience. He felt that it tended to dull and impoverish and tie up the naturally quick and brilliant and supple Indian intelligence, to teach it bad intellectual habits and spoil by narrow information and mechanical instruction its originality and productivity. The movement began well, and many national schools were established in Bengal [and in other provinces as well] and many able men became teachers, but still the development was insufficient and the economical position of the schools precarious. *Sri Aurobindo had decided to take up the movement personally and see whether it could not be given a greater expansion and a stronger foundation, but his departure from Bengal cut short this plan.* [Italics mine] In the repression and the general depression caused by it, most of the schools failed to survive. The idea lived on, and it may be hoped that it will one day find an adequate form and body ... [7].

I found this passage to be of great import since it indicated the deeper essence of the quest for a philosophy of national education centring around, in this case, the central figure of Sri Aurobindo. Otherwise, a small part of a rather long autobiographical note, I saw in the passage Sri Aurobindo's personal acceptance of the responsibility for the national education movement, for developing

7. Sri Aurobindo, *Autobiographical Notes and Other Writings of Historical Interest,* 2006.

its potential, giving it a solid foundation, and for making it the base on which a future superstructure of a national education in the country could be really created. This came across as significant. For a leader known to be reticent and usually impersonal these words expressed and exuded a sense of personal involvement with a crucial aspect of the movement even after a hiatus of three-odd decades.

The passage was part of a note he dictated on his political life decades after he had retired from it. Sri Aurobindo, it appeared to me from the above note, never really disassociated himself from the national education effort or ceased to be preoccupied with it. This is what prompted me to undertake an exploration of the national education effort, and in order to take it up from a different dimension, I made it into a narrative giving a wide overview of the age and of the debate itself. I have tried to essentially understand how Sri Aurobindo tried to organise the movement or make his contribution to the effort and to the debate and of how those around him also made their contribution to the quest. These are, to begin with, the essential fundamentals that came to my mind while revisiting this particular statement of his.

Does a particular philosophy of national education then emerge from this? Did the quest for a philosophy of national education finally culminate into some distinguishable or definable physical or intellectual manifestation? These are some of the essential questions that arise. I have chosen to name the study, 'The Master: Sri Aurobindo and the Quest for National Education' essentially because, as I saw it, the accumulated effort of the leading thought-leaders of this period was towards trying to evolve or formulate a system and a philosophy of national education. Their quest was essentially one which tried to define an ideational base to what they hoped would be an eventual national system of education. Along with political movement for freedom, these thought-leaders considered a movement for Swadeshi education as an essential parallel or corollary. While they spoke of freeing Indian education from the control of the colonial machinery and mindset, they were also concerned with the fundamentals, the shape and direction that free India's education would take. In the process there came a spurt of ideas on a new education in India, there was a virtual explosion of educational ideas as well as experiments. The goal of national education thus began to assume a certain centrality it hitherto lacked, and it became one of the defining pillars of one of the largest political mass movements against colonial rule in the world. In the course of my study, it clearly appeared to me that the quest for a philosophy of national education did never really culminate – each phase was followed by another and the debate too, did not die out.

At times, for instance, during the phase under examination here, it assumed a central focus and other times, such as later in the 1920s and beyond, it was side-tracked and manifested mainly through selected educational experiments, as it did during the phase when Mahatma Gandhi assumed leadership of the national movement, and decades later when he formulated his revolutionary idea of 'Basic Education'.

The first phase of the quest for national education did not succeed in making a long-lasting physical impact, as stated by Sri Aurobindo, mainly due to a precarious economic base and also due to the unwillingness of large number of students and their guardians to switch systems because of a perceived uncertain future. Sri Aurobindo saw another reason for the failure of the first phase and especially for its limited impact, and I have discussed it in the study. He saw it happen, as he said, because the new education institutions chose to steer away from the larger national movement at a certain point of time. This was done mainly to avoid administrative wrath and for survival. Though the reasons may be varied, this was one of the principal reasons for failure, as Sri Aurobindo saw it. His observation that the 'idea lived on' itself shows and, as I have also argued, that the quest was an ongoing one, and the thinking on an education system for independent India was also a continuous process with many a leader later. It never ceased to exercise the minds of those leaders who followed the pioneers of national education in the first phase. Therefore, if not in terms of physical manifestation, the impact of the early national education quest did leave behind a lasting impression in terms of ideas and influences. The philosophy kept being reformulated, redefined, restated, and revisited and it is through such a framework that the quest ought to be perhaps judged and studied. Its greatest impact eventually came through the ideas that it succeeded in disseminating, and it was through this dissemination that it saw a certain perpetuation of the quest.

Sri Aurobindo's central role in the movement ended with his resignation as principal of the National College, but I have also tried to argue that his intellectual and spiritual involvement with the movement continued, in a sense, till his last year when in 1949, he penned a series of articles on the importance of the body, and issued a message on the role of physical education in a national scheme of education for his Ashram's newly created department of physical education. It is also clear from his writings during his second political phase in 1909, that he had a drastically different plan for national education work than that followed by the National Council of Education. But, as I have pointed out, he did not have sufficient time and support for carrying these out. My discussion has not been so much on the physical and statistical aspects of the education system then prevalent, although I have included a section which surveys the Indian education scenario some time prior to, and during the Curzonian era, but as that would be entering into the history of Indian education and would basically be a repetition of an analysis of educational statistics, I have kept it short and quite shorn of statistics. I have made it a point though, to discuss India's once widespread network of an indigenous education system and how it gradually withered, and was eventually starved, under the colonial set-up.

Why, some may wonder, have I insisted on discussing ideas that were actually debated a century ago. How does it serve to remember and revisit these, or for that matter what is the relevance or purpose of such an exercise today in an age that is drastically and radically different from that age, when the prospect of freedom itself was seen by the majority as a vain chimera. In an age that is dazzled by glamour and swaggering success, thinkers of the past may appear to be an incongruent lot, running after a pipe dream or perhaps demanding too much *tapas* and sacrifice from their countrymen! What attracted me, however, to them and their educational thought and vision and especially to Sri Aurobindo's early observations and speeches on education, was the continuing relevance of their ideas to the educational debate today. Their ideas, their arguments, their examination and lamentations appear to be still shedding light on current educational problems in either diagnosing its various maladies, or in acting as signposts on the way forward towards possible solutions.

Against the backdrop of the National Education Policy, formulated by Prime Minister Narendra Modi's government and ably drafted by a group of leading educationists and thinkers, the educational ideas of our thought-leaders from the past assumes greater relevance and significance. The essential position, objective, and vision of the NEP comes across as being in tune with the fundamental articulations of these nationalist thought-leaders.

The other significant aspect that attracted me was the sheer sweep and depth of the whole educational debate, the indomitable urge to undertake fresh experiments while castigating the old system, and the effort that they (the thinkers) made to apply themselves to a very crucial aspect of national reconstruction. Their preoccupation and concern with a future education system for a free India was in itself inspiring. To gradually absorb the fact that Sri Aurobindo was actually deeply involved with the movement and attempted to take it to the masses was a remarkable aspect. In fact, the British intelligence had noted with alacrity his educational activism and his personal initiative in forming national schools all over the province.[8] He was, apart from being recognised as the principal ideologue of the nationalist party, also seen as one of the pillars of the national education movement. While going through the material I felt that these could very well be revisited, and the whole effort narrated so as to bring the spotlight back on the effort of developing a national system of education for India.

Another aspect that fascinated me was the fact, that even when the cry for complete freedom was not yet widely accepted, and was yet to percolate deep within the masses, some of these leaders and thinkers were attempting to plan an education for a free India – a new India, which they saw deriving inspiration from her past civilisational experience, and resolutely dealing with the present, while aspiring towards a greater future. These thinkers were quite certain, as Sri Aurobindo put it, that the national education effort

8. Amiya.K.Samanta, ed. *Terrorism in Bengal*, 1995.

was not a 'return to the fifth century but an initiation of the centuries to come', it was not to 'ignore modern truth and knowledge, but to take our foundation on our own being, our own mind, our own spirit'.[9] The gradually evolving national movement was preparing the possibilities of just such a foundation and national education formed an intrinsic part of it.

On their part, these thinkers were creating the edifice of a future India, expressing their ideas or observations while speaking out against overburdening the learner with too many subjects and the pressures of a mechanical examination system, destroying the teacher's aptitude for taking initiative, and learning by rote without entering into the deeper meaning of the subject or the topic. These are issues that even today generate much debate and heat.

As far as my principal protagonist, Sri Aurobindo was concerned, he too, with his inimitable ardour and manner, was assisting in shaping the mighty chariot of nationhood and in that, he perceived the national education effort to be one of the chief wheels. He was, as his wont, constantly leaping towards the future, and after a while, what preoccupied him constantly, was the thought of how best to preserve freedom having wrested it. For this he saw as imperative, the need to develop a national system of education for India.

This narrative then basically looks at the concerted effort made at developing a philosophy of national education in the early decade of the last century in India. Centring itself on Sri Aurobindo, it makes an effort to study some of the most dynamic minds of our national history during that period and seeks to highlight the contemporaneity of their thoughts and hopes. And in that it seeks its continued relevance, its deeper utility, and contemporary resonance.

---

9. *CWSA* vol.1, op.cit.

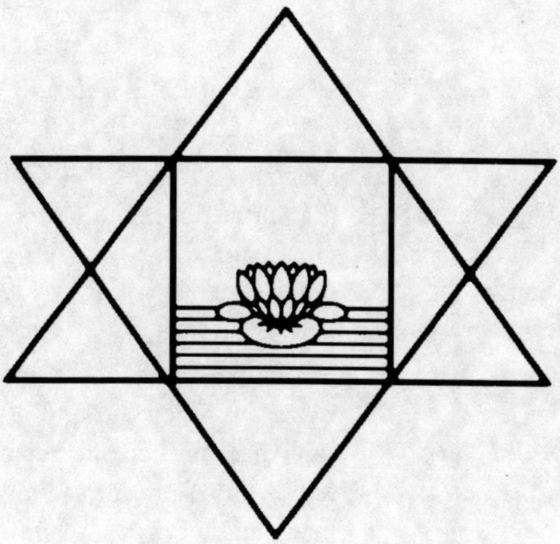

1

Early Realisations

Understanding the Indian System

"

Do you see this map? It is not a map, but the portrait of Bharat-Mata: its cities and mountains, rivers and jungles form her physical body. All her children are her nerves, large and small. Their literature is her memory and her speech; their vitality is her life; their cultural aspirations her soul; their freedom and happiness her self-fulfillment. Concentrate on Bharat as a living mother; worship her with the nine-fold *bhakti*.

– Sri Aurobindo to K.M. Munshi in Baroda

Aurobindo lacked no proficiency in Sanskrit. While studying the Ramayana and the Mahabharata he never sought any help from their English versions...His knowledge of the essence of literature and his subtle and deep insight into its spirit surprised me. Thus, I would learn much more from than what he would from me.

– Dinendra Kumar Roy, Aurobindo Prasange

I.1. AN EDUCATIONIST IN A PRINCELY STATE: BARODA

A major line of action that Sri Aurobindo had supported for national resurgence during his days as the leader of the advanced nationalist group fighting for India's freedom from British rule, was the task of setting up an edifice of National Education. In fact, along with Swaraj (self-rule), Swadeshi, and Boycott, National Education became a principal plank of the new nationalist platform. The demand for establishing a system of national education was not a mere agitational programme, but one that attempted to bring about a systemic change in the educational framework of colonial India. The earnestness was evident when a serious attempt was made to open a national college in Calcutta in August 1906. The attempt was also to systematically set up a chain of national schools and colleges all over Bengal and other parts of the country to try and provide a viable alternative to those who felt the colonial academic set-up to be mind-stunting and denationalising. Dictating a general note on his political life sometime around 1946, necessitated in order to rectify misconceptions about his stand and policies while in politics, Sri Aurobindo stated that, '... national education was another item [of the political action] to which [he] attached much importance. He had been disgusted with the education given by the British system in the schools and colleges and universities, a system of which as a professor in the Baroda College he had full experience. He felt that it tended to dull and impoverish and tie up the naturally quick and brilliant and supple Indian intelligence, to teach it bad intellectual habits and spoil by narrow information and mechanical instruction its original productivity'.[1] These were the ideas that he would constantly seek to address in his writings and speeches, first during his active nationalist phase and later too. The emphasis here is not so much on the preservation of self-identity as the principal motivating factor of a new educational movement, but the fact that the loss of inherent psychological and intellectual prowess of the Indian mind would eventually lead to the loss of a distinct national identity.

Sri Aurobindo spent a total of thirteen years (1893–1906) in Baroda in the service of the princely state. He worked in different departments on official and formal assignments which included 'working in different departments of the Secretariat of the Baroda Raj' as a personal assistant to the Maharaja Sayaji Rao Gaekwad III (1863–1939) and drafting 'important speeches for him and preparing his reports and replies to the colonial Indian Government'.[2] However,

1. Sri Aurobindo, *Autobiographical Notes and Other Writings of Historical Interest*, 2006, p. 58.
2. Manoj Das, *Sri Aurobindo: Life and Times of the Mahayogi* (*The Pre-Pondicherry Phase*), Pondicherry: Sri Aurobindo International Centre of Education, 2020, p.117. The collection of Sayaji Rao III's speeches compiled into volumes give an idea of the speeches that Sri Aurobindo had drafted for him. For instance the speech on the 'Revival of Industry in India' delivered by the Gaekwad at the inauguration of an industrial exhibition in Ahmedabad on 15th December 1902, was drafted in entirety by Sri Aurobindo. The speech's second paragraph, clearly points at Sri Aurobindo's literary and political touch. That the Maharaja also addressed it verbatim, indicated his advanced position among Indian princes who were nationalists as well. '... Famine, increasing poverty, widespread disease, all these bring home to us the fact that there is some radical weakness in our system and that something must be done to remedy it. But there is another and a larger aspect of the matter and that is that this economic problem is our last ordeal as a people. It is our last chance. Fail there and what can the future bring us? We can only grow poorer and weaker,

his chief roles in Baroda were that of an educationist and a student

more dependent on foreign help; we must watch our industrial freedom fall into extinction and drag out a miserable existence as the hewers of wood and drawers of water to any foreign power which happens to be our master. Solve that problem and you have a great future before you, the future of a great people, worthy of your ancestors and of your old position among the nations...' (*Speeches and Addresses of His Highness Sayaji Rao III, Maharaja of Baroda*, Vol.1 (1877–1910), 1927, p.83. Also see: CWSA Vol.1 p.694. Around the time Sri Aurobindo lived and worked in Baroda, the state was among the more progressive of the princely states. It covered an area of around 8.100 square miles and had a population of two and half a million. Of Sayaji Rao's record, his biographer Stanley Rice, writes, 'it is no mean achievement, to have raised Baroda from the position of a medieval State, full of corruption and oppression, and dependent for its life on the whims and caprices of the ruler, to a foremost place among the States of India, with a government framed on constitutional lines, with just and reasonable laws, and instinct with all the progress of modern science and modern wisdom.' (Stanley Rice, *Life of Sayaji Rao III, Maharaja of Baroda*, Vol.1, 1931, p.viii). Baroda, 'had come to be regarded as a model state for other princes. Sayaji Rao III was considered a highly cultivated and well-travelled man with a head full of progressive ideas, which other rulers could emulate.' (Uma Balasubramaniam, *Sayajirao Gaekwad III: the Maharaja of Baroda*, New Delhi: Rupa Publications, 2019, p.187.) Baroda had evolved an extensive public education system under Sayaji Rao. Among the Indian princes, Sayaji Rao's predecessor, Sayaji Rao II 'had started schools for the Untouchables in 1833'. Dr. Babasaheb Ambedkar's foremost biographer Dhananjay Keer, reminds us that it was Sayaji Rao III who had sponsored Babasaheb's education in the Elphinston College and had also enabled him to go abroad for his higher studies. (See eg. Dhananjay Keer, *Dr. Babasaheb Ambedkar: Life & Mission*, Mumbai: Popular Prakashan, (1954), 5th ed. 2016) Sayaji Rao had his nationalist leanings and had differences with the colonial authorities. In 1904, for instance, he accepted an invitation to 'preside at the Social Conference of the Indian National Congress in Bombay'. He delivered the inaugural address and 'spoke at length on the two most dominant of the Indian classical scriptures, of which he undertook a wide and meticulous study, and of all his functions in Baroda, 'teaching alone seems to have been close to his heart'.[3] 'Through uncertainties, intervals and altering functions, Sri Aurobindo continued to teach till the end of his Baroda service'.[4] Not only teaching students, but also teaching himself seemed to have been an absorbing passion with him during his years in Baroda.

'In England he had received, according to his father's express instructions, an entirely occidental education without any contact with the culture of India and the East. At Baroda, he made up the deficiency, learned Sanskrit and several modern Indian languages, assimilated the spirit of Indian civilisation and its forms past and present'.[5] A look at Sri Aurobindo's study of the Indian languages and classics in Baroda makes an interesting read. In Baroda, he also worked on the translation of the Mahabharata. Bengali novelist and

issues acting as impediments to India's progress: caste prejudices and the status of women', '(1) Difficulties arising out of the caste system; (2) Difficulties in connection with the status of women.' Can one perceive Sri Aurobindo's style in the following lines from Sayaji Rao's speech at the Conference, 'There is, of course, some truth in the position that reform must work along lines natural to the country and our national characteristics. There are some features in our environment which are sufficiently powerful to modify the practical application of any idea, and these account for certain tendencies in national history which persist even through long centuries of foreign influence. It is also true that servile imitation is no reform and is often worse than the original evil. But the truth behind the phrase is, that it is the general advance of the nation which is the aim of reform: that only is national reform which subserves national interests'. (*Speeches and Addresses of His Highness, Sayaji Rao III Maharaja of Baroda*, Vol.1 op.cit., pp 155–157, (Uma Balasubramaniam, op.cit., p.227).

3. Ibid., p.117.
4. Ibid., p.120.
5. *Sri Aurobindo Birth Centenary Library* (*SABCL*), Vol-30, 1976, p. 1.

author Dinendra Kumar Roy (1869–1943),[6] who had been engaged 'to help [Sri Aurobindo] to correct and perfect his knowledge of

---

6. Once a well-known name in the world of Bengali literature, Dinendra Kumar Roy's account of his days in Baroda with Sri Aurobindo, between 1898 and 1900 or 1901, gives an interesting account and is perhaps the only detailed description of Sri Aurobindo during his Baroda days. Originally serialised in the Bengali literary journal *Sahitya* between 1911–1912, the series was brought out as a book, *Aurobindo Prasanga*, in 1923. 'Aurobindo spent a few years of the earlier part of his active life at Baroda,' wrote Roy in his memoir, 'It is doubtful whether any of his biographers know anything worthy of mention about the period of his stay in Baroda ... whatever little I know is the result of my personal contact with Aurobindo'. Roy recalled leaving for Baroda 'sometime around the beginning of winter' in 1898. 'I had been given the charge of teaching Bengali to Aurobindo .... From his childhood, Aurobindo had lived in England; he stayed there from the age of five or six till he was past his teens. For this reason he had not had the chance to learn his mother tongue well; but he was very eager to learn Bengali, since from his childhood he felt strongly attracted to it'. Roy's description of Sri Aurobindo in Baroda, was full of wit and perceptive, 'It goes without saying that I was very disappointed with my first meeting with Aurobindo. Old-fashioned slippers with ends turned up on his feet; his clothes of coarse, flounced Ahmedabad-mill khadi, the end of his dhoti hanging loose; a tight-fitting waistcoat on his back; on his head, a mane of long, thin hair parted in the middle and hanging down over the neck; tiny pockmarks on his face; his eyes with a gentle, dreamy look – who would have thought that this thin, dark-skinned young man was Sriman Aurobindo Ghose, a living fountain of English, French, Latin, Hebrew, Greek! Had someone pointed out the hills of Deoghar and told me, "These are the Himalayas", I would have been less surprised and confounded.'(Dinendra Kumar Roy, *With Aurobindo in Baroda*, (trans.2006), pp.4–5. It is perhaps one of the most reliable and moving accounts of Sri Aurobindo, seen at close quarters, in his early days as an educationist, student of Indian classics and languages and as a revolutionary in the making.

the language and to accustom him to conversation in Bengali'[7], observed that he was engaged in translating the Mahabharata and that he understood the Sanskrit Ramayana and Mahabharata quite well and that he wrote poems based on some of the episodes of the Mahabharata. "Occasionally he used to read out poems to me", recalled Dinendra Kumar Roy, and '[he] would open the Ramayana and Mahabharata and read out the original words to verify whether his rendering had been faithful'.[8] From his own observations, it appears that Sri Aurobindo learnt both Bengali and Sanskrit on his own – regarding the learning of Bengali, he commented that 'before engaging [a] teacher [he] already knew enough of the language to appreciate the novels of Bankim and the poetry of Madhusudan'.[9] Around 1899, Romesh Chandra Dutt (1848–1909) historian, litterateur, and a senior member of the ICS, whose 'poetic translations' of portions of Ramayana and Mahabharata had just been released and highly acclaimed in England, had come to Baroda, and on hearing that Aurobindo had translated certain parts of Ramayana and Mahabharata, he expressed an eagerness to see the translations .... Mr. Dutt, discerning as he was in literary matters said, "Seeing your poems, I regret all the trouble I went to trying to translate the Ramayana and the Mahabharata! Had I seen your poems earlier, I would have never published my own writings. It all seems like child's play now."[10] For a while in 1900–1901, Sri Aurobindo developed the habit of noting down the books he was studying and also the number of pages he read every day. A closer look at these notes gives an idea of the system he followed while reading the classics, and of exactly what he read and the time taken to cover

7. *Autobiographical Notes*, op.cit., pp.43–44.
8. Dinendra Kumar Roy, *With Aurobindo in Baroda,* (trans.2006), p. 18.
9. *Autobiographical Notes*, op.cit., p.44.
10. Dinendra Kumar Roy, op.cit. pp. 18–19.

the subject – 'in September 1900, Sri Aurobindo was [studying] a Sanskrit text of the Mahabharata. On the fourth of September, besides correcting his class's examination papers, he read the 63 slokas of *suktas* 53 and 54 of the *Virataparva*. He had read up to this point (i.e. *suktas* containing 1533 slokas) in just eight days. In three more days, he read twice over the whole first part ('Purvamegha') of Kalidasa's famous *Meghaduta* or Cloud-Messenger'. A further delving into the extracts from his notebooks will give an idea of the phenomenal range that he covered during this period. It shows his involvement with education, first for himself in the form of acquisition of knowledge, self-culture, and self-study, and also as he was inclined to often observe, in an immerse in the spirit of Indian civilisation and culture, and then in the form of his academic duties as an educationist. The extract from the notebooks reveals his meticulous and unsparing self-preparation:

On Thursday 3rd January 1901, he began the study of another of Kalidasa's poem the *Raghuvansha* – Canto-I. 95 slokas read with reference to Mallinatha's Tika [commentary]; understood; a number of words unknown, a few slokas baffling till commentary consulted.

Fri. Jan 4th: *Raghuvansa*. Canto I. Reread with dictionary; meaning of unknown and imperfectly known words ascertained. Wealth and success slokas of the Hitopadesh entered in Collection. Tennyson's *Coming of Arthur* read with notes; also the whole introduction.

Sat. Jan 5th. *Raghuvansa*. Canto II. 75 slokas read with Mallinatha's Commentary. As canto I. Freytag's *Die Journalisten* [A play written in 1852 by German playwright Gustav Freytag (1816–1895)], a page and a half. Fate slokas of Hitopadesha entered in Collection.

Sund. Jan 6th *Raghuvansa*. Canto II, reread with dictionary. *Die Journalisten* 16 pages i.e. to end of scene I.[11]

11. Roshan and Apurva, *Sri Aurobindo in Baroda*, 1993, p. 101, 102.

We have a glimpse of how Sri Aurobindo must have studied and read while in Baroda, from a description of one of his erstwhile students Rajaram N. Patkar. 'Passion for reading [with Sri Aurobindo] was very great ... and not confined to any particular subject and was extended to various compartments of human knowledge .... After reading a book, he used to brood for a time and commit his views to paper'. Patkar had seen, 'volumes of such writings in his room in different languages such as Greek, Latin, French and English' and 'his concentration was so great that he felt himself the least perturbed by any outside disturbance'.[12]

'Aurobindo's library', recalled Dinendra Kumar Roy, 'contained piles of books in various European languages, all sorts of books in French, German, Russian, English, Greek, Latin, Hebrew .... His collection contained works by all the English poets from Chaucer to Swinburne. Numerous English novels were stacked up in cupboards, piled up in corners of the room, and locked away in steel trunks. Homer's *Illiad*, Dante's great epic, our *Ramayana* and *Mahabharata*, books by Kalidasa and other such poets were all there in his library'.[13] Could it be that Sri Aurobindo's habits and methods of self-study, which enabled him to successfully master subjects of which he had had no exposure prior to his arrival in India, contributed to developing in him a disgust for the mechanical, snippet-oriented education, that he found being encouraged by the official colonial machinery in India then?

Ever since his return to India from England in 1893, Sri Aurobindo was associated with the imparting and organising of education in some capacity or the other. At Baroda, among other

---

12. *Sri Aurobindo Ashram Archives Collection*, cited in Manoj Das, *Sri Aurobindo: Life and Times of the Mahayogi* (*The Pre-Pondicherry Phase*), 2020, p.121.
13. Dinendra Kumar Roy, op.cit. p. 23.

duties, he taught French in 1897 as a part-time lecturer at the Baroda College and then taught English as a permanent professor from 1900 onwards. In 1904, he was appointed vice principal of the College and was the acting-principal from March 1905 to February 1906. In 1905, he was also appointed temporarily the 'In Charge Minister of Education' of Baroda State. These various stints gave him an opportunity to observe, at close quarters, the colonial educational structure, and its effect on the Indian mind and life, although, it must be mentioned, that Baroda was one of the more progressive princely states in India. Sri Aurobindo's opinion of the Maharaja of Baroda, Sayaji Rao, Dinendra Kumar Roy tells us, 'was very high. He told me that the Maharaja was worthy of governing a far greater empire and that it was hard to find in India a politician like him'.[14]

Thus, in a sense, his association with the education system of this country began ever since his return and as he himself admits, this association with the academic world made him contemplate on its current nature and future possibilities and thus, the quest for evolving 'a true education' began. Recalling later his teaching experience at Baroda, Sri Aurobindo observed that, what had surprised him was that students would "take down everything verbatim and mug it up." This sort of a thing, he felt, would never have happened in England.[15] Since the age of seven when he was taken to England for his education, Sri Aurobindo had a thorough exposure to the British and European system of education and was deeply conversant with it. Back in India, he saw first-hand the application of a colonial system of education and realised its drawbacks. Commenting on the methods followed by the students in the Baroda College, he once said, 'the students, besides taking my

14. Dinendra Kumar Roy, op.cit., p.18.
15. K.R.Srinivas Iyengar, *Sri Aurobindo – A Biography and a History*, 5th ed., 2006, p. 52.

notes, used to get notes of some professor from Bombay .... Once I was giving a lecture on Southey's *Life of Nelson*. My lecture was not in agreement with the notes. So the students remarked that it was not at all like what was found in the notes ...'[16] It may have been these experiences, which one finds in evidence even today, and his keen observation of the human mind that, presumably, compelled Sri Aurobindo to critically examine the entire system.

Writing during this period (1893–1906) on the degradation of the faculties of the Indian mind brought about by the misapplication of educational principles, he observed, rather scathingly, that the 'university system' was threatening and had initiated the process of irretrievable degradation and final extinction of whatever was left of the 'intellectual alertness, quickness, and originality of the Indian mind'.[17] 'The first fundamental mistake' therefore, of the educational approach, as Sri Aurobindo argued, in this early and incomplete piece on education, was to 'confine ourselves to the training of the storing faculty memory and the storage of facts and to neglect the training of the three great manipulating faculties, viz. the power of reasoning, the power of comparison and differentiation, and the power of expression'. These faculties, according to him, exist 'to a certain extent in all men', but they 'demand cultivation, they demand that bringing out of natural abilities which is the real essence of education'. Sri Aurobindo warns that if this 'fundamental mistake' is perpetuated and these three mental powers are not cultivated at the appropriate stage of growth of the human mind, it can bring about an eventual and general intellectual degeneration of the whole race.[18] To him, the 'easy assumption' that the primary and, may be the sole, duty of education is to simply supply the mind

---

16. Roshan and Apurva, op.cit., p. 78.
17. *Complete Works of Sri Aurobindo* (*CWSA*) vol. 1, 2003, p.359–360.
18. Ibid., pp. 359–360.

with information and facts and that the rest will develop on its own, is an erroneous one. He expressed a vehement disapproval of the supply-information approach and argued that the 'amount of knowledge is, in itself, not of the first importance but to make the best use of what we know.

The easy assumption of our educationists that we have only to supply the mind with a smattering of facts in each department of knowledge and the mind can be trusted to develop itself and take its own suitable road, is contrary to science, contrary to human experience, and contrary to the universal opinion of civilised countries'.[19] His point that the gathering of knowledge is not the primary but one of the duties of education, and what is of a more fundamental importance is the development of faculties that would assist in making a right and cogent use of that knowledge, can be found all through his observations and arguments on education. Commenting on this incomplete manner of looking at education, asmerely for information gathering, Sri Aurobindo argued, 'To give the student knowledge is necessary, but it is still more necessary to build up in him the power of using his knowledge. It would hardly be a good technical education for a carpenter to be taught how to fell trees so as to provide himself with wood and never to learn how to prepare tables, chairs, and cabinets or even what tools were necessary for his craft'.[20] And yet, Sri Aurobindo rather caustically pointed out, 'this is precisely what our system of education does. It trains the memory and provides the student with a store of facts and secondhand ideas. The memory is the woodcutter's axe and the store he acquires is the wood he has cut down in his course of tree felling. When he has done this, the University says to him, "We now declare you a Bachelor of Carpentry; we have given you a

19. *CWSA* vol.1, op.cit., p. 360.

20. Ibid., p.359.

good and sharp axe and a fair nucleus of wood to begin with. Go on, my son, the world is full of forests and provided the Forest Officer does not object, you can cut down trees and provide yourself with wood to your heart's content." Now the student who goes forth thus equipped, may become a great timber-merchant but unless he is an exceptional genius, he will never be even a moderate carpenter'.[21]

Calling for revolutionising the whole 'aims and methods' of our education as a 'very first step in reform', Sri Aurobindo argued that teachers must be accustomed to 'devote nine-tenths of their energies' to educating the 'active mental faculties', the power of reasoning, the power of comparison and differentiation, and the power of expression], 'while the passive retaining faculty' [which he calls memory], 'should occupy a recognised and well-defined but subordinate place ...'. His keen observations of the educational scenario made Sri Aurobindo realise that a mere rearranging of the curriculum could not bring about such an approach. It made him enumerate various subjects which, if taken up with a different attitude, could be of help in developing these faculties. His incisive and profoundly accurate analysis also shows the extent to which he was involved in trying to reform Indian education:

> It is true that certain subjects are more apt to develop certain faculties than others; the power of accurate reasoning is powerfully assisted by Geometry, Logic and Political Economy; one of the most important results of languages is to refine and train the power of expression, and nothing more enlarges the power of comparison and differentiation than an intelligent study of history. But no particular subject, except language is essential, still less exclusively appropriated, to any given faculty. There are types of intellect, for instance, which are constitutionally incapable of dealing with geometrical problems or even with the formal machinery of Logic, and are yet profound, brilliant, and correct reasoners in other intellectual spheres. There is in fact hardly any subject, the sciences of calculation excepted, which in the hands of a

21. Ibid., p. 359.

capable teacher does not give room for the development of all the general faculties of the mind...'.[22]

At the Baroda College, Sri Aurobindo did not limit himself only to taking classes and self-study, but actively participated in various other recreational activities, such as being the Chairman of the Baroda College Union and Debating Society. This brought him in closer contact with a larger number of students and thus, gave him a greater opportunity to not only observe the effects of education imparted on the students, but to also share some of his views with them. His task as Chairman of the College debating society was to mainly introduce visiting lecturers to the Union and 'to regulate the course of the debate in such a way that the best in the students came out and they didn't miss the spirit of intellectual inquiry in the excitement of the moment'.[23] Rajaram N. Patkar, Sri Aurobindo's former student in Baroda recalled decades later:

> It was a treat to hear [him] on the platform. He used to preside occasionally over the College Debating Society. When he used to preside, the College Central Hall which is sufficiently large was almost packed to the full with the audience which not only consisted of the College students but many educated people from outside .... When he rose to speak there was a pin-drop silence and the audience used to listen to him with rapt attention. Without any gesture or movement of limbs he stood like a statue, motionless and the language used to flow like a stream from his lips with a natural ease and melody that kept his audience almost spellbound. Every sentence that he uttered was full of meaning and set the audience thinking for days together. He was at his best when the subject pertained to religion and philosophy. He rarely dabbled in politics, but references were made now and then to the down-trodden condition of India and illiteracy and ignorance of the masses.[24]

---

22. *CWSA* vol.1, op.cit., p.360–61.
23. Roshan and Apurva, op.cit., p. 87.
24. Sri Aurobindo Ashram Archives Collection, Sri Aurobindo Ashram, Pondicherry cited in Manoj Das, op.cit., pp.121–123.

Even after a passage of more than five decades, Patkar could still remember his erstwhile teacher's figure on the Baroda College platform and hear the ring 'of his sweet melodious voice'.[25] Another former student, H. Kantavala, writing for *The Baroda College Golden Jubilee Commemoration* volume brought out in 1933, recalled, how the speech which 'Professor Ghose' delivered was a 'piece of chaste and polished English, the like of which' he had never heard.[26]

Through the Baroda College debating society, Sri Aurobindo took the opportunity to project his idea of what Indian educational institutions ought to strive to achieve, in order to reach not only a certain degree of academic excellence but also to be able to create an atmosphere which would be congenial to an all-round personality development of the learner. This is evident from the content of the only recorded talk of his, during this period delivered on July 22, 1899, before the College Social Gathering. The subject of the talk was Oxford and Cambridge and what Indian universities ought to learn from them. He describes the changes that the atmosphere of these ancient European seats of knowledge bring about in the character and outlook of a pupil who had spent three years within their precincts. It is instructive to read his assessment of the effects that ancient seats of learning with established methods of teaching have on young minds:

> He goes up from the restricted life of his home and school and finds himself in surroundings which, with astonishing rapidity, expand his intellect, strengthen his character, develop his social faculties, force out all his abilities and turn him in three years from a boy into a man. His mind ripens in the contact with minds which meet from all parts of the country and have been brought up in many various kinds of trainings, his unwholesome eccentricities wear away and the unsocial, egoistic elements of character

25. Manoj Das, op.cit., p.123.
26. Ibid., p.126.

are to a large extent discouraged. He moves among ancient and venerable buildings, the mere age and beauty of which are in themselves an education. He has the Union which has trained so many great orators and debaters, has been the first trial ground of so many renowned intellects. He has, too, the athletics clubs organised with a perfection unparalleled elsewhere, in which, if he has the physique and the desire for them, he may find pursuits which are also in themselves an education. The result is that he, who entered the University a raw student, comes out of it a man and a gentleman, accustomed to think of great affairs and fit to move in cultivated society, and he remembers his College and University with affection, and in after days if he meets with those who have studied with him, he feels attracted towards them as to men with whom he has a natural brotherhood.[27]

This was the kind of 'social effect' he wanted 'the Colleges and Universities of India also to exercise, to educate by social influences as well as those which are merely academical and to create the feeling among their pupils that they belong to the community, that they are children of one mother'.[28]

Sri Aurobindo refers here to the aspects of intellectual training and character training. The pupil having come in contact with others, expands his mental horizon, develops a certain degree of reciprocity and his idiosyncrasies of character and conduct usually driven by the thought of self-first, give way to a larger sense of accommodation and assimilation resulting in the development of a sense of brotherhood and companionship which brings about a greater social integration and equality. He felt these to be the results of education in premier educational institutions in the West and which could, according to him, be worked out in the Indian context.

He sounded a note of caution though, for those who thought that education was complete once one successfully completed the university course. He didn't subscribe to that view and observed

27. *CWSA* vol.1, op.cit., p.354.
28. Ibid.

that the university merely equips the pupil to continue his onward journey of self-development, 'There is too much of a tendency in this country to regard education as a mere episode, finished when once the degree is obtained. But the University cannot and does not pretend to complete a man's education; it merely gives some materials to his hand or points out certain paths he may tread, and it says to him, "Here are the materials I have given into your hands, it is for you to make of them what you can," or "These are the paths I have equipped you to travel; it is yours to tread them to the end, and by your success in them justify me before the world"'.[29]

We get a hint here of another one of his fundamental positions on education – that education is an ongoing process and does not halt with the end of academics.

I.2. EARLY PUBLIC EXPRESSIONS OF THE EDUCATIONAL MALAISE: THROUGH AN ANALYSIS OF BANKIM'S LIFE AND HIS EDUCATION

During his stay at Baroda, Sri Aurobindo witnessed, first-hand, the application of the university system in India and it is evident that the situation he witnessed, as well as its adverse effects on the Indian mind, had disturbed him much. Though he formulated his educational regeneration strategy during his active political phase in Bengal, he had started highlighting the defects and deficiencies of the system much earlier. We have analysed his address on education at the Baroda College Union gathering in 1899, and it would be interesting to observe that as early as 1894, in his first years in India after return from a 14-year stay in England, Sri Aurobindo had started making scathing public attacks on colonial educational and political system in the pages of the Bombay-based Marathi-English

29. *CWSA* vol.1, op.cit., p. 355.

weekly *Indu Prakash*. His articles in the *Indu Prakash* announced the beginning of Sri Aurobindo's public activities. A series, of nine articles, 'New Lamps for Old', written at the behest of his Cambridge friend, K.G. Deshpande, 'vehemently denounced the then Congress policy of pray, petition, and protest and called for a dynamic leadership based upon self-help and fearlessness'.[30] The series created an uproar, leading some eminent moderates of the era to warn the editor of a reprisal from the colonial administration. Sri Aurobindo was asked to tone down his attacks and soon lost interest. His political activities would be underground and secret till around 1905.

An interesting 7-part article he wrote in the *Indu Prakash* between 16th July and 27th August 1894 was on the bard of Indian nationalism, Bankim Chandra Chatterjee (1838–1894), who had just passed away. In it, Sri Aurobindo made some very bold and perceptive observations on the education that was then imparted in India; these observations were, in seed form, the first expressions of his later political programme and his philosophy of education. The biographical series is also replete with delectable snipes that he takes at the British system and its attitude in India and its many idiosyncrasies. For instance, on Bankim's famous clash with the British masters, he writes:

> He was shipwrecked again in a collision with Anglo-Indianism. Walking in Eden Garden, he chanced across Munro, the Presidency Commissioner, a farouche bureaucrat with the manners of an Englishman and the temper of a badly educated hyena. Bankim examined the queer curiosity, as one might any queer curiosity, with a certain lazy interest, but no signal of respect. He was unaware at this time that to Salaam any stray European you may

30. Sri Aurobindo, *Autobiographical Notes & Other Writings of Historical Interest*, Pondicherry: Sri Aurobindo Ashram Publication Dept, 2006, p.51.

meet is the highest privilege of a Hindu and the whole duty of a Deputy Magistrate.[31]

Our focus in this series is on the part about education. It provides an insight into Sri Aurobindo's early thinking on the subject. Sri Aurobindo discussed the various facets of Bankim's life and work, drawing a background of the society he lived and worked in, of his literary output, of his contributions to Bengal and the Bengali people, and of his hand in creating a national consciousness. In short, he analyses Bankim's contributions towards creating 'a language, a literature, and a nation'.

In the analysis on 'His Youth and College Life', Sri Aurobindo revealed how Bankim's genius was already coming to the fore and he was fortunate to be saved, by being unconventional in his approach to the system of education which was prevalent during those times. Describing Bankim's educational progress, Sri Aurobindo wrote, "He [Bankim] ascended the school by leaps and bounds; so abnormal was his swiftness that it put his masters in fear for him. They grew nervous lest they spoil by over-instruction the delicate fibre of his originality, and with a wise caution they obstructed his entrance into the highest class ..."[32] That over-instruction at the formative stage, impedes the natural growth of the child and prevents the surfacing of his latent qualities and talents is one of the ideas found in seed form in these words. This would become a constant in Sri Aurobindo's educational articulations. In preventing Bankim from being promoted and thus being over-instructed with non-essentials, his masters, Sri Aurobindo felt, did him a very good turn and assisted in the growth of his genius.

---

31. *CWSA* vol.1, op.cit., Bankim Chandra Chatterji, III – His Official Career, p.101.
32. *CWSA* vol.1, op.cit., Bankim Chandra Chatterji, I – His Youth and College Life, p. 91.

He continued, in the same vein, looking at Bankim's higher education, "Bankim had always, an extraordinary luck. Just as at school, his fine promise was saved by the prudence of its guardians from the altar of High Education, the Moloch to whom we stupidly sacrifice India's most hopeful sons, so it was saved at Hugly College by his own distaste for hard work ..."[33] Higher education prevalent in colonial India did not allow the qualities of the student to emerge. To those like Sri Aurobindo, who saw its structure closely, it came across as more of a routine drudgery that was indulged in, in order to acquire an official position in the vast colonial machinery. That lifeless and mechanical education decimated or could not cultivate most of the innate qualities of the students and did not give them scope to explore themselves and their surroundings. Sri Aurobindo's use of the word 'sacrifice' – the individual immolates himself and his unique possibilities at the altar of higher education in order to simply survive and follow a routine existence, best describes his strong views of this diluting education. Bankim, however, Sri Aurobindo felt, refused to do that. He refused to undergo the grind of cramming and of unthinking regurgitation. Instead, what Bankim did was to initiate himself in the process of *swadhyaya* [concentrated self-study and self-training], having easily won laurels within the existing system without, as one would say, much effort. He indulged himself in his 'caprices'. "He conceived at this time", Sri Aurobindo observed, "a passion for Sanskrit and read with great perseverance at a Pandit's *tol* [Sanskrit school]. In a single year, he had gone through the *Mugdhabodh*,[34] *Raghuvansa*,

---

33. Ibid.
34. Vopadeva, a grammarian who is said to have flourished in the latter half of the 13th century at the court of Himadri, King of Deva-giri, wrote a grammar for beginners on a system of his own called the *Mugdha-bodha*, which is much valued as an authority in Bengal, and referred to by many native commentators. (Source: Monier Williams,

Bhatti[35] and the *Meghaduta.* Advancing at this pace, he managed in something under four years to get a sense of mastery in the ancient tongue and a feeling for its literary secrets which gave him immense leverage in his work of creating a new prose ...".[36] Sri Aurobindo further commented that this method did not bog Bankim down in the pedantry of the classical language but rather he, along with the poet Madhusudan Dutta, 'broke the tyranny of the Sanskrit tradition', and introduced a new direction.[37] Could it then be argued that Bankim, having attended the classes at a *tol* system, extracted from them the essence that these systems had to offer and having thoroughly imbibed from them, could give an altogether original direction to the language that he began expressing himself in?[38]

Indian Wisdom or Examples of the Religious, Philosophica,l and Ethical Doctrines of the Hindus, (1875) rpt 2006, p.178).

35. Indian poet, flourished between 6th or 7th CE A.D. Sanskrit poet and grammarian, author of the influential *Bhattikavya* which is a *mahakavya* [epic poem] composed of a variable number of short cantos. Bhatti lived in the ancient Indian city of Valabhi and was patronised by Shridharasena. He is said to have taught Sanskrit to the Princes at the Court. Comprising a total of 22 cantos and 1,650 verses, his *Bhattikavya* recounts the story of Rama and Sita based on the Sanskrit epic of *Ramayana.* At the same time, it illustrates the principle rules of Sanskrit grammar and poetics that were codified by the grammarian Panini. (Source: *Britannica Online Encyclopedia*)

36 Bankim's tryst with Sanskrit pundits was indeed acknowledged in the annals on Bengal, 'When about 15 years of age he began to study Sanskrit literature and rapidly learnt enough to be able to criticise the works of Sanskrit authors.' (See. C.E. Buckland, *Bengal Under the Lieutenant Governors: being a narrative of the principal events and public measure during their period of office from 1854 to 1898, vol.2*, Calcutta: S.K. Lahiri & Co, 1901, p.1077).

37. *CWSA* vol.1, Bankim Chandra Chatterji, op.cit., p. 92.

38. Pre-British Bengal had a wide and intricate indigenous super-structure of education which taught a wide variety of subjects. An intricate and thriving network of Sanskrit *tols* – schools, colleges,

Following Sri Aurobindo's line of thought, it may be argued that Bankim could do this because first, he decided to break away from

---

and universities also functioned across the province. That these educational institutions also followed a structured and well-developed system of instruction is evident from a very detailed and interesting 18th century account of the Sanskrit University of 'Nuddeah' (Navadvip in Nadia) in present day West Bengal. In its heydays, Sanskrit universities such as the one at Nadia admitted over 5000 students, around the late 1700s, there were 1100 students and 150 masters. In this education system, all valuable works, [were] committed to memory; and to facilitate this, most of their [pundits] compositions, even their dictionaries, [were] in metre. But they, by no means, trust their learning entirely to this repository: on the contrary, those who write treatises, or commentaries on learned topics, have at Nuddeah, always met with distinguished encouragements and rewards'. The method of teaching followed was dialogic, 'two of the masters commence a dialogue, or disputation on the particular topic they mean to explain. When a student hears anything advanced, or expressed, that he does not perfectly understand, he has the privilege of interrogating the master about it. They give the young men every encouragement to communicate their doubts, by their temper and patience in solving them'. It was an established injunction and rule among the teachers at these universities and schools, 'that a pundit who lost his temper in explaining any point to a student, let him be ever so dull and void of memory, absolutely forfeits his reputation, and is disgraced'. (Source: Dharampal, *Archival Compilations*, Vol. IX, 'British Narrations on India – Its Conquest, Its Dominance, And Destruction 1600–1900 A.D.,' Sevagram: Ashram Pratishtan, 2000, p.6) The student was accorded primacy, he was encouraged to question, to differ, to express and to display his personality in the process of learning. These are dimensions which have often been lost sight of, or were marginalised in the discussion on indigenous Indian education. They go to show the kind of encouragement that was given to learning and to developing the faculties of creative thinking and reasoning in the traditional Indian educational scheme of things. Bankim benefitted from it.

the routine of an artificial instruction and second, because he had the urge to pursue his interest. It was his urge, his *swabhava* (his innate propensity for a perfect self-expression), that gradually led him to his *swadharma* (his unique duty in life).

The next step, considered unnatural for the period, was the cutting short of 'his attendance at Hugly [Hooghly] College' at the age of seventeen because, as Sri Aurobindo analysed, "His spirit needed larger bounds than a school routine could give it, and refused, as every free mind does, to cripple itself and lose its natural suppleness. It was his constant habit, a habit which grew on him with the lapse of time, to hide himself in a nook of the College Library and indulge his wandering appetite in all sorts of reading. At the eleventh hour and with an examination impending, he would catch up his prescribed books, hurry through them at a canter, win a few prizes, and go back to his lotus-eating." This, as Sri Aurobindo held it, was the case with brilliant minds in 'all countries', and its positive side was that, "it save[d] [these minds] from the sterilising effects of over instruction ...".[39]

Sri Aurobindo argued here for allowing the pupil at least some time to engage in activities, which are after his heart, his inclinations, and his interests. According to Sri Aurobindo, these contribute immensely to the moulding of character, outlook, and personality, and in unfolding the latent genius in the individual. This idea was stretched across a spectrum of half a century and was put into practice when the International Centre of Education named after Sri Aurobindo was established in Pondicherry in 1951. The realisation that every child had a uniqueness, and had the capacity to express that uniqueness if given the possibility and provided with the right environment, was one of the dominant ideas of the Centre. Therefore, it created such an ambience, refusing to bind itself in a

39. *CWSA* vol.1, Bankim Chandra Chatterji, op.cit., p. 92.

method of routine instruction, and allowed the uniqueness of the child to flower by providing a variety of activities that could attract the interest of the growing mind, which at an early stage, is full of natural inquisitiveness.

A continued look at the series on Bankim will reveal the existence of some more of Sri Aurobindo's educational ideas, which were then in an early stage of crystallisation. Discussing briefly Bankim's sojourn at the Presidency College at Calcutta, Sri Aurobindo mentioned that he was preparing himself for law with the intention of qualifying as a High Court pleader. Then came a decisive turn in Bankim's life and Sri Aurobindo says, "At the right moment for literature, the Calcutta University came into being and Bankim took literary honours instead of legal. The court [thus] lost a distinguished pleader and India gained a great man."

Though Bankim found time from 'hard official drudgery and larger literary toil to appear with his usual distinguished success for the B.L.', it is to be observed that it was finally in his area of interest that he made lasting and original contributions and these acquired for him, an exalted place in the annals of Indian nationalism.[40] Sri Aurobindo essentially tried to argue through the series that the capacity of identifying one's area of interest, an area where one could deeply train oneself and widely excel, the opportunity for self-educating oneself in these areas, and the growth of thought that one could, through one's calling in life, make a unique contribution to national life were all denied by the colonial education machinery in India.

The series on Bankim is interesting, in that they throw up a number of early ideas on education which Sri Aurobindo had begun to develop. Let us explore of few more of these through his observations.

---

40. *CWSA* vol.1, pp.92–93.

The Indian mind, as Sri Aurobindo saw it, had a scholastic tendency that was dominant. The dominant preoccupation of the Indian mind, as it was trained and shaped by the colonial system in the field of education, was one of passing examinations and the acquiring of academic degrees. Sri Aurobindo saw this as the summit of the aim of the majority of the Indian students during those times. "We are a scholastic people," he commented, "and in our life, examinations and degrees fill up half the book. But examinations and degrees are a minor episode in the history of a mind."[41]This was to be another of his educational fundamentals – that the education which had as its principale objective the obtaining of a degree and the successful passing of examinations, was not the true kind of education. It did not really develop the faculties and powers of the mind, encouraged an unthinking retention and therefore, played a very limited role in the actual growth of the mind.

This approach in application was evident in the workings of the Centre of Education at Pondicherry, where the role of examinations and degrees, as understood in the conventional sense, is non-existent or at the most negligible. It may appear strange to those accustomed to the usual frantic pace of exam-oriented education, but this was the approach followed at the Centre of Education right from its inception. During an early period, exams were conducted, although even then they were never the area of primary focus, and a system of free growth, focusing on developing the powers of the mind and other dimensions of the personality, was attempted. At a later stage of the institution's growth, examinations were discontinued altogether. Unbridled pursuit of competition and examination, the concept of excelling at any cost, even at the cost of the other, prevent the spontaneous growth of the qualities of empathy, compassion, and brotherhood. The lack of this growth in young

41. *CWSA* vol.1, p. 93.

minds, or rather the prevention of this growth, as all of these positive qualities are already present in the individual, heavily contributes towards dislocating the balance and harmony of collective life. Like Tagore's early stand at Visva-Bharati, examinations in the Centre of Education at Pondicherry too, were never given primacy and did not emerge as the base of its educational system.[42]

---

42. The Visva-Bharati prospectus stated: 'The system of examination will have no place whatsoever in the Viswabharati, nor is there any conferring of degree.' Vide. Abhik Kumar De, *Rabindranath O Charu Chandra Dutt: Kayekti Prasanger Prekhite* [Beng] in Chaturanga Vol.67 No.1 for Tagore's letters on the subject. Charu Chandra Dutt (C.C. Dutt I.C.S (1876–1952), a close revolutionary associate of Sri Aurobindo, an important financier of the revolutionary movement, and one of the first historians of the Indian National Congress, who was given the charge of writing it in the 1928 session of Congress, was associated with Tagore at Visva-Bharati between 1931–38, out of which he held the post of Vice-Chancellor for five years. Dutt later joined Sri Aurobindo Ashram at Pondicherry in 1946 where, till his passing in 1952, he was actively involved in the educational experiment of the Ashram. On January 7, 1936, Tagore expressed his anguish at having to institutionally bow down before the examination system structure of the Calcutta University because there was a demand/clamour for it. This compromise, Tagore felt, was gradually narrowing the manifestations of his educational ideal. This article contains some revealing letters on this aspect and gives an insight into Tagore's thinking on the issue. It must be mentioned here the educational reforms were initiated during this period in the Calcutta University under Dr. Syama Prasad Mookerjee, the youngest Vice Chancellor of the University, between 1934 and 1938. Tagore and Syama Prasad shared a deep bond which was also reflected in the educational sphere. In 1932, much before he became Vice Chancellor, Dr. Mookerjee, active in the academic administration of the University had specially invited the Poet to accepted the position of University Professor waiving all the ordinary rules that went it, fixing an honorarium of Rs.5000 per year, for a period of two years, and inviting him to 'deliver a course of lectures each year on

Interestingly, the seed of his first principle of teaching that nothing can be essentially taught, is also found in in Sri Aurobindo's observations made in the piece. '... [N]othing which is worth knowing can be taught', remarks Sri Aurobindo, and then goes on

---

selected topics connected with Bengali language and literature for the benefit and guidance of post-graduate students' and to promote study and research in Bengali. In 1937, Syama Prasad invited Tagore to deliver the Calcutta University's convocation address in Bengali, the first time that an Indian was invited to do so in an Indian language. (See Dinesh Chandra Sinha 'Syama Prasad O Kolkata Visvavidyalaya' in *Satabarsher Aloy Syama Prasad* [Syama Prasad in the Light of a Hundred Years], [Beng], Kolkata: Sristi Prakashan, pub. by: Dr. Syama Prasad Mookerjee Smarak Samiti, 2002, pp.37–58). The prospectus of Sri Aurobindo International Centre of Education contains the following words printed in bold: 'the Centre of Education awards no degrees or diplomas' and 'one of its objects being to provide an atmosphere where knowledge is sought for the sake of knowledge and for the building up of the character'. In its note on the higher courses of the Centre of Education, the prospectus states that 'there is no system of conventional examinations or tests and the system of continuous assessment and evaluation of the student is continued'. Vide: handbook brought out by the Centre of Education on its system of education and its aims and objectives. Thus, the parallel between the two regarding the examination system and awarding degrees is evident. The difference being that Tagore's experiment was, perhaps, on a wider scale and his institution *did* finally succumb to the demands of the conventional examination system whereas the Centre of Education, though smaller in scale, refused and still refuses to follow the examination line and the awarding of degrees, thus retaining its original essence and objectivel. The Mother of Sri Aurobindo Ashram, in fact, dropped the nomenclature 'University' from the institution's name in 1959, and replaced it with 'Centre' in order to avoid being entangled into the official web of regulations and routines, which she felt, would dilute the primary aims of Sri Aurobindo's educational philosophy and its experiment. It was a difficult decision but it ensured, in a sense, the unsullied continuation of an altogether new educational attempt.

to present another one of his fundamental principles of education:

> Not what man learns, but what he observes for himself in life and literature is the formative agency in his existence, and the actual shape it will take is much determined by the sort of social air he happens to breathe at that critical moment when the mind is choosing its road. All else is mere dead material, useless without the breath of a vivifying culture. If examinations and degrees are the skeleton of university life, these are its soul and lifeblood, and where they exist poorly or not at all, education, except for the one or two self-sufficing intellects becomes mere wind and dust.[43]

This is probably the essence of Sri Aurobindo's early critique of the education system. His perception that real education can and must necessarily be discovered beyond the mechanical pedagogic framework, had begun to develop. Sri Aurobindo's educational conviction that examinations and degrees were just a part of the whole system, and that the real formative acquisitions were those that the individual observes and absorbs in and from his surroundings, and that the environment indeed had a decisive influence on the growth of the mind, all emerge through these observations.

Sri Aurobindo discusses the environment in which Bankim grew and developed his faculties. He describes the then Bengal as a 'theatre of a great intellectual awakening', where a 'sort of miniature Renascence was in process'. While describing the Bengali temperament and intellectual constitution, Sri Aurobindo points to another crucial aspect, one that was then being widely discussed as being one of the principal reasons for constricting the intellectual growth of the Indian student, which was the use of English as the medium of instruction rather than the vernacular. Talking of the Bengali mind and temperament, Sri Aurobindo observes that when the individual – here, the Bengali student – is 'tenderest and

---

43. *CWSA* vol.1, Bankim Chandra Chatterji, op.cit, p. 93.

needs the most careful rearing', it is then subjected to 'the wicked and wantonly cruel strain of instruction through a foreign tongue' and an 'enormous academic labour'.[44] These, he felt, pushed the individual towards premature exhaustion and decline. Talking about the positive contribution of the environment Sri Aurobindo concludes that whatever Bankim lost by being exposed to a rigid and unresponsive academic system, he made up through 'his youthful surroundings' from which he gained much 'emotional experience and great flexibility of mind'. But what was it that saved Bankim and helped preserve and nurture his exceptional talent, asks Sri Aurobindo.

> It was the initial stimulus and the cultured environment .... With a limited creature like man, the power of the environment is immense. Genius it is true, exists independently of environment and, by much reading and observation, may attain to self-expression, but it is environment that makes self-expression easy and natural; that provides sureness, verve, stimulus. Here lies the importance to the mind in its early stage of self-culture of fine social surroundings; that sort of surroundings which our Universities do nothing and ought to have done everything to create.[45]

This was another cardinal principle of Sri Aurobindo's educational philosophy – the importance of the environment in moulding the individual. The education system then, as Sri Aurobindo felt, did not provide the opportunity for the young mind to consciously imbibe from his surroundings. The mind was exposed, right from the beginning, to an artificial environment which pumped into it artificial contents in a language that was artificial and alien to it. This reference to the environment is also found in Sri Aurobindo's later formulations on the philosophy of national education. It was to be the cornerstone of his third

44. *CWSA* vol.1, p.97.
45. *CWSA* vol.1, p.98.

educational principle – the aim of working from 'the near to the far, from that which is, to that which shall be,' and in that he describes the importance of the environment in shaping the individual. "The basis of a man's nature," he argued, "is almost always, in addition to his soul's past, his heredity, his surroundings, his nationality, his country, the soil from which he draws sustenance, the air which he breathes, the sights, sounds, habits to which he is accustomed. They mould him not the less powerfully because insensibly. From that then we must begin."[46] It is to the environment that the child feels an organic affinity and pull and therefore, to make him conscious of his milieu and allow the milieu to mould and shape his growth, was an important consideration.

The early usage of English as a medium of instruction hampered the growth of this awareness and brought in a certain amount of artificiality. The mother-tongue is the proper medium of education and therefore, the first energies of the child should be directed to the thorough mastering of the medium. Tagore had already highlighted this issue in 1892–93,[47] and it grew to become one of

---

46. *CWSA* vol.1, pp. 384–85.
47. In his celebrated speech on 'The Centre of Indian Culture', Tagore makes a pointed reference to this problem, "For the perfect irrigation of learning", observed Tagore, "a foreign language cannot be a true medium ... when we are compelled to learn through the medium of English, the knocking at the gate and turning of the key take away the best part of our life. The feast may be waiting for us inside the room, but the difficulty and delay of admission spoil our appetite and the long privation permanently injures our stomach. The ideas are very late in coming to us, and the tediously long trial of our teeth over the grinding of grammar, and a system of spelling, which is devoid of all conscience, takes away our relish for the food when it does come at last." Tagore saw two fundamental reasons for the large majority of Indian boys not being able to master the English language. One, it was difficult to 'accommodate this language in their minds, whose

the main demands of the national education movement. It was driven by the realisation that instructions being given in a foreign tongue right from the start prevented a free growth of the faculties of the mind, as an immense amount of energy usually went into mastering the techniques of the language itself. "When the mental instruments are sufficiently developed to acquire a language easily and swiftly, that is the time to introduce him [the child] to many languages easily and swiftly," notes Sri Aurobindo, to be the issue that ought to be handled.[48]

It would be relevant to recall here that Sri Aurobindo's maternal grandfather, Rajnarayan Bose (1826–1899) one of the early advocates of nationalism and cultural self-recovery in Bengal and the ideologue many of whose ideas announced a new era of cultural awakening, had founded in 1866, a 'Society for the Promotion of National Feeling among the educated Natives of Bengal'.[49] The objective of Raj Narayan's society was 'to resist the powerful tendency of imitating the West by reviving the old ideas, traditions, and customs in every walk of life. Indigenous gymnastic exercises, Indian music, Hindu medicines, Bengali food, dress and etiquette' and more were to replace the foreign forms. The insistence was on learning the mother-tongue before English and 'cultivation of Sanskrit was to be encouraged' among other things.[50]

---

ingrained habit has been to think in an Eastern tongue'. He compared the feat to trying to fit an 'English sword into the scabbard of a scimitar', and two, very few boys had the means 'of getting anything like a proper grounding in English at the hands of a competent teacher – the sons of the poor certainly have not'. (Rabindranath Tagore, The Centre of Indian Culture' in Sisir Kumar Das ed. *The English Writings of Rabindranath Tagore,(EWRT) vol.2*, .2008, pp.477–478.

48. *CWSA* vol.1, p. 394.
49. R.C.Majumdar, *History of the Freedom Movement in India*, Vol.1, (1962, 1971) Rpt.1997, p.295.
50. Ibid.

Sri Aurobindo, circa December 1907

Sri Aurobindo, Calcutta, 1907

Sri Aurobindo with his students of Baroda College

Sri Aurobindo presiding over the Nationalist Party conference in Surat after the split of the Congress, December 1907. Also seen in the picture is Lokmanya Tilak, standing and delivering his address. Seated to Sri Aurobindo's right is nationalist leader from Maharashtra G.S. Khaparde.

Sri Aurobindo in Surat, December 1907. Front row seated left: G.S. Khaparde, seated right: Ashwini Kumar Dutt; middle row, from left to right: Sardar Ajit Singh, Sri Aurobindo, Lokmanya B.G. Tilak, Syed Haidar Reza; top row standing left: Dr. B.S. Moonje, Ramaswamy, K. Kuverji Desai

Sri Aurobindo (seated first right), Uttarpara, 1908. On the first left seated: Bipin Chandra Pal

Sri Aurobindo, Alipore Jail, 1908

Sri Aurobindo, Alipore Jail, 1908

Bal Gangadhar Tilak

Lala Lajpat Rai

Bipin Chandra Pal

Lala Lajpat Rai with Madan Mohan Malaviya and Kodilayam V Rangaswami Iyengar

The Nationalist Triumvirate of Lal-Bal-Pal, (left to right): Lala Lajpat Rai, Lokmanya Bal Gangadhar Tilak, Bipin Chandra Pal

Rabindranath Tagore came to meet Sri Aurobindo in Pondicherry – 1928. At the Pondicherry old Pier, sitting in a cutbarrel alongwith his secretary Nirmal Kumari Mahalanabish, Smt (Rani), which was being lifted by a crane to bring it to the sea shore

Brahmabandhab Upadhyay, editor of the fiercely nationalist paper *Sandhya*

Annie Besant

Maharaja Sayajirao Gaekwad III

Dinendra Kumar Roy

Raja Subodh Chandra Mullick

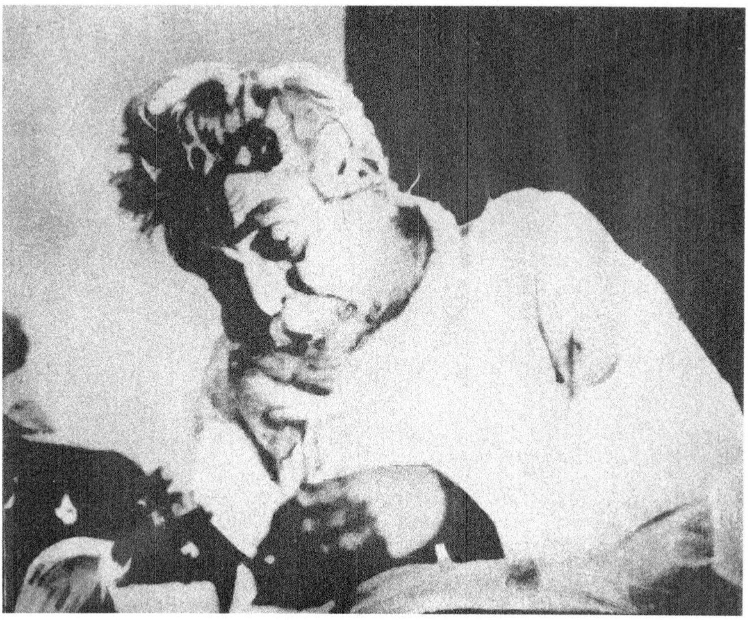

Acharya Satish Chandra Mukherjee

Raj Narayan's ideas were to be taken up by the likes of Nabagopal Mitra (1840–1894) with the founding of the Hindu Mela with the aim of promoting 'national feeling, sense of patriotism, and a spirit of self-help among the Hindus'.[51] There were altogether fourteen editions of the Hindu Mela between 1867 and 1880 and it became a dynamic platform which crystallised the early aspirations for a cultural and political self-assertion. Speaking of Raj Narayan's impact on his era, Bipin Chandra Pal observed that 'his writings and speeches did a good deal to create that spirit of self-respect and self-assertion in the educated classes that have since found such strong expression in our recent political activities'.[52] Raj Narayan, who was often referred to as the 'Grandfather of Indian Nationalism',[53] was especially fond of his grandson Sri Aurobindo. He had arranged for Dinendra Kumar Roy to be sent to Baroda for tutoring Sri Aurobindo in Bengali.[54] While Raj Narayan lived in Deoghar, Sri Aurobindo visited him several times. Of these visits, Sri Aurobindo recalled, 'My politics were shaped before I came to India; he talked to me of his Nationalist activities in the past, but I learned nothing new from them. I admired my grandfather and liked his writings "Hindu Dharmer Sreshtatwa" and "Se Kala r E Kal" ...'.[55]

Sri Aurobindo speaks rather forcefully in this piece, of how the system of public instruction usually burdens the mind with the learning of too many subjects, steam-rolls individuality, and prevents the individual from specialising in something which is

---

51. R.C.Majumdar, *History of the Freedom Movement in India*, Vol.1, op.cit., p.294.
52. Bipin Chandra Pal, *Indian Nationalism: Its Principles and Personalities*, 1918, p.162.
53. Ibid., p.164.
54. Dinendra Kumar Roy, op.cit., p.3.
55. Sri Aurobindo, *Autobiographical Notes & Other Writings of Historical Interest*, 2006, p.45.

after his heart and suitable to his nature and temperament. "To find your vocation and keep to it," Sri Aurobindo argues,

> ... is not indeed a showy, but it is a simple and solid rule of life. We forget that the mind is as mortal and as much subject to wear and tear as any perishable thing, forgetting that specialism is one condition of the highest accomplishment, forgetting that our stock of energy is limited, and that what we expend in one direction, we lose in another. We insist on burning the candle at both ends. This spirit appears in our system of public instruction, the most ingeniously complete machine for murder that human stupidity ever invented, and murder not only of a man's body but of a man's soul, of that sacred fire of individuality in him ...[56]

This was Sri Aurobindo's concern; he felt that the decimation of individuality perpetuated alien rule by killing the urge for initiative and of freethinking. In his series of essays published sometime in 1906 at the height of the Swadeshi movement, cultural historian and philosopher Ananda Coomaraswamy also echoed this aspect of the failures and adverse impact of colonial public instruction on the Indian mind, when he argued that one of the 'remarkable features of British rule in India' was the fact that 'the greatest injuries done to the people of India, have taken the outward form of blessings' and of this, Education was a 'striking example'.[57]

Later, when writing exclusively on the subject of a national education, Sri Aurobindo pointed at the negativities of trying to teach a number of subjects all at once by giving an imperfect little of each. He called it the method of teaching by 'snippets' and compared it to the old Indian system of instruction.

> A subject is taught a little at a time, in conjunction with a host of others, with the result that what might be well learnt in a single year is badly learned in seven, and the boy goes out ill-equipped, served with imperfect parcels of knowledge, master of none of the great departments of human knowledge

56. *CWSA* vol.1, p. 105.
57. Ananda Coomaraswamy, *Essays in National Idealism*, 1906, p.96.

.... The old system was to teach one or two subjects well and thoroughly and then proceed to others ... [58].

It disturbed Sri Aurobindo to see that the prevailing method of learning was by highlighting and memorising only that which was useful for passing an examination. This method came into vogue after the public instruction system was introduced by the colonial education department. It ushered in the era of 'textbook culture' which made the passing of examinations with the assistance of textbooks the primary educational objective. By the time Sri Aurobindo looked at this, it was becoming or had become, the established procedure.[59] Sri Aurobindo felt that this not only reduced the capacity of the Indian mind for an in-depth reflection but also affected the growth of concentration, sustained application, and turned the individual into a mere passive receiver. His method of teaching was innovative and demonstrated his disregard for established norms of teaching through hired notes and repetition. His students remembered the fact that his method of teaching 'was a novel one'. Sri Aurobindo would start by giving a 'series of introductory lectures for initiating the student to the subject-matter of the text .... After preparing the student to understand the text in this manner, he used to start reading the text, stopping wherever necessary to explain the meaning of difficult or obscure sentences. Then he used to dictate general lectures bearing on the various aspects pertaining to the text',[60] recalled one of his students in Baroda, Rajaram N. Patkar. Another of his students, P.B. Chandwani,

---

58. *CWSA* vol.1, On Education: Simultaneous & Successive Teaching, p. 393.
59. See. Krishna Kumar 'Origins of the Textbook Culture' in *What is Worth Teaching* (Hyderabad: Orient Blackswan, 2009) for a greater debate on the issue.
60. Cited in Manoj Das, op.cit., p.121.

a member of the 'Servants of the people Society' who attended Sri Aurobindo's classes during the 'last phase of Sri Aurobindo's sojourn in Baroda', remembered attending his classes on Burke's '*Reflections on the French Revolution*'. Chandwani recalled, 'while many students complained that he made no effort to coach us for examination, I felt his teaching was so exhaustive that no examiner could ever ask a question which we could not answer with the flood light thrown on it by the learned Principal'.[61] A contemporary of Chandwani, at Baroda College, Shankar Balwant Didmishe, gives a precise description of how Sri Aurobindo taught:

> His method consisted in going to the roots, one could never forget what he taught, even though the whole text was not completed. His mastery of the English language was phenomenal .... He had no books or notes with him; everything was extempore.[62]

Laying emphasis on the advantages of instruction in the mother-tongue, Sri Aurobindo argues that Bankim's mastery of his mother tongue gave him the capability of a rich and unique literary output. Talking of learning a foreign language and using it as a medium of expression, Sri Aurobindo observes, "in a language [one has learnt], [one] may write graciously, correctly, pleasingly, but [one] will never attain to the full stature of [one's] genius." He draws a comparison between Bankim and one of his contemporaries in the Bombay Presidency, Kashinath Trimbak Telang.[63] Telang, according

61. Manoj Das, op.cits., p.125. Chandwani rose to become the Deputy General Manager of the North-Western railways, associated with Mahatma Gandhi, and is said to have stayed with him during his last days in Birla House at Delhi.
62. Ibid., p.125.
63. Kashinath T. Telang (1850–1893): Judge, educationist, Indologist, and social-reformer. Telang, a graduate of the Elphinstone College, Bombay, had great command over the English language. In 1889, he accepted a seat on the High Court bench where he gave authoritative

to Sri Aurobindo, was a man of '... large abilities, [and] the most considerable genius a highly intellectual people has produced, yet left nothing to which the world will return with unfailing delight

---

judgments on the Hindu Law, which, due to his mastery of Sanskrit, he was able to interpret first-hand. He was a syndic of the Bombay University from 1881, and Vice-Chancellor from 1892 until his death in the following year. In the same year, he became the President of the Asiatic Society of Bombay, the first Indian to hold both these posts. A follower of Dadabhai Naoroji in politics, he formed the Bombay Presidency Association along with Sir Pheroze Shah Mehta, the famous moderate leader of Congress in the Bombay Presidency. Along with Badruddin Tyabji and Mehta, he formed the Bombay Triumvirate. His political activities involved the writing of a number of articles, especially protesting the Vernacular Press Act of Lord Lytton, then Viceroy of India and giving addresses, the most famous one being on 'Should social reform precede political reform', which was intended as an answer to the then Lieutenant-Governor of the United Provinces, Sir Auckland Colvin, who had patronisingly advised members of the newly formed Congress to set their house in order first and then demand political rights. His studied Sanskrit deeply and translated the Bhagavad-Gita into English prose. His translation became a standard work and found place in Max Mueller's *Sacred Books of the East*. He is also known for his criticism of Albrecht Weber's (1825–1901, German Indologist and historian) hypothesis that the Homeric epics influenced the Ramayana. (Source: *Encyclopaedia* Britannica *11th ed.* and *Dictionary of National Biography, Vol.- IV* ed. S.P. Sen, Calcutta, 1974, *The Indian Nation Builders, Part-III,* Madras: Ganesh & Co Publishers, date not stated). In fact, Bankim in his commentaries on the *Srimad-Bhagavad-Gita* makes copious references to Telang's work on the Gita. (See his commentaries in J.C. Bagal edited *Bankim Rachanabali, vol.2*, 16th imp., [Beng], 1417). Living in Baroda during that period, Sri Aurobindo must have known all about Telang. Sri Aurobindo's friend from Cambridge, K.G. Deshpande, editor of the *Indu Prakash,* for which Sri Aurobindo wrote regularly for a while, was known to a number of leading social reformers of the Bombay Presidency.

…'. This was because, as Sri Aurobindo observed, Telang wrote mainly in English and as pointed out earlier, in a language that one learns, according to him, one could not express oneself uniquely and with impact. But Telang's more radical mistake, according to Sri Aurobindo, was that he allowed himself to dissipate and did not stick to his true calling. While referring to Telang's power as pre-eminently literary, Sri Aurobindo argued that Telang 'allowed it to run in every direction except the very one that nature had marked out for it,' and therefore, could not contribute anything lasting through his talent. Sri Aurobindo says this with a feeling of regret and is in no way trying to minimise Telang's contribution to India's national life, which he says, could have been richer had he focused on literature in the vernacular.[64]

Sri Aurobindo's belief that one ought to respond to one's inclinations and find the right vocation is also seen here. But Bankim was more fortunate, says Sri Aurobindo, because he 'wrote in his own beautiful mother-tongue' and could therefore, unravel himself near completely. Bankim's originality, Sri Aurobindo observes, "would in any case have forced its way out," and only had he worked 'single-heartedly' in the field of his rich harvests, and did not have to undergo the strains of a daily official drudgery, could Bankim's output have been far greater than is otherwise available.[65]

Assessing Bankim's contribution to Bengal, Sri Aurobindo observes, among other things, that he contributed towards the making of Bengali into the principal language of public expression for the Bengali. "Bankim's influence has been far-reaching," observes Sri Aurobindo at the end of the assessment, "and every day enlarges its bounds. What is its result?" He supplies the answer himself saying, "Perhaps, it may very roughly be summed up thus. When a Maratha

64. *CWSA* vol.1, Bankim Chandra Chatterji – His Versatility, op. cit., p. 105.
65. Ibid., p. 105.

or Gujerati has anything important to say, he says it in English; when a Bengali, he says it in Bengali. That is, I think, the fact which is most full of meaning for us in Bengal. It means besides other things less germane to literature, that, except in politics and journalism which is the handmaid of politics, English is steadily driven out of the field. Soon it will only remain to weed it out of our conversation."

Sri Aurobindo mentions here the work of Kali Prasanna Ghosh[66] who had, he felt, already given a shoulder to the wheel that would finally drive out the usage of English in public domain. "Not long ago," observes Sri Aurobindo, "anyone moving in that province of the mind, which Babu Kali Prasunna has annexed, would have held it beneath the dignity of his subject to write in any medium

---

66. Kali Prasanna Ghosh (1843–1910): Bengali scholar and litterateur who learnt Persian, Sanskrit, and Bengali during his childhood and learnt English at the age of ten in the Dacca Collegiate School. He studied the *Mugdhabodh*, *Raghuvamsha*, and *Meghadutam* at entrance level, and then studied English literature, history, psychology, logic, theology, etc at Calcutta. In 1870, he became the editor of *Subhasini*, a journal of the Brahmo Youth and in 1874, edited the journal *Bandhab*. While working as the principal officer of the Raja of Bhawal, Ghosh established the Sahitya Samalachana Sabha (literary discussion society) and was equally dexterous in speaking English. Kali Prasanna became a distinguished member of the Bangiya Sahitya Parishad, later became its Vice-President, and became the President of the Sahitya Sammelan. (Source: *Bangali Charitabidhan, Vol.1* 2nd ed. 2002, Kolkata. Kaliprasanna followed a Sankritised Bengali style and it resembled that of the early writings of Vidyasagar. He was conferred the honorific of 'Vidyasagar' by the Pundits of Dacca, and came to be known popularly as the Vidyasagar of East Bengal. The reflective essays collected in his *Prabhatchinta* ('Morning Thoughts', 1877) and *Nisithachinta* ('Midnight Thoughts', 1896) enjoyed a vogue for a long time as school textbooks. Source: Sukumar Sen, 'Essays and Essay writers (1850–1914)' in *Studies in Bengal Renaissance*, 3rd revised ed., 2002.

but English. Work, like Babu Kali Prasunna's, marks an important stage in the great revolution of sentiment which our literary class has set going, the revolution of sentiments which promises to make the Bengalis a nation .... Young Bengal gets its ideas, feelings, and culture, not from schools and colleges, but from Bankim's novels and Robindranath Tagore's poems; so true is it that language is the life of a nation."[67] And if 'a renaissance creates a new mind, brings about a reawakening'[68] then it certainly did that in Bankim. It presented him as a new mind, which brought about a new awakening. The renaissance had already begun spurting forth new ideas; it had begun to give shape to a distinct Bengali identity. It was this identity, Sri Aurobindo argued, that Bankim consolidated through his life and work, gave further shape, crystallised, and symbolised. It was this 'revolution of sentiments' that nurtured Bankim and he, in turn, gave his energies into making a nation through the power of his language and imagination.

The standard school and college, the routine mechanism of instruction as imposed by the colonial machinery, and the foreign medium of instruction, Sri Aurobindo realised early, and as is evident from this series, was limiting the impact and influence of this revolution of sentiments and of this re-birth which was gradually wielding the Bengalis into a nation again, consolidating a collective consciousness. Therefore, he urged its rejection and instead pushed for the evolution of something new, suited to the needs of the age in its place. Language, he felt, was one instrument that could rapidly bring about this consolidation, which could ignite this awareness, and gradually pave the way forward for united action on various other fronts. Years later, in an eloquent piece on

67. *CWSA* vol.1, Bankim Chandra Chatterji –What He did for Bengal & Our Hope in the Future, op cit., pp. 115, 118.

68. R.K. Dasgupta, Introduction to the 3rd ed. of *Studies in the Bengal Renaissance*, 2002.

'Rishi Bankim Chandra', Sri Aurobindo would revisit these aspects of Bankim's life and contribution, and in conclusion would pen his famous lines describing Bankim's contribution to the awakening of Indian nationalism, speaking of his 'supreme service' to the nation as that of giving 'us the vision of our Mother'. 'It was thirty-two years ago that Bankim wrote his great song and few listened', wrote Sri Aurobindo, 'but in a sudden moment of awakening from long delusions, the people of Bengal looked around for the truth and in a fated moment somebody sang *Bande Mataram*. The mantra had been given, and in a single day a whole people had been converted to the religion of patriotism'.[69]

A detailed study of Sri Aurobindo's series on Bankim was thus necessitated, because in it, lie scattered, a number of key ideas on education that Sri Aurobindo was to develop later. These ideas indicated a way towards a future philosophy of national education. These ideas also exposed the adverse impact that an alien education system had on the mind.

Some of these key ideas found in this early series by Sri Aurobindo could be summarised thus: the concept that nothing can be truly taught, that the environment had a deep impact on the formative mind, that one should have the leisure to follow one's own inclinations and to develop oneself in one's chosen field of interest and thereby make one's unique contribution to the national life, the importance of the vernacular in expressing oneself and in forming one's identity, the importance of not dissipating oneself in a maze of subjects, and the necessity of delving deep into the given subject and try and absorb it superficially, can all be read in this piece.

These are the earliest known public formulations of Sri Aurobindo's educational ideas, and they gradually find voice later through his other writings and speeches.

---

69. Sri Aurobindo, *Bankim-Tilak-Dayananda*, (1940), 6th ed. 2006, pp.13–14.

I.3. EARLY SUGGESTIONS FOR REFORMS: AS AN EDUCATION ADMINISTRATOR

Sri Aurobindo was appointed, for a brief while in 1905, as the Minister-in-Charge of Education and held, simultaneously, the post of the acting Principal of the Baroda College. While carrying out this dual responsibility, he wrote a minute on a '*Proposed Examination for Teachers*' dated August 9, 1905, for the consideration of 'The Minister of Education' – BARODA. In it, one finds some of his early opinions on the examination system. "I have gone very carefully," wrote A.A.G. Ag. Principal, Baroda College, "through the scheme of the proposed examination for teachers ... [&] I do not quite see the object of introducing this severe and stringent examination into our State. Our schools are working quite well enough on the whole for the purpose of education as given in this country. I do not myself think very highly either of the principle or methods or results of that education but, being subject to the Bombay University, we have to take things as they are and cannot attempt anything ideal ...."

One notices here Sri Aurobindo's dissatisfaction with the present university system in India, which had also disgusted Tagore and had turned him into an inveterate opponent of the system. Sri Aurobindo, writing here as an official of the Baroda state, could not then demand a radical disaffiliation with the official system. This demand he made later when he moved into the political field.

The examinations, Sri Aurobindo suggested, could be modified by 'a mild test'. Analysing the proposed examination, Sri Aurobindo argued that the sort of examination here proposed is such as might be prescribed in a European country where the science and art of education are really advanced. Here it is likely to degenerate into a formality harassing to the teachers but useless to the State .... Undoubtedly the teachers will cram up the subjects learning by rote as is the habit in this country, and a percentage of them will pass, but there it will end; a few of the brighter and smarter young men may understand and make the attempt to apply the principles they learn, but that will be all ...."

Reading the note on the 'Junior Examination' in Part-II of the minute, we find, again, some of Sri Aurobindo's brief reflections on methods pursued, "Instead of the elaborate affair [proposed system of examinations] it will be enough to see whether the teacher can make the boys understand the lesson, explain a subject correctly and command their attention ...."[70]

One also finds a detailed note on the necessity of a 'Head Assistant for the High School'. In it, Sri Aurobindo discusses the working of the Baroda High School, and it is seen that he did have first-hand experience and knowledge of the administrative aspects of the colonial education system and the running of schools under it.

Sri Aurobindo was not only concerned with creating a new philosophy of education but he also realised that the whole educational structure and educational approach would have to be reconstituted and re-shaped if national education had to really play the role of nation building. In one of his last articles on education while in Bengal in January 1910, Sri Aurobindo argued for setting up a wholly new system of teachers' training classes that would train teachers, keeping in mind the national requirement and temperament.[71] It was this aspect that was missing from the

70. *CWSA* vol.1, op.cit., Opinions Written as Acting Principal, Baroda College: 1905, pp. 745–54.

71. In his article on National Education in the *Karmayogin* of 1st January 1910, Sri Aurobindo points to the problem of inadequacy of trained teachers. He pointed out that the necessity of 'providing a regular and plentiful supply of teachers trained in an entirely new system

national education experiment initiated by the National Council of Education. Sri Aurobindo realised that the teachers trained at training colleges instituted by the colonial education department, could never really be expected to give a radically new direction to Indian education.

Perhaps, the following words, meant for public delivery, best illustrate the direction that his mind had started pursuing towards the demand for national education, and its use as an instrument for self-determination. Drafted in 1902, this incomplete speech was perhaps meant to be delivered by Sri Aurobindo:

> The subject on which I wish to address you this evening ... is Education. Some of you may ask yourselves, why this subject rather than any other? It is not a new subject but rather quite a threadbare one; you have already heard and read much about it and probably listened to much better lectures on the subject than any I can give you; it has besides been handled by a great many men in high places of authority; most of all, it has been taken up by no less a person than Lord Curzon himself, and measures are to be formulated and perhaps carried into execution for the reform of what is defective in the present system. "What more do you want," you will perhaps

---

of instruction' [as he hoped the national education system would eventually evolve] still remained because the Council, he observed 'has systematically ignored [it], and not even the elementary steps of establishing a Teacher's Training Class in Calcutta and issuing a series of suitable books in the vernacular has been attempted'. [*CWSA* vol.8, *Karmayogin*, 1997, p. 388.] Sri Aurobindo argued that a completely new system of teachers' training ought to have been initiated by the Council in order to make a lasting impact on the education system. He felt that the teachers' training course prescribed by the colonial education department was not equipped to induce new thinking and develop the faculties of the student. . The vision and understanding of a teacher's training remained much the same *vis-à-vis* teachers' training programmes, remain much the same in a post-colonial India until the National Education Policy (2020) introduced a fundamental course correction to its approach.

ask, "or why should we trouble ourselves about it? The Government of India will in its own good time reform the whole business and of course when their new system is in force, the Baroda Schools and Colleges will assimilate themselves to it. Meanwhile it is quite superfluous for us to bother our heads about the matter." Now in answer to that attitude I have to say this, that the Government of India is, in the first place, not the fit body to formulate the necessary improvements and in the second place, not the fit instrument to put them into force. It is not fit to formulate them because it cannot realise and feel as we do where the shoe pinches us and therefore in mending it ....[72]

The early formulations of an uncompromising critic of the colonial educational machinery had indeed begun.

72. *CWSA* vol.1, On Education, op.cit., p.357.

2

Survey of the Indian Educational Scene

A Prelude to the National Education Movement

"

Rammohan Ray arose with a new religion in his hand, which was developed on original lines by men almost greater one thinks than he, by Rajnarain Bose and Debendranath Tagore. The two Dutts, Okhay [Akshay] Kumar and Michael Madhu Sudan, [Dutt] began a new Prose and a new Poetry. Vidyasagara, scholar, sage and intellectual dictator, laboured hugely like the Titan he was, to create a new Bengali language and a new Bengali society, while in vast and original learning Rajendra Lal Mitra has not met his match. Around these arose a class of men who formed a sort of seed-bed for the creative geniuses, men of fine critical ability and appreciative temper, scholarly, accomplished, learned in music and the arts, men in short not only of culture, but of original culture...

– Sri Aurobindo,
Bankim Chandra Chatterji

It would be worthwhile to have a look at the various educational initiatives that had sprung up during the last part of the nineteenth century and in the early part of the twentieth. It was a period when Sri Aurobindo was still enlisted in the service of the Baroda Raj and when nationalist sentiments were crystallising, especially in the province of Bengal. A spirit of dissatisfaction was being nurtured and expressed in various spheres in the province and the country as a whole.

A critical appraisal of the colonial education framework had already begun, and efforts were being made to try and provide a direction to Indian education which would be more in consonance with Indian needs, conditions, and ethos. In short, a 'quest for self-identity' in the field of education had begun. It is known that during his Baroda stay, Sri Aurobindo was actively, albeit secretly, already engaged in revolutionary activities and was closely following developments in Bengal while attempting to prepare the ground for a larger revolutionary movement in that province. It may be assumed that Sri Aurobindo was also aware of the currents of educational thought that had begun to gather speed in that province.[1] His first

1. Sri Aurobindo arranged for Jatindranath Banerjee – later Niralamba Swami – (1877–1930) who had come to Baroda sometime around 1899, to undertake military training under the assumed north Indian name of Yatinder Nath Upadhyay in the Baroda state army. Jatin entered the 4th Baroda Infantry as a sepoy to learn discipline from the ground up. After a year, he was transferred to the Gaekwar's Bodyguard and perfected his riding skills. Sometime around 1902, Jatin came back to Bengal with the direction from Sri Aurobindo to start organising secret revolutionary societies and begin recruitment throughout

political move, so to say, while in Baroda, was when 'he sent a young Bengali soldier of the Baroda army, Jatin Banerji, as his lieutenant to Bengal with a programme of preparation and action which he might occupy a period of thirty years before fruition could become possible'.[2]

Maharaja Sayaji Rao III of Baroda clearly nursed nationalist sentiments despite his state being among the highest ranking five states to be entitled to the customary, but indicative '21-gun salute'.

---

the province. Jatin was to put into effect one side of Sri Aurobindo's political action namely the organising of armed insurrection. In 1906, he undertook *sannyasa* and assumed the name of Niralamba Swami. In 1908, he was arrested in connection with the Alipore Bomb Case but was acquitted due to lack evidence. During this period, Sri Aurobindo had also begun contacting revolutionary societies of western and central India in order to try and create a network of such societies; he was in the process of gauging the temper and situation in Bengal: Vide: *Samsad Bangali Charitabhidhan* –Biographical Dictionary, ed. Dr.Subodh Chandra Sengupta and Anjali Bose, vol.1, 2nd imp, 2002, p. 43, Peter Heehs, *The Bomb in Bengal*, rpt, 2004, Roshan & Apurva, op.cit. Of Jatindranath Banerjee's activities from 1906 onward, after he left Bengal, historian of the pre-Gandhian phase of the Indian freedom movement, Prithwindra Mukherjee writes in his opus, 'Jatin Banerjee had left Bengal and under the name of Niralamba Swami, had undertaken a tour from Tibet through the mountain regions of Garhwal up to Punjab and Uttar Pradesh. Bearer of Sri Aurobindo's revolutionary ideas, he contacted and inspired leaders such as Sardar Ajit Singh and Kishen Singh (father of the future martyr Bhagat Singh), Lala Lajpat Rai, Har Dayal, Sufi Amba Prasad, Obeidullah Sindhi, doctors Haricharan Mukherjee of Ambala and Charu Ghose of Peshawar. Each of them collaborated with the Extremists of Bengal...' (*The Intellectual Roots of India's Freedom Struggle (1893–1918)*, (Eng Trans of the original French), New Delhi: Manohar, 2017, p.149)

2. Sri Aurobindo, *Autobiographical Notes & Other Writings of Historical Interest*, p.49.

He was one of those few among princes who 'demanded from the British courtesy and consideration an equal deserved'.[3] On occasions when the British would 'ask him to stop statements hostile to them emanating from his territory', Sayajirao countered them, by 'telling them to stop criticism of their policies and actions by British officials and Anglo-Indian press inside the territory directly ruled by the British'.[4] According to one of his most reliable biographers, Sayaji Rao, like 'most sensitive Indians of his age had been drawn under the spell of the advanced guards of the freedom movement' and was 'perfectly aware' of Sri Aurobindo's 'political views and activities' and is said to have 'secretly sympathised with them'.[5] This was a time, when 'princes who called themselves progressive were closely watched to see if their liberalism strayed into the sphere of politics, and any prince who was not properly subservient at all times was marked down as disloyal'.[6]

A note on Sayaji Rao's progressive governance measures and the scepticism with which the British looked at it may be relevant for here. It was perhaps James O'Grady, Labour Member of Parliament and trade unionist who raised the issue in the British Parliament in March 1908, when he asked whether the Secretary of State for India was aware that the 'Maharaja of Baroda had separated the judicial from the executive functions, has restored local self-Government, has instituted popularly elected members in his Legislative Council?'

---

3. Manoj Das, *Sri Aurobindo: Life and Times of the Mahayogi: the Pre-Pondicherry Phase*, 2020, p.93.
4. Manoj Das, op.cit., p.93.
5. Fatehsinghrao Gaekwad, *Sayajirao of Baroda: The Prince and the Man*, 1989, p.183.
6. Ibid. The Raj's trouble with Sayaji Rao was that 'while his administration was first-rate and his private life unexceptionable, his loyalty was not wholehearted', their grievance was that he had 'ceased to be a good prince'. p.218.

O'Grady asked whether the Council of India would consider applying these reforms to other 'Native States' and to the rest of India. The Secretary of States for India replied with caution that 'the results of these measures in Baroda would be watched with interest' but 'he could not undertake forthwith to suggest the introduction of similar measures in the whole of British India, he would not interfere with discretion of the rulers of other states'.[7]

Despite knowing that to 'harbour a well-known extremist' in his service, was, for someone in his position, a grave risk, he had, asserts Sayaji Rao's biographer, 'gone on supporting Aurobindo, to the extent of giving military training to one of Aurobindo's friends, Jatin Banerji, in the Baroda Cavalry, and thereby defying a ban imposed by the British government against employment of Bengalis in the army'.[8] Residency Records of that epoch refer to Sayaji Rao's behaviour as 'openly suspicious' and speak of him as a being 'in sympathy with the extremists'.[9]

The British administration's anger at Sayaji Rao for having displayed nationalist sentiments, for often being unyielding on his attitude to it and for his harbouring Sri Aurobindo in his service, is seen from a letter Lord Hardinge, Governor General and Viceroy of India, in a secret communiqué to the British government recommended 'an uncompromising tougher line with the Gaekwad' and pointed out how the Gaekwad had once displayed the audacity of having employed Aurobindo Ghose 'the noted extremist' and of having covered up on his anti-Empire activities. Hardinge wrote, "For a time he [Sri Aurobindo] acted as His Highness's Private Secretary and ... a Vice-Principle of the Baroda College ... There can be no question but that his employment in the State gave a great

7. Ibid., pp.205–206.
8. Ibid., p.206.
9. Ibid., p.184.

impetus to the anti-British movement."[10] This was written years after Sri Aurobindo had left the Baroda service and moved on to politics in Bengal.

In Baroda, Sri Aurobindo instilled the spirit of nationalism and the aspiration for freedom in a number of his students. One of them would eventually become a famous leader of the freedom movement, a Gandhian who displayed an independent streak, uncompromising in his political stance. K.M. Munshi, avant-garde nationalist, founder of the Bharatiya Vidya Bhavan, an institution he formed with the aim of projecting India's cultural and educational ideals, later member of the Constituent Assembly and union minister for agriculture, rebuilder of the Somnath Temple and eventually among the founder leaders of the Swatantra Party, had the opportunity of a few close interactions with Sri Aurobindo in Baroda as his student.

The other was Munshi's friend Mohanlal Pandya, who 'was completely under the influence of Sri Aurobindo' and had organised some of his fellow students 'into a revolutionary group'. Pandya had also started experimenting with bomb-making while in Baroda,[11] and in 1909, is said to have been involved in the attack on Viceroy Lord Minto during his visit to Ahmedabad. As they were driving through the city two bombs were hurled at their carriage, neither which exploded, a third exploded some distance away, blowing off the hand of a bystander. 'The bomb throwers made their escape in the excitement'.[12]

---

10. Fatehsinghrao Gaekwad, op.cit., p.215. For riveting narration of Sri Aurobindo and Sayaji Rao see eg. Manoj Das, *Sri Aurobindo: Life and Times of the Mahayogi*, op.cit.
11. *Munshi: His Art & Work*, Vol.1: *Early Life & Career as Lawyer*, (1956), 2nd ed. 2015, p.40.
12. 'Bombs are Thrown at the Viceroy of India' in *New York Times*, November 15, 1909. .

In 1911, Pandya was dismissed from 'Baroda state service for his belief in violence'.[13] He would eventually grow into one of the leading satyagrahis and Gandhians of Gujarat, leading the famous Kheda Satyagraha along with Sardar Patel and others in 1918. Arrested because he had outsmarted the colonial district administration by preventing them from confiscating the onion crop of a peasant who had participated in the Satyagraha, Pandya and his associates 'were Gujarat's first satyagraha prisoners'. It earned him the endearing sobriquet 'Dungri Chor' or 'Onion Thief'.[14] Referring to Pandya's role in Vallabhbhai Patel's life and political career, one of Patel's early biographers observed that without Pandya, 'there would have been no Kheda stir in 1918 and perhaps no Bardoli in 1928, without whom there might not have been a "Sardar" Patel'.[15]

Munshi's own interactions with Sri Aurobindo in Baroda, would leave a lasting impression on him. In Baroda, Munshi went to meet Sri Aurobindo, then officiating principal of the Baroda College. Munshi asked him, "How can one become patriotic?" With a 'disarming smile, Aurobindo pointed at the wall map of India and said:

> Do you see this map? It is not a map, but the portrait of *Bharat Mata* – its cities and mountains, rivers and jungles form her physical body. All her children are her nerves, large and small. Their literature is her memory and her speech; their vitality is her life; their cultural aspirations her soul; their freedom and happiness her self-fulfillment. Concentrate on Bharat as a living mother, worship her with the nine-fold *bhakti*.[16]

When he asked his teacher how he should concentrate on that vision, Sri Aurobindo asked him to read Vivekananda. Munshi

---

13. Rajmohan Gandhi, *Patel: A Life*, 1991, p.43.
14. Rajmohan Gandhi, op.cit., p.67.
15. Ibid., p.249.
16. *Munshi: His Art & Work*, Vol.1, op.cit., p.46.

confessed to have become an 'ardent nationalist, under the influence of Sri Aurobindo' with the *Bande Mataram*, edited by him, becoming a 'political gospel' for some of them.[17] In 1907, Munshi recalled decades later in his memoirs, "I was one of the young men who appointed themselves volunteers in the Extremist camp of militant nationalism, led by Lal-Bal-Pal (Lala Lajpat Rai, Lokmanya Tilak and Bepin Chandra Pal), of which Prof Aravind Ghosh, whom we adored was the prophet."[18] While in Baroda, Sri Aurobindo had clearly attracted, for good, a number of such young minds into the vortex of the freedom struggle.

A distinct nationalist character was the hallmark of these movements for self-recovery in the fields of education, art, physical training, technical training, and historical research etc – areas which played a key role in developing the mind, the physique, and pushed for the growth of a distinct national consciousness. Besides this, the demand for the 'Indianisation of services' was a demand made by 'educated Indians since the time of Raja Rammohun Roy'.[19] All these were gradually shaping a narrative of freedom and of cultural and political self-assertion.

Disenchantment grew with the existing system of education because, its critic argued, it divested the students of their cultural roots. The need was felt for re-instilling pride in one's civilisational heritage and religious identity, the need for the mother-tongue and Indian languages to be the medium of instruction was advocated, the necessity of developing the students' personality inspired by the perennial spiritual knowledge of India was argued for, and the necessity of imparting an updated and modern technical education

17. K.M. Munshi, *Pilgrimage to Freedom*, Vol.1 (1967), 2nd ed. 2012, p.2.
18. Ibid., p.3.
19. See eg. Biman Behari Majumdar, *History of Indian Social and Political Thoughts: from Rammohan to Dayananda*, (1934), rpt, 1996.

– were some of the demands that were made through most of these educational movements. For the nationalist, education played a pivotal role in his 'quest for self-identity'. It was in education that the cultural agenda of colonisation had been most succinctly and subtly expressed.[20] The demand for educational reform, for a national system of education, for the indianisation of the education framework, essentially aimed at a cultural decolonisation. Cultural colonisation, as philosopher K.C. Bhattacharya was to argue later in one of his seminal addresses, 'Swaraj in Idea', occurs when 'one's traditional cast of ideas and sentiments is superseded without comparison or competition by a new cast representing an alien culture which possesses one like a ghost. This subject is slavery of the spirit…'[21] The national education movement aspired to liberate the Indian mind.

'The quest for self-identity' gave rise to a conflict in the minds of educated Indians. The conflict was between the perceptions that English education was on the one hand enriching India's culture and on the other, was casting a shadow over it and gradually altering its characteristics and identity itself.[22] Thus we find in the early attempts at evolving an indigenous educational system, around the end of the 19th century, an emphasis on cultural re-assertion. The near total absence of religious and moral training inspired by the ancient Indian scriptures – which would give due attention to the psychological development of the learners and would instill in them greater confidence and pride in the merits of their civilisational achievements, and empower them to be forthright about them

---

20. Krishna Kumar, *Political Agenda of Education – A Study of Colonialist and Nationalist Ideas*, 2nd edition, Sage, New Delhi, 2005.
21. 'Swaraj in Ideas' in Sisir Kumar Ghosh edited, *Four Indian Critical Essays*, 1977, p.13.
22. Krishna Kumar, op.cit.

– was seen as a major lacuna of the colonial system. The cultural and religious dimension therefore became an important component of the new educational thought. It was beginning to be realised that Indians would have to revive the narrative of a civilisational and cultural identity, and comprehensively revive and assert it as a precursor to a greater national awakening.

II.1. NEW EXPERIMENTS AND LIGHTS: THE YEARNING FOR A NEW SYSTEM

The Dayanand Anglo-Vedic College institutions, of the Hindu reform movement, the Arya Samaj, had been set up from 1886 onwards in Lahore and had started attracting attention. Around 1896 it began establishing girls' schools too. The Arya Samaj Schools had already been in existence for quite a while prior to the founding of these institutions of higher learning because Swami Dayananda Saraswati (1824–1883) its founder, 'had a great interest in early childhood education and had developed a scheme for infant instruction and training which was to be carried out by the mothers'.[23] Dayananda long ago realised that without 'imparting education compulsorily to all the boys and girls of school-going age it was impossible to revive the glory of India'.[24] So firm was Dayananda in this demand of his that he even called for punishing those parents who did not send their children to school to be punished under the law. His realisation and advocacy of education as a precursor to a greater national awakening led Dayananda to establish a well-defined system of education and network of schools and other educational institutions. Yoga and physical education were made compulsory

23. Kathleen M. O'Connell, *Rabindranath Tagore: The Poet as Educator*, 2002, pp. 34, 35.
24. Biman Behari Majumdar, *History of Indian Social and Political Ideas: From Rammohan to Dayananda*, (1934), rpt 1996, p.413.

in these schools and, as a great champion of women's right and empowerment, Dayananda called for absolute equality for women in education. The Arya Samaj had founded the girls' school, the Arya Kanya Pathshala in Jullundhur, Punjab in 1890. In 1896 it became a high school, and by 1911 graduated to become a women's college. It eventually became the centre 'of a women's educational movement with its own journal and its graduates were active in starting other schools for girls and women elsewhere in north India'.[25]

Dayananda's scheme of education was 'ambitious and all-round, the twenty-two years period of education would comprise of philosophy, medical science, music, arithmetic, science of government, among other subjects'. In his scheme of things the education curriculum was to be divided into two parts – 'civil and military' – the 'art of governing people, protecting their life and property, developing the wealth and resources of the country, making people happy and contented by the right administration of justice'. The military dimension consisted of drills, training in the usage of firearms, principles of military organisation, tactics, and strategy'. Dayananda's approach to education was revolutionary in all aspects keeping in mind the socio-political climate of his era. The statement of objective of the Dayananda Anglo Vedic College at Lahore, spoke of making education 'national in tone and character' in order to obtain its best advantages.[26] It spoke of an education which should be so devised so as to 'strengthen the ties which naturally bind individuals into a common nationality'. It argued that

---

25. Carey A. Watt, 'Education for National Efficiency: Constructive Nationalism in North India, 1909–1916' in *Modern Asian Studies*, May 1997, Vol. 31, No. 2 (May 1997), pp. 339–374, published by Cambridge University Press.
26. Lala Lajpat Rai, The *Arya Samaj: an account of its origin, doctrines and activities, with a biographical sketch of its founder*, 1915, p.181.

though 'English literature' had enlightened and improved 'many thousand minds' in the country, it nevertheless created a schism, a class which was not connected to the masses of India. This was the 'inevitable consequence of the one-sided policy of education imparted through a foreign agency, for whom it was impossible to appreciate the indigenous wants, and to apply a suitable method'.[27] The Arya Samaj's educational mission and institutions, as stated in 1885, proposed thus the following, while charting out a new course that it hoped would transform Indian education:

> We propose to establish an educational institution which will supply the shortcomings of the existing systems, and combine their advantages. The primary object will, therefore, be to weld together the educated and uneducated classes by encouraging the study of the national language and vernaculars; to spread a knowledge of moral and spiritual truths by insisting on the study of classical Sanskrit; to assist the formation of sound and energetic habits by regulated mode of living; to encourage sound acquaintance with English literature; and to afford a stimulus to the material progress of the country by spreading a knowledge of the physical and applied sciences.[28]

Swami Dayananda had clear views, on India's colonial subjection and her eventual liberation. He articulated these in an indirect manner and carried 'the spirit of nationalism to the masses of northern India'. Valentine Chirol, (1852–1929) the notorious British journalist and author who openly displayed his intense disapproval and disdain for Hindus and the nationalist assertion, in his infamous 'Indian Unrest' argued that the Arya Samaj which was 'spreading all over the Punjab and United Provinces, represents in one of its aspect a revolt against Hindu orthodoxy, but in another it represents equally a revolt against Western ideals'.[29] Chirol saw

27. Ibid.
28. Ibid., pp.182–183.
29. Valentine Chirol, *Indian Unrest*, London: Macmillan & Co Ltd, 1910, p.27.

in Dayanand's teachings an attempt to range Hinduism 'into active resistance to the alien influences which threatened, in his opinion, to denationalise it'.[30] The Arya Samaj institutions never asked for aid from the colonial government, did not invite officials to its functions, and had adopted Hindi as the medium of instructions in their schools and educational institutions. This often generated friction with the colonial administration, often acting against its institutions.

Describing the British attitude towards the Arya Samaj, Lala Lajpat Rai, one of the most well-known Arya Samajists among the leading nationalist figures, noted that 'the foreign rulers of India have never been quite happy about the Arya Samaj. They have always disliked its independence of tone and its propaganda of self-confidence, self-help, self-reliance .... They cannot look with favour on an indigenous movement which, according to them, can do big things without their help and guidance, and which has established a government within the government'.[31] Rai described the Arya Samaj as 'perhaps the greatest indigenous educational agency'. The Arya Samaj, Rai listed in his *History of the Arya Samaj* (1914), 'have founded and are maintaining a large number of boys' schools, Primary and Secondary, Gurukulas and Patchalas. A good many of these are high-class educational institutions, and are being carried on at great cost, and with a great deal of self-sacrifice'.

Dayananda's activism symbolised the aspirations for a cultural self-assertion. Describing Dayananda's work and impact, Sri

---

30. Cited in, Sumitra Gupta, 'The Arya Samaj and the Indian National Movement', *Proceedings of the Indian History Congress*, 2002, Vol. 63 (2002), pp. 722–732 Published by: Indian History Congress; also see, Lala Lajpat Rai, The *Arya Samaj: an account of its origin, doctrines and activities, with a biographical sketch of its founder*, London: Longman Greens & Co, 1915.
31. Ibid.

Aurobindo spoke of a 'spontaneous power and decisiveness' stamped 'everywhere in his work' which aimed at going back 'trenchantly to the very root of Indian life and culture, to derive from the flower of its first birth the seed for a radical new birth'.[32] To be national for Dayananda, was 'not to stand still', it was rather to 'seize on a vital thing out of the past and throw it into the stream of modern life' which was the 'most powerful means of renovation and new-creation'.[33] Dayananda's work, argued Sri Aurobindo, 'brings back such a principle and spirit of the past to vivify a modern mould'.[34]

At a time when the summit of political demand was for the 'transplanting of political institutions of England in Indian soil' with the 'educated young men of India', without 'paying any heed to the genius and culture of the Indian people' and 'slavishly copying the superficial aspects of European civilisation', Dayananda 'boldly hurled India's defiance against the social, cultural, and political domination of the West. He was the very embodiment of India's instinct of self-preservation' but a self-preservation which did not mean a 'total and utter exclusion of foreign influence...'.[35] Possessing advanced ideas in politics in India, Dayananda, one of his assessors noted, 'succeeded in carrying his ideas of Liberalism and Nationalism to the very heart of rural India and to the masses tied down to agelong ignorance and superstition'.[36]

Swami Shraddhanand's (1856–1926) founding the Gurukul at Kangri, near Haridwar in 1902, was a major educational initiative of the period, the objectives of the institutions were stated to be

---

32. Sri Aurobindo, *Bankim-Tilak-Dayananda* (1940), 2006, p.49
33. Ibid., p.50.
34. Ibid.
35. Biman Behari Majumdar, *History of Indian Social and Political Ideas: From Rammohan to Dayananda*, (1934), rpt 1996, p.387.
36. Ibid.

the 'reviving [of] the ancient institution of *Brahmacharya*, of rejuvenation and resuscitation of ancient Indian philosophy and literature, conducting researches into the antiquities of India, of building up a Hindu literature incorporating into itself all that is best and assimilable in Occidental thought, of producing preachers of the Vedic religion and good citizens possessed of a culture compounded of the loftiest elements of the two civilizations, which have made their home in this ancient land of sages and seers'. [37] Most of the experiments of the period talked of the acceptance from western educational thought of all that was considered to be beneficial for the growth and expansion of the Indian identity. It would be useful to have a look at some of these educationists, educational philosophers, thinkers, and institutional builders, who shaped the Indian aspirations for a new education in the decades preceding the national education movement.

While discussing the evolution of the nationalist demand for a new education for India it would be useful to keep in mind that before the British came to India on their colonising mission, India possessed a wide and extensive network of indigenous schools. The British gradually starved these and allowed them to wither away.[38] The penetration of British influence in the interiors of the country 'brought serious deterioration in the conditions faced by the populace. This in turn resulted in their inability to support many indigenous institutions of which indigenous education

---

37. O'Connell, op. cit., pp.82–83.
38. For a detailed understanding of pre-British indigenous Indian education see eg. Dharampal's seminal *The Beautiful Tree: Indigenous Indian Education in Eighteenth Century*, (1983), Goa: Other India Press, 2000; Joseph Di Bona edited, *One Teacher, One School: The Adam Reports on Indigenous Education in 19th Century India*, New Delhi: Biblia Impex, 1983; Gita Dharampal edited, *Essential Writings of Dharampal*, New Delhi: Publications Division, Govt of India, 2015.

was but one'.[39] One of the measures that the colonial government took which 'hastened the demise of indigenous institutions' was 'the withdrawal of support for vernacular schools'. There existed throughout India, 'lands that had been reserved for the support of scholars and teachers' but gradually these were appropriated by the colonial administration, leading to the desiccation and starvation of the indigenous system.[40]

II.2. ANNIE BESANT: A FOUNDATION OF EDUCATION FOR INDIA

In 1882, theosophist and later an articulate voice in the struggle for India's freedom struggle, Annie Besant (1847–1933) arrived in Madras. Prior to her arrival, the Theosophists had already begun establishing schools in the Madras area, 'which emphasized the accomplishments of ancient India and the need for Sanskrit study'. [41] Upon her [Mrs. Besant's] arrival, education became 'a high priority' as she set about raising funds for a university modelled on Hindu tradition and culture. By 1895, she had learned Sanskrit and made plans for building a library and preparing textbooks for a Central Hindu College which she founded in 1898 in Benares.[42] Of Annie Besant and the Theosophists, Valentine Chirol, whose reactions and assessments were an accurate reflection of the reading of the British Indian administration of situations and individuals, wrote:

> No Hindu has done so much to organise and consolidate the movement [Hindu awakening] as Mrs. Annie Besant, who, in her Central Hindu College at Benares and her Theosophical Institution at Adyar, near Madras, has openly proclaimed her faith in the superiority of the whole Hindu system to the vaunted civilisation of the West. Is it surprising that Hindus should

---

39. Joseph Di Bona, op.cit., p.30.
40. Joseph Di Bona, op.cit., p.31.
41. O'Connell, op. cit., p.83.
42. Ibid.

turn their backs upon our civilisation when a European of highly-trained intellectual power and with extraordinary gift of eloquence comes and tells them that it is the key to supreme wisdom; that their gods, their philosophy, their morality are on a higher plane of thought than the West has ever reached?[43]

In 1897, while discussing the educational issue and advocating a greater national control and choice over its content and dissemination Besant made the following remark, which reflected the line of thought on the demand educational reform. 'Boys of the upper classes', she felt, must receive, keeping in view the necessities of the age, 'an English education. Without this, they cannot gain a livelihood'; she realised the practical necessity of such an approach necessitated by the prevailing material realities.[44]

But she also advocated a reform in the method, content and orientation, 'a reform in the books' [studied] she felt was necessary and that 'efforts should be made to substitute a detailed knowledge of Indian history and geography for the excessive amount of foreign history and geography' that was being then taught.[45] Mrs. Besant articulated the core of the early nationalist thought on education, when she argued in the same discussion that foreign history was not to be negated altogether, but had to be taught in a balanced and a broader manner so as to give the learner a rich exposure to the whole gamut of Western Civilisation and culture. This would, she felt, widen the mind, but at the same time a more complete and 'fuller' knowledge of one's own history was also necessary not only to create a mind conducive to the growth of patriotism, but also to be able to form sound judgments when the question of evolving

43. Valentine Chirol, *Indian Unrest,* op.cit., p.28–29.
44. Haridas and Uma Mukherjee, *The Origins of the National Education Movement*, 2nd rev. ed., 2000, p. 8.
45. Ibid.

and implementing changes to the 'national genius' arose.[46] This perception was widened and expanded later during the national education movement.

This would become a constant argument of the national education movement. Besant's 'boys' college was to be a combination of 'Hindu monastery and English public school' [and] the 'curriculum drew on both Western and Hindu models. Part of the day was spent in meditation and scriptural study, with the role of *Brahmacharya* held up as the ideal'. 'Strong emphasis' was also laid on the study of science 'with lessons that were based on practical experiments using laboratory equipment'.[47] A number of teachers were brought over from England, extension lectures were organised through visiting academics. Mrs. Besant undertook extensive lecture tours all over India to disseminate her educational ideas, and influential personalities of the period, such as Motilal Nehru and the Maharaja of Kaṣhmir, extended support to her educational endeavours.

The Theosophists philosophy of education can be gleaned from an article entitled, 'The Foundations of Education' by Mrs. Besant that appeared in the London Theosophical Review in September 1899. Satish Chandra Mukherjee's *Dawn* magazine reprinted parts of the 'very useful article...' in its December, 1899 issue.

Apart from giving a succinct view of the educational thoughts that guided the Theosophists in their various educational experiments, one finds a number of similarities with it of the later formulation of the concept of '*Integral Education*' as evolved and practiced, inspired by Sri Aurobindo's educational philosophy. One of the first thing that comes across as similar to the vision of Integral Education, is Mrs. Besant's stand that education must be imparted at different levels to nurture the various parts or aspects of the

46. Ibid.
47. Kathleen M.O'Connell, op.cit. pp. 83, 84.

individual. Integral Education speaks of the physical, vital, mental, psychic-spiritual education of the individual, because its essential formulation is that education must have five principal components connected to these 'five principle activities of the human being'.[48]

These dimensional bifurcations of the individual broadly match the educational model enunciated by Mrs. Besant. A more detailed look at the article reveals that the Theosophists' educational concept did contain a number of integrative and holistic educational formulations, which focused on the integrated and harmonious development of the individual and her various capacities, including paying attention to the individual's positive role in the sustenance and the cohesive growth of the collectivity. Besant argued that 'the teacher must regard his pupil as an individual, and must accept it as his duty to draw out and train the capacities he finds already existing' and not focus on merely preparing a crammer for the successful passing of examinations, but rather help the individual unfold the various capacities and talents and help develop 'its powers harmoniously and with balance, cultivating the reason in preference to the memory, training the powers of observation, comparison, judgment more than that of memorising and reproducing statement of facts...'[49]

Besant's educational ideas were advanced and militated against the aims and methods of the prevailing colonial system of education in India, and contributed to the articulation of the philosophical bases of the later educational demand. It went against the industrial approach of *commodifying* education and spoke of providing scope for the individual's growth and unfolding.

---

48. Pavitra (P.B. Saint-Hilaire), *Education and the Aim of Human Life – Sri Aurobindo's Integral Education*, 1999, p. 52.
49. Annie Besant, 'The Foundations of Education' in *The Dawn*, September, 1899, Reprint Vol.-III, 2004, p. 127.

Sri Aurobindo's stand on education since the beginning of his activities in India had seen him similarly disapproving the notion that education was merely an information-gathering system through the instrument of memory. His educational principles emphasised the 'child-centred' approach. Sri Aurobindo argued that 'every man has in him something divine, something his own, a chance of strength and perfection in however small a sphere, which God offers him to take or refuse. The task is to find it, develop it, use it'. The chief aim of education therefore, he argued, 'should be to help the growing soul to draw out that in itself which is best and make it perfect for a noble use'.[50]

The identification of those qualities and propensities which in the student is best, and then to draw it out, can be possible only if the system and in it, the teacher, regards the pupil, the learner as an individual whose latent potential and capacities needed to be drawn out, as Annie Besant argues, or as a soul with a possibility of achieving a distinct and particular perfection as Sri Aurobindo elucidates the issue.

The ideas formulated a century ago giving primacy to the individual, retain their relevance even in the present national education scenario where the child-centric paradigm in education is being very gradually taken note of, and there is a debate on its efficacy and its imperative for bringing about a paradigm shift in the educational approach and discourse.

Going against the prevailing trends of the times, Besant insisted that 'the individual should be aided to grow along his own line, not forcibly twisted into a set shape',[51] while Sri Aurobindo enunciating his 'second principle' of true teaching about a decade later, felt that

50. Sri Aurobindo, 'The Human Mind' in *A System of National Education*, *CWSA* vol.1, op.cit., p.384.

51. *The Foundations of Education*, op.cit., p. 127.

the 'mind had to be consulted in its own growth', and that 'the idea of hammering the child into the shape desired by parent or teacher' [was] 'a barbarous and ignorant superstition'.[52] The child must be encouraged to follow a trajectory of growth which is in accordance with his nature.

The habit of pre-deciding the line of a child's development, to fix the nature and path of the development of his qualities, capacities, ideas, and virtues, or to prepare him for a 'prearranged career' decided by the parent, was considered by Sri Aurobindo to be a great error that mutilated and discouraged any further possibility, in the student, of an independent development.[53] Incidents of the child being forced to take a line of development contrary to his nature and inclinations still abound, the result being an unhappy phase of growth, followed by a dissatisfied professional life, and as a corollary, a mediocre or meagre work-output lacking in originality or depth.

But what must necessarily also attract our attention was Besant's recognition that the constitution of man had natural divisions to it, and education should be imparted in such a manner so as to be able to nourish each of these divisions. Besant divides this nature into four parts 'closely allied yet distinctly marked out': the physical nature comprising the bodily activities, the emotional nature consisting of feelings, the intellectual nature containing thoughts, and the spiritual nature comprising of the individual's 'yearnings after that which is greater than himself'.[54]

She argued that all these dimensions are 'integral parts' of man's nature and an education which neglects any of these parts will leave the individual 'lop-sided'. An education that recognises

---

52. Sri Aurobindo, 'The Human Mind' in *A System of National Education, CWSA* vol.1, op.cit., p.384.
53. Ibid.
54. *The Foundations of Education,* op.cit. p. 127.

this 'fourfold nature of man' and meets it by a fourfold education comprising of the physical, emotional, mental and spiritual, Besant considers to be a well-directed one. Her stress on physical education was quite innovative, for the system followed in India then lacked a comprehensive physical education curriculum in schools. Her exposition of physical education is one of the most detailed parts in the write-up.

For Besant, the aim of physical education, should be to raise the level of efficiency of the physical body and to make it 'the best possible instrument for man's activities .... It must neither be pampered nor tortured, but trained'. She saw physical education as an integral part of a 'true education' and even formulated a brief sketch of a physical education programme where the eyes and ears should be trained to develop a power of accurate observation, the fingers 'deftness and sensibility' and the whole body must evolve a 'gracious and rhythmical motion'. This, she saw as mandatory for education in the kindergarten and at home, and must be completed by the age of seven. She spoke of the necessity of developing 'alertness, agility, swift adaptability, strength, grace, quick resourcefulness, prompt obedience, in school through drills, gymnastic, drills and games – the components that a physical education programme must possess. Because, the body is an animal and remains in need of deliberate training and should not be neglected, and the early years were the best period for good habits to be imposed on the body.[55]

A parallel may be drawn to the educational experiment at Pondicherry based on Sri Aurobindo's philosophy. After the opening of the Sri Aurobindo Ashram School in 1943, the Mother (1878–1973)[56] encouraged the implementation of a systematic programme

55. *The Foundations of Education.*, pp. 127–28.
56. Sri Aurobindo's principle spiritual collaborator, who gave a practical shape – in the form of the Ashram at Pondicherry from 1926 onwards – to Sri Aurobindo's philosophy of the Integral Yoga. The Mother

of physical education for different age categories from 1945 onwards. It was one of the few comprehensive programmes to be undertaken in colonial India and which continues unabated even to this day. The programme was a detailed one for various age groups ranging from elementary levels to senior ones and was approved by Sri Aurobindo, who extolled the virtues of physical education in one of his last messages in 1949 to the members pursuing this physical education programme, saying that such 'an intensive physical training programme' was to be 'an important part of their development'.[57]

---

was also the principle guiding light of Sri Aurobindo International Centre of Education from its inception in 1951, when a national memorial convention was convened under the chairmanship of Dr. Syama Prasad Mookerjee, educationist, former and the youngest Vice Chancellor of Calcutta University, statesman, and free India's first Industry & Supply Minister, and attended by a number of eminent citizens, thinkers, public personalities and educationists from across India – till her passing in 1973. For the Centre of Education, the Mother succeeded in gathering around her a number of well-known experts in their fields and in a way, reminiscent of Tagore's action at Visva-Bharati, she gave practical shape to Sri Aurobindo's philosophy of education, which eventually acquired the nomenclature 'Integral Education'. Through extensive talks and writings, question and answer sessions, interviews, classes etc. the Mother provided, for over two decades, a practical insight into the growth of an educational experiment inspired by the principles of Sri Aurobindo's philosophy. These materials, because of their empirical value may, among other things, also serve as a guide to those wanting to set up institutions patterned on the same philosophy. The Centre of Education remains today one of the best practical examples of a system of education evolved from the bases of Sri Aurobindo's thoughts in that field.

57. Vide his Messages and articles on Physical Education in the *Bulletin of Physical Education* [*CWSA* vol.13, 1998, pp. 517-592.] between 1949 and 1950; the series which dwell in detail on the aspects of physical education, inner, outer as well as national, remained incomplete on

Besant also spoke of the emotional nature of man as she argued

Sri Aurobindo's passing in December 1950. In this series, Sri Aurobindo also dwells at length on his conceptions of the Supermind, the Divine Body, the Mind of Light, Supermind and Humanity, etc., some of the defining themes of his philosophy. The Mother also wrote a series of articles in the *Bulletin of Physical Education* of the Ashram from 1949 onwards on various aspects of physical education – such as 'Concentration and Dispersion', 'Energy Inexhaustible', where she provided deep insights into the benefits, objectives, and higher aims of physical education in the child's growth. In an article on physical education that appeared in April 1951, she pithily formulated three 'principle aspects' of physical education – (1) control and discipline of the functioning of the body, (2) an integral, methodical, and harmonious development of all the parts and movements of the body and (3) correction of any defects and deformities. [Vide the Mother's articles on physical education in The Mother – *Education-Part III-Physical Education*, 2nd Imp., 1997.] Physical Education according to the Mother was 'meant to bring into the body, consciousness and control, discipline and mastery, all things necessary for a higher and better life'. She constantly encouraged the 'members of the Ashram to lead active and healthy lives'. The first two decades of the Ashram's existence saw physical activities limited to informal exercises such as walking, gardening and the work of the individual seekers. It was only after children were admitted to the community in the 1940s, that a systematic programme was drawn, beginning with the founding of a Department of Physical Education in May 1945, with a mandate to 'establish a formal exercise programme both for the children and the members of the Ashram'. The Mother, for whom physical education was an important aspect of man's search after perfection, since it symbolised the quest for physical harmony and balance, and a 'valuable adjunct' to the spiritual life, herself took active interest in the growth of the department and for many years spent the evening hours with those taking part in physical activities. The physical education programme followed at the Centre of Education continues to be broadly based on these three principle aspects of the subject, as enunciated by the Mother and is coordinated by instructors known as 'captains', who train the learners following a an integral part of his constitution, 'all the relations between a man

systematic programme in games, gymnastics, combative-sports, swimming, athletics, weight-lifting, and asanas. [The Mother – *Education-III*, 'Physical Education', op. cit.] The Joseph Bhore Committee constituted in 1943 – and which submitted its report in 1946 – to provide a 'blue-print for health services development in independent India', and which 'devoted a substantial section on the need and importance of school health programmes for school going children', laid stress, among other things, on the promotion of positive health which would include physical culture 'through games, sports, and gymnastic exercises'. [*Position Paper-National Focus Group on Health and Physical Education*, NCERT, 2006] The Mother's encouragement of a systematic programme of physical education anticipated this recommendation and provided an alternative framework that could be applied, with modification, across the country as an important constituent of a national education programme. The need for physical education was realised by most of the early thinkers. It is well known that Swami Vivekananda stressed the need for developing the physique; referring to this aspect of the Swami's message, one his foremost interpreters, Sister Nivedita, made an interesting observation when she said, "On the last Charok Puja day of his life, a gymnastic society came to the Math for sports and prizes, and he spoke of his desire that the Hindu Lent should be celebrated henceforth by special courses by athletic exercises. The energy that had hitherto gone into the mortification of the body, might rightly, in his opinion, under modern conditions, be directed to the training of the muscles." Inspired by the Swami's message of developing physical strength and prowess, a number of young men began organising physical culture societies. These were to later form the base for the revolutionary movement in Bengal. Satish Bose, founder of the Anushilan Samiti, also refers to this inspiration of the Swami and of his insistence on the young men getting into relief work, sanitation work, and physical culture. Sister Nivedita, he recalled, also encouraged them along these lines. Hemchandra Ghose, another veteran of the early revolutionary movement in Bengal, also reports similar exhortation of the Swami. (*CWSN, vol.1,* 5th imp, 2006, p.42, Sankari Prasad Basu, *Nivedita Lokmata, vol.2*, 2nd imp.

and his surroundings have their bases in feelings, and emotions

1414, p.84, Bhupendranath Dutta, *Swami Vivekananda: Patriot-Prophet – a study*, 1954, pp.331–335, Prithwindra Mukherjee, *Les Racines Intellectuelles*, 2010, p.23–24). It may also be relevant here to point out that Bankim also emphasised the need for developing awareness on physical education in his treatise on 'Anushilan' – culture. The entire Chapter Eight of the analysis is dedicated to the theme of physical culture. Bankim speaks of four dimensions of education and elucidates on the primacy of physical education: 1) Physical (*shaririki*), 2) Knowledge – intellectual (*gyanarjani*), 3) Practical – vocational (*karyakarini*), 4) Entertainment – developing the *kalas* (*chittaranjani*). For Bankim, physical strength, fitness, and health was central to all that one did. It provided a sound support to the entire gamut of human activities. He argues that without a modicum of physical fitness even religious practices would be impossible to conduct because the state of the mind and the state of body were interdependent and intertwined. European thinkers and scientists, he says, have well proved this link. Bankim's main complaint against the Indian education system as he saw it then was that it neglected developing this interest in physical fitness amongst the students, and such neglect would, in the long run, degrade not only the body but the mind as well. But the other, more serious fallout of a lack of awareness for the need of physical strength was the incapacity for self-defence. Bankim talks of three human actions – *atmaraksha* (self-defence), *swajanraksha* (defence of one's own people/family), *swadeshraksha* (defence of one's own country/nation), which he sees as indispensible for survival and for which physical training and education was necessary, it was necessary to develop a strong muscular body as well. Saying that in the present times physical education was extremely necessary Bankim, interestingly, draws up a regular curriculum of physical education. His recommends the following activities in a curriculum of physical education, including paying attention to nutrition: exercise (*vyayam*), wrestling (*mallayuddha*), (which he says has special benefits), training in handling weapons (*astrashiksha*), horse riding (*aswarohan*), swimming (*santaran*), hiking (*padavraje duragaman*). Along with these one had to develop physical resistance/resilience/tolerance

are but rationalized feelings,' she argues and points out that 'moral education is the culture of the emotions, and bears to the emotional nature the same relation as the culture of the mind bears to the intellectual nature.' For Besant the cultivation of emotions was an important aspect of education because it succeeded in establishing a certain degree of balance, harmony and reciprocity in his dealings–because 'on its right culture all social evolution depends.'

Besant accuses the State of neglecting emotional education and of focusing only on the physical and intellectual dimension of education leaving the culture of emotions in the hands of 'parents and ministers of religions' who may be incompetent to handle such a sensitive issue which is far more vital to the welfare of the State than the physical and intellectual aspects. She saw emotional education in two streams, one that would stir the learner with 'noble tales' – 'tales of heroism, of patience under wrong, of endurance through bitter hardships, of truth held fast in face of all temptations...', such

---

– one should be able to tolerate all extremes of heat, cold, thirst, hunger, and fatigue etc. An all-round curriculum had to focus on 1) exercise (*vyayam*), 2) education (*shiksha*), 3) nutrition (*ahar*), and 4) controlling/sublimating the senses, (*indriyasanyama*). It is interesting to note the great detail that Bankim goes into in arguing his case for the need of a robust curriculum of physical education in India. There was a tradition of physical exercise in the country – people regularly took to push-ups, wrestling, mace wielding etc, observed Bankim. But what really intrigued him was why in the process of assimilating the English culture was such a robust tradition given up or forgotten by the Indians. ('*Shaririki Britti*' in *Dharmatatva – Anushilan* in *Bankim Rachanabali*, op.cit., pp.546-551). Though these thoughts were part of his *Dharmatatva*, which appeared as a book sometime in 1888, they nevertheless made an impact on young minds of that period. The national education movement did try to pay attention towards this aspect as well. We shall have a look at other aspects of Bankim's educational thought in another section.

tales that would 'mould the plastic life into shape heroic' and the other should be an attempt to teach the learner as he grows older, 'to understand the roots of virtues and vices…'.[58]

Describing the varied interests that are intrinsic to a child and speaking of the possibilities of tapping and developing those interests, Sri Aurobindo observes that because 'every child is a lover of interesting narrative, hero-worshipper and a patriot' an appeal ought to be made to evoke 'these qualities in him and through them let him master without knowing it, the living and human parts of his nation's history'.[59] The call was for establishing a growing and an organic link with one's nation's evolution, which is different from the dry and lifeless absorption of mere historical facts and figures which, in any case, is unable to kindle a living empathy with one's country and its constituent elements.

Sri Aurobindo argues that the child has in him those qualities that push man towards self-excelling and a greater perfection, but that the education system is unresponsive to these qualities and does not give scope for these to surface. Therefore, if it at an early stage one can place before the learner some of the best efforts of humanity in forms of inspiring narratives, one will be able to strengthen the possibilities of positive growth.

In her scheme of education Besant speaks of training the intellect. She terms this as intellectual education and points to the necessity of training the mind to impart rapid impulses which would enable the students to develop 'quick responsiveness'. The development of 'clear and accurate perception' and 'attention', a 'power that lies at the root of all mental effort' ought to be the focus of intellectual education. At an early age the memory must be strengthened, the

58. *The Foundations of Education,* op. cit., pp. 128–29.
59. Sri Aurobindo, *Simultaneous and Successive Teaching in a System of National Education,* op.cit., p. 395.

pupil must be encouraged to learn different languages because the brain continues to be 'plastic' and the strengthening and training of his reasoning faculty must be encouraged.

Besant observes that little can be done with the 'average youth' in terms of developing the reasoning faculty before the age of 14 and that it was only after crossing that threshold can the training of the reasoning faculty begin in right earnest. Summing up the role of intellectual education, Besant's point was that it must strive to develop an individual who is 'observant, reasoning [and] well judging' counting these as being far more pertinent to personality training than the formation of a 'well-arranged encyclopaedia'.[60] The role of mental education in the scheme of Integral Education is not to focus on the 'capacity of storing knowledge gained from others, so as to keep it ready at hand, at least for the time of examination',[61] and if successful, the effects of a precise mental education is far more complex and enduring in terms of results.

Besant also highlights the need for spiritual education. She calls it the 'educational arch' and admits that it is at once the 'most important and most difficult part of education'. She suggests a simple framework of what came to be eventually termed while arguing that the 'spiritual nature' of man always responds to 'higher emotions'. She speaks of describing these higher emotions to the pupil through his heroes, and by portraying that religion was the principle motivating factor of the heroes, Besant argues, 'one could link religion in the young minds with heroism, strength and tenderness.' While this approach seems to have its portion of risks, if one keeps in mind the conflicts that arise and are inspired by religious appeal, especially of religions which are violently

---

60. *The Foundations of Education,* op. cit., p. 129.
61. Pavitra (P.B. Saint-Hilare), *Education and the Aim of Human Life*, op. cit., pp. 61–62.

proselytizing in nature, Besant rounds off the edges by suggesting an assimilative approach. She calls for infusing the memory of the pupil with 'verses from great Scriptures, and with noble poems of strong and deep devotion' [and] the holding up the examples and lives of those 'Masters of Wisdom who have given religions to the world' before the pupil as 'objects of reverent adoration, as the living exponents of Wisdom....'[62] As the pupil grows older, Besant suggests a daily practice of meditation which becomes a mode of expressing his noblest self.

Concluding his section in the *Karmayogin* on the training of the 'Moral Nature', Sri Aurobindo succinctly observes, speaking of moral and religion training, that the essential concepts of religion 'to live for God, for humanity, for country, for others and for oneself in these' must be made the ideal of schools that call themselves 'national'.[63] A certain direction may be discerned in these early thoughts on moral and value education. Sri Aurobindo and Annie Besant based their early thoughts on religious education on the essence and timeless tenets of Hinduism. These, they believed, contained universal and integrative elements which could appeal to adherents cutting across religious lines and divides.

Finally, an education based on these ideals, according to Besant, will be capable of creating 'agents' who shall strive for a nobler society. The principle objectives of the education system as suggested by Annie Besant, thus, will eliminate the competitive element in education, and by transforming it into a cooperative endeavour and turning the school into a 'larger family', will succeed in training students to realise their obligation to the 'wider family of the township, of the nation, of the race....'[64]

---

62. *The Foundations of Education,* op. cit., pp. 129-30.
63. Sri Aurobindo, *The Moral Nature in a System of National Education,* op. cit., p. 392.
64. *The Foundations of Education,* op. cit., p. 130.

Besant was clear that for the cause and sake of national regeneration it was essential that India maintain her differences of culture, of living, and of identity. As early as 1895, while speaking on 'The Means of India's Regeneration', Besant argued for rediscovering and maintaining the essential differences of identity. This was necessary, she explained, for a long-term plan of national regeneration to be effective. The centrality of her scheme was the maintaining of this identity which would eventually consolidate national feelings, 'the encouragement of national feeling, by maintaining the traditional dress, ways of living ... by promoting Indian arts and manufactures, [and] by giving preference to Indian products over foreign'.[65] She saw this approach as going to the 'very root of Indian revival'. One could not afford to undervalue or ignore it:

> Do not undervalue the importance of sentiment, and do not try to do away with everything which differentiates India from other lands; rather strive to maintain the immemorial costumes, and follow the immemorial tradition, instead of trying to look as little Hindus as possible, as many of you are inclined to do. It is true, of course, that these are outside matters, but they have a very real effect on the generation and maintenance of national feeling. [66]

This reflected the core objective and ideals of Besant's educational experiment. These would also grow to become among some of the essential ideas that were to propel the national education movement. In her Hindu College, Besant tried to synthesise what she called the two Hindu nations – one of the Pandits with their profound knowledge of the scriptures, of Indian languages, systems etc, and the other of westernised Indians oblivious of their traditions and ways. The actualisation of such a synthesis would prove to be

---

65. 'Swadeshi Movement' in Annie Besant, *The Birth of a New India: A Collection of Writings and Speeches on Indian Affairs*, 1917, p.67.
66. Ibid.

a major challenge to the protagonists of the national education movement. Besant wrote:

> We have one peculiar thing in the Hindu College. Every boy who comes into the English department is obliged to learn Sanskrit. We have also a Pathshala and every boy who comes to join it is obliged to learn English, so that the English-educated boys have to know English. This is a great innovation. You may say: Why do you do it? Do you not see that there are two Hindu nations in this land – one of Pandits, profound in their learning, scholarship, thought and knowledge, but knowing nothing outside Sanskrit literature? They know nothing of modern thought, modern life, the modern spirit. On the other side there is a Hindu nation growing up, knowing nothing of Sanskrit literature and the Sacred Books, growing utterly Westernised. There is a great gulf between them and the nation of Pandits. The Pandit cannot influence the English–educated boy, because he does not sympathise with him in his hopes and aspirations. You cannot influence the young unless you sympathise and feel with them. We want to bridge the gulf between these Hindu nations, and we build this double bridge of Sanskrit and English. We lead both classes over it, so that both shall know English and both know Sanskrit; we thus hope to join the two Hindu nations and make them one in the service of their Motherland.[67]

The Indian educational question remained vital for Besant even later in her active political phase. In a lecture delivered in Bombay in 1903 on 'Education as a National Duty', Besant discussed the educational issues in India and called for re-shaping it by those who identified with the land and loved it. '...Education is not so much a matter for the Government as it is the duty of the people. To be really successful it must be taken up, designed, guided, and carried out, by those who are not only lovers of their country, but who are also men who understand its needs and are well aware of its peculiarities, of its characteristics, and of its tradition'. [68]

---

67. 'Education as a National Duty' in Annie Besant, *The Birth of a New India: A Collection of Writings and Speeches on Indian Affairs*, 1917, p.105.
68. *The Birth of a New India.*, p. 89.

Besant perceptively defined the fundamentals of a national education – it was in consonance with the ideologues of the national education movement who would shape its narrative and impart it direction. 'To be truly useful, Education must be founded on a knowledge of the past of the country as well as of its present'. Besant wrote, 'it must be designed in accordance with the ancient traditions and national habits, and adapted to modern necessities, to meet at every point the growing needs of an ever-increasing nation'.[69]

Besant continued to push the cause of national education. In a speech on the subject in 1914, she calls upon Indian educators and education planners to study the systems of the West, examine western educational ideas and theories in order to fully utilise these new ideas and to avoid making mistakes that had been made in the past. A system that urged Indian educators to study and adapt to Indian conditions was the Montessori system which, as she argued, though a fundamentally Eastern idea, was gaining greater acceptance in the West:

> The idea that the child who comes into your hands is not a mere child to be coerced, but an intellectual and spiritual nature to be give full opportunity of development along its own natural line of evolution, instead of having forced upon it the line of its elders, who are supposed to be naturally its superior.... It is seen more and more that it is the duty of the parents and the teachers to study the child, in order that they may help it along its own line of natural evolution, and not to endeavour to strive to force it into a line uncongenial to the child's own nature, to the instincts, the qualities, the faculties of the child.[70]

Her advocacy of the indigenisation of Indian education however, remained in place. Besant also insisted on the need for education for depressed classes and village education. In a public address on

---

69. Ibid.
70. 'National Education' in Annie Besant, *The Birth of a New India: A Collection of Writings and Speeches on Indian Affairs*, 1917, p. 176.

'National Education' delivered in Bombay in 1914, she spoke about making village education less literary, "teach in the village schools handicrafts and agriculture. Take in the next schools above them a higher course of agriculture, the teaching of simple chemistry, of the nature of soils and the suitable manures, which will enable them to learn how to improve the soil on which they live."[71] Besant argued against taking the villager away from the village 'still more to overcrowd the town, but make the life of the village fuller and more prosperous by stimulating the intelligence of the villager'. The best way would be through self-help:

> Organise yourselves, and do not leave the Government to do the work that you are not doing. Government cannot do it. You ought to do it. And then your cultivated villagers will form the strength of your nation, and will pay you back in intelligent patriotism that which you spend upon them today in effort and in labour.[72]

While she created nationalist education institutions, she also demanded that the official system open up to further reform and accommodation, '... what we want in the Senates of our Universities now is that they should be bodies recruited from all that is most thoughtful, most cultured, most patriotic, and most self-sacrificing in the country. They should not be half filled with nominees who know nothing of Education...'.[73]

II.3. EARLY CALLS FOR CHANGE: GURU DAS BANERJEE AND RABINDRANATH TAGORE

Guru Das Banerjee – a few thoughts on education

Public criticism of the English education system had already begun in the 1890s, when the first Indian Vice-Chancellor of Calcutta

71. 'National Education' in Annie Besant, *The Birth of a New India*, op.cit., p.190.
72. Ibid., pp.190–191.
73. *Education as a National Duty*, op.cit., p.94.

University, Sir Guru Das Banerjee (1844–1918), criticized it in his first and subsequent convocation addresses. In his first convocation address, Banerjee said that the vernacular literature of India would be enriched if it assimilated all that was 'valuable in western learning', and vice versa. This was no narrow approach but an exhortation for a greater exchange which would instill pride in Indian knowledge systems and languages.

In his second convocation address in 1891, Das made a clear case for education through the medium of Indian languages. Unless this was done, Banerjee felt that the possession of 'any thorough and extensive culture as a nation' was impossible. Finally in his third convocation address in 1892, he reiterated his stand on the need for a vernacular medium of instruction, "One great reason why our university education fails to awaken much original thinking is because it is imparted through the medium of a difficult foreign language, the genius of which is so widely different from that of our own."[74]

During his tenure as Vice-Chancellor, Guru Das Banerjee sought to promote the usage and study of Bengali, and to resist undue government interference in the affairs of the university. Banerjee's dissenting note, in a sense, set the pace for the education debate closer to the period when the national education movement itself would gather momentum. It would be relevant to have a brief look at some sections of his dissenting note in order to set it in the backdrop of the larger education debate that was to soon emerge.

On the appointment and restructuring of the Senates among Banerjee's views was that 'Indians and Europeans may be fairly, and if possible, equally represented'. It went contrary to the prevailing view of the epoch which was that since 'a University is a Western institution, the European element should predominate in the

---

74. R.K. Dasgupta, National Education' in *Concept of National Education in India,* 1967, pp. 12, 13.

Senate, with only a small admixture of the Indian element to enable the European members to know what the views of the Indians are upon any question affecting them'.[75]

On the issue of fixing fees for educational institutions Banerjee countered the colonial practice and spoke in favour of the poor but talented Indian student, who wished to pursue higher education: "The principle of excluding students from University education by a fee limit is open to further objection, that it will, on the one hand, exclude not only the undeserving but also the deserving poor student; while on the other hand, it will fail to exclude the undeserving rich student."[76]

Banerjee also objected to the provision that the private schools recognition by the University will 'depend upon its recognition, by the Director of Public Instruction'. Such a thing, he argued, undermined a host of private institutions which ran on their efforts and resources. This point was crucial, it supported an argument which was made later that the colonial system gradually destroyed and starved the indigenous education system in India. Banerji argued:

> So far as the Government and aided schools are concerned, there can be no objection to this recommendation. But as regards unaided private schools, the propriety of recommendation is open to question. These schools receive no aid from Government; and it does not seem to be right to place them practically under the control of the Education Department, to subject them to the rules made by the Director of Public Instruction, and to compel them to adopt the scheme of studies prescribed by them. It would amount to an undue interference with their freedom of action in directions in which they might be left free to move, with benefit to themselves and without harm to others; and it would tend to reduce the school education of each Province to a dead level of uniformity not always conducive to progress. [77]

---

75. *Report of the Indian Universities Commission, 1902*, pp. 73, 74.
76. Ibid., p.77.
77. *Report of the Indian Universities Commission, 1902*, p.80.

In a letter written a few years later to one of his Western disciples, Swami Vivekananda lamented this destruction of Indian education. 'All property and lands granted by the previous [Indian states] governments, for supporting education have been swallowed up, and the present government spends even less than Russia on education. And what education? The least show of originality is throttled ...', the Swami wrote to Mary Hale on October 30, 1899.[78]

Regarding the prevention of cramming through abolition of textbooks Banerjee argued that it would not be 'safe to assume that we shall suppress cramming by abolishing text books, unless we also improve our methods of teaching and examination'.[79] Sir Guru Das's arguments were cogently placed stemming from his long and close experience of the system itself. We shall not enter into a detailed analysis of it but make brief references to some observations that are immediately relevant to the debate – especially those on the improvement of school education.

In spite of the rapid multiplication of schools and colleges in the past few years, Banerjee argued that the quality of education imparted left much to be desired. He saw four primary reasons for this: ' i) unsuitable textbooks and course of study, ii) inefficient teaching, iii) injudicious methods of examination, iv) insufficient encouragement for post-graduate studies'.[80]

The first resulted in boys learning bad English and in developing the habit of 'mechanically [committing] to memory many things without understanding them'. That happened mainly because often reading books in English were only 'imperfectly intelligible to them, by reason of their relating to scenes and incidents wholly foreign to the Indian student'. Inefficient teaching was because the

---

78. *Letters of Swami Vivekananda*, pp.395-396.
79. *Report of the Indian Universities Commission, 1902*, op.cit, p.81.
80. *Report of the Indian Universities Commission, 1902*, p.84.

teachers were 'untrained and ill-paid' and were forced to 'teach large classes'.[81] While the method of examination and papers set for the examination had an 'injurious effect on the infant mind' and generally 'encouraged cramming', while poverty was a major deterrent for a large number of Indian students from advancing in studies.[82] The dissent note actually summed up some of the essential and glaring defects of the colonial Indian education system.

Sir Guru Das was among those distinguished individuals who were present at the 'historic conference that met on November 16, 1905' to deliberate on the proposal of setting up a National Council of Education. Writing a preface for Guru Das's book, *A Few Thoughts on Education* in 1904, Banerjee briefly identified the problems of Indian education. It was a reiteration of his earlier stand as Vice-Chancellor. The problem was that of the student 'having to acquire knowledge through the medium of a difficult foreign language which not only overtaxes their energies, but also cramps their thoughts'.[83]

About the applicability of foreign systems and the control of education in foreign hands, Guru Das argued, '...while on the one hand, the circumstances of the country and the habits and sentiments of its people, make Western methods and systems in their integrity often inapplicable to them, on the other hand the control of Education rests with those who, from their early training and imperfect knowledge of the East, naturally consider those methods and systems equally efficacious here, and seek to enforce them accordingly'.[84]

It was these issues – English unsuited as the medium of instruction, and the control of Indian education by foreigners

---

81. *Report of the Indian Universities Commission, 1902,* p.85.
82. Ibid., p.84.
83. Gooroo Dass Banerjee, *A Few Thoughts on Education*, 1904, p.v.
84. Ibid.

seeking to apply Western methods to what was essentially an Eastern setting – which became some of the key arguments of the national education movement. The philosophers of the national education movement repeatedly stressed the need to introduce Indian languages as the medium of instruction and to hand over the control of the entire Indian education set-up into Indian hands.

Being one of the early thinkers on a new education for India, Sir Guru Das discussed the whole question of national education in his 1904 book. But being conservative and moderate in his political outlook, Guru Das's book dealt mainly with the method, pedagogy of education, and attempted to formulate alternative suggestions without entering into the politics of the issue.

Interestingly, in his chapters on the 'Instruments of Education', Banerjee discussed the link between Universities and Colleges, and also argued that the government of the day ought to have a greater representation in the Universities. He emphasised that the government, being responsible for 'the peace and prosperity of the country' should, through this representation, make sure that 'no revolutionary or mischievous doctrines are inculcated to the youth of the country'.[85] However this representation must not be overbearing as that would, Banerjee stressed, destroy the independence of the University and its scope of flexible functioning.

On the involvement of the 'Europeans' in the Universities, Banerjee, observed that since the present University was a 'Western institution', the 'active and sympathetic-cooperation of learned Europeans in its administration' was 'absolutely necessary' at the 'present moment'.[86] But this had to be balanced with a greater degree of Indian representation too, 'as the Indian Universities work for the training of Indian youths, educated Indians also ought to have an

85. Ibid., p.271.
86. Ibid., p.273.

effective voice in their management, so as to adapt their working to the wants and habits and the sentiments and susceptibilities of Indian students'.[87]

Banerjee called for a 'gradual reformation, and not sudden destruction, of the existing educational fabric'.[88] He could not accept the official view that it was the educated class that spread disaffection in the country. These people, Banerjee argued, were concerned about the state of their fellow countrymen and thus raised their voices, but all of it was done in a loyal and constitutional manner. [89]

On the whole, though certainly not an educational treatise that supported the demand for an Indian control of education, Banerjee's thoughts on education contained in them a masterly analysis of the prevailing University system and suggestions for its improvement and expansion. Of great relevance and interest, however, in the work is Banerjee's word of caution to the European educators in their attitude towards their Indian pupils and vice- versa. 'I would beg,' he wrote:

Of the European professors to disabuse his mind of the impression, if any there be, that the Indian student is wanting either in intelligence or in respect for authority; and I would on the other hand ask the Indian student to free his mind of all apprehensions that the European professors may treat him with unkindness of discourtesy. The Indian student (I speak from personal knowledge and not from partiality for my countrymen, pardonable as it may be) is mild and docile; reverence for his teacher whether secular or religious is strictly enjoined by his religion and is deeply ingrained in his nature; he may be somewhat sentimental and may expect to be treated gently; and a little kindness is enough to win his heart. If he occasionally appears to be unmannerly or disrespectful, it is due more to his ignorance of the English code of manners or of the English language than anything else. .... I have

87. Ibid., p.273.
88. Ibid., p.274.
89. Ibid., p.275.

earnestly entreated our European professors not to accept as correct the view sometimes entertained, that the Indian student is intellectually inferior to students in Europe ...[90]

The above attitude in the Western educator was a major challenge for the national education movement. The national educational institutions also sought to dispel that entrenched perception. Sir Guru Das's thoughts on education, though not part of the pantheon of revolutionary educational thinkers, were nevertheless needed in order to popularise the educational debate. As the first Indian Vice-Chancellor of the University of Calcutta, he was, thus, an honoured invitee in the first national education conference.

Tagore's Early Educational Demand

Rabindranath Tagore was also among those early thought-leaders who called for the usage of the mother tongue in education at the elementary level. In his pioneering speech, *Sikshar Herpher* ('The Discrepancies in Education') which was read at a public meeting in Rajshahi [East Bengal] in 1892, Tagore mooted the idea. Tagore highlighted the 'discrepancies' between the responses of English children and Bengali children to the English-medium curriculum by pointing out that to an English child, the language and references are all inherent to his/her background; but to a Bengali child, the same system would be distanced by a foreign language [which was often taught by someone who was not proficient in it] and unrelated to the Indian environment'.[91] Moreover, this gave rise to the habit of learning by rote, blocked the development of the power of imagination and thought, and neglected an all-round development of the individual.[92] Education in the mother tongue, Tagore had

90. Ibid., pp. 279-281.
91. Kathleen M.O'Connell, op.cit. p. 87, 101.
92. Haridas and Uma Mukherjee, 'Jatiya Shiksha Andalone Rabindranath' in *Swadeshi Andolone O Banglar Nabajug* [Beng] rpt 2004, pp. 63—64.

then argued, needed to be developed at such a level, the language itself moulded in such a manner so that it could 'facilitate thought and express the cultural ethos'.[93]

1901 saw Tagore start his first experiment at alternative education with the setting up of his *Brahmacharyashram* inspired by the ancient Hindu concept of the pupil living with the master and learning from him. Tagore was one of those few, who would, throughout his life, continue unbroken to creatively pursue his mission of evolving a national system of education. Tagore's educational thought, philosophy, and vision have been extensively discussed across the world and therefore I have limited this portion to just mentioning his well-known demand of Indianising the imparting of education. I have, however, in another section, focused on his early education experiment – the *Brahmacharyashram* 1901 – because that was undertaken in collaboration with the fervently nationalist Brahmabandhab Upadhayay (1861–1907) and emphasised the traditional Indian method and approach to education while also introducing innovative teaching methods.

Dr. M. O'Connell mentions *Sikshar Herpher* as a speech first delivered at Rajshahi in 1892, and published in the December 1892 issue of the journal *Sadhana*. Prof. Haridas and Uma Mukherjee quote from the article in Sadhana but give its publication date as March-April 1893 of the Sadhana issue. They make the interesting point, that in 1893, Swami Vivekananda delivered his epochal address at Chicago and pushed India on the world-scene, Sri Aurobindo began writing his series, 'New Lamps for Old', where he began publicly attacking the then Congress policy of mendicancy and thereby introducing a radical terminology and direction in Indian politics, and Rabindranath Tagore, through his *Sikshar Herpher* publicly spoke of the deficiencies of the then prevailing English education system in India – all three actions contributed towards ushering in a new era in national life.

93. Kathleen M. O'Connell, op.cit. p.101.

II.4. SISTER NIVEDITA: HINTS TOWARDS AN EDUCATION FOR THE NATION

Mention must be made here of Sister Nivedita (1867–1911), Swami Vivekananda's Hinduised Irish disciple who played a decisive role in the Swadeshi movement and the movement for educational and cultural self-recovery in India.. Sister Nivedita had an exposure to Western educational thought prior to her coming to India. Her access to the literary circles of London brought her in contact with leading intellectuals of the day such as G.B.Shaw, T.H.Huxley, and W.B.Yeats etc. Nivedita founded a kindergarten school at Wimbledon based on the methods of Froebel and Pestalozzi.[94]

Nivedita's familiarity with thoughts on education of both these western pedagogues is evident from her expositions of their methods. She wrote of Pestalozzi thus in 1903:

> He [Pestalozzi tried to discover the law, the psychology of education ... he discovered that most people are unable to think clearly because they have no clear knowledge. Now what is knowledge? It is something that is the result of experience. Without experience, there can be no knowledge ... No knowledge without experience – then how to acquire experience? Pestalozzi answered: Through the senses – by sensation.... He came indeed to the conclusion that in the act of realising any piece of knowledge there are three processes, 1) sensation; 2) thought-germination; and 3) expression. Pestalozzi concluded that we must base all education on concrete sensation.[95]

Writing about the methods followed by the Kindergarten and of their adaptability under Indian conditions, Nivedita summarised the concept of both these western education pioneers thus:

---

94. Friedrich Froebel (1782–1852) creator of the word Kindergarten based his educational methods on the recognition that children have unique needs and capabilities. Johann Pestalozzi (1746–1827), Swiss pedagogue & educational reformer.
95. Kathleen M. O'Connell, op.cit. p. 228.

... [T]o Pestalozzi ... it was clear enough that the science of education could only be built up, on as keen and continuous observation of the laws of mind. Over and over again Pestalozzi refers to the modern problem as that of the "*psychologising* of education". In this *psychologising*, he made two great discoveries. First came the law that abstract thought has to be gathered from concrete experience. Second was the generalisation, that the child in its development follows the race. One hardly knows which of these two is the more important. In the first place, all knowledge begins with the concrete, that is to say, with the senses. Through the senses to the mind! Never by ignoring or thwarting the senses, can we build up education. By controlling, certainly! For control presupposes development, and training is only a larger name for it. But always from experience of the concrete, through the senses, to the power of the abstract thought, is the great Veda of modern education ... It was on the basis of the laws thus enunciated by Pestalozzi, that his disciple, Froebel, devised the Kindergarten. For years he watched the play of children, and analysed the subjects they had to learn, trying to connect the one with the other. Finally he invented the collection of toys known as his 'gifts'; tabulated a certain number of materials, such as string, sticks, sand, chalk, paper, and others; left on record a wonderful series of games and observations. All these together constitute what is known as the Kindergarten system. It is a system in which all knowledge is supposed to receive a foundation in concrete experience and all work to appear to the child as 'play'. The 'gifts' consist of balls, building-materials, and titles, for pattern-making. The 'occupations' – such as stick-laying, mat-weaving, paper-folding, colour-drawing, and so on – are of perennial interest, being in fact based on the primitive occupations of humanity. And these games which do not occur simply as parts of lessons, are for the most part observations of the crafts, or of natural phenomena, turned into action-songs ...[96]

After her arrival in India in 1898, Nivedita opened her own girl's school, disseminated knowledge on the latest Western educational theory and became an active pillar of the national education

96. Sister Nivedita, 'The Place of the Kindergarten' in Indian Schools, *The Complete Works of Sister Nivedita*, (CWSN), Vol. 4, 1996, pp.404-405. Also see e.g. Pravrajika Atmaprana, *Sister Nivedita: of Ramakrishna-Vivekananda*, 6th ed., 2007, pp.3,4.

movement.[97] Education was a key area of Sister Nivedita's action in India. She took it up as part of her ordained mission as envisioned for her by her Master, Swami Vivekananda. Nivedita saw the 'giving of knowledge' as another way of 'making the unity of our country effective'.[98] At the time when the national education debate was raging, Nivedita spoke of the sacredness of imparting education. She talked of the need to develop an 'army of education'. Drawing a parallel with the system of a compulsory three-year military training in the West on completion of education, why should it be impossible, she wondered, for every Indian student to give 'three years to the people' when his own education is over?

> ...[I]t is of course understood that just as the only son of a widow is, in the West, excused from military service, so one whose earnings are absolutely necessary to others must be excused the educational service. The villagers, on the other hand, would easily maintain a single student, living amongst them as a school-master. And when his own three years were over, it is to be supposed that he could, from his own old school or college, arrange for another to take his place. Some would learn to love the simple village life, and elect to live and die, poor school-masters. Most, however, would serve the years of their vow, and pass on, returning to the city, to bear their part in the life of a more complex community. On the one hand, the duty of teaching, on the other, the duty of maintaining, so teacher and taught make the perfect social unit. And so the great masses of the people might be swept within the circle of articulation. It takes thirty years to make a whole people literate, even supposing that an idea like this were carried out in its fullness.[99]

Nivedita was, of course, clear that such a scheme could not be arranged or implemented by any 'central organisation', but would have to be built up and sustained 'only by a common impulse of the people and the students themselves'.[100]

---

97. Kathleen M. O'Connell, op.cit. p. 39.
98. 'Primary Education: A Call for Pioneers' in *CWSN, Vol. 4*, op.cit, pp.329–330.
99. Ibid., pp.330–331.
100. Ibid., pp.331–332.

Nivedita did not see it as an impossible task, but all depended, in the last resort, on the 'quantity and quality of human life that can be sacrificed to it ...' The question was 'how many will give up comfort, place, opportunity, ease, even perhaps their whole life, for this, the elementary education of the Indian people?'[101] This was also a central question before the national education movement, and on it depended its overall success and longevity. Nivedita was closely involved with the movement right from its inception, profusely contributed to its intellectual framework by being involved with the activities of the National College, the *Dawn* magazine and encouraged young scholars to develop their expertise in their chosen field of work.[102] For Nivedita, the future of India depended on education and educational self-help and self-reliance. As she wrote in her masterly treatises on education, which appeared later as 'Hints on National Education':

> We all know that the future of India depends, for us, on education. Not that industry and commerce are unimportant, but because all things are possible to the educated, and nothing whatever to the uneducated man. We know also that this education, to be of any avail, must extend through all degrees, from its lowest and humblest grades. We must have technical education and we must have also higher research, because technical education, without higher research is a branch without a tree, a blossom without any root. We must have education of women, as well as education of men. We must have secular education, as well as religious. And, almost more than any of these, we must have education of the people, and for this, we must depend upon ourselves.[103]

101. Ibid., pp.331–332.
102. See, eg. *Origins of the National Education Movement*, op.cit., pp. 34, 35, 216, 218, *CWSN Vol.4*, op.cit., pp.389–396, ' A Note on Historical Research' – a letter written to Radha Kumud Mookerjee, then a budding scholar at the Bengal National College.
103. 'Primary Education: A Call for Pioneers' in *CWSN, Vol. 4*, p.329.

The reason for dwelling at some length on Sister Nivedita's as well as Annie Besant's educational initiatives and thoughts is because both of them, through their work and ideas, had interactions with Sri Aurobindo. In 1908, Sri Aurobindo wrote a rather strong editorial in the *Bande Mataram* discussing the proposal of setting up a national university that had been mooted by Mrs. Besant, and a decade later from his perch in Pondicherry, he wrote a message on national education, for the *New India* issue of April 8, 1918, a journal edited by Mrs. Besant, for a national education week that was being organised by her. It appeared under the heading: "Message from Sons of the Motherland to Their Brothers"; Sri Aurobindo's was the longest of nine messages contributed by India's "leading patriots".

Sister Nivedita, was Sri Aurobindo's close associate in the nationalist movement. After Swami Vivekananda's passing in July 1902, Sister Nivedita's arrangement with the Ramakrishna Order changed and her work was regarded henceforth as 'free and entirely independent of their [Ramakrishna Order] sanction and authority'. Thus, for nine years until her death in 1911, her activities were 'centred mainly on the national movement in its various aspects'. Two months after this, Sister Nivedita undertook a fund-raising tour of Western India and this brought her to Baroda in October, where she had come ostensibly on a lecture tour. But the actual intention was to try and rope in the Gaekwad to support revolutionary activity. It was during this visit that she met Sri Aurobindo, in fact he received her at the station, and 'brought him up to date with developments in Calcutta'.[104]

Though Sri Aurobindo recalled later that whenever he and Nivedita met they would discuss revolution and politics, it is not unlikely that they discussed education as well. The other point of reference is the *Karmayogin*, the English weekly that Sri Aurobindo launched from prison in 1909. It was in the pages of this journal that Sri Aurobindo first began systematically formulating his ideas on

104. Peter Heehs, *The Bomb in Bengal*, op.cit., p. 40.

education. Sister Nivedita was constantly in touch with him during this period and took keen interest in the running of the journal. In early 1910, when Sri Aurobindo suddenly moved to Chandernagore, he asked Sister Nivedita to carry on the work of the *Karmayogin*. The series on education that Sri Aurobindo began writing in *Karmayogin* were published in eight installments between February 12 and April 2, 1910. Sri Aurobindo departed for Chandernagore sometime in the middle of February 1910, and his association with the journal ended.

It is evident that he must have left the manuscript of 'A System of National Education' behind and Sister Nivedita took charge of publishing the remaining eight chapters in the *Karmayogin*.[105] Sister Nivedita's connection with the exposition of Sri Aurobindo's educational thought, apart from her advanced formulations on education, can be seen in their association with the *Karmayogin*. A separate analysis of these early educational thoughts shall be undertaken in later sections to give us an insight into how the early thinkers attempted to implement a nationalist agenda of education which was forward-looking, inclusive, heritage-conscious and spiritually alive while focusing on the individual's growth of the powers of the mind and personality.

II.5. SWAMI VIVEKANANDA: VEDANTIC SEEDS FOR A FUTURE SYSTEM OF NATIONAL EDUCATION

While discussing Sister Nivedita's educational thoughts, one has to briefly turn to Swami Vivekananda's educational ideas as well. During the period in discussion, as one of the ionic figures of the Indian renaissance, Vivekananda strove to give directions in several areas of human growth and development to the rising national consciousness, which he himself helped to awaken in no mean measure. For Sri Aurobindo, the appearance of Swami Vivekananda at Chicago 'showed the spiritual ideas for which India stands, no longer on their defence but aggressive and invading the materialised

105. *CWSA* vol.1, Note on the Texts, op. cit., p. 772.

mentality of the Occident'.[106] The rise of new educational ideas for national regeneration were a result of that assertion of the deeper Indian identity that Vivekananda's Western sojourn symbolised. Since his educational ideas have been, and are, extensively, continuously and widely discussed I shall focus on a few limited texts.

In an illuminating conversation on education around 1890s, Vivekananda discussed the defects of the education system as he saw it, and articulated his ideas on education.

Vivekananda emphasises the efficacy of the age-old Hindu system of *Guru-griha-vasa* [living with the master in his abode], and thus imbibing and learning from him; 'my idea of education', remarked Swamiji, 'is *Gurugriha-vasa.* Without the personal life of the teacher, there would be no education. One should live from his very boyhood with one whose character is a blazing fire, and should have before him a living example of the highest teaching'.[107]

That the old system would have to be modified in keeping with the backdrop of the present, was clear to Vivekananda, and he clarified that the system would be as of old, 'but with this education has to be combined modern Western science. Both these are necessary'. Vivekananda saw the prevailing university system as a 'perfect machine for turning out clerks' and those who went through this system were becoming increasingly deracinated.[108]

Sri Aurobindo too found the old Indian system of the 'guru commanding by his knowledge and sanctity the implicit obedience, perfect admiration, reverent emulation of the student' a far superior

---

106. Sri Aurobindo, *The Renaissance in India and Other Essays on Indian Culture*, 2002, p. 63.
107. T.S. Avinashilingam, *The Educational Philosophy of Swami Vivekananda*, 1983, p. 33.
108. *The Complete Works of Swami Vivekananda*,(CWSV) *Vol.5*, 2009, pp. 364–365.

method of evolving and inculcating moral discipline than the English boarding school system. In the English boarding school system though the master 'at his best stands as a moral guide and example' for the pupils to emulate and influence each other to follow the example, it nevertheless spoilt things by forcing adherence to an excessive outer discipline. This Sri Aurobindo felt commanded obedience out of fear and not out of understanding and need.

Sri Aurobindo also argues that it is impossible to 'restore that ancient system' under modern conditions, but advocates that at least the instructor can embody the qualities that the guru did in an earlier age – that of being a 'wise friend, guide and helper' – and not a mere 'hired instructor' or 'benevolent policeman' who are out to dutifully perform their task by following an outward routine and system but who, in the long run, fail to lead by example and establish a living relationship with the pupil.[109]

The embodiment of the qualities of a guru – who, in the Indian context, is a compassionate teacher and comrade having already lived through the experience of growing and learning – appeared to be for our thought-leaders an essential requirement for the imparting of moral education. A successful application of it excludes the use of fear as an instrument of instruction and enables the creation of an environment of mutual trust.

The system [*gurugriha-vasa*] is not to be replicated in its physical entirety or even partially, for modern systems and conditions will not perhaps allow its complete working out. What, however, is to be replicated or sought to be applied under modern conditions are its psychological dimensions, objectives, and ideals. Swami Vivekananda as well as Sri Aurobindo looked to such an application and contextualisation when they spoke of applying this aspect of the Indian system.

109. *CWSA* vol.1, op.cit., p. 390.

Vivekananda also says that 'no one can teach anybody' and that 'the teacher spoils everything by thinking that he is teaching'. He defines the roots of a Vedantic philosophy of education; one perceives its similarities with Sri Aurobindo's first educational principle, which says that 'nothing can be taught', that the teacher is 'a helper and a guide', that he does not impose himself on the child but only 'shows him where [knowledge] lies and how it can be habituated to rise to the surface'.

Both insist that the teacher must maintain an unobtrusive manner of functioning, desist from imposing his own notions and ideas, and must rather encourage the growth of spontaneity in the child and help give rise in her a natural curiosity which is the starting point of any true, healthy, and effective process of learning. '...Vedanta says that within man is all knowledge,' contended Vivekananda, 'even in a boy it is so – and it requires only an awakening, and that much is the work of a teacher. We have to do only so much for the boys that they may learn to apply their own intellect to the proper use of their hands, legs, ears, eyes, etc., and finally everything will become easy ... Our pedagogues are making parrots of our boys and ruining their brains by cramming a lot of subjects into them'.[110]

If the Swami's chief message in the field of education was 'based on the divinity of the human soul' and the belief that 'all souls are potentially different and that education should be the manifestation of the divinity already in man',[111] then cramming, and a mechanical approach to learning had no place in it. The teacher, in his vision of education, had to assist in the manifestation of this divinity by 'positive help, encouragement, and [by] his own example'.[112]

110. *CWSV vol.5*, op.cit., pp. 366,367.

111. Avinashilingam, op.cit., p.20.

112. Ibid.

Vivekananda's educational thought was futuristic, and one finds further similarities in the thoughts that he enunciated with Sri Aurobindo's formulation of educational ideas presented towards the end of the first decade of the last century. It is necessary therefore to look at these in some detail.

The refusal to accept the cramming of the mind with information as a process of education is a stand that Vivekananda adopted throughout his discussions on education. A similar stance is also adopted by Sri Aurobindo when he consistently opposed the notion that education is primarily about the imparting and assimilating of information. Vivekananda laid great stress on developing the powers of the mind and in it specially the power of concentration. He was categorical that the very essence of education was the concentration of mind and not collection of facts.

The education system as he saw it around him, Vivekananda felt, prevented the growth of originality in the individual. 'Every man of originality that has been produced', lamented Vivekananda, 'has been educated elsewhere, and not in this country', articulating his famous retort :

> Education is not the amount of information that is put into your brain and runs riot there, undigested, all your life. We must have life-building, man-making, character-making assimilation of ideas. If you have assimilated five ideas and made them your life and character, you have more education than any man who has got by heart a whole library .... If education is identical with information, the libraries are the greatest sages in the world, and encyclopaedias are the Rishis.[113]

---

113. *CWSV vol.3*, p. 302. In a letter to Swami Rangathananda (1908–2005), Julian Huxley (1887–1975) once wrote, 'The Swami gives a splendid definition of what education ought to be and sometimes is. But my visits to India showed me that the aim of a large number of Indian undergraduates was not to enjoy an education of this sort, but to pass examinations and obtain a degree which was useful in getting jobs'.

The Swami left no opportunity to reiterate this point and of emphasising the need to develop the power of thinking. In a talk delivered sometime in 1896, he argued 'No amount of books can help us to become pure. The only power is in realisation, and that lies in ourselves and comes from thinking. Let men think. A clod of earth never thinks; but it remains only a lump of earth. The glory of man is that he is a thinking being. It is the nature of man to think and therein he differs from animals'.[114]

On another occasion in 1898, while in dialogue with some of his *grihastha* disciples, Vivekananda clarified what he actually meant by education – 'By education I do not mean the present system, but something in the line of positive teaching. Mere book-learning won't do. We want that education by which character is formed, strength of mind is increased, the intellect is expanded, and by

---

Swami Ranganathananda accepted that India 'is wrestling with the problem of introducing ethical and spiritual values in education' and yet she had a wealth of ideas in this field from which to draw upon. He also drew attention to one of Gandhi's observations on Vivekananda's educational philosophy, "Writing a foreword to a small book of selections on Education by Vivekananda, Mahatma Gandhi observed that the 'current Indian education is basically a continuation of what the British introduced in India in the last century, with its aim of turning out clerks. It has quantitatively expanded immensely but has gone down qualitatively. It has neither the virtues of the ancient Indian system nor the modern British system, but the weakness of both. It turns out every year not men, but functionaries of society – so many lawyers, doctors, engineers etc, etc. But India is also silently engaged in education and there is much silent constructive thinking and discussion also on the subject. We may hope to feel the impact of all these on our education in the coming decades...'" (Swami Ranganathananda, *Role & Responsibility of Teachers in Building up Modern India*, 2006, pp.25–26.)

114. *CWSV vol.* 2, p.336.

which one can stand on one's feet'. [115] And at times, in his inimitable style, Vivekananda categorically denigrated the entire practice, 'Getting by heart the thoughts of others, in a foreign language and stuffing your brains with them and taking some university degrees you consider yourself educated. Is this education? What is the goal of your education?' [116]

---

115. *CWSV vol.5*, p.342. In an earlier conversation Vivekananda defined 'negative education'. His usage of the term 'positive' as well 'negative' education, is thought provoking: 'We have had a negative education all along from our boyhood. We have only learnt that we are nobodies. Seldom are we given to understand that great men were ever born in our country. Nothing positive has been taught to us .... We master all the facts and figures concerning the ancestors of the English, but we are sadly unmindful about our own. We have learnt only weakness. Being a conquered race, we have brought ourselves to believe that we are weak and have no independence in anything...' (Ibid., p.332) The Swami, through such argumentations, contributed in no mean measure to laying the ideological foundations of the national education movement.
116. Cited in S. Narain, *Examinations in Ancient India*, 1993, p.1. The ideals of ancient Indian education quite clearly defined what education was not – it was not mere book learning, or learning by rote. The Swami was referring to that tradition which was intrinsic to the Indian system. For example, in Chandogya-Upanishad in Rishi Sanat Kumara's conversations with the Sage Narada, one finds one such supporting example. Narada approaches Sanat Kumara and asks to be taught by him. On being asked what he has already studied, Narada says, "Most reverend Sir, I have studied: The Rig Veda, the Yajur Veda, the Sam Veda, the Atharva Veda, and Ayur Veda, Itihasa - Purana, Grammar, and the Pitrya, the Arithmetic, ... Astrology, Logic, the Deva Vidya, the Brahma Vidya, the Bhuta Vidya, the Military Science, the Sarpa and Deva Jnana Vidya, the science of making perfumes, dancing, singing, playing and other fine arts. All these I have studied Sir, but still I am in sorrow. Lead me thee over, I pray, to the further shore that lies beyond sorrow." Sanat Kumara's reply to Narada perhaps sums up the entire Indian educational vision:

Vivekananda was also clear on the need of developing a national system of education under national control, 'the ideal, therefore, is that we must have the whole education of our country, spiritual and secular, in our own hands, and it must be on national lines, through national methods as far as practical'.[117] The Swami, it appears, was clear on the need for the indigenous control of education and of the fact that such a control alone could really do away with the negative education.

Sri Aurobindo too assailed the habit of seeing education as a mere information-gathering process. While writing a preface on National Education in his philosophical review *Arya* between 1920–21, where he initiated a detailed discussion on the nature and identity of a possible national education for the country – though this also like some of his other writings remains incomplete – Sri Aurobindo made observations which were similar to those found in his incomplete writings on education at Baroda and which were in line with Vivekananda's arguments on the essence of education.

Sri Aurobindo observes that those who argue against the concept of a national education believe that the central matter of education is the 'acquiring of this or that kind of information'. 'But', he argues, almost in the same vein as Vivekananda:

> The acquiring of various kinds of information is only one and not the chief of the means and necessities of education: its central aim is the building of

---

'What you have studied is but words.' (Narain, op.cit., p.3) The Indian ideal thought of education as liberating – and liberation could come when one went beyond the text, beyond the word into the deeper meaning and dimensions of the topic. Self-knowledge as the Swami stressed was the *summum bonum* of Indian education and when both he and Sri Aurobindo discouraged the notion of mere book learning or information-gathering as education they were point back at that classical Indian vision of education.

117. *CWSV vol.3*, p.302.

the powers of the human mind and spirit, it is the formation, or, as I would prefer to view it, the evoking of the knowledge and will and of the power to use knowledge, character, culture – that at least if no more.[118]

The term 'evoking' in the context of education is central to Sri Aurobindo's thoughts on education. He continued to harp on the point that the child cannot be subjected to an external volley of unrelated information served as knowledge but has to be instead guided and assisted in first knowing where to look for knowledge and then in assimilating it.

The question that comes to mind here is that of knowledge and information and the use of knowledge. Similarity and synchronicity of perception is evident between Vivekananda and Sri Aurobindo in defining the term 'knowledge' – which according to them, meant knowledge of the self, knowledge of the workings of one's mind and nature, ones inclinations and temperament, the controlling of reactions as well as actions, the formulations of the object of one's life – and its application in solving and dealing with the challenges and problems of life.

Both these thought-leaders believed that mere information-gathering does not equip one to face life in a balanced manner and if information-gathering was the sole objective of education, would not libraries and encyclopedias qualify as all-round educators, as Vivekananda stated the issue! The 'evoking of knowledge' aspect still remains an issue subject to perception and application. It requires a deeper understanding of the pupil's mind, a constant observation of its propensities and requirements and demands a greater understanding on behalf of the teacher and instructor.

The discouragement of originality, the inclination to treat the individual as an automaton to be saturated with information,

118. *CWSA* vol.1, op.cit., pp. 420–421.

the neglect of the character-building dimension, the deliberate denial of technical knowledge were all part of an education system that appeared to most protagonists of national education to be mercenary and soulless by nature and character.

Vivekananda was conscious of the fact that technical education also needed to be a vital part of indigenous education. He spoke of the need 'to study independent of foreign control, different branches of the knowledge that is our own, and with it the English language and Western science; we need technical education and all else that may develop industries so that men, instead of seeking for service, may earn enough to provide for themselves ...'[119]

The need for a sound technical education was also one of the driving factors of the national education movement. To train the individual to be financially self-supporting was one of the objectives of the national schools and the College. While speaking on National Education at Bombay in 1908 during a tour of Maharashtra, the other citadel of extremist politics, at the invitation of Lokmanya Tilak, Sri Aurobindo dwelt at length on the experiment of national education undertaken in Bengal. It was perhaps his longest recorded verbal exposition of the theme, [examined in detail in the second part of the discussion]. Sri Aurobindo spoke of technical education being imparted at the National College and described its objective as that of ensuring that the student did not have to make somebody else carry him on his shoulders but to become self-reliant himself. It is done, he explained, through the teaching of 'many vocational subjects, such as carpentry and smithy, along with science. The result [being] when a student comes out of [such] schools, he does not find it difficult to earn a monthly wage ...'[120] A precursor in certain respects

119. *CWSV vol.5*, op.cit., p. 368.

120. Sri Aurobindo, *Speeches – On Indian Politics and National Education,* 2005, p. 175. Aparna Basu in her National Education in Bengal:

of the Basic Education concept evolved in the 1930s by Mahatma

1905-1912 (in *The Contested Terrain —Perspectives on Education in India* ed. Sabyasachi Bhattacharya, Orient Longman, 1998) has argued that compared to one of the distinguishing features of Gandhian education – the importance of manual work in the education scheme – 'manual work was not a part of the curriculum of the national schools of Bengal, as the pupils and teachers were *bhadralok* who were divorced from manual work'.(p.66) Sri Aurobindo's observation in the above mentioned public speech does not support that argument. Prof. Haridas and Uma Mukherjee in their seminal '*The Origins of the National Education Movement*' (pp. 102, 112) show how the newly founded Bengal National College attempted to provide adequate attention to the vocational and technical training of the pupils. They point out, based on primary material, that The National Council of Education held periodic exhibitions of 'articles, implements and apparatus manufactured in the laboratories and workshops of the Bengal National College'. The *Dawn* Magazine in its February issue of 1908 carried a report on an exhibition that was held between January 2–19. A list of the articles exhibited will show that most of them required direct manual labour to be manufactured. 'Apparatus for physics, apparatus and appliances for chemistry, cardboard work such as drawing models, medicine cases etc, furniture work such as folding tables, almirahs etc, drawing appliances such as drawing boards, set squares, T-squares, compass ... miscellaneous things such as candle-stands, inkstands, picture frames, penholders, office stationery case, gardening tools' etc. were some of the items on display. The National College had developed a system which sought to graft technical training and workshop practice on a system of general education.(p.109) It is also seen that the concept of vocational and manual training was encouraged even in the district (*mofussil*) national schools such as the Jessore National School specialising in clay models and 'iron implements of carpentry'. The Santipur School's area of specialisation was 'chiefly furniture' the Rangpur School achieved distinction in ivory work, Mymensingh schools specialised in teak-wood boxes, cane-covered sticks, bamboo-punkhas, folding-chairs and cane strips' etc. (p.110). All these items were then centrally displayed in the exhibition and they had each a price tag attached to

Gandhi, where manual training, learning of crafts was a mandatory

them. The whole activity thus had a commercial as well as educational value. The *Dawn* Magazine in a report in May 1909, mentions that in the workshop of the College, 'the visitor has the opportunity of seeing the students at their labours, and the business practicability of the school is here attested by the repairs now in course of operation in respect to sundry articles'. (p.111) One perceives here a similarity with the later narrative on manual work in the Gandhian Basic education system. The commercial viability of the manual and technical work were kept in mind at the NCE. The other aspect that the *Dawn* article clearly reports, goes contrary to Prof. Basu's assertions on manual work and the so-called '*bhadralok*' angle, 'It is one of the intentions of the institution to beat down existing caste prejudices against manual labour, and it is interesting, in this connection, to observe a high-caste Brahmin in the Smithy's shop toiling at a boring cutter and a polishing lathe. The felicity of labour seems to be the keynote of the system in vogue in the workshops...' (p.111) It is evident that the '*bhadralok*' prejudice did not play a part here or at least it shows that the '*bhadralok*' was consciously trying to outgrow his mindset and mingle with the other caste-elements who were being welded into a single national life, and he did not in any way, at least in the national education experiment, remain aloof or sequestered. It must also be accepted that caste prejudice was not what kept the movement from growing and becoming viable. In fact another interesting point is made on the issue of manual work. Joseph Bara of the Educational Records Research Unit (ERRU) at the Jawaharlal Nehru University, New Delhi, in his essay '*Colonialism and Educational Fragmentation in India*' that appeared in the same anthology, mentions that by the time the Wardha Scheme of education was formulated, 'the colonial system had irreparably distorted the popular mind [and] Education and manual labour came to be considered opposites, and any new experiment was judged in terms of its expediency in leading to a white-collar job in town'. (p.158) Probably this is one of the reasons why the Wardha Scheme of Basic Education was vehemently opposed by a section. I argue that the national education movement in Bengal sought to root out this prejudice against manual labour, and had it continued for a longer period, had it succeeded in creating

principle with the aim of making the individual and institution self-reliant. After the Congress ministry had assumed office in the provinces in 1937, Gandhi urged them to aim at restructuring Indian education. A mega education conference was convened at Wardha on October 22, 1937, which saw eminent educationists, Gandhians, Congress ministers and many 'distinguished people' participate. The conference met for three days and in his inaugural address Gandhi described the tenets of basic education. For Gandhi, the 'principal means of stimulating the intellect should be manual training ... because the intellect of our boys is being wasted. Our boys do not know what to do on leaving schools'. True education for him, was that which 'draws out and stimulates the spiritual, the intellectual, and physical faculties of the children'. Such an education, he argued, would be for them a 'kind of insurance against unemployment'. Gandhi lamented that because educational and manual training was divorced, the importance of village crafts were overlooked.

---

a wider base for itself things on this front would have been different. The larger question is whether this divorce between education and manual work still exists in society at large and whether the majority education system now followed has succeeded in bridging this gap? The National Education Policy (NEP) 2020, which has come up with path-breaking suggestions in revamping Indian education, speaks of 're-imagining' vocational education by overcoming the 'social status hierarchy associated with vocational education and requires integration of vocational education programmes into mainstream education in all education institutions in a phased manner. Beginning with vocational exposure at early ages in middle and secondary school, quality vocational education will be integrated smoothly into higher education. It will ensure that every child learns at least one vocation and is exposed to several more. This would lead to emphasising the dignity of labour and importance of various vocations involving /Indian arts and artisanship.' (*National Education Policy 2020*, Human Resources Ministry, Govt of India, p.44)

'Manual work has been regarded as something inferior...'. Gandhi told the Wardha educational conference that his scheme was not about the 'teaching of some handicrafts side by side with the so-called liberal education', for him, 'the whole education should be imparted through some handicrafts or industry'.[121] Through his handicraft-based and handicraft-oriented Basic Education, Gandhi saw the possibilities of a comprehensive rejuvenation of India's village economy and society.

Sri Aurobindo also stressed the importance of disseminating technical education among the masses along with literary education. While discussing the constructive programmes undertaken by organisations and institutions involved in the freedom struggle, Sri Aurobindo observed that it would be appropriate to provide the masses, especially rural, 'education, technical training and [to] give them (fundamentals or principles of) organisation, not on political but on business lines'.[122] He was referring to the need for achieving self-reliance through the growth of rural industry and commerce.

While in Baroda, Sri Aurobindo had very early highlighted the need for systematically imparting technical education.

In a report he had drafted on trade in the Baroda State in 1902, Sri Aurobindo analysed, in great detail, the whole 'depressing' scenario of trade in the state and made suggestions for its expansion and improvement. Enumerating the 'hindrances to expansion of trade he spoke of '(a) the want of technical education', as a first impediment.' He felt that technical and agricultural education was

121. For a detailed and interesting expose and report of the Wardha educational conference and the philosophy of Basic Education, see eg., D.G. Tendulkar's *Mahatma: Life of Mohandas Karamchand Gandhi*, Vol.4, New Delhi: The Publications Division, (1952), 2016, pp.186–203.

122. A.B. Purani, *Evening Talks with Sri Aurobindo,* 1995, p. 566.

an imperative and suggested the establishing of technical schools in each 'division' and 'Kasba' and also highlighted the fact that the state must sponsor the technical education of some students in its existing technical institution, and must also loan capital for starting factories to students who pass out successfully.

The suggestion that students must be sent to, 'foreign countries for technical instructions', also finds mention in his report. The report also sees Sri Aurobindo focus on the imparting and improving of agricultural education. Analysing the need for agricultural instruction in the same report Sri Aurobindo made precise suggestions. His suggestions could have been easily passed off as part of a nationalist programme or movement for achieving national self-reliance in agriculture. The steps suggested by Sri Aurobindo, then still in service in Baroda, were (a) Agricultural schools or classes teaching the children of cultivators free and other classes for a 'light fee', (b) Public lectures by competent persons, (c) Publication of Agricultural Pamphlets, books or a magazine, (d) Skilled cultivators should be sent to Europe along with English-knowing students to learn. They should take implements with them to learn from the European; Sri Aurobindo also suggests the holding of (e) Agricultural Exhibitions and (f) the development of Model Farms.[123]

It is interesting to note that though written for a princely State, the note could very well serve as a guide for technical and agricultural education in the early years of independence. The document stressed the point that that Indians must be exposed to the technical advances of Europe and must implement those skills in their working conditions. The suggestion for launching an agricultural magazine and distribution of pamphlets on the

---

123. *CWSA* vol.1, op.cit., 'Report on Trade in the Baroda State 1902', pp. 730–31, pp. 738–39.

subject appears to be very modern, keeping in mind the prevailing condition in India then, showing that Sri Aurobindo, even in an official capacity, while submitting a routine report, always spoke for innovation, upgradation, and assimilation of the latest scientific development.

Vivekananda too, had emphasised the education of the masses. It was an issue which was dear to him and one which he unequivocally highlighted. Vivekananda spoke of the deprivation of the masses by the ruling clique and men of authority, and blamed this attitude for being at the root of India's degeneration. 'I see it before my eyes,' he wrote in 1897, to Sarala Devi Ghosal (1872–1945), editor of the Bengali journal *Bharati* and later, one of the pioneers of the secret society and physical culture movement in Bengal, and an early nationalist collaborator of Sri Aurobindo, that '...a nation is advanced in proportion as education and intelligence spread among the masses' and a regeneration of India will come by 'spreading education among the masses. The chief cause of India's ruin has been the monopolising of the whole education and intelligence of the land, by dint of pride and royal authority, among a handful of men. Education, education, education alone!'[124] [Among the masses, would regenerate the country].

The letter was one of those lucid and succinct elucidations of the Swami's insight of India's educational needs and it made a few fundamental points. He compared the comfort and education of the poor in the West with his own poor countrymen and pointed out that it was education that made all the difference – 'Through education comes faith in one's own Self, and through faith in one's own Self, the inherent Brahman is waking up in them, while the Brahman in us is gradually becoming dormant'.[125]

---

124. *CWSV vol. 4*, pp. 482–83.

125. Ibid., p.483.

Vivekananda was perhaps 'the first Indian leader to recognise the role of the working class in building a new India'. He used the term 'proletariat' to describe them. He was extremely conscious 'of our national sin', of having exploited them for centuries together. 'It is they', he said, 'who from time immemorial, have been working silently, without even getting the remuneration for their labours'. He spoke of this neglect of the masses as a 'great national sin' and 'one of the causes of our downfall'. He called for awakening them through 'mass education on positive lines'. His method, 'let hundreds of young men go from village to village, bringing not only religion to the door of everyone, but also education'.[126]

The education that Vivekananda saw being imparted in the West embedded ardour and confidence into the learner. On the other hand the education that was imparted to the boys at home, he argued, was very negative and mind-numbing. It was the surest instrument for sowing seeds of confusion and doubt and self-deprecation:

> The schoolboy learns nothing, but has everything of his own broken down – want of Shraddhâ is the result. The Shraddhâ which is the keynote of the Veda and the Vedanta – the Sraddhâ which emboldened Nachiketâ to face Yama and question him, through which Shraddhâ this world moves – the annihilation of that Sraddhâ! ... The ignorant man, the man devoid of Shraddhâ, the doubting self runs to ruin. Therefore are we so near destruction. The remedy now is the spread of education. First of all, Self-knowledge.[127]

The Swami clarified what he meant by Self-knowledge – it was not a retrogression, it was rather the attainment of a liberating knowledge which not only showed the path towards true freedom, but also made possible the mastery of the material field:

126. See eg., P. Parameswaran, *Marx and Vivekananda: A Comparative Study*, 1987.
127. Ibid., pp.483-484.

I do not mean thereby, matted hair, staff, kamandalu, and mountain caves which the word suggests. What do I mean then? Cannot the knowledge, by which is attained even freedom from the bondage of worldly existence, bring ordinary material prosperity? Certainly it can. Freedom, dispassion, renunciation all these are the very highest ideals... [128]

Along with this awareness of Self-knowledge, a system of imparting that education had to be put in place. The Swami suggested a nationwide band of itinerant teachers – 'there are thousands of unselfish, kind-hearted men in our country who have renounced everything. In the same way as they travel about and give religious instructions without any remuneration, so at least half of them can be trained as teachers or bearers of such education as we need most...' [129]

Self-knowledge, rekindling the nearly lost or weakening Shraddhâ, and a complete negation of a negative and confusion-embedding education are some of the keynotes of Vivekananda's educational thought, formulated at a time when Sri Aurobindo ensconced in the Baroda service, was himself also applying his mind to the key questions of education in India.

Realising the need to spread education far and wide and at all levels, the early nationalist discourse on education believed that national schools must be started on a wide scale. Every nationalist movement that began in different regions and districts had as one of its first agenda the founding of a national school. These schools had as their aim, among other things, making the youth aware of the depravities of the colonial administration, awaken them to the rich cultural and civilisational legacy, nurturing in them a collective consciousness and training them become self-reliant not only psychologically, but also economically.

---

128. *CWSV vol. 4*, p.484.
129. Ibid., pp.484–485.

The organic link between the school and society that once existed in the past was sought to be revived. Though a large portion of resources for the movement came from the wealthy land-owning class it did not seek to perpetuate the hold of the privileged over the deprived classes. A genuine attempt was made to restructure education from the grassroots. It will be unfair to overlook the fact that it was for the first time that a mass movement on educational lines was initiated and the degenerative sense of elitism in it was conspicuous by its absence.

The rapid pace with which national schools were set up and founded had its infrastructural and organisational drawbacks, and eventually led to many of them collapsing, though that happened mostly because of administrative repression. Nevertheless it was instrumental in giving rise to this realisation that education was one of the principle paths to Swaraj.

Though a section of the populace continued to support the existing education system from fear of compromising the future prospects of their wards, the national education movement had, apart from the aim of political protest, a serious objective of broad basing education. Swami Vivekananda germinated the seeds of that awareness. It is known that most of the early revolutionaries read his works for inspiration.[130] Sri Aurobindo gave a political voice to

130. For a detailed discussion on Swami Vivekananda and India's struggle for freedom see for instance, Sankarai Prasad Basu's multi-volume magmum opus, *Vivekananda O Samakalin Bharatvarsha*, vol.6, (1985), Kolkata: Mandal Book House, 6th rpt, 2012. Speaking of Vivekananda as the hero of young Bengal, Dunlop Smith, British officer, then Private Secretary to Viceroy Lord Minto, admitted to Lady Minto in a letter dated March 11, 1908, at the height of the political ferment brought about in Bengal and the country because of the new revolutionary politics, that 'The key to a great deal of what is happening is a remark I read in an Indian magazine... "Kehsub Chander Sen has ceased to be

that awareness by consistently and persistently harping on the issue of national education as one of the major actions that needed to be initiated and undertaken by the nationalists. He considered it to be one of the main pillars that would ultimately uphold the 'house of Swaraj'.

II.6. A NEW APPROACH ACROSS THE SEAS: JOHN DEWEY'S CONCERN FOR THE CHILD'S NATURE

Across the seas, a new approach to education had already begun. John Dewey's (1859–1952) Declaration concerning education was first published in *The School Journal* in 1897. The Declaration indicated a radical attempt at transforming education and making it child-responsive and friendly. Similarities with Dewey's educational Declaration emerge in Sri Aurobindo later writings on education. It would suffice here to a draw parallel in approaches on some aspects. Dewey declares:

> I believe that ... the teacher is not in the school to impose certain ideas or to form certain habits in the child, but is there as a member of the community to select the influences which shall affect the child and to assist him in properly responding to these influences.

Sri Aurobindo while elucidating his first principle of teaching argues that the teacher is not an instructor or task-master; he is a helper and a guide. Dewey argues [he believes]:

---

a national hero, young Bengal is looking now to the ideals of Rama Krishna and Swami Vivekananda." Tilak is the apostle of this new evangel. We have ourselves to blame for over-Anglicising our system of education and this reaction is only natural. But it will be serious if it proceeds to extreme lengths and actually reaches the masses.' ('*Servant of India: A Study of Imperial Rule: from 1905–1910, As told Through the Correspondence and Diaries of Sri James Dunlop Smith, Private Secretary to the Viceroy*' cited in Sankari Prasad Basu, Vol.6)

That we violate the child's nature and render difficult the best ethical results, by introducing the child too abruptly to a number of special studies, of reading, writing, geography, etc., out of relation to this social life.

In his third principle of education Sri Aurobindo argues that it is always better to apply the principle 'from the near to the far, from that which is to that which shall be'. He insists that the surrounding environment of the child need to be respected and the child made gradually aware of it – 'We must not take up the nature [of the child] by the roots from the earth in which it must grow or surround the mind with images and ideas of a life which is alien to that in which it must physically move. If anything has to be brought in from outside, it must be offered, not forced on the mind. A free and natural growth is the condition of genuine development.'[131]

On the child, his environment, and on the type of approach to his education, Dewey makes a significant observation which reminds one of Sri Aurobindo's exhortation to teach from the near to the far. Dewey's expressions also verge on the poetic when he says that the key-note in handling the child are 'affection and sympathy' and that the child's world is a narrow world of touch and 'personal contact' and the course of study that he usually meets in school:

... [P]resents material stretching back indefinitely in time, and extending outward indefinitely into space. The child is taken out of his familiar physical environment, hardly more than a square mile or so in area, into the wide world – yes, even to the bounds of the solar system. His little span of personal memory and tradition is overlaid with long centuries of the history of all peoples. [132]

---

131. Vide – the *Informal Education Archives* at http://www.infed.org/archives/e-texts/e-dew-pc.htm & Sri Aurobindo, *On Education – A System of National Education, ch-1, The Human Mind*, p.384–85, *CWSA* vol.1.

132. John Dewey, 'The Child and the Curriculum' in J.J. Findlay edited, *The School and the Child: Being Selections from the Educational Essays of John Dewey*, 1906, p.19.

Interestingly, Dewey also talks of the child's life as being 'integral', though his formulation of it was made in a different context. Dewey talks of the child quickly transitioning from one object to another, from one topic to another without necessarily being aware of it or absorbing either. His explanation of this phenomenon and of the system's inability to understand it reminds one of Sri Aurobindo's disapproval of the habit of teaching by 'snippets'. Referring to this, Dewey argues:

> ... [The child] passes quickly and readily from one topic to another, as from one spot to another, but is not conscious of transition or break. There is no conscious isolation, hardly conscious distinction .... Whatever is uppermost in his mind constitutes to him, for the time being, the whole universe. The universe is fluid and fluent, its contents dissolve and re-form with amazing rapidity. But, after all, it is the child's own world. It has the unity and completeness of his own life.[133]

And then comes the school and the tailor-made curriculum and the attitude of division, and of compartmentalising:

> He goes to school, and various studies divide and fractionise the world for him. Geography selects, it abstracts and analyses one set of facts, and from one particular point of view. Arithmetic is another division, grammar another department, and so on indefinitely ...[134]

Dewey interestingly talks of 'three typical evils' in curriculum-setting *vis-à-vis* the child. They are, he argues: first, ' ...the lack of any organic connection with what the child has already seen and felt and loved makes the material [of the curriculum] purely formal and symbolic. The second evil that Dewey identifies is the 'lack of motivation', '...when material is directly supplied in the form of a lesson to be learned as a lesson, the connecting links of need and aims are conspicuous by their absence. What we mean

133. Ibid., pp.20–21.

134. John Dewey, 'The Child and the Curriculum', p.21.

by the mechanical and dead in instruction is a result of this lack of motivation. The organic and vital mean interaction – they mean play of mental demand and material supply.'[135] For Dewey, the third evil was the fact that however logically one arranged the matter, a lot of it would be lost to the child with an as yet inadequately developed reasoning and logical faculty:

> ...[T]he most scientific matter, arranged in most logical fashion, loses this quality, when presented in external, ready-made fashion, by the time it gets to the child. It has to undergo some modification in order to shut out some phases too hard to grasp, and to reduce some of the attendant difficulties. What happens? Those things which are most significant to the scientific man, and most valuable in the logic of actual enquiry and classification drop out. ...The child's reasoning powers, the faculty of abstraction and generalisation, are not adequately developed. So the subject-matter is evacuated of its logical value, and, though it is what it is only from the logical stand-point, is presented as stuff only for 'memory'...[136]

For Dewey, it was imperative that the educator 'determine the environment of the child' and allow the 'child's nature fulfil its own destiny, revealed ... in whatever of science and art and industry the world now holds as its own'. The child was the centre, but the teacher and his link with the child was always interfered with by the curriculum, as Dewey quite bluntly puts it:

> It is his [the child's] present powers which are to assert themselves; his present capacities which are to be exercised; his present attitudes which are to be realised. But save as the teacher knows, knows wisely and thoroughly, the race-experience which is embodied in that thing we call the Curriculum, the teacher knows neither what the present power, capacity, or attitude is, nor yet how it is to be asserted, exercised, and realised. [137]

Whether Sri Aurobindo was aware of Dewey's pioneering declaration is difficult to ascertain; his close and active involvement

---

135. Ibid., p.41
136. John Dewey, 'The Child and the Curriculum', p.41.
137. Ibid., pp.46, 47.

with, and an interest in education allowed him to independently assess the condition of the Indian mind which was exposed to the British education system as implemented in India. That he was aware of developments in education in the West was because of his exposure to the system from an early age. In his unfinished article on education started in Baroda, Sri Aurobindo writes, that 'the first thing needed therefore is the entire and unsparing rejection of the present methods of teaching in favour of those which are now being universally adopted in the more advanced countries of Europe'.[138]

Sri Aurobindo did not entirely reject one system for another, 'he was not against accepting new ideas and knowledge from the West, but he had at the same time deep regard for Indian values. He was very much against disregarding India's own culture and knowledge, its own requirement and temperament'. [139]

The ideologues of the national education movement were in general open to the latest educational developments in the West. Most of them had an exposure to the Western system of education, and in their demand for examining the advanced educational ideas of the West and of exploring their applicability in India, they were unanimous.

While defining national education during the height of the movement, Sri Aurobindo clarified this perception – 'We must acquire for her [India] the best knowledge that Europe can give her and assimilate it to her own peculiar type of national temperament. We must introduce the best methods of teaching humanity has developed, whether modern or ancient'.[140]

---

138. *CWSA* vol.1, p. 361.
139. Indrani Sanyal, 'What it is to be Educated? In the Light of Sri Aurobindo's Philosophy' in *Understanding Thoughts of Sri Aurobindo,* 2007, p. 102.
140. *CWSA* vol.7, p. 895.

He had, in a way, resolved the 'conflict of identity' by trying to follow what he did throughout his life in his philosophical thoughts and formulation – the method of integration. In his view, all systems had some benefits which needed to be observed and if found conducive, assimilated in the new system and remodeled according to the environmental and temperamental requirements of the adapting people and civilisation. This was also the broad theme and demand of the national education movement.

Such then was the educational scene, Indian as well as international, when Sri Aurobindo, then Prof. Arvind Ghose, as Chairman of the Baroda College Union and Debating Society, addressed the College Social Gathering in July 1899. Within the next few years, he was to play an active role in trying to usher in an alternative indigenous system of education, and his participation in this grand movement for a philosophy of national education would help to further crystallise his thoughts on education – his philosophy of education.

II.7. EARLY ARGUMENTATIONS FOR AN INDIGENOUS EDUCATION

A number of Indians who were products of the new awakening in Bengal eventually became the ideational symbols and active voices in the quest for freeing and Indianising Indian education. Since much has been written on this aspect and a great deal of analysis has gone into the unraveling of the thoughts of some of the leading minds of that period, I shall confine myself towards making brief allusions to them. It shall help in setting the context of the debate as well as help us in situating Sri Aurobindo in the entire environment and movement.

A number of those who spearheaded the movement for India's political, social, commercial, and educational regeneration saw the need for the crystallisation of a distinct national consciousness. This broadly meant being conscious of the fact that India consisted of a particular geographical space, possessed a distinct cultural identity, and had a unique spiritual heritage through which she has civilisationally contributed to the evolution and flowering of human thought and life. Such a national consciousness, they argued, ought to precede any great movement at regeneration. The likes of Vivekananda, Dayananda, Bankim and little later Sri Aurobindo and Lokmanya Tilak, to name a few, ushered in a new dimension to India's struggle for freedom. For long it had become, for some leaders and their politics, to look upon British occupation of India as providential, 'extreme westernisation' and 'cultural alienation' dominated. As philosopher and thinker Ram Swarup observed, 'Europe's superiority was taken for granted by the ruled' and the 'majority of India's educated and articulate class paid allegiance to Western ideals, and wanted to bring their own beliefs and customs which they had learnt secretly'.[141]

Even for those who spoke of political reform, freedom for the country was a 'distant goal' and the British connection was an 'ordained' link 'in the inscrutable dispensation of Providence, for India's good'. Even self-government within the Empire would require, they argued, 'years of earnest and patient effort and sacrifices'.[142] While these leaders 'wanted a parliament where representatives of the people could decide crucial questions of the day', they believed at the same time, 'in the legitimacy of British rule in India'. Many of them claimed to be 'loyal to the Raj to his backbone'. For them, there was no contradiction 'between the aim of representative government and their faith in British rule'. Among

141. Ram Swarup, *Hinduism & Monotheistic Religions*, (2009), New Delhi: Voice of India, 2015, p.268.

142. Ram Swarup, op.cit., p.269.

the leading ideologues who propounded such a political line were Dadabhai Naoroji, R.C.Dutt and G.K.Gokhale. They spoke of the drain of India's resources by Britain, made brilliant exposés of it, spoke of the economic disparities between India and Britain and yet, 'they seemed to think that, ideally, British Imperial and Indian interests were perfectly compatible'.[143]

In the avant-garde thought-leaders, who were social and cultural thinkers and philosophers, sadhakas also, such as Dayananda, Vivekananda, Bankim and Sri Aurobindo, a clear shift away from such an attitude was evident, leading to an awakening. These thought-leaders, these pioneers, were not, as Ram Swarup lyrically describes it, 'politicians as we understand the word today', instead:

> They spoke of Gods, humanity, larger life, truth, *Sanatana Dharma*, and of *Ramarajya*. They fought a national battle without ceasing to be great humanists. They serve the immediate national struggle, but they were also great futurists of humanity. They were great reformers, but their inspiration was their love and respect for their people. They were also great educationists. They wanted a system of national education based on the larger spiritual premises ...[144]

They led to the questioning of old premises, they closely scrutinized Western culture and 'found it wanting in deeper matters'. The questioning of old assumptions led to the old politics becoming outdated. These new spokesmen, argued Ram Swarup,

> ... taught us to look at the country and its Independence struggle in a particular way. They taught that India was more than a geographical entity, that it was a holy land, a sacred trust, a spiritual idea, a power of the spirit, even a deity; they taught that India was rising for the truth it embodied, for recovering its *svabhava*.[145]

---

143. Leonard A Gordon, *Bengal: the Nationalist Movement (1876–1940)*, (1974), rpt 1979, p.16.
144. Ibid., pp.220–221.
145. Ibid., p.269.

These words and vision, dynamised the whole nation and gave a 'deeper ideation' to the struggle for freedom; they imparted a new focus and direction to the nationalist movement and_'set up new tasks, new goals' for it.[146] Political historian, Biman Behari Majumdar, succinctly describes this new direction imparted by these thought-leaders thus:

> If Nationalism means simply the devotion to one's nation, there is plenty of evidence of the prevalence of this sentiment in India before the return of Swami Vivekananda from his tour to the West in January 1897. But if it signifies a policy of national independence, it is difficult to find any definite trace of it, except in some stray utterances of a few advanced thinkers. The first four decades since the outbreak of the movement of 1857 witnessed the germination of the seed of patriotism in our country. The ideal of national unity and of love for the motherland was preached in this period indeed, but no concrete suggestion was made by any individual or organisation as to the best way of achieving independence for India. It was reserved for Swami Vivekananda, Sister Nivedita, Lokmanya Tilak, Sri Aurobindo, Lala Lajpat Rai and a band of active revolutionaries during the two decades following the murder of Rand and Ayerst [June 1897], to chalk out plans for making India free from bondage.[147]

The logic of nationalism, that only 'self-rule offered the possibility of eventually fulfilling national self-interest'[148] started becoming evident to many.

It was clear to those in the forefront of moulding thought and opinion that the colonial education system which had exposed a certain number of people to the latest in Western thought and political ideas, was also a deracinating agency that was retarding

---

146. Ibid.
147. Biman Behari Majumdar, *Militant Nationalism in India: And Socio-Religious Background (1897–1917)*, Kolkata: General Printers & Publishers, 1966, p.1.
148. Leonard A Gordon, *Bengal: The Nationalist Movement (1876–1940)*, op.cit., p.16.

the growth of that national consciousness which they believed to be an essential pre-requisite for a multidimensional national regeneration. The need, therefore, for an alternative was beginning to be acutely felt.

The educational scene in Bengal was never the same from 1902 onwards. It was in this year that public expression of dissatisfaction with the prevalent system of education became more strident, and set in motion events that would eventually culminate in the formation of the National Council of Education and the founding of the Bengal National College. The perceptions and ideas on education had long been building up, and in 1902, when the Indian Universities Commission Report was published along with Gurudas Banerjee's note of dissent, which advocated a broadening of the base of the educational fabric, the opposition to the system further crystallised.[149] It was a part culmination of the intellectual phase of the educational awakening which had started decades back. This awakening was kindled by the likes of Bankim, Vivekananda, Dayananda and many others who had spoken out on the need for a new education for India. When he was once asked how he had seen India during his visit in 1902 compared to the India he was returning to in 1915, Gandhi replied:

> So far as I have been able to observe, and so far as I am competent to compare things today with things as I observed them in 1902, during my brief visit to India, I notice that there is a greater eagerness amongst the younger generation to be of service to the Motherland, and that there is also great willingness to undertake work which may require a measure of self-sacrifice.

Among a number of political developments globally, post-1902 generated political enthusiasm in India. Japan's victory over Russia in 1905 and its emergence as a major power signifying a shift also

149. Karan Singh, *Prophet of Indian Nationalism: A Study of the Political Thought of Sri Aurobindo Ghosh: 1893–1910*, 1991, p. 128.

proved that Western powers were not invincible. This made a major impact on the Indian and the Asian mind. The reaction to this momentous feat in India is perhaps best described in the words of the nationalist missionary '*Deenabandhu*' C.F. Andrews:

> [In 1904] The air was full of electricity. The war between Russia and Japan had kept the surrounding peoples on the tip-toe of expectation. A stir of excitement passed over North of India. Even the remote villagers talked of the victories of Japan as they sat in their circles and passed round the huqqa at night. One of the older men said to me, "There has been nothing like it since the Mutiny [1857] .... Asia was moved from one end to the other, and the sleep of centuries was finally broken.[150]

A brief retracing of the intellectual aspects and origins of this educational awakening would be relevant at this point. The political demand had not yet reached a crescendo, while the effects of Western education on Indian society was being closely examined and scrutinised. Amidst these new changes that society was witness to, the effects of English education on the Indian mind, the limits of that education system, in terms of its effect, was being gradually felt. On the one hand, the sweep of the Young Bengal movement had a widespread effect and swung to extremes a section of Bengali youth, on the other an intense questioning also began on the long term effects on society, culture, and education of such a radical swing.

Initially these thoughts on education mainly dwelt on the mode of instruction in education and then they gradually developed into a deeper questioning on culture, identity, and nationhood. The question of utilising education as an instrument for challenging colonial rule did not arise at the beginning. These were at first early thoughts aimed at simply improving the education system and thereby facilitating the spread of literacy and giving gradual rise

---

150. C.F.Andrews, *The Renaissance in India: Its Missionary Aspect*, 1912, p.5.

to a discourse on nation, race, and religious identities, on national awakening and consciousness and traditions.

The discourse reflected the quest of a collective mind bewildered at the extremes it was being exposed to and beginning to seek for some balance from the very traditions that it had initially rejected as obsolete. The idea was not to readmit unchanged those very traditions, but rather alter them where necessary and fit them into a rapidly and radically changing social scene. 'The new cultural sons of the West' sought to rebuild India on the Western pattern and thought-leaders came forward with a new approach to their ancient ideals, while the orthodox section faced the challenge by a stiffening of their stance in support of their cherished values. It was those who, having been exposed to Western education, having once thoroughly rejected India's traditions, who made turning back to their Indian cultural and civilisational roots and become some of the early proponents of a cultural and educational self-recovery.

The efforts of the new thought-leaders were a sincere attempt to 'get at the truth of India's past and to appraise it in the light of reason which their Western contact had kindled in them'.[151] Was it a synthesis, an interpenetration, a compromise, or adjustment? Was it some, or all of these that they were seeking? What was, however, discernible was their attempt to reinterpret a number of dimensions of India's traditions under a different set of knowledge.

Raja Rammohun Roy and others, who aired views on reforms, represented therefore, the first attempt to achieve this synthesis. By 1822, Rammohan had already opened 'on his own account an Anglo-Indian School for imparting a free education in English to Hindu boys' and for which 'with the exception of a few subscriptions from other friends, the whole of the funds required were supplied'

151. Sisir Kumar Mitra, *The Liberator: Sri Aurobindo, India & The World*, 1954, p. 21.

by him.[152] Rammohan's contention was whether the Government should 'seek simply to develop and deepen the education already in vogue in India? Or should it boldly endeavour to introduce the innovations of European science and European culture?'[153]

Rammohan aired his objections in 1823 to the setting up of a Sanskrit College; his case was for the promotion and for the spread of the English language because he felt that the teaching of Sanskrit would strongly retard the diffusion of modern knowledge, 'it would load the minds of youth with grammatical niceties and metaphysical distinctions of little or no practical use'.[154] 'The Sanskrit system of education,' he wrote in a letter to the then Governor-General Lord Amherst:[155]

> ... would be the best calculated to keep this country in darkness, if such has been the policy of the British legislature. But as the improvement of the native population is the object of the Government, it will consequently promote a more liberal and enlightened system of instruction embracing Mathematics, Natural Philosophy, Chemistry, Anatomy, with other useful sciences, which may be accomplished with the sums proposed by employing a few gentlemen of talents and learning, educated in Europe, and providing a college furnished with necessary books, instruments and other apparatus.[156]

The Raja's criticism of Sanskrit was hard, but it has been argued that he actually objected to the orthodox method of teaching followed by the Pandits rather than the language itself. He was

---

152. Sophia Dobson Collet, edited, *The Life and Letters of Raja Rammohun Roy*, 2nd edition edited by Hem Chandra Sarkar, 1914, p.106.
153. Sophia Dobson Collet, edited, *The Life and Letters of Raja Rammohun Roy*, p.107.
154. Ibid.
155. William Pitt Amherst (1773–1857) was Governor-General of India from 1823 to 1828.
156. Nemai Sadhan Bose, *Indian Awakening and Bengal*, 1990, p. 110., *The Life and Letters*, op.cit., pp.108, 109.

convinced that the British government should promote and spread English learning which he believed, could alone free his countrymen from the clasp of orthodoxy and empty ritualism.[157] Sri Aurobindo too later criticised the *Tol* system of education, saying that it was not a fit one to be followed in the scheme of India's educational regeneration.[158]

---

157. Nemai Sadhan Bose, *Indian Awakening and Bengal*, pp. 110–111.
158. However, regarding Sanskrit, Sri Aurobindo felt that it had a unique place in the Indian system and was one of the best languages to bring one in close touch with the Indian ethos and spirit, and also help one to develop a right appreciation of Indian classical culture. But he was clear that it had to outgrow its heavy and therefore discouraging style. Writing a review in his journal *Arya* in 1916 of the 'Sanskrit Research', an 'Anglo-Sanskrit Quarterly' brought out by the Sanskrit Academy of India, Bangalore and edited by one Pundit Lingesha Mahabhagawat, Sri Aurobindo concluded that, 'Sanskrit ought to still have a future as a language of the learned and it will not be a good day for India when the ancient tongue ceases entirely to be written or spoken. But if it is to survive, it must get rid of the curse of the heavy pedantic style contracted by it in its decline with the lumbering impossible compounds and the overweight of hair-splitting erudition.' [Source: *CWSA* vol.1 Reviews: "Sanskrit Research" p.613] At the Centre of Education at Pondicherry, therefore, Sanskrit was accorded great importance and along with French is taught right from the primary levels. A simple Sanskrit is taught and the child is encouraged to imbibe it by listening to stories, speaking, singing, play-acting at a very early age. In fact the spread of simple Sanskrit for the benefit of all, and finally making it the national language, was strongly advocated by the Mother. This point made here is to briefly illustrate the importance of Sanskrit in Sri Aurobindo's scheme of things. Rammohan was of another age and if one keeps in mind the stranglehold that orthodoxy had on society during that period, it was but natural for Rammohan to favour the English language and education as principal agents of change and ones that could shake society out of its degenerative stupor.

The later minds who inspired the national education movement were not closed to Western education either. In fact they encouraged its dissemination and its power to change the features of an education which they felt was too literary, but at the same time they did not shut their minds to the utility and necessity of traditions. The journey of ideas was an evolving one and what began primarily as expressions of requirements for educational improvement gradually turned into a movement for educational regeneration, which became one of the principal drivers of greater demand for national emancipation.

Sri Aurobindo's assessment of Rammohan's contribution and direction towards taking the national reawakening to its next stage sums up his whole effort and its effect. Sri Aurobindo saw Rammohan as having given a 'triple impetus' to the Renaissance movement – '(a) awakening the critical and intellectual faculty that was temporarily eclipsed; (b) transmitting the desire of a new creation; (c) orienting India's new awareness towards new conditions, new ideals, [and] the imperious necessity to understand, assimilate and conquer them'. Sri Aurobindo saw this impetus providing the nationalist movement the ability to not only rediscover the significance in India's past culture but to simultaneously realise that that rediscovery must necessarily lead to its re-evaluation in the context of modern ideas and knowledge.[159]

Peary Chand Mitra (1814–1883), who had entered Hindu College in 1827 as a disciple of Henry Louis Vivian Derozio (1809–1831), was one of those early ones to be affected by this questioning. Mitra began developing ideas of a national education. At an early age he developed the 'propensity for diffusing knowledge' and started a

159. Prithwindranath Mukherjee, '*Les Racines Intellectuelles du Mouvement de d'Indépendence de L'Inde (1893–1918)*, (Intellectual Roots of the Indian Fight for Freedom – 1893–1918), 2010, p.48.

school at home for instructing neighbourhood boys. He 'advocated the use of simple colloquial Bengali for communicating useful knowledge to the people'. Mitra must be, however, remembered for the early advocacy of the need for agricultural education in the 1870s, and for his belief that students ought to take interest in both commerce and agriculture as also for his opposition to the 'exclusively literary education' propounded by the Young Bengal movement.[160]

Peary Chand combined in himself the twin roles of 'a political philosopher and a practical reformer' and was an 'enthusiastic member of the Society for the Acquisition of General Knowledge'. His activities were multifarious and especially in his advocacy for the ryots, he called for the spread of education among them as a significant step towards mitigating their miseries. Peary Chand was one of those early thinkers and reformers who realised the need for a widespread education among the masses especially the subalterns. He 'appealed to the Government to spread vernacular education and to teach agriculture in all schools and colleges'. In a meeting of the Bengal Social Science Association held on January 22, 1869, he argued that 'there was an intimate connection between crime and the spread of education. The condition was not so obvious in England, because there was no universal system of popular education, but it might be seen in operation on the continent'.[161]

The legendary Rajnarayan Bose (1826–1899), Sri Aurobindo's maternal grandfather and, as we have seen, often called the 'Grandfather of Nationalism'[162] and 'one of the makers of modern

---

160. Biman Behari Majumdar, 'Reaction against Derozians and Young Bengal' in *Concept of National Education in India*, op.cit. p.4.
161. Biman Behari Majumdar, *History of Indian Social and Political Ideas: from Rammohan to Dayananda*, 1996, pp. 135, 136, 140.
162. 'As some people called him the father of Indian Nationalism,

Bengal' did his share of thinking in this area. Though he 'caught, as fully as anyone else among his contemporaries, the impulse of the new illumination, [yet] he did not lose so completely as many of them did, his hold on the fundamental spirit of the culture and civilisation of his race'.[163] It was this that exercised him with the de-rooting effects of a westernised education on Indian society.

Along with Bhudev Mukhopadhyay, Rajnarayan set his face 'against the wholesale imitation of Western civilisation and preached the beauty and grandeur of Hindu culture'.[164] He gave his attention to the needs of vernacular instructions and, as we saw earlier, in 1866 established at Midnapore in Bengal the Society for the Promotion of National Feelings (*Jatiya Gaurava Sancarini Sabha*). Its aim was to infuse in the young minds an enthusiasm for the Bengali way of life including a love for the Bengali language. He condemned the practice of mixing up English words while conversing or writing in Bengali and championed the usage of Bengali at public meetings, while writing letters and conversing – 'those who had not been able to learn their own language' remarked Rajnarayan, ' cannot easily master a foreign one'.

Sri Aurobindo's arguments on the need for using the mother-tongue as the medium of instruction and his views that a thorough mastery of one's mother-tongue paves the way for mastery of other

---

Rajnarayan humorously styled himself as the grandfather of Nationalism. He could not foresee at that time that he would deserve the title literally because of the momentous part played by his daughter's sons, Sri Aurobindo and Barindra Kumar Ghose in the history of the freedom movement of the country.' (Biman Behari Majumdar, *Militant Nationalism in India*, op.cit., p.7.

163. Vide. Bipin Chandra Pal, *Indian Nationalism: Its Principles and Personalities*, 1918,

164. Majumdar, *History of Indian Social and Political Ideas*, op.cit., 154.

foreign tongues, is also reflected in the above remark.[165] Though manifesting a non-parochial mindset and a mind that recognised the modern contributions of the West and the need to assimilate them for developing a greater sense of national resilience, Rajnarayan, having been himself published in leading British journals (e.g. the *Times* of London), endorsed the need and utility of learning Sanskrit, one's mother-tongue and English.[166] Bepin Chandra Pal summed up best Rajnarayan's influence when he wrote that though Rajnarayan 'did not openly take any part in politics, ... his writings and speeches did a good deal to create that spirit of self-respect and self-assertion in the educated classes' that [later] found strong expressions in political activities.[167]

Bepin Pal lists Rajnarayan as one of the originators of composite nationalism and observed that he 'represented the high watermark of the composite culture of this country – Vedantic, Islamic, and European. When he discoursed on Brahma-Jnan or knowledge of God, he brought to mind the ancient Hindu gnostics of the Upanishads. When he cited verses from the Persian poets, filling the ear with their rich cadence ... he reminded one of the old Moslem devotees.[168] And when he spoke on the corruption of current religion, or the soulless selfishness of modern politics, he appeared as a nineteenth century nationalist and iconoclast of Europe'.[169]

Rajnarayan is usually dismissed as the founder of the Hindu Mela and referred to as one of the revivalists. His life actually saw multi-dimensional activity, and his thoughts on reform – societal

---

165. Dr. Biman Behari Majumdar, *Concept of National Education in India*, op.cit. pp. 4– 5.
166. Prithwindra Mukherjee, *Les Racines Intellectuelles,* op. cit., p. 66.
167. Bipin Chandra Pal on Sri Aurobindo, op.cit., p. 189–190.
168. Mukherjee, *Les Racines*, op.cit., p. 67.
169. *Bipin Chandra Pal on Sri Aurobindo,* op.cit., p.190.

and educational – stemmed from his profound study of various religious and social systems and traditions. They were the result of a deep intellectual quest. His deliberations on the exigencies of the age had an integral characteristic and do not seem to be dominated by isolated passions of thoughtless imitations or revivalism. Bepin Pal marks him as one of those who have had a great influence on Sri Aurobindo. 'Aravinda' he wrote, 'owes not only his rich spiritual nature but even his very superior literary capacity to his inherited endowments from his mother's line' [as represented by Rajnarayan].[170] To Rajnarayan, India's 'multiple crisis – economic, moral and intellectual' – arose from an insufficient national spirit.[171] He foresaw the necessity of an active attempt at generating that spirit of nationalism. The political element was present in Rajnarayan's approach, actively contributing to the awakening of political consciousness.

He was one of the originators of a vigilant public life whose hall mark was the growth of 'a number of leagues, associations and *sabhas* in important cities of the country ... [which helped] foster the new-born political consciousness and give it some shape according to the need and temper of the time'.[172] Rajnarayan too formed a secret society which had young Rabindranath Tagore as a member and established an institution for revolutionary propaganda and action.[173] While not much came out of this early attempt it goes to show that Rajnarayan realised that such bodies would eventually take the action into the political arena. Rajnarayan's action was not limited to intellectual articulations of social problems but also covertly spread into the revolutionary field. His life presented a synthesis of ideas and actions.

170. Ibid., p.191.
171. Prithwindra Mukherjee, *op*. cit., p.66.
172. Sisir Kumar Mitra, op.cit. p. 20.
173. K.R.Srinivasa Iyengar, op.cit. p.62.

Bhudev Mukhopadhyay (1827–1894), another student of the Hindu College, though exposed to the same influences of the Young Bengal Movement, felt the need for rekindling an interest and respect in, and for, the Indian traditions and culture. Among the early initiatives that he took, in the course of a long life of prolific intellectual output, was the organising of the Vernacular Literature Society with the aim of publishing 'educative works in Bengali'. Bhudev founded a Bengali educational monthly, *Siksadarpan,* in May 1864, and in one of its first issues he advocated the necessity for every nation to preserve its distinct qualities which, if lost, announces the loss of nationhood itself. As with Rajnarayan Bose, Bhudev also realised that the nation's distinctive qualities have to be rediscovered, preserved, nurtured, and disseminated in order to gradually recreate and reignite a national consciousness.

In another issue of his *Siksadarpan,* Bhudev criticized the then dominant habit of imitating anything western ... as a sign of unmanliness peculiar to a de-nationalised people. Bhudev argued that 'ever since western civilisation penetrated this land, we began to lose our religion, our sense of nationality, our freedom ... in fact even our identity'.[174] He was especially critical of the educated Bengali for their habit of extreme imitation, 'the latter's [English-educated Bengali] ways of walking and speaking, jokes, accent, gestures, manners, in fact everything about them smells English a little', he caustically observed.[175] English education, he argued, was degenerating the Hindus who were developing arrogant behaviour and self-centeredness, 'the growth of English [education] and the initiation of the English were aggravating egotistic propensities'.[176]

---

174. Tapan Raychaudhuri, *Europe Reconsidered*, 2002, p.58.
175. Tapan Raychaudhuri, *Europe Reconsidered*, 2002, p.59.
176. Ibid., p.60.

For Bhudev, Western education was 'tinsel rather than gold'. From an early stage all education was acquired 'through the medium of an ill-understood and difficult foreign language'. A foreign tongue was always an ill-suited and unsatisfactory medium of instruction and was full of words 'denoting unfamiliar objects, and, even more unfamiliar ideas'. Thus the western-educated Indian developed the habit of learning without 'full comprehension' and the true scientific spirit was always missing.[177]

But one of the most serious consequences of Western education, Bhudev argued, was the 'alienation of the elite from the masses. Having invested a lot of effort in learning English and western education, the new elite naturally held dear what they had acquired, no matter what its intrinsic worth'. This barrier of language and exposure created a chasm between these two sections of society.[178] Bhudev did accept, though, that one of the redeeming features of the period was the decline of this habit of senseless Western imitation.

In another issue of *Siksadarpan*, Bhudev interestingly called for promoting 'national culture through a system of national education imparted by teachers with a national consciousness'. Education was also the subject of Bhudev's first published work.

The educational reform discourse thus began gathering substance and moving towards consolidation. Bhudev 'was not anti-British in the political sense; but he upheld a form of nationalism in education and culture'.[179] This was the characteristics of the age, the political demand had not yet organised itself, but it is noticeable that social and religious reform occupied the thoughts of the leading minds of the age and the need for educational reform began receiving greater attention.

---

177. Tapan Raychaudhuri, *Europe Reconsidered*, pp.61–62.
178. Ibid., p.62.
179. R.K.Dasgupta, *National Education*, op.cit., p. 9.

Akshoy Kumar Datta (1820–1886), among leading figures of the cultural awakening in Bengal who did much for the growth of Bengali, was in favour of vernacular instruction. A rationalist with a scientific bent of mind who had questioned the infallibility of the Vedas, Akshoy Kumar argued in 1856 in his *Dharmaniti* in favour of 'compulsory education for all children up to the age of fifteen [and that] children of even the poorest citizens should not be apprenticed to any trade or occupation without his education'.[180]

He believed that young men must be exposed to technical and vocational education, and urged the colonial government to take steps to this effect. Akshoy Kumar also spoke for, and supported, the early demand for using the mother tongue as the medium of instruction not only at the primary level but also at the secondary stages, and in higher education. Since 1840, when he began teaching at the *Tattvabodhini Pathashala*, he 'constantly pondered over the problem of educating the masses'.[181] He observed that those who were educated in English expressed a 'lively distaste for the indigenous language and culture' giving rise to a generation that had become 'servilely English'[182].

Seeing the need for putting together a scheme of education that would reverse that trend, Akshoy Kumar articulated a method that would teach a vast range of subjects in successive stages, starting with Arithmetic, Algebra, Trigonometry, then Geography, Natural History etc. He placed the principles of religion, theology, literature, and painting towards the end. It was probably

---

180. Majumdar, *History of Indian Social and Political Ideas*, op.cit., p.109.
181. Ibid., p.108.
182. Sri Aurobindo uses this expression to describe the then prevailing attitude among 'Anglicised-Babus' towards the Bengali language, *Bankim Chandra Chatterji*, op.cit. p. 116.

a reaction to the trend of a purely literary education that had set in with the Young Bengal movement.[183]

Interestingly, Akshoy Kumar had also drawn up an 'elaborate scheme for the different stages of education' recommending sending children to schools at the age of two. They would be schools which would come across and make 'children believe them to be play-grounds' in which they would be taught cleanliness and other 'elementary laws of health' through practical demonstrations.[184] The next type of schools that Akshoy recommended was to cater for children from the age of six or seven, up to the age of fourteen or fifteen. In attempt to draw a precise curriculum and ambience for such schools, Akshoy even described the premises of these schools. They should 'contain shady tress, bowers and various plants, amidst which some seats are to be provided. In the by-paths of the groves and bowers, statues of men like Socrates, Bacon, Newton, Franklin, Pascal, Washington, Aryabhatta, Bhaskaracharya' etc. should be placed. 'Pictures, drawings and practical demonstrations' were to form the chief means for conveying education' at this stage. He emphasised the need for physical training and argued that 'many of the civilized nations have disappeared from the face of the earth for want of physical prowess'. [185]

In the third kind of school in his scheme of education, Akshoy argued that only selected students were to be admitted who would pursue their studies up to the twentieth or twenty-second years of age. His educational prescription for the majority was the imparting of technical and vocational education, 'instead of theoretical university education'. Akshoy also envisaged the opening of libraries

183. Biman Behari Majumdar, op.cit. pp. 6–7.
184. Majumdar, *History of Indian Social and Political Ideas*, op.cit., p.110.
185. Ibid., p.111.

and reading rooms in every village in the country,[186] and his writings sought to draw official attention to this very useful tool of mass education.

Though he did not advocate the giving up of English, Akshoy was, nevertheless, a strong votary of the use and spread of the vernacular language. He spoke of how it was difficult to 'learn the foreign tongue, and of how the poorer classes cannot afford to spend the time necessary for picking up the knowledge of the English language'. He also argued that the knowledge imparted through the vernacular normally filtered down to 'the lowest strata of society, but the knowledge imparted in a foreign tongue necessarily remains confined to a few educated'.[187] Akshoy seems to have firmly believed that the Government of the day alone was capable of spreading mass education and left no opportunity to remind it to get down energetically to achieving that task.[188]

At any rate one perceives in these efforts an early attempt to give some cohesion to the thought of educational reform. The predominant points in the discourse on educational reform was the emphasis on an education imparted through Indian languages, the need to awaken cultural awareness through imparting a knowledge of traditions and religion, and the need to impart technical and vocational education to reverse the disproportionate focus then given to the literary dimension of education.

Bankim Chandra Chattopadhyay (1838–1894), one of the giants of his age who contributed profusely and epically towards creating a language, a literature, and a nation, had definitive views on education too. Our earlier survey of Sri Aurobindo's study of Bankim's

---

186. Ibid., pp.111, 112.
187. Ibid., p.112.
188. Ibid.

education and environment revealed the strength of Bankim's mind and his capacity at self-education. Though Bankim had developed a deep mastery of the vernacular he was 'less dogmatic in his criticism of the English language' and expressed his view that 'the best Bengali books [were] the productions of Bengalis who [were] highly cultivated English scholars'.[189] Bankim also expressed his admiration for the scientific knowledge that 'European research has revealed'. Though, and as Sri Aurobindo pointed out, Bankim studied Sanskrit with 'great perseverance' at a Pandit's *tol* and mastered the language, however, in 1873, he criticised 'the philosophy of the *tols* [as] the most barren and unprofitable study in which the human intellect ... engage[d] itself'. [190] It could be that Bankim's innate talent helped him absorb the essence of Sanskrit even in a *tol* structure, he had the requisite quality for self-development, usually absent in a vast majority and therefore the ambience or content may not have mattered to him much. But for the average mind, used to the passive instructional and rote method, Bankim must have felt *tol* education to be a constricting factor.

Like a number of his contemporaries, Bankim wanted to synthesise the acquisitions of a new knowledge with the fundamental elements of his culture, and for this he believed the rise of a national consciousness to be indispensable. Through his writings, he had already initiated a movement towards it and he began to now feel that a 'sound system of education' could further ignite the process. In an essay, '*Loksiksa*' in his *Bangadarshan* in 1878, Bankim regretted 'the decline of all forms of popular education' due to the progress of English learning. He perceived that this was 'mainly due to the fact that the educated classes do not care for the uneducated'.[191] For

189. R.K.Dasgupta, op.cit., p.11.
190. Ibid.
191. Ibid., p. 12.

him, since education did not percolate to the lower strata of society, it was not education for the country as a whole and was therefore not national.

The process of deracination that was in progress had not escaped Bankim's eyes. While accepting that some liberal ideas came from the West he also pointed out that the prevailing system of education was meant to produce 'a race of Babus who think knowledge of English [to be] the most important intellectual accomplishment'.[192] One finds in Bankim one of the earliest concepts of an 'integral' education, formulated in his *Dharmatattva*, the 'idea of the development of the human personality through a harmonious cultivation of all faculties' and the acceptance that a simultaneous development of faculties was imperative for a successful and complete education. His study of the classical systems of India had given rise to such a view in him.[193] The principal, or overweening idea, from Bankim's educational thoughts that inspired the 'exponents of national education' decades later, was the belief that 'ancient Indian thought had a great deal to offer to modern civilisation and that a disproportionate enthusiasm for anything foreign was a danger to our intellectual progress'.[194]

Sri Aurobindo's assessment of Bankim made in 1894, summed up the vibrancy, ingenuity, and the rich intellectual output of that age. It stated some of the fundamentals of that age which shaped Bankim and gave directions to thinking in diverse fields. Sri Aurobindo called that era the 'young Bengal of the fifties', and saw it as 'a society electric with thought and loaded to the brim with passion' which 'was at that time the theatre of a great intellectual awakening', where a 'miniature Renascence was in process'. 'An ardent and imaginative race,' wrote Sri Aurobindo:

---

192. R.K.Dasgupta, op.cit, p.12.
193. Ibid.
194. Ibid.

> ... long bound down in the fetters of a single tradition, had suddenly put into its hands the key to a new world thronged with the beautiful or profound creations of Art and Learning. From this meeting of a foreign Art and civilisation with a temperament differing from the temperament which created them, there issued, as there usually does issue from such meetings, an original Art and an original civilisation. Originality does not lie in rejecting outside influences but in accepting them as a new mould into which our own individuality may run. This is what happened and may yet happen in Bengal. The first impulse was gigantic in its proportions and produced men of an almost gigantic originality. Rammohan Ray arose with a new religion in his hand, which was developed on original lines by men almost greater one thinks than he, by Rajnarain Bose and Debendranath Tagore. The two Dutts, Okhay Kumar and Michael Madhu Sudan, began a new Prose and a new Poetry. Vidyasagara, scholar, sage and intellectual dictator, laboured hugely like the Titan he was, to create a new Bengali language and a new Bengali society, while in vast and original learning Rajendra Lal Mitra has not met his match. Around these arose a class of men who formed a sort of seed-bed for the creative geniuses, men of fine critical ability and appreciative temper, scholarly, accomplished, learned in music and the arts, men, in short, not only of culture, but of original culture...[195]

It is this call for an open and ever-evolving originality that one constantly discerns in Sri Aurobindo's educational and cultural thoughts. It was such an idea of originality that the thought-leaders of the Bengal Renaissance attempted to formulate and manifest, and it was this sense of originality that had to permeate a system of national education. The age thus was replete with ideas on education and educational reform. The education debates and propositions were rich and vibrant and created an entire tradition and bedrock for the quest for a national education that was to follow soon.

It was just two years after Bankim's educational exposition in the *Dharmattatva* that the then Vice Chancellor of Calcutta

---

195. Sri Aurobindo, *Bankim Chandra Chatterji,* op.cit., p. 94.

University, Gurudas Banerjee, in his first convocation address in 1890, dwelt on the need to not only accept Western education and enrich the indigenous vernacular but also to contribute to the West the treasures of India's classics. In his subsequent convocation addresses, as we have discussed, Gurudas highlighted aspects of education that needed to be reformed; this led the discourse on educational reform out into the open in an organised and in a vocal manner for the first time. It led to its further crystallisation when he put forth his note of dissent on the Universities Commission in 1902. It brought to a culmination the first phase – an intellectual one – of the demand for India's educational regeneration. The ideas that were created, formulated, expounded, and aired during this phase served as powerful pointers to the emerging national education movement.

II.8. WESTERN PERCEPTIONS OF INDIAN EDUCATION

A number of Western intellectuals and educators also joined this debate and demand for reform in Indian education. These were leading English intellectuals and old India-hands, who articulated their views on the Indian education system and its content. The educational discourse and debate often referred to their ideas and arguments. By interacting with them, Acharya Satish Mukherjee, one of the pioneers of the national education movement, helped to highlight the issues of education and gave the debate a wide publicity through his journal. Though this section does not strictly discuss the educational ideas of selected thinkers it has been included here in order to give an idea of the Western perceptions of Indian education. My choice of these Western thinkers are selective because I have concentrated for the present on those personalities who made a major contribution towards promoting Indian culture and art and who had, to a great extent, assimilated themselves to Indian life and society.

Sir George Birdwood (1832–1917),[196] who kept up a lively interest in India, regularly contributed to Indian journals, and whose views on Indian affairs were valued mainly because of the author's vast knowledge of the subcontinent, was one such scholar whose opinions on Indian education became public. In a letter to Satish Chandra Mukherjee in 1898, Birdwood noted with satisfaction that Indians, especially those that were coming to England, were giving attention to the industrial development of their country, [i.e. they were taking interest in the technical aspect of education]. Further in the letter Birdwood discussed the role that Indians must take upon themselves to bring about a change in the educational scene, 'the first thing' he felt Indians must do is to take the whole of the higher education into their hands. 'In our English system of education', Birdwood told Satish Chandra Mukherjee, 'far too much of time and energy is spent on English Literature and far too little on Hindu i.e. Sanskrit...' and other languages.

---

196. Sir George Christopher Birdwood (1832–1917) naturalist, writer, official, was born in India. He entered the Bombay Medical Service in 1854, became professor at the Grant Medical College, registrar of the University, curator of the Museum, secretary of the Asiatic and Horticulture Societies and Sheriff of Bombay. He returned to England in 1868 and entered the revenue and statistics department of the India Office (1871–1902). While there, he produced among other things, volumes on the industrial arts of India and monographs on Indian art. He was also a journalist and while in India, helped to convert *The Standard* into the *Times of India,* and edited the *Bombay Saturday Review*. He kept up his India connection by regular contributions to the Indian press, was created K.C.I.E. in 1887, and was also conferred the *Legion D'Honneur.*

For the study of modern science, Birdwood felt that India must look towards Europe, 'It is to modern Europe ... that you must directly look for your scientific culture' and as for the Indian 'spiritual culture, as he termed it, he advocated that India must look to her own for that, and must never surrender it. And as far as possible under present circumstances, that culture must, Birdwood argued, be strengthened and its influence extended. But he also conceded that if India is to be part of the greater international life and preserve her worthy cultural space, she cannot remain isolated and that her culture will face modifying influences from the 'literary, artistic and religious culture of the West'. With impulses of modernisation, Birdwood felt that this was inevitable.[197] But, Birdwood argued,

197. Sri Aurobindo dwelt at length on 'Indian culture and external influence'. While he saw technological innovations bringing cultures closer, increasing their frequency and depth of interaction, and anticipated the process of interculturation and interconnectedness, Sri Aurobindo also spoke for an 'assimilative appropriation'. Writing on 'Indian Culture and External Influence' in the March 1919 issue of his journal *Arya*, Sri Aurobindo made the following point, 'I take it as a self-evident law of being applicable to group-individuality, that it is neither desirable nor possible to exclude everything that comes in to us from outside. I take it as an equally self-evident law that a living organism, which grows not by accretion, but by self-development and assimilation, must recast the things it takes in to suit the law and form and characteristic action of its biological or psychological body, reject what would be deleterious or poisonous to it, – and what is that but the non-assimilable? – take only what can be turned into useful stuff of self-expression. It is, to use an apt Sanskritic phrase employed in the Bengali tongue, *atmasāt-karana*, an assimilative appropriation, a making of the thing settle into oneself and turn into the characteristic form of our self-being. The impossibility of entire rejection arises from the very fact of our being a term of diversity in a unity, not really separate from all other existence, but in relation

nothing could be forced upon the Indian mind by an alien system. He concluded:

> ... [T]he point is that it [the modifying influences] must not be forced upon you under alien compulsion through the Government schools and the not less official Indian Universities. The modification must come naturally and spontaneously and gradually, as if *subjectively*, through inevitable commercial and social intercourse .... You can acquire no ingrained, no immanent, and instinctive, no natural and enduring culture save in this voluntary and slow and sure way; and you will never assimilate and receive real nourishment from an alien culture imposed on you under the compulsion of the drill-sergeant's cane...[198]

This was a fundamental point, the forced modification of the Indian way of life by a foreign culture and system. While the positive modifying influences were acknowledged and constant attempts made to try and make them part of the mainstream, the idea of a complete rejection of the indigenous systems and traditions as having nothing to provide was being seriously contested.

Ananda Coomaraswamy[199] in his seminal '*Essays in National*

---

with all that surrounds us, because in life this relation expresses itself very largely by a process of interchange. The undesirability of total rejection, even if it were entirely possible, arises from the fact that interchange with the environment is necessary to a healthy persistence and growth; the living organism which rejects all such interchange, would speedily languish and die of lethargy and inanition'. [Sri Aurobindo, *The Renaissance In India and Other Essays on Indian Culture*, op. cit., pp. 47, 48.]

198. Haridas and Uma Mukherjee, *The Origins of the National education Movement*, op.cit., pp. 315–16–17. George Birdwood's letter to Satish Chandra Mukherjee dated September 9, 1898.
199. Ananda K. Coomaraswamy (1877–1947) metaphysician, pioneering historian and philosopher of Indian art, art history and symbolism and an 'early interpreter of Indian culture to the West' was a prolific writer, and during a brief period, was also involved in the Swadeshi

Idealism' published around 1906, referred to George Birdwood on the deleterious effects colonial education had on the Indian mind's attitude towards her own traditions and culture. 'Sir George Birdwood truly says' wrote Coomaraswamy, that 'our education has destroyed their [Indians] love of their own literature ... and their delights in their own arts and, worst of all, their repose in their traditional and natural religion. It has disgusted them with their own homes – their parents, their sisters, their very wives. It has brought discontent into every family so far as its baneful influences have reached'.[200] It may be a partially defeatist expression, but it reflected quite acutely the dilemma of the age and shows how Birdwood's thoughts on education were widely followed in forward-thinking circles of that age.

---

movement. His views of cultural Swadeshi, cultural regeneration and cultural education reflecting issues of that age continue to remain relevant even today. Our interest in him, apart from his massive output on Indian culture, metaphysics & art is also because of Sri Aurobindo's interest in his works and the fact that he closely followed Coomaraswamy's trend of thought and interpretations. Sri Aurobindo made a number of observations on Coomaraswamy through his own writings in his years in Bengal as well as during his later stay at Pondicherry. In fact, in August 1910, he took up the pen to defend Dr. Coomaraswamy and Sister Nivedita against whom an art critic in an article entitled, 'Comment and Criticism: The Indian Fine Art Critics' that appeared in the *Modern Review* of Calcutta had made disparaging remarks. In it Sri Aurobindo referred to Coomaraswamy as 'a critic of established reputation, whose contributions to the study of Indian Art are valued in every country in Europe and Asia, where the subject itself is studied'. [For Sri Aurobindo's incomplete article vide. *CWSA* vol.1 p. 468, and Note on Texts p. 773.]

200. Ananda Coomaraswamy, *Essays in National Idealism*, 1915, pp. 102–03. This quotation appears in the chapter '*Education in India*'.

Quoting at length in the same work from a letter written to him by Sir Patrick Geddes (1854–1932)[201] – a Scottish biologist, innovative urban planner and educationist, who participated in Tagore's experiment at Santiniketan and who maintained a correspondence

201. Patrick Geddes shared with Tagore 'a suspicion of the Examination system and did not take any degrees'. 'Geddes had a deep disdain for all academic drudgery, and he adamantly refused to take a degree examinations.' Tagore too abhorred all types of formal education. 'Geddes' criticism of the Edinburgh University system failed to get him a chair there' and he moved to University College, Dundee, as a part-time professor of Botany. At Dundee, he could implement some of his educational ideas. Geddes agreed with Tagore's educational ideas and refuted the 'rote method and the unnecessary fanfare that goes before actual education can start; where the student is the least considered object and where humanity is missing'. It was to Geddes that Tagore movingly wrote in May 1922, regarding the growth of the institution at Santiniketan, '... I merely started with this one simple idea, that education should never be dissociated from life. I had no experience of teaching, no special gift for organisation; and therefore I had no plan which I could put before the public in order to win their confidence ... All I could do was to offer to the five little boys who were my first students my company, I talked and sang to them, played with them, recited to them our epics, improvised stories specially given to them by evening, took them on excursions into neighbouring villages ... My first idea was to emancipate children's mind from the dead grip of a mechanical method and a narrow purpose. This idea has gone on developing itself, comprehending all different branches of life's activities from Arts to Agriculture. Now it has come to a period, when we are fully aware of the absolute necessity of widening, across all barriers, the human sympathies of our students, – thus leading them to the fulfilment of their Education'. [For a detailed treatment of the Tagore-Geddes relationship and the insights on education in it see eg. '*The Tagore-Geddes Correspondence*, 2004, compiled & edited by Bashabi Fraser of the Centre for South Asian Studies, Edinburgh University.]

with him on wide-ranging issues which included education. Coomaraswamy highlighted the whole issue – 'the trouble is not only with the vested interests of the official class (which are sure to be protected in any change)', wrote Prof. Geddes, 'but in the wooden heads, the arrested minds, the incompetent hands, etc. etc. of those who have gone through this machine, whether here, or with you in India. It lies in your thousands of barristers and clerks and crammers, who know all the programmes of the University of London in its darkest days ... but who know nothing of the vital movements in literature, science, art, etc., by which we in some measure here escape, or at least mitigate, our official oppression, or even begin to modify it'. In some measure, Geddes found the same problem in the European system of education. He observed:

> In short, then, the strife is not between '*Eastern* and *Western Education*' ... but between *Cram* and *Education,* and for both alike, in West as in East. It is very hard indeed, upon *your* thousands of graduates to say that they must be considered as lost victims of a mistake, and put aside as useless for practical purposes, save here and there the man who has the will and power to re-educate himself; but the same is true here at home, and nothing could be more disastrous, I think, than for you in India to give your present Europeanised graduates the re-organizing of things; that would be continuing our mistakes not correcting it. But recover your own arts, etc., on one hand, and utilise also the Western progress .... Learn from France – non-official France primarily, of course – from America on her non-philistine side, from Germany at her best (though this is being materialised in most of the universities or elsewhere), from the small countries you as yet practically ignore – Scandinavia, Netherlands, etc., and so on. Don't believe the usual contempt of South American States; they are far more advanced than most Europeans know: in short, open yourselves more widely to the Western influence...[202]

202. Ananda Coomaraswamy, op.cit., pp. 110–11.

Commenting on Prof. Geddes' letter, Coomaraswamy in support made the following exhortation:

> From such advice there is not a little to be learnt. But this does not mean that any others can do for us the work that is our own; the re-organisation of Indian education, if it is to be of any use, must be accomplished by Indian hands. The most denationalised Indian is still more Indian than a European. It is for Indians to nationalise Indian education. Given the responsibility and the power to act, and even Europeanised India will rise to the occasion; ... Let Indians place the control of education in the forefront of the nationalist programme. By control, let absolute control be meant, not merely a half control, or a control sanctioned by some royal charter that may be withdrawn as easily as given.[203]

The development of the 'Indian intelligence through the medium of Indian culture' was one of the main themes of Coomaraswamy's educational philosophy. And such a turn of vision could not be envisaged and worked out by a colonial education system. 'The real difficulty at the root of all questions of Indian education', argued Coomaraswamy, 'is this, that modern "education", this education which Englishmen are so proud of having 'given' to India, is really based on the general assumption – nearly universal in England – that India is a *savage* country, which it is England's divine mission to *civilize*. This is the more or less conscious underlying principle throughout'.

In his essay on Indian education, [though written much later, in 1919] John Woodroffe (1865–1936), a recognised and prolific Indophile, whose work on Tantras was widely read, discussed some of the fundamentals of education in India. Woodroffe argued that since education means 'to "educe" or "bring forth" what is within

203. Ananda Coomaraswamy, pp. 111–12.

the child, we cannot bring forth that which is not there, though it is possible to superimpose something from without. Woodroffe however saw such an acquisition as transient. In the case of the education of an Indian, the aim must be to bring forth the 'Indian *Sangskâra*.'[204] Referring to a criticism then leveled at him by one of the members of the Indian Educational Service who argued that in that case, the 'child of the Thug should be brought up to be a Thuggi, and the child of a member of a criminal tribe should be brought up to be a thief', Woodroffe argued that 'probably in every man there are some bad elements. Education does not mean the fostering of these, but of the good elements of character'. The 'evil elements' are to be eliminated by 'appeal to and encouragement of, those which are good'.

In Indian education, Woodroffe observed:

> ... as it exists today, the matter of first importance is to give the inherited *Sangskâra* a full, free, play. It will then, with some guidance, develop itself rightly. This means that the primary process is a *negative* one, that is the clearing away of all the foreign incongruous stuff, which is piled over and choking the *Sangskâra*, as it were a mass of mixed earth and rubbish thrown upon a young shooting plant. Clear this away and let the plant grow. The next stage of the process is a *positive* one. Nourish the plant properly. [205]

Woodroffe clearly felt that English education in the past has always threatened to smother the Indian *Sangskâra*. In answer to the criticism that he was more of a reactionary, Woodroffe is careful to clarify that he does not advocate the dumping of English education altogether. He countered:

---

204. John Woodroffe, *The Seed of Race: An Essay in Indian Education*, 1919, p.21.
205. Ibid., pp.21, 22.

I have repeatedly said that English education has had some good, as well as some evil result. The knowledge of the English language, which is that of a vast and increasing part of the world, and of Western science, is essential to the progress of this country, and only one who was either without sense, or an enemy of its advancement, could hold otherwise.[206]

But in the process of giving free development to the *Sangskâra* the medium, 'the instrument by which education is given' – the language used – was extremely important. And at present, he argued, 'the education is generally a Western education given by Englishmen or English-educated Indians, whose outlook is often more an endeavour to follow that of their own teachers – the English, than the outlook of their own people; that is, the education is substantially an education by aliens'.[207] What was needed was an increase in the number of Indians who can give what is called nowadays a "national education". Woodroffe also argued that 'knowledge is not the property of any people. Whether the term "national" be appropriate or not, what is meant is an education suited to the needs of the Indian people'. Indian life, Indian conditions, he argued, were understood and interpreted by Indians themselves, hence the Indian control of education was seen as a thing desirable:

The fact of Indian life must be considered. These *prima facie* are best known and understood by the people who take part in that life. It seems to me obvious that a qualified and properly educated Indian teacher will better understand his boys, than the best of English teachers are likely to do.[208]

---

206. John Woodroffe, *The Seed of Race: An Essay in Indian Education*, p.23.
207. Ibid., p.24.
208. Ibid., pp.28, 29.

The demand was therefore for Indians to control Indian education. This demand was to become among the foremost demands of the nationalist programme that Sri Aurobindo had drawn up.

3

Towards a National Education

First Stirrings

"

National Education was another item to which Sri Aurobindo attached much importance. He had been disgusted with the education given by the British system in the schools and colleges and universities...He felt that it tended to dull and impoverish and tie up the naturally quick and brilliant and supple Indian intelligence, to teach it bad intellectual habits and spoil by narrow information and mechanical instruction its originality and productivity.

– Sri Aurobindo,
Autobiographical Notes

It thus was in the 1890s that the early stirrings of the national education movement began. The intellectual base for the movement was prepared by developing a varied discourse on the issue. One of the first platforms to support discourse was the *Dawn* journal started in 1897 by Satish Chandra Mukherjee (1865–1948) – one of the legendary pioneers of the national education movement in Bengal who not only began experiments in education but also initiated critical debates on the prevailing education system. Satish Chandra lucidly articulated the educational problems and their possible solutions. His Dawn Society and its journal had as one of its principal objectives the aim of spreading Indian moral and spiritual ideals while also retaining a lively and legitimate interest in the development and progress of other systems. The journal proposed 'to make a special study of Hindu life, thought and faith, in a spirit of appreciation, while remaining fully alive to the usefulness and the necessity of the existence of all other systems, secular or religious, Eastern or Western'.[1]

A contemporary of some of the intellectual giants of his era such as Swami Vivekananda, Brajendra Nath Seal, Bipin Chandra Pal and Aswini Kumar Dutt among others, Mukherjee had studied at Presidency College at the same time as Vivekananda and had struck up a friendship with him. A disciple of Acharya Bijoy Krishna Goswami, Mukherjee had cast a deep influence on young scholars who had involved themselves in the national education movement. Benoy Kumar Sarkar (1887–1949), formidable polyglot,

1. *The Origins of the National Education Movement*, op.cit., p. 215.

phenomenally prolific author and public intellectual, considered to be one of the founders of sociological studies in India and who was himself one of the best products of the national education movement[2], recollected the influence Mukherjee had on him when they met at the Hindu Hostel of the Calcutta University around 1902:

> Country, service to one's country, about the country, sacrifices for the sake of one's country, selfless service for the sake of one's country – these sentiments I first heard from Satish Babu. Before meeting him, I had just heard of Vivekananda's name. I did not know anything else; I had no idea of the vastness of his personality and work. It was while participating in Satish Babu's discussion circles, that I heard him speak of Vivekananda .... I realised that Satish Babu himself was a living example of Vivekananda's definition of an 'inspired fanatic'.[3]

His regular interaction with the young students at Calcutta University brought together many young scholars who would later form the first batch of educator-researchers at the Bengal National College.

Imbued with an 'all-embracing cosmopolitan spirit', Satish Chandra's journal *Dawn* served as a forum for highlighting many of the 'general criticism of the English medium of instruction.' It spoke of education through the medium of English as being too literary,

---

2. From 1906 to 1914, Sarkar 'was actively engaged with the National Education Movement of Bengal and National Council of Education... During this period, he organised several national schools at Maldah, [Bengal] wrote five books in Bengali language furnishing guidelines for national education, and campaigned for the use of vernacular as the medium of instruction in various schools and colleges of India.' (Suhrita Saha, 'Benoy Kumar Sarkar (1887–1949): A Tryst with Destiny' in Source: *Sociological Bulletin*, January-April 2013, Vol. 62, No. 1 (January-April 2013), pp. 4–22.
3. Sankari Prasad Basu, *Swami Vivekananda: Notun Tathya, Notun Alo* (New Facts, New Light), (2005), rpt 2011, pp.189–190.

not technical enough and hampered by the language barrier. These criticisms were being levelled from various quarters at that time. Some of the leading thinkers of that era argue that education, as we have seen, was also deracinating. Bipin Chandra Pal speaking of his youth, recollected how the education which they received, 'in their schools and colleges had very seriously unsettled their faith not only in the traditional religion of their own people but, more or less, in all religion.'[4]

When the leaders of the national education movement insisted on the need for Indian students to study their way of life, their traditions and their faith, they did not base their demand on a compelling ethnocentric urge. It was their quest for re-creating, for re-discovering and articulating once again a national cultural self-identity, an identity that they argued had been submerged under the weight of colonial systems. This self-identity could be rediscovered not only by re-assessing India's past civilisational achievements, but also by exposing the young learners to advanced achievements from across the world. This led them to also emphasise the need for an awareness and interest in the modern scientific and material advancements of the West.

Before launching the journal *Dawn*, Satish Chandra had launched other literary ventures as well. In September 1892, he launched a journal *The Light of the East*, a 'Hindu Magazine Devoted to Aryan Philosophy, Religions and Occultism'. The magazine had a twofold objective: 'for the European readers' it would 'supply expositions of the Hindu system of philosophy by its ablest expositors.' A precursor to his *Dawn* magazine, Mukherjee wanted *The Light of the East* to become an authentic forum for interpreting and explaining India's traditions, philosophies and scriptures to the West, a sort of forum for talking back. The other, and 'by far the most important object'

4. Bipin Chandra Pal, *Memories of My Life and Times*, 1932, p.233.

of the journal was 'to help those who sincerely wish to lead the life but are hindered from doing so for want of a trustworthy guide.'[5] Mukherjee saw the journal offering a serious practical guide to those who wanted to undertake the rigours of India's yogic systems and wanted to lead a life of seeking:

> There are various ways pointed out in the Shastras leading up to the sublime beatitude of Nirvana, and each individual has to select for himself that path which will suit him best. As most of the important articles in our paper will be from the pen of those who, by virtue of *yoga,* are in a higher level of spiritual consciousness than the mass of mankind, the practical hints given in this magazine will greatly benefit this class of our readers.

The idea also was to invariably compare the Hindu system with 'theories of the great European thinkers from Plato downwards in order to make it more palatable to the over-refined European of today.'[6] The journal existed till about 1902, after which it ceased publication altogether.

In 1895, Mukherjee also founded the *Bhagavat Chatuspathi.* It was an early attempt at developing a model for national education. The inadequacy of the prevailing education system that discouraged originality, had a weak technical and industrial side and which failed to impart education with a 'living sense of idealism' were the factors that led Satish Chandra to start his first experiment in education. Though its principal aim was to encourage the study of the Hindu religion, philosophy and Sanskrit literature, Satish Chandra made sure that adequate technical and industrial training was also imparted along with moral and physical education. All in all, it attempted to create a band of selfless workers who would

---

5. *The Light of the East,* Vol.1 No.1, September 1892, edited by S.C. Mukhopadhyay, Printed & Published by: L.M. Das, pp.13–14.
6. Ibid., also see Sankari Prasad Basu, *Swami Vivekananda: Notun Tathya, Notun Alo* (New Facts, New Light) op.cit.

dedicate themselves to the goal of a national awakening through national education.

The main charges levelled against the prevailing system were that it was not rooted in the soil, that a foreign methodology and foreign concepts were sought to be imposed on the Indian mind. When they started occupying parts of India, the British discovered the existence of an elaborate system of indigenous education, which was widespread especially in Bengal and the southern parts of the country. The schools in such a system had an organic link to the community, was supported by its members and the teacher in it had greater freedom of action and innovation. The child in it was given an education in consonance with his environment, something to which he could feel akin and connected. The early nationalists felt that the colonial education system negated these precepts.

III.1. DISTORTION IN APPLICATION: ANALYSING THE COLONIAL SYSTEM OF EDUCATION

The chief contributions of the colonial education system that was implemented in India in the 1850s – the Wood's Despatch of 1854 suggested the creation of an education department and a structured education system – was the starting of high schools in each district, initiating the concepts of grant-in-aids to educational institutions founded with the object of spreading English education. The destruction and starvation of India's well-defined indigenous education system, especially in its vast rural hinterland is a separate subject altogether. For any serious scholar of the history of Indian education, it is disconcerting to see how that network and system was deliberately destroyed, how the system was de-rooted leading to illiteracy and deracination. In the 1930s this debate was renewed in India with Mahatma Gandhi publicly accusing the colonial rulers of destroying indigenous Indian education and of uprooting a well planted tree which had deep roots and had successfully nourished and trained India's generations across centuries.

The Wood's Despatch, also called the 'Charter of Indian Education', promoted the centralisation of the education system. It also initiated the method of training teachers and introduced an impartial examination system to pass, which was to become, henceforth, the ultimate goal of all education.[7]

---

7. Historically it would be relevant to note that almost simultaneously with the creation of the Lieutenant-Governorship the education scheme of Bengal and the whole of India was given an impetus by the issuing of the Education Despatch No.49 of the Court of Directors on July 19th 1854. Lord Dalhousie then Governor General of India saw the Despatch as containing 'a scheme of Education for all India, far wider and more comprehensive than the Local or the Supreme Government could ever have ventured to suggest, and that "it left nothing to be desired, if indeed it did not authorise and direct that more should be done than is within our present grasp." Under this dispatch the office of the Director of Public Instruction was constituted...; (*Bengal under the Lieutenant Governors*, op.cit., pp.6-7) Among the recommendations of the Despatch were 1) the constitution of a separate Department for the administration for education; 2) the institution of Universities at the presidency towns; 3) the establishment of institutions for training teachers for all classes of schools'. It also talked of promoting indigenous and vernacular education while introducing the grant-in-aid system. (Ibid., p.7) Though the Despatch called for supporting vernacular schools so that Indians could 'become useful members of society instead of making them ambitious only for the Clerkship', there was not much evidence of an intention to support indigenous schools. The shift from the vernaculars to the language of the colonial rulers, alienated Indian education from the land and eroded 'traditional culture' and 'vitality of rural institutions diminished' as well. (Joseph Di Bona, *One Teacher, One School*, op.cit., p.33)

With this came the introduction of textbooks and with it was injected into the national psyche the 'textbook culture' – a sacred and near total unquestioned adherence and allegiance to whatever the prescribed textbook dished out as necessary education. The concept of learning by rote only whatever was necessary to successfully pass the examination – in Sri Aurobindo's parlance learning by 'snippets' – and just learning enough to successfully pass the examination was another effect of this system. The habit of fathoming the depths of a subject in order to, if not master, at least gauge the wideness of the topic gradually ceased to be of any value. The practical exigencies of empire building demanded the creation of subordinate officers and clerks and therefore the colonial machinery felt the need to evolve a different system of education to meet that demand. Our intention here is to simply point to the fact that among the numerous changes that the colonial education department introduced in the indigenous system, some had a long term debilitating effect on the Indian mind and society.

The destruction of the indigenous school network especially hit hard rural Indian society. As 'traditional schools disappeared so too did the folklore, and history that gave the rural community its stability and appeal.' This happened all across the Indian subcontinent. As G.W. Leitner (1840–1899) British Orientalist, Principal of Government College in Lahore who had studied and reported on the extensive network of indigenous schools in Punjab, caustically commented, 'it is only where the influence of a government school has extended that these signs of a national intellectual life are disappearing.' The symbolic effect of this erosion was evident with the disappearance of the minstrels who praised 'the exploits of Ranjit Singh or the glories of the Dharm Raj.'[8] It

8. Jospeh Di Bona; quoting G.W. Leitner, op.cit., p.34.

symbolised the decimation of traditions and an entire class of those who carried it to the masses, disseminated their core thoughts and values in a very simple and absorbing manner and kept it alive.

Snapping of the organic link of the school and the community was a glaring contribution of this new system. It altered the existing balance. The first to suffer were the teachers of these indigenous schools. His links with local society was weakened and eventually ruptured. The teacher henceforth was paid by the colonial administration and the village did not have to look after his upkeep. This not only impoverished the teacher materially, for he was better off under the village maintenance system, but it also made him emotionally dependent on the administration and its officers – especially the inspectors of schools – to please whom, and thus preserving his job became his sole driving force.

Under the new regime, while fixing the teacher's pay scale for the primary level, 'colonial officers did recognise that the village teacher had access to incomes other than the small cash he received from his pupils, but they greatly minimised the value of these other earnings.'

Alexander Duff, the influential Scottish missionary and educationist, who, it is said, inspired the Wood's Despatch, felt that the Bengali teacher's earnings part in money and part in clothes, vegetables and other commodities 'did not exceed Rs.3 a month.' This was a gross underestimate. There are descriptions of the village teacher's earnings which show otherwise, 'apart from the total of roughly two rupees that the pupil paid every month, the teacher received from every pupil a monthly *siddha* consisting of rice, pulses, vegetables, salt and mustard oil', and each of these 'often supplied material for the breakfast and dinner', of the teacher and his family for one day and thirty such units kept him supplied for the whole month. Moreover, the teacher received other gifts too during different occasions in the village. An addition of all of these will show that the villager school-master was not so badly off under the old structure.[9] But as soon as the teacher 'started to get a government salary ... earnings of this kind began to dry up. Thus the village teacher was squeezed from both ends – the government paid him a low wage on the ground that his income had always been small, and his extra earnings from the community started to shrink as soon as he entered the government's payroll.[10]

---

9. E.g. in his essay *'A Peep into the Ideal of Education in Indo-Aryan Society'*, Mahamopadhyaya Vidhusekhara Bhattacharya deals with this aspect of the subsistence of the teacher while referring to the classical Indian system, '...as regards the expenses for the education of the boy. Who was to meet them? Why, the education was absolutely free, and there was the question of expenses to be paid by a student. Yet, was not there the question of at least the daily food for both the student and the teacher? How was it provided for, and by whom? Evidently by the society itself and in the most remarkably economical and simple way that could be thought of. The food was daily collected by the students themselves begging from door to door, and it was a religious and obligatory duty of every householder to supply a student with as much food as he could afford.' This duty of supplying the student, Bhattacharya argues, was enjoined especially on 'the wife of a householder (and not on the householder himself, as the latter might be more often absent from the house than the former owing to his outdoor works), that when a student approached her for food she must not refuse him, otherwise all her previous good actions would be of no avail.' (D.R. Bhandarkar, et.al. edited, *B.C.Law – Volume Part-II*, 1946, p.50.) The representation may appear as an idealized but it at least confirms the arrangement that the teacher in the Indian society was supported by the people themselves and did not generally lead a materially marginalised life.
10. Krishna Kumar, op.cit., pp.77–78. It is well recorded that Duff was the prime mover of the Educational Despatch of 1854. His biographer gives him chief credit for its formulation and propagation. From

This was quite a strong demoralising factor and, coupled with the teacher's lack of say in the formulation of the curriculum, the

---

Duff's own admission one of the objectives of this move was the gradual abolition of the indigenous system which till then received some kind of state patronage. Duff called for the entire education to be controlled by the government. When asked, during his presentation before the Parliamentary Committee to the President of the Board of Control, 'Will you state what you would propose the Government should do towards the further improvement and extension of education in India', Duff's answer was rather revealing: 'Fall back on the resolutions of Lord William Bentinck in March 1835, resolutions, which, without damaging or interfering with the existing vested rights of any one, would lead to the gradual abolition of these oriental colleges as seminaries for the educational training of natives, and thus liberate the funds so wastefully lavished upon them for the purposes of a sound and healthful education throughout the land. If the learned oriental languages are to be taught at all in the Government institutions, they ought to be taught simply as languages by one or two native professors, under general European superintendence...' Duff further observed that imparting centrally an expressly designed education was the only way of spreading and retaining the English dominion in India, '...I have never ceased to declare, that if our object be, not merely for our aggrandisement but very specially for the welfare of the natives, to retain our dominion in India, no wiser or more effective plan can be conceived than that of bestowing this higher English education in close and inseparable alliance with the illumining, quickening, beautifying influences of the Christian faith.' Duff saw such an education consolidating and perpetuating the British Empire in India 'for years, or even ages to come'. His mark was evident all over the contents of the Despatch, 'not only in the definite orders, but in the very style' of the entire document. This promulgation by Parliament, Duff's biographer contends, was possible because of the missionary pressure in 1830–34. Those demonstrations then, he admits, had 'for its chief end the destruction of Hindooism, and the Christianisation of the hundred and thirty millions of Eastern and Northern India.' (George Smith, *Life of Alexander Duff, vol.2*, 1879, pp.241–245).

'dominant role' of the examination system gradually rendered the teacher static in terms of creativity. His job was downgraded to merely preparing the student with the right kind of answers which they would reproduce in the examination copybook. The rational way to do this was to restrict teaching to the content of the textbook.[11]

The teacher thus lost his innovating zeal, he turned into a mere keeper of the textbook, he strictly adhered to its contents, did not deviate from it, did not innovate, did not enliven and enthuse and ceased to make an effort to become a living example worth emulating. His sole duty was to see to it that pupils under his jurisdiction would perform successfully in their annual examinations. To this was added a number of clerical duties too – such as maintaining of accounts, registers etc., which further divested the teacher of all urge for educational creativity. Hitherto he was well provided for by the community but under the new dispensation he struggled to make both ends meet and this added to his demoralisation. Eventually the low remuneration of a teacher's job attracted only those who had failed to make forays into other professional avenues. The prescriptive qualification required to apply for a teacher's job was deliberately kept very low.

The other aspect of the system introduced was the process of de-linking the child from his environment. The subject taught ceased to have a link with the pupil's surrounding and with his daily living. This was seen to affect the natural inquisitiveness of an infant mind which felt confused and bewildered at having been exposed to concepts, examples, and situations quite foreign to his environment – the epistemology itself was an alien one. It is clear from a number of path breaking studies undertaken towards the latter half of the last century. Dharampal's opus, *The Beautiful Tree*, inspired by

---

11. Krishna Kumar, op.cit., p.86.

Mahatma Gandhi's statement in 1931, at London's Chatham House, that the British had destroyed the existing system of indigenous education in India and had thus pushed India towards greater illiteracy, still stands as one of the best study of India's indigenous education system.

While on his visit to England and the West in 1931 to attend the Round Table Conference, Mahatma Gandhi was invited to speak at the Royal Institute of International Affairs, Chatham House. The meeting was held on October 20, 1931 and is said to have been attended by 'influential Englishmen and Englishwomen drawn from all parts of England and was presided over' by the British politician diplomat Lord Lothian.[12] The Mahatma spoke on 'The Future of India'. His observations on illiteracy in India 'seemed to have made sparks fly.' Gandhi made two main points on India's growing illiteracy under the British – he said, i) 'that today India is more illiterate than it was fifty or a hundred years ago', ii) 'that the British administrators, instead of looking after education and other matters which had existed, began to root them out. They scratched the soil and began to look at the root and left the root like that and the beautiful tree perished.' Gandhi asserted that he was 'without fear' of his 'figures being challenged successfully.'[13] These observations unleashed an intense and long-drawn debate among colonial educators and Gandhian educators and activists, many of whom had painstakingly gathered solid evidence in support of the Mahatma's claim.

---

12. Gita Dharampal, *Essential Writings of Dharampal*, op.cit., p.247.
13. Ibid., pp.246–247. As early as 1804, William Bentinck, then governor of the Madras Presidency writing to the President of the Board of Control, confessed that 'we have rode the country [India] too hard, and the consequence is that it is in the most lamentable poverty ...' (Cited in Ibid., p.246).

In a long and detailed letter, for instance, to Philip Hartog, one of the founders of the School of Oriental Studies, London, and a former Vice Chancellor of the University of Dacca, who was the first one to challenge the Mahatma and to continue a public debate with him over the next few weeks, Professor K.T. Shah, Gandhian, economist and scholar, wrote basing himself on a number of records including that of W. Adam and G.W. Leitner:

> I need hardly mention what every member of the Board knows as well as I do, that there is hardly a village, great or small, throughout our territories, in which there is not the least one school, and in larger villages more; many in every town, and in large cities in every division; where young natives are taught reading, writing and arithmetic, upon a system so economical, from a handful or two of grain, to perhaps a rupee per month to the school master, according to the ability of the parents, and at the same time so simple and effectual, that there is hardly a cultivator or petty dealer who is not competent to keep his own accounts with a degree of accuracy, in my opinion, beyond what we meet with amongst the lower orders in our own country; whilst the more splendid dealers and bankers keep their books with a degree of ease, conciseness, and clearness I rather think fully equal to those of any British merchants.[14]

For example, the indigenous rural schools, especially the small ones with but one teacher, 'with their limited resources were able to train quality professionals and specialists for the wide range of social needs in Bengali society. These village schools turned out the accountants, the lawyers, the doctors, the priests, logicians and the bureaucrats that were required in 19th century Bengal.'[15] In his first report on the state of education in Bengal, William Adam, for instance, spoke of the existence of about '1,00,000 village schools in Bengal and Bihar around the 1830s.' Similar statements were also made before Adams, for the Madras Presidency by Thomas Munro,

---

14. *Essential Writings of Dharampal*, op.cit., pp.249–250.
15. *One Teacher, One School*, op.cit., p.3.

who noted that 'every village had a school', for the Bombay Presidency areas, senior colonial officials like G.L. Pendergast pointed out that there was 'hardly a village, great or small throughout our territories, in which there is not at least one school, and in larger villages more.' G.W. Leitner also spoke of a similar network and spread of education in 'Panjab around 1850'.[16]

It was left to Dharampal to unravel and put together a large number of records that documented the existence of a wide network of indigenous schools with a uniform caste representation, with the lower castes doing well and attending schools in high numbers. His finding also revealed that India's indigenous education was based on the child and his environment and made use of the surroundings to awaken in the child the first stirrings of awareness. Dharampal's work remains the most authoritative and authentic argumentation on the tradition and structure of Indian education and how it was eradicated and starved by the colonial administration.

The teacher training system initiated by the colonial education department structured its whole training methodology on the assumption that the pupil was a passive learner who had to be prepared to be able to internalise definitions and at the appropriate forum of the examination to be able to reproduce them at ease. The teaching demonstrations that the trainee teacher had to perform as a replica of classroom teaching had hardly any bearing on the reality of classrooms outside the teacher's training school. It was a make believe system that one had to follow in a routine manner just to acquire the requisite permission to teach.[17]

---

16. *Essential Writings of Dharampal*, o.cit., p.206.
17. Directions for some of the ideas expressed here were inspired by Dharampal's – *The Beautiful Tree*, Vol. III of Collected Writings, 2007, *Essential Writings of Dharampal*, 2015, Prof. Krishna Kumar's *Political Agenda of Education: A Study of Colonialist and Nationalist Ideas on Education*, 2005.

All this is not to say that the indigenous education system in India was perfect and needed no alteration, far from it. Sri Aurobindo argued it was not feasible to replicate the old method of education nor would it be fruitful to revert to the instructional method of the *tols.* Realising this, the nationalist advocates of an Indian controlled and directed education spoke in favour of the introduction of western scientific knowledge and opposed those aspects which disturbed the organic societal support system for education, reduced the role of the teacher and de-linked the child from his environment.

All these, they argued, had a long term detrimental effect on the overall growth of the national mind. The effects of these alterations were adversely felt within six decades of their implementation and it were these basic changes that the movement for national education questioned and sought to reverse.

In fact Sri Aurobindo's main principles of education, which he argues are applicable to any nation, were evolved observing the effects of these changes at close hand in India. He strongly felt that the system as applied in India had an atrophying effect on the Indian mind by discouraging it to think originally, a quality, he argued, which was intrinsic to it. What the colonial administration essentially wanted to structure through its education system was a community of translators who could convey their sense and priorities to the teeming millions, to govern whom was their ordained duty. It was to be an education that would basically prepare and mould those whom the British colonialists would assign to assist them in their *mission civilisatrice.*

A brief review, thus, of this background gives us an idea of the state of education in India and some of the causes of its stagnancy and its inability to relate to Indian needs and temperament. It will help us in better understanding this debilitating system against which some among the 'natives' decided to raise their voices and struggled to provide an alternative.

III.2. SATISH CHANDRA MUKHERJEE – THE EARLY PIONEER: A REVISIT

Let us revert to Satish Chandra Mukherjee and to his early experiment in indigenous education. Similar to some of the leading minds of his age, Satish Chandra believed that the emulation of the ancient Indian ideals of teaching was the one thing needed to bring about a comprehensive national intellectual regeneration. In this, one perceives a similarity of his views with that of Rabindranath Tagore, who started his Brahmacharyashram at Santiniketan, and Upadhyay Brahmabandhab, who was part of Tagore's early initiative. Brahmabandhab too had ideas on national education and on promoting indigenous knowledge systems.

Talking of the ancient Indian ideal of education in an article in *The Dawn* around 1898, Satish Chandra argued that the intellectual development of the student in the ancient Indian system of education was 'a means to an end, the end being the development of the higher, the spiritual nature of man.'[18] Education in India of the past was therefore a 'perpetual regulation of conduct, and the intellectual growth was part of an all embracing scheme of education,'

For our interest in this aspect of education, it would be appropriate to make a diversion in order to link the perceptions and to briefly delve into a system that kept, as a key-note, spiritual education. The concept of developing the spiritual nature of man is an intrinsic and fundamental aspect in Sri Aurobindo's

---

18. Haridas and Uma Mukherjee, op. cit., p. 10.

educational thought. This aspect of developing the 'higher, the spiritual nature of man' which is essentially an effort to sublimate his nature towards a greater perfection, a greater harmony, leading to a spontaneous response to all that is ennobling and inspiring in the environment, to encourage an inspired effort at recognising and appreciating individuality and at the same time realising the truth of the existence of a pervading and uniting thread amidst an abundant diversity – are some of the key contents of the spiritual aspect of education. An education that is based on the spiritual principle broadly seeks to evoke these dimensions in the individual. As discussed earlier, Sri Aurobindo's core educational vision was reflected in a concrete form later in the early 1950s, when the Mother gave a major emphasis at the Centre of Education on the spiritual dimension of education – the development of the 'higher' nature in man. The method of implementing a spiritual education or the question of the curriculum to be followed for it, is part of another discussion altogether. It must be, however, pointed out here that that in order to weave this concept into the new educational experiment at Pondicherry, the Mother did not rely on any outward ritual or mechanism to which the student could be latched on, and then shaped. She firmly believed that a process initiated through compulsion would inevitably give rise to a routine and unthinking adherence rather than an inspired one that is generated from a compelling inner need. She relied on the environment, the community of the Ashram, that she and Sri Aurobindo had founded.

The Ashram itself was devoid of any ritual method of living and of initiation. It was a cosmopolitan community where the child received an exposure to a rich diversity at an early age. As his awareness increased, he witnessed the harmonious coexistence of that diversity. The atmosphere of learning was permeated by a great sense of freedom, rules were kept to a minimum and the personal example of the teacher – the Mother insisted on the instructor/teacher setting high standards of personal conduct and thus serve as a living example – was placed at a premium.

The teacher in the Ashram was like the centre of education, an organic part of the community. She/he was part of the community, was sustained by it and had dedicated his/her life to practicing the yoga of Sri Aurobindo. Thus what one taught and lived were co-related, a link in one's life, in and outside the school was sustained. Moreover the teacher at the Centre of Education retained a great degree of freedom in formulating the curriculum and in making innovations in it based on her/his understanding of the students need and inquisitiveness. The educator here thus broke free from the colonial mindset and did not become a mere executor of the text-book's will. The outdated notion that the pupil was a passive learner was done away with right from the start.

Some of the essential features of education in Pondicherry based on Sri Aurobindo's thoughts were this: the master led, by example, to create an environment which would, by itself, become an early instructor to the child, encouraging an atmosphere of freedom in learning – an aspect which Tagore too, vigorously and militantly defended and implemented in his experiment at Visva-Bharati, and about which the Mother was no less emphatic. Sri Aurobindo had insisted, in one of his principles of education, that the child must not be hammered into a pre-determined mould, and that he must be allowed a great degree of freedom of growth. This aspect was particularly stressed upon at the Centre of Education at his Ashram.

The teacher's freedom to innovate and formulate and act as a guide, and the belief that the child was not a passive receiver but could be moulded into an active participant in his own growth and evolution, were some of the other essential features of this education

– features, that the early nationalist thought on education had also held to be of great importance in an earlier era. It is interesting to note how a number of these were successfully implemented at the Centre of Education in Pondicherry later.[19]

Continuing with Satish Chandra's article on Indian and western ideas of education, one sees him point to the utilitarian trait of western education. He talks of its aim of seeking greater worldly comfort, greater worldly prospects [and the] acquisition of wealth and power. The training of the mind is undertaken but 'all mental discipline subordinates itself to the requirements of the age, the race for greater worldly enjoyment, greater worldly power'.[20] The Indian ideal of education, on the other hand, encouraged the notion of self-development and the joy of learning and discovery. The material benefit and growth dimension was not of primary importance to it.

These ideals Satish Chandra set out to rework in a new system of education, whose time he felt had come. He had quite early

19. I have done away here with any academic reference and have solely relied and drawn on my understanding and memory of the system of education as followed in the Centre of Education at Pondicherry having myself been a part and product of it. For a more detailed discussion of the system and philosophy of education as practiced and pursued at the Centre of Education in Pondicherry see e.g. Jugal Kishore Mukherjee, *Principles and Goals of Integral Education: and the experiment at Sri Aurobindo International Centre of Education*, Pondicherry, 2005, *Sri Aurobindo and The Mother on Education*, 2006, Pavitra (P.B. Saint-Hilare), *Education and the Aim of Human Life*, 2006, *The Mother on Education Part I-III*, (1997, 2001, 2002), Pranab Kumar Bhattacharya, *A Scheme of Education,* 1952, Kireet Joshi, *A National Agenda for Education*, 2007, Kireet Joshi, *Education at the Crossroads*, 2000, Prithwindranath Mukherjee, *Pondicherrir Dingulo* (Bengali) (Pondicherry Days), 1988.
20. Haridas and Uma Mukherjee, op.cit., p. 10.

realised that the colonial education system had produced no men of originality and that it had not enabled the people to be 'self-reliant, self-dependent, self-sacrificing, patriotic.' Commenting on the examination system he said that it had 'failed to bring to the front the stamp of men who can hold their own in the great industrial struggle which is the marked feature of the great civilisations amidst which [people] lived'[21]

He clearly felt that the education imparted did not prepare men to face the challenges and struggle of the new age that had dawned with the growth of industrialism, a period when civilisations and societies were undergoing a process of restructuring and new systems were being constantly evolved and experimented with.

No less an India baiter than Valentine Chirol, in his much publicised as well as criticised work, *Indian Unrest*, that appeared in 1910, argued that the fundamental weakness of Indian education was that 'the average Indian student [could not] bring his education into any direct relation with the world in which, outside the class or lecture room, he continues to live.' Though Chirol refers to this Indian world as the old world of the forefathers of the Indian students, he was nevertheless right in his assessment of the predicament of the Indian student.[22]

Chirol interestingly cites the statement of a leading missionary of that epoch, Dr. Garfield Williams, on Indian education and on

21. Haridas and Uma Mukherjee, op.cit., p. 7.
22. Valentine Chirol, *Indian Unrest*, 1910, p. 216. However Chirol, as was his wont, went off to the other extreme by arguing that since the majority of Indian students – he gave the example of Calcutta, where the figures that he found, showed 1000 students out of 4,500, living in hostels – did not live in the hostels attached to colleges and universities, they were liable to be constantly compromised ideologically. They were, he concluded, living under 'conditions intellectually, morally, and physically deleterious.' (p. 217).

Indian students. It would be instructive to read that statement in some detail as it aptly describes the status of the Indian student and his principal aim in being educated. We have amply discussed the views of some leaders of nationalist thought on how the colonial system of education, implemented over the last five-odd decades, had majorly contributed in debilitating the Indian student. At a Missionary Conference in Calcutta sometime in the winter of 1909, missionary educationist Garfield Williams scathingly observed:

> The conditions and environment of the student in Calcutta are such as to make the formation of character almost impossible.... He is not a student in the best sense of the word, for he has not the scholarly instincts of a student – I speak, of course, of the average student, not of the exceptional one. His parents send him to the university to pass one or two examinations, and these have to be passed in order to enable him to attain a higher salary.... His work is sheer "grind". The acquisition of good notes for lectures is the first essential for him, and the professor who gives good clear-cut notes so that a man can dispense with any textbooks, is the popular professor – and for two reasons: first of all, it saves the expense of buying the textbook, and then, of course, it helps to get through the examination.... The question is how to prevent this ridiculous wastage of students; how to prevent the production of this disappointed man, who was a student only in name. He never had any desire to be a student in nature; he was brought up without that desire ... and indeed, if he be a boy with real scholarly instincts, and he happens to fail in his examinations, it makes it all the worse, for his parents will not recognise those scholarly instincts of his – all they want is a quick return for the money spent on his education, and he will have to make that return from a Rs.30 salary instead of a Rs.50 one.[23]

Garfield's compatriots had actually brought such a passé in India. They were driven, on the one hand, by the desire to create a batch of managers, through whom they would manage and perpetuate their Indian Empire and on the other hand, they were convinced that the 'natives' were to be lifted out of their dark faith and exposed

23. Chirol, op.cit., pp.217, 218.

to the light of Western education and Christianity. As early as 1797, Charles Grant, then a member of the Court of Directors of the East India Company, in his observations before the Court on the 'state of Society among the Asiatic subjects of Great Britain', summed up the dominant colonial attitude which drove both administration and education in India:

> Upon the whole we cannot avoid recognising in the people of Hindustan, a race of men lamentably degenerate and base, retaining a feeble sense of moral obligation, yet obstinate in their disregard of what they know to be right, governed by malevolent and licentious passions, strongly exemplifying the effects produced on society by great and general corruption of manners, and sunk in misery by their vices.[24]

The situation, as described by Garfield, greatly perturbed a number of the nationalist educational idealists, and they envisioned a new system that would reinstall the thrill of study in the Indian student. Through the pages of the *Dawn*, Satish Chandra provided a platform for initiating debates on various facets of Indian polity, including the education scene. He eminently succeeded in this, *Dawn* soon became a vibrant forum, advocating new thought in Indian education. Day after day, in its pages, Satish Chandra forcefully and cogently discussed the deficiencies of the colonial system of education and its debilitating effect on the Indian mind.

The colonial government's educational policy had been deliberately framed so as to direct 'the ambitions and aspirations of educated Indians along a narrow line of thought, along the line merely of seeking official patronage, or professional advancement, without their being able to bring into operation forces that tend towards a wider rapprochement with the higher Western thought,'[25]

---

24. H.R. James, *Education and Statesmanship in India (1797 to 1910)*, 2nd ed. 1917, p.16.
25. *Origins of the National Education Movement*, op.cit., p. 11.

was how Satish Chandra Mukherjee described it. The government, he argued, was never serious about imparting true and advanced education to the Indians – an education that reflected the progress and advancement of the West and, at the same time, blended the best of Eastern thought and ethos, and trained the student to develop a wider outlook of thought, action and assimilation. It encouraged the Indian mind only to run in the narrow rut of a professional track under the benedictions of 'official patronage'.[26]

III.3. LIVING WITH THE GURU – THE CATHOLIC VEDANTIN AND THE POET: IN SEARCH OF AN INDIGENOUS EDUCATIONAL ROOT

The principal concept behind Satish Chandra Mukherjee's *Bhagavat Chatuspathi* was that of living with the master and imbibing knowledge from him – the Indian ideal of *guru-griha-vasa*. Though it blended its lines of activity in demand with requirements of industrial training, it had, as one of its primary objects, the 'regulation of the daily life and habits of the scholar under a system of Hindu discipline' according to the traditional 'plan of ... residence with the Guru at his Asrama and under his complete control.' It was modelled on the ideals of the ancient *tols* but had a wider ambit that included scientific and industrial training. It may be observed that the experiments that were undertaken in education during this period aimed at replicating this system. Rabindranath Tagore's and Brahmabandhab Upadhyay's early educational experiments are

26. It would be necessary to look at Satish Chandra's educational thoughts in some more detail later, as his views and voice contributed greatly in enriching and strengthening the early nationalist educational discourse. His ability to identify in a precise manner the ills of the system, made accessible the problems of education to a wider public. The part above may be treated as a preliminary exposure to his educational opinion.

cases in point. A brief look at the experiment would not only serve to widen the ambit of the survey but also illustrate the varieties of experiments that were undertaken in the field of education in that era.

In the Tagore-Brahmabandhab educational experiment, one saw an adherence to tradition and to strict codes of conduct which were developed based on the *shastras.* This arose from an urge to replicate a system which in its original pristine form had, in the past, succeeded in creating men of originality imbued with spirituality and with clear objectives in life. These kinds of men, it was felt, were needed to awaken India to the vision of her nationhood. The originators felt that such a system would restrain the youth from rejecting altogether the contributions of Indian civilisation and culture. This relook was of another kind, it was inspired more by a genuine quest of the past rather than by the political habit of one-upmanship. Tagore, in his later experiment of Visva-Bharati, did away with all constricting rules and codes.

Tagore's early experiment was similar in spirit to Satish Chandra's *Bhagavat Chatuspathi.* This gives us an idea of some of the educational initiatives undertaken in early years, before Sri Aurobindo came to Bengal. This gives us the background for better understanding Sri Aurobindo's action in the educational field during his nationalist activities.

During the course of his hectic life, Brahmabandhab Upadhyay, the Catholic–Vedantin, had evolved ideas on national education and it was a happy turn of events when, through the medium of positive reviews written by Upadhyay of a number of Tagore's poems, the two developed a mutually admiring relationship and began exploring ways of giving a practical shape to their vision of education.

By July 1901, Tagore envisaged the setting up at Santiniketan of an educational establishment along traditional lines. He was in search of a couple of 'self-denying celibate teachers' for running it. In a letter in July 1901 to his friend, the scientist and nationalist Acharya Jagadish Chandra Bose, Tagore refers to the system that he intended to implement in the school. All rules in it, he wrote, 'must conform to living with the guru as in ancient times. There mustn't be a trace of luxury; everybody, well-off and poor, will have to adopt a strictly celibate way of life.' For this, Tagore had already Upadhyay in mind and the collaboration began.[27]

Brahmabandhab on his part had also started a school in north Calcutta; it was conducted on the ancient Aryan ideal, the students were charged no fees and the paraphernalia that fill the ordinary schools were conspicuous by their absence. Some six students of respectable families attended the institution.[28] Upadhyay's idea behind the school was to build up a cultural identity among the students based on the study of Sanskrit and through conformity to traditions. It was then decided that the Bolpur experiment would start with the existing students of Upadhyay's Aryan school at Calcutta.

A reconnaissance trip to survey the infrastructure and land for the new project in Bolpur was made by Tagore, Upadhyay and others. And on December 22, 1901, the Santiniketan School was inaugurated with Upadhyay's students being transferred to the estate at Bolpur. In his inaugural address, Tagore talked to the students of the ancient education and discipline, 'what kind of education and discipline did our ancient forefathers follow?' he asked, 'they left their house

---

27. Julius.J.Lipner *Brahmabandhab Upadhyay: The Life and Thought of a Revolutionary*, 1999, p. 86.
28. B.Animananda *The Blade: Life and Work of Brahmabandhab Upadhyay*, (c.1946), p. 93.

at an early age and went to live in the guru's house in a secluded area. There the students used to restrain themselves through rigid rules.' In the path to be followed here; 'you will have to stay in the guru's house and similarly pass through all the hardships and rigid regulations, minimising all aspects of self-importance.'[29]

Nature was an inseparable part of Tagore's educational scheme. He considered it to be one of the greatest and spontaneous educators, and therefore, the forest hermitage of the ancient sages where the pupil lived amidst undisturbed pristine surroundings and received his education, attracted him. The central place of nature in his later scheme of education at Santiniketan, and even in his literary creations, is a testimony to that fact. It would be useful to see the routine and the manner of instruction followed by the students of the *Brahmacharyashram*:

> ... [t]he students got up at quarter to five, swept, had a swim in the pond, dressed. The Brahman boys in white silk, the Vaidyas and Kayasthas in red silk, and Vaisha lads in yellow silk: the various colours representing the various castes; then they said their individual prayers in Sanskrit each under a separate tree, and their breakfast which consisted of gram soaked in water and halwa, and dug the ground for cultivation for about half an hour. The classes opened at 7 a.m. with prayer in which both the master and pupil joined. At ten, class teaching was over, the boys had various outdoor games or practiced on the harmonium or read story books, each according to his taste. At 11.30 they had their dinner, the Brahmans dining separately. At 12.30 the school re-opened. There was recreation for 15 minutes at 3, and the lessons were finished exactly at 4.30. Cricket and football were over by 6.30. The evening prayers being done as in the morning, the boys had lessons in music, followed by supper and exciting games or stories; and when the clock struck 9, all the students were fast asleep ... The boys were divided into groups according to their attainments and each group with its master sat under a tree for instruction.[30]

---

29. Kathleen M.O'Connell op.cit., p. 57.
30. Animananda, op.cit., pp.94,95.

'The whole scene ... reminded one of the happy, glorious days of the ancient acaryas,' wrote Animananda, then Rewachand, Upadhyay's assistant and later his biographer, who was in-charge of the students at the ashram.[31]

The experiment at Santiniketan was to last for about a year and then the parting of ways took place. Tagore preferred to continue working at the educational experiment while Upadhyay was attracted to the revolutionary movement and started the fiercely nationalist paper, *Sandhya*. For Tagore, this period was one more step towards formulating his vision of the World University. He had his contacts with 19th-century education reformers and this education experiment, therefore, may be seen as a result of that contact and its influence.[32] It stemmed from his belief that India's indigenous education systems were still capable of directing a new way towards national regeneration and an attempt, therefore, had to be made to replicate some of its aspects under present conditions. The emphasis was on shaping personality-building through the influence and appeal of traditions.

Brahmabandhab meanwhile – even when absorbed in the vortex of nationalist politics, where he created a wave with his uncompromising opposition to colonial rule and by facilitating the initial printing of the *Bande Mataram* which, edited by Sri Aurobindo, introduced in its short life span the 'New Thought' in Indian politics – continued to evolve his thoughts on, and experimented with education. His school in north Calcutta continued to function and in 1902, when Upadhyay left for England, it had eight students on its rolls and was left in the care of his assistant. Gradually within two years the number went up to 35 and in 1904, a formal opening took place with the name *Sarasvat Ayatan* or *Collegium Sophia* – 'goddess

31. Ibid., 95.
32. Kathleen M. O'Connell, op.cit., p. 62.

of learning or better, the aspect of Wisdom in God – Sophia, as Holy Scripture calls Him'. This was how Animananda described the whole concept.

The idea was to train Hindu boys in the traditional Hindu way and to foster an indigenous identity that would counter the de-rooting effects of the then prevailing education system. According to Upadhyay, traditional practices and values were to be given importance but aspects of Western knowledge and skills, which were important and which, could give, on the one hand a 'scientific edge' and also 'show the depth of Hindu culture' on the other, could be included. Upadhyay's 'grand design was to train experts in this tempered Hindu wisdom who would themselves found similar establishments in other parts of India.'[33]

A similarity here is therefore discerned between Satish Chandra's *Chatuspathi* and Upadhyay's *Ayatan* – both based on tradition, both upholding the traditional way of learning, and yet both including the industrial and scientific dimension of the West as a necessary component of the whole scheme. In 1905, just two years before his death while in detention, Upadhyay issued an appeal for a National College. During Lokmanya Tilak's Calcutta visit in June 1906 to inaugurate the Shivaji festival and express solidarity with the Bengal nationalists, Upadhyay interacted regularly with Tilak on various matters and took the opportunity to 'read out his paper on National Education'.[34] Tilak was also an *avant-garde* exponent of national education and hugely contributed to promote it in his home province.

A look at the appeal for a National College reveals Brahmabandhab's plan. He spoke of an effective blending for education to be able to make a wide impact on the national mind.

33. Lipner, op.cit., p. 318.
34. Animananda op.cit., pp. 152–53.

The aims of the proposed college were to be 'a training in various forms of learning in accordance with Dharma' and 'the practice of good conduct ... the study of various useful occupations as well as of agriculture, trade and handicrafts for carrying out one's livelihood.'[35]

It may be recalled that the national education movement emphasised manual training for self-sufficiency. Sri Aurobindo dwelt on this in his speech on national education delivered at Bombay in early 1908. Apart from Sanskrit and grammar, the study of the epics and mythology, the subjects included in the primary stage were geography, astronomy, study of society, 'especially facts about Bengal and India', physics, handicrafts' etc. In the later stages, the study of estate management and agriculture were included, besides English literature, arithmetic and other scientific subjects.

Upadhyay laid emphasis on manual training and included such subjects as carving, casting, dyeing, weaving, electrical expertise and 'training in other such skills'. At the senior stage, medicine, economics, philosophy – the six systems – and the study of European psychology was also included. Students were to 'follow the dharma and custom of his own caste' and 'no fees' were to be accepted although 'voluntary contributions' were welcomed 'from the children's guardians'.[36] The ancient concept that education cannot be sold was pursued in his system. Upadhyay's scheme attempted to 'blend Indian and western knowledge and skills'; he realised the necessity of Western knowledge, but at the same time he did not want to see them 'overwhelm' indigenous facets and norms of life. He preferred developing a patriotism that was informed and yet retained an 'indigenous identity'. The syllabus was well rounded with an emphasis both on theory and practice and manual training,

35. Lipner, op.cit., p.319.
36. Ibid., p. 319–321.

and the necessity of establishing an organic contact with the land. The objective was to able to churn out individuals 'equipped to lead lives useful to themselves and to society.'[37] Interestingly one of the chief features of Brahmabandhab Upadhyay's 'National College' was the 'compulsory study of Hindi as the *lingua franca* of the country' and 'foreign learning was to be brought in as an auxiliary, the main line of culture being chiefly national', while English was to be taught as a second language.[38]

Though his appeal for a National College did not receive much response and the idea never really took off in the sense that he wanted it to, what is striking in Upadhyay's personality was his versatility, energy and wideness of thought. It also showed that most thinkers during that era who were intensely involved in nationalist politics also paid attention to education as a vital component of the freedom struggle.

The close association of Tagore and Upadhyay with Sri Aurobindo during his nationalist phase in Bengal necessitated this brief study of the experiments undertaken by them. Both Upadhyay and Tagore had hailed Sri Aurobindo's arrival in Bengal in wake of the anti-partition movement as the beginning of a new age for nationalism, Bengal and India. On the eve of the launching of *Bande Mataram* as the official paper of the 'Nationalist Party', Brahmabandhab paid glowing tributes to Sri Aurobindo describing him as 'the immaculate white lotus, full bloomed, hundred-petalled flower on India's lake of inward mental splendour' whose 'power of writing' fills one with 'patriotism, awakening an eagerness to worship the Mother ...'[39]

---

37. Lipner, pp. 321–322.
38. Animananda, op.cit., 153, 154.
39. Chanda Poddar, Mona Sarkar, Bob Zwicker edited, *Sri Aurobindo and the Freedom of India*, op.cit., p.109.

A study of these experiments also shows that the idea of national education did not evolve merely as a reaction to some repressive laws or originate to satisfy some revivalist instinct. The idea grew from the realisation that any movement for national regeneration had to include education as a necessary component and the leading minds of the day gave it attention in their own characteristic ways. In some, the dominant emphasis were past systems applied to modern conditions, in others, it was the need for an exclusively technical education and in yet others, it was a balance of the past and the present. The common thread, however, in all of these was the restoration of self-confidence in the nation, in its youth and therefore in its future. The fact that the nation could move ahead, without crutches, towards a future of its own making was emphasised through these experiments.

4

Education and National Education

The Political and Intellectual Debate

“

Aurobindo the new idol of the nation was hardly known then by his face, and at every small and big station a frantic crowd rushed about on the station platform looking for him in the first and second class compartment, while all the time Aurobindo sat unobserved in a third class compartment. By the time this fact became known and he was found out, the train was about to start.

– **Barindra Kumar Ghose,**
Sri Aurobindo: As I Understand Him

Aurobindo's power of writings will fill you with patriotism. Awakening, an eagerness to worship the Mother. Your fear will vanish on reading the Bande Mataram's message and your arm shall strike like thunder. A fiery warmth will course through your veins. Your fear of death will be replaced by a feeling of joyous participation in spring-time festival.

– **Brahmabandhab Upadhyay, *Sandhya***

Sri Aurobindo finally came to Bengal in 1906 after a 14-year stay at Baroda – in between he had been a visitor to the province in order to survey the political situation and to initiate the first steps towards developing a movement of revolutionary nationalism. To be precise, Sri Aurobindo's sojourn in Baroda lasted '13 years, 4 months and 11 days.'[1] In December 1905, after he had attended the Benares Congress, Sri Aurobindo returned to Baroda. At the Benares Congress, Sri Aurobindo 'made his presence felt without, perhaps, actually participating in the open debates'. The 'new party', the Nationalist Party, led by Lokmanya Tilak and Sri Aurobindo 'supported by contingents from Bengal, Maharashtra and Punjab' applied political pressure and saw to it that Swadeshi and Boycott made entry into the Congress's programme. The Congress would never be the same.[2]

In February 1906, Sri Aurobindo took two months of privilege leave to which he 'attached the summer vacation and spent the whole time in Bengal.' He utilised this time to further consolidate the nationalist links that he had established, and in sorting out various issues in the centres of revolutionary activity that had started under his inspiration and guidance and also in general, in studying the political situation in the province. Events took place in quick succession, on 12 March, the 'declaration of *Yugantar*' [Jugantar], a Bengali journal was filed.[3] At Barindra's suggestion, Sri Aurobindo

---

1. Manoj Das, *Life and Times of a Mahayogi*, op.cit., p. 88.
2. K.R. Srinivasa Iyengar, *Sri Aurobindo: a Biography and a History*, 1985, pp.216, 217.
3. A.B. Purani, op.cit., p.85.

had agreed to start this paper which was to 'preach open revolt and the absolute denial of the British rule and include such items as a series of articles containing instructions for guerilla warfare.' Sri Aurobindo wrote a number of opening articles and exercised a 'general control' over the paper.[4]

Sri Aurobindo attended the Barisal Conference held on April 14, 1906. 'The conference was declared illegal by the government and the participants were ordered to disperse.' On the day of the conference:

> A number of policemen were found stationed in different parts of the town with regulation *lathis.* In the Police lines ... the number of these policemen armed with *lathis* was the largest. Besides, dozens of guns were placed near the Police lines so that the public might have a clear view of them from the road. Reports were also circulated throughout the town that the Police would fire and shoot down those uttering 'Bande Mataram'.[5]

The leaders and delegates refused to oblige the administrations strictures for dispersal, 'there was a procession to protest against the government's action'. Sri Aurobindo, Bipin Chandra Pal and others were in the first row, 'behind them were delegates to the conference in rows of four. The procession was charged by the police. They allowed the leaders to pass and stopped the delegates from proceeding further'. The procession was lathi-charged and dispersed leaving some of them injured.[6] The police attempted to snatche the badges worn by the delegates and started raining lathis blows on them. Each time they were struck, the delegates chanted '*Vande Mataram*' and did not disperse. A number of them were injured and continued to chant '*Vande Mataram*'.[7]

---

4. Sri Aurobindo, *On Himself*, p.24.
5. Paramananda Dutt, *Memoirs of Motilal Ghose*, op.cit., p.166.
6. A.B. Purani, op.cit., 85.
7 For a description of the Barisal Conference, see Krishna Kumar Mitra's, *Atmacharit*, (1937) edited by Supriya Bhattacharya, reissued, 2017.

After the conference, 'Sri Aurobindo went round the districts of East Bengal in company with Bepin Chandra Pal ...' so that he could study the political situation in these parts and 'also to bring political awakening by personal contact'.[8] Recollecting later the effect of the Swadeshi period, Sri Aurobindo observed that 'there was a sudden transformation during the Swadeshi days. Before that, people used to tremble before an Englishman in Bengal. And then the position was reversed. I remember when I wanted to do political work, I visited Bengal and toured the districts of Jessore, Khulna etc. We found the people steeped in pessimism, a black weight of darkness weighing over the whole country. It is difficult nowadays to imagine those times'.[9]

As long as he was in Baroda, Sri Aurobindo 'could not take part publicly in politics. Apart from that, he preferred to remain and act and even to lead from behind the scenes without his name being known in public ...'[10] While in Baroda, Sri Aurobindo had 'already joined with some of the more advanced leaders to organise bodies for political action which would act when the time for action came'.[11] It was only later in 1906, when the decision to establish the Bengal National College and his name was proposed as its first Principal, that it gave him the 'opportunity he needed [of coming permanently to Bengal] and enabled him to resign his position in the Baroda Service and join the College ... [it made him free] 'to give his whole time to the service of the country'.[12]

We must, however, remember that it was in Baroda that he wrote the scathing nine-part series, 'New Lamps for Old', in the

8. A.B. Purani, op.cit., p.85.
9. Ibid., pp.85, 86.
10. Sri Aurobindo, *Autobiographical Notes & Other Writings of Historical Interest*, op.cit., p.52.
11. Ibid., pp.70,71.
12. Sri Aurobindo, *On Himself*, 1989, pp. 27, 28.

Indu Prakash, indicting the Congress party's policy of mendicancy towards the British. In these series, Sri Aurobindo repeatedly called for the Congress to open itself up and become the actual spokesperson of the 'silent and suffering people of India.' He called for the Congress to turn itself into a mass organisation, only then could it become a true representative platform of the people of India, representing the aspiration for freedom.

Sri Aurobindo was clearly the first leader to make such an appeal. He was perhaps the first leader to speak of the 'proletariat' as a 'very great potential force' and the need to understand and elicit its strength. He spoke of the need for an 'adroit management of the proletariat', to awaken and organise it for the eventual success of the movement. Such a demand was anathema for most leaders of that era, used to petitioning the colonial government for some grant and concessions. He indicted the Congress for not having made an honest effort to be 'a popular body empowered by the fiat of the Indian people in its entirety'.[13]

Sri Aurobindo decried the policy of holding 'our supplicating hands to the English Parliament, like an infant crying to its nurse for a toy'; this way, national renovation was impossible, the need was to 'recognise the hard truth that every nation must beat out its own path to salvation with pain and difficulty...'[14]

No one had spoken in that tone before. A leading historian of India's struggle for freedom, R.C. Majumdar, speaking of Sri Aurobindo's series in the *Indu Prakash*, wrote of how his was the first 'emphatic protest against the Indian National Congress.' The

---

13. 'New Lamps for Old' in Sri Aurobindo, *Bande Mataram*, 1972 (1997).
14. 'India and the British Parliament' in *Bande Mataram*, CWSA vol. 6, p.10.

'new chord struck by Aurobindo', wrote Majumdar, 'caused alarm in the Congress camp and he was not allowed to continue his series of articles in the same strain...'.[15]

In 1905, while in Baroda, Sri Aurobindo had written *Bhawani Mandir*, without appending his name to the pamphlet. The ideas discussed in the pamphlet were more Barindra's and laid out a plan for the 'revolutionary preparation of the country. It was smuggled out of Baroda into Bengal and other parts of India and thousands of copies made and distributed amongst the youth. The pamphlet was of great interest to the colonial intelligence since it explained "the ideas underlying the revolutionary movement..." and particularly spoke of the establishment of a sort of monastic retreat, or Ashram as it is called, for the teaching of revolutionary work.'[16]

His former student remembered the day when Sri Aurobindo's plan to shift base to Bengal had finally worked out. "One day he appeared to me in a jubilant mood", recollected R.N. Patkar, "I forthwith made bold to ask him how it was that I see him like that and without the least reservation he replied, 'Don't you know, brother, that my time for my service to the Mother has arrived! My prayer is heard, and I am leaving Baroda very soon'."[17] As one of Sri Aurobindo's most well-known biographers noted:

> For all practical purposes, he was leaving the Baroda service for good. He hardly gave a thought to the settled salary, and the seductive prospects. The Mother had called him to Bengal, he would go! Was he taking a blind leap into the Unknown? – He did not know, and he did not care, and he did

15. R.C. Majumdar, 'The Genesis of Extremism', *Studies in the Bengal Renaissance*, edited by Atul Chandra Gupta (1958), 3rd revised ed. 2002, p.165.
16. J.C.Ker, *Political Trouble in India (1907–1917)*, (1917), New Delhi: Oriental Publishers, rpt 1973, p.35.
17. Manoj Das, ibid., p.126.

not hesitate either. Here was work for him to do, here was Bhavani Bharati summoning him to action – nothing else mattered.[18]

The province of Bengal which had just undergone the first pangs of partition was in the throes of massive protests which had captured the imagination of the whole country. A build-up was visible prior to the partition of the province, 'The whole of India and more specially Bengal was surcharged with a deep feeling of humiliation and resentment at her political subjugation. She was like a store house of gunpowder and a spark was only needed to set her on fire'. Curzon supplied 'the spark to this storehouse of gunpowder'. His move to partition Bengal, 'threw the country into a great conflagration'.[19] Patriotism, noted an observer, 'which was hitherto almost limited to the arm-chair politicians began to be practical and men learned to suffer for their country'.[20] Sri Aurobindo realised that this was a supremely opportune moment to begin a movement that would 'establish and generalise the idea of independence in the mind of the Indian people, and at the same time, to push first a party and then the whole nation into an intense and organised political activity which would lead to the accomplishment of that ideal'.[21] Addressing a large audience in Madras on the partition of Bengal, Bipin Chandra Pal, dripping with sarcasm told those gathered:

> We had been given for too long a period the beautiful and charming baby-comforter to keep ourselves quiet ... But God be thanked, Lord Curzon threw the baby-comforter away, and by throwing it away made us feel the hunger that is in us, the hunger for *Swaraj*, the hunger for political autonomy, the hunger for occupying our definitely appointed place in the council of

18. K.R. Srinivasa Iyengar, op.cit., p.217.
19. Paramananda Dutt, *Memoirs of Motilal Ghose*, Calcutta: Amrita Bazar Patrika, 1935, p.155.
20. Ibid., pp.155, 156.
21. Sri Aurobindo, *On Himself*, 1989, p. 26.

nations, the hunger for entering upon our own rights in the universal life of humanity, with a view to deepen, broaden, to quicken that life by the provisions of our special culture, civilisation and ideals. This is the work that God has done, and he chose, in the mysteriousness of his Providence, Lord Curzon as the main instrument for doing his work.[22]

Curzon, Pal told his Madras audience, had 'awakened the dormant consciousness of the nation' but he had not created it. 'The consciousness was there. It lay latent, it flowed as an undercurrent, and recent movements only helped to bring the latent forces in the nation to the surface'.[23]

Protest meetings against partition were held 'in almost every village' and were not confined to Bengal. 'It soon became an all-India question and other provinces sympathised with Bengal in her trouble. The policy of the powers that be was condemned from a thousand platforms'.[24] 'Bruised by the mutilation of the Motherland' people all over India 'observed a ritual mourning' accompanied by an unusual act and vow, 'to boycott British goods, burning them in bonfires, and to use home-made products only'. Purchase of Manchester cloth was completely shunned, dealing such a 'terrible blow to the turnover that a petition of importers demanded the government to revoke the Partition of Bengal'.[25]

In Baroda, at a public meeting on September 24, 1905, to protest against the partition of Bengal, Sri Aurobindo, 'though he did not speak because he was in the Baroda service' moved a resolution in which he said, "The present wave of support for the movement is

---

22. *Speeches of Bipin Chandra Pal: Delivered at Madras*, Madras: Ganesh & Co, 1907, pp.6,7.
23. Ibid., p.7.
24. Paramananda Dutt, *Memoirs of Motilal Ghose*, op.cit., p.157.
25. Prithwindra Mukherjee, *The Intellectual Roots of India's Freedom Struggle (1893–1918)*, 2017, p.157.

very strong, and we should make comprehensive efforts to prevent the wave from receding. We must ensure that the movement is sustained."[26] 'Such was the content of the second resolution put forward by Principal Ghose in his fluent English' reported the Poona's *Kesari* on 3 October 1905.

Sri Aurobindo argued for openly using boycott as a 'political weapon'. This would be realised in the Benares session of the Congress held a few months later. From Baroda he wrote 'asking whether it would not be possible to bring in the industrialists and manufacturer ... and create an organisation in which men of industrial and commercial ability and experience and not politicians alone could direct operations and devise means of carrying out the policy'[27] of Swadeshi.

Sri Aurobindo also began drafting a proposal during the period 1905–06 to set up '*A Sample-Room for Swadeshi Articles*' at Baroda, where Swadeshi products could be displayed: '1. I propose that a permanent sample-room should be maintained by the Baroda Industrial Association in its own offices fulfilling the following purposes (1) an ocular demonstration to the public and the merchants of the number and kinds of goods they can have from their own country; (2) a standing advertisement of Swadeshi articles procurable in the local market; (3) a register of information available to all interested in the industrial development of the country ...' As mentioned, most of these were not published, maybe constrained by the terms of his services, Sri Aurobindo kept these to himself but they certainly reflect his active interest in the developments in Bengal.[28]

---

26. *CWSA* vol. 6, *Bande Mataram*, p.96, Peter Heehs, *The Bomb in Bengal*, 1993, p.77. A.B. Purani, *The Life of Sri Aurobindo*, op.cit., p.84.
27. *On Himself*, op.cit., p.31.
28. Vide *CWSA* vol.6, section: Writings and A Resolution -1893–1906, 2002.

Interestingly in September, a 'monster meeting' held in Chandernagore with 'its Mayor Leon Tardival in the Chair, passed resolutions for the vigorous conduct of the boycotting of British goods'. Surendra Nath Banerji, among others, 'delivered fiery speeches on the occasion'. A protest meeting against the Partition of Bengal was also held in distant Mandalay in early September.[29]

The Boycott 'suggestion', as historian R.C. Majumdar noted, 'spread quickly all over the country' and public meetings were 'held in all important towns and hundreds of villages, in which resolutions were passed endorsing the Boycott proposal'. Henry Nevinson describes the boycott that was spreading across the country and especially in Bengal:

> In towns and villages young men formed themselves into associations to preach Swadeshi and boycott. Shops that continued the sale of foreign goods were surrounded by youths who implored customers for the sake of their country to depart without purchasing. Boys threw themselves prostrate in supplication before the customer's feet. This form of picketing was never violent .... But in some places the boycott took the form of destroying British goods, especially "Liverpool salt"... [30]

According to official intelligence reports:

> Meetings and processions took place daily in towns and large villages. In Barisal, at one meeting, an effigy of Lord Curzon was burnt, and mock *Sradh* ceremony performed ... shouting of *Bande Mataram* was adopted as the war cry of the agitation, and the general attitude of the Bengalis towards Europeans became insolent and aggressive.[31]

For Sri Aurobindo, the 'general outburst of revolt' which followed the partition of Bengal favoured the rise of the extremist party and

---

29. R.C. Majumdar, *History of the Freedom Movement in India*, Vol.II, p.19.
30. Henry W. Nevinson, *The New Spirit in India*, 1908, pp.184, 185.
31. Ibid., pp.14,15.

the great Nationalist movement'. Sri Aurobindo turned his attention more and more towards the consolidation of this movement.

In October 1905, from a letter written to his wife, Mrinalini Devi, we gather how deeply and proactively, although secretly, Sri Aurobindo was involved in the political movement. Sri Aurobindo's Baroda friend, Khaserao Jadhav's brother Madhavrao, was 'sent to Europe to get military training, learn to prepare bombs, get arms etc'. 'I have to keep money to send to Madhavrao. He was sent to England on a special mission. I have spent a lot in the Swadeshi movement, and I have another work yet to be done which requires enormous wealth'. This 'work' was the revolutionary work. From 1902 onwards, 'Sri Aurobindo's interest had moved more and more towards politics and the service at Baroda ceased to interest him'.[32] We are also told that while in Baroda Sri Aurobindo had joined a secret group in Bombay, led by 'a noble of the Udaipur State with the title of Thakur'. The aim of this group was to organise 'Maharashtra and Mahratta States'. This 'Thakur' had, it appears, 'worked principally upon the Indian Army of which he had already won over two or three regiments'. Interestingly, 'Sri Aurobindo took a special journey into Central India to meet and speak with Indian sub-officers and men of one of these regiments'.[33]

The reactions to the partition of Bengal also hardened the line between the Moderates and those they dubbed 'Extremists', termed by Sri Aurobindo and Tilak as the 'new party' and brought to the surface their fundamental differences. Historian of the Indian nationalist movement, Leonard Gordon, describes this schism thus, "The new nationalist leaders, the Extremists, felt themselves representative of a higher stage in Indian nationalism. They

32. A.B. Purani, *Life of Sri Aurobindo*, op.cit., p.85.

33. Sri Aurobindo, *Autobiographical Notes & Other Writings of Historical Interest*, p.70.

embodied nineteenth-century cultural and religious trends which were barely evident in the views and work of the earlier Moderates." Some of them called 'for a return to ancient Indian ideals, widening the scope of nationalism to include all aspects of culture, and called for revival in art, education, literature, historical research and morality'.[34] This demand for widening the movement was led by Sri Aurobindo and the Nationalist Party in Bengal and educational regeneration formed a crucial part.

Sri Aurobindo's political programme had a public dimension to it – 'a public propaganda intended to convert the whole nation to the ideal of independence', a proposition then regarded by the vast majority as an almost 'insane chimera'. Sri Aurobindo was the first to call for 'independence', the English equivalent of *Swaraj*, and 'reiterate it constantly in the *Bande Mataram* as the one and immediate aim of national politics'. In the pages of the *Bande Mataram*, he argued that the new movement must aim 'not only at national Government responsible to the people but a free national Government unhampered even in the last degree by foreign control'.[35]

---

34. Leonard Gordon, *Bengal: The Nationalist Movement 1876–1940*, op.it., p.77,78.
35. Sri Aurobindo, *Bande Mataram*, p.92 in Sri Aurobindo's series 'The Doctrine of Passive Resistance'. These words, never uttered or put to paper before, publicly served to galvanise youth, a number of whom decided to join the ranks of the revolutionaries. See e.g. Upendra Nath Banerjee, *Nirbasiter Atmakatha*, c.1921, translated into English as 'Memoirs of a Revolutionary', (K.L. Chakravarty, Kolkata, c.1921). Upendra Nath begins his narrative of how a chance copy of the *Bande Mataram* thrown by fate into his way in the winter of 1906, drove him to join the revolutionaries, "In its leader, devoted to a speculative discussion about the political aspirations of India, the paper remarked, 'We want absolute autonomy free from British control'. Such an observation is now [1920s] heard up and down the land on everybody's lips; but in those days even the big political

This public political programme also included the creation of an organisation that would carry on sustained and united opposition to the government through 'increasing non-cooperation and passive resistance'. The secret side of the programme was the initiation of 'a secret revolutionary propaganda and organisation of which the central object was the preparation of an armed insurrection'.[36]

National Education was to be a crucial component of the open programme and it was accorded great importance and priority by Sri Aurobindo. This is evident from his own statement while discussing his political programme, where he says, as mentioned earlier, that he attached much importance to the programme of National education.

Assessing the movement, Sri Aurobindo observed that, 'the movement began well, and many schools were established in Bengal and many able men became teachers, but still the development was insufficient and the economical position of the schools, precarious'.[37] It is known that insufficient funds and the ever-growing number of schools rendered the situation challenging. Sri Aurobindo's statement reveals that he was greatly concerned with national education and was trying to give it a more concrete shape and make it relevant to the needs of the nation even after his disassociation from the National College in 1908.

---

bogeys could hardly muster courage enough to give it voice. So those few words put in blazing print made my heart jump. Such candour was a rarity in an age when the champions of National politics would never call a spade a spade. Even when these great men happened to grow thundering eloquent over questions of 'self-government', they always qualified their ideal with a prudent epithet 'Colonial'. By this, they managed to bag the game without burning their powder; for the trick left the law inviolate and at the same time commanded clapping applause from a credulous audience."

36. Ibid., p. 21.
37. Ibid., pp. 32–33.

By his own admission, Sri Aurobindo had 'decided to take up the movement' 'personally, and see whether it could not be given a greater expansion and a stronger foundation', this idea was 'cut short' due to his 'sudden departure from Bengal' in April 1910.[38] After his acquittal in the Alipore Conspiracy Case even when he 'found the whole political aspect of the country altered', Sri Aurobindo decided to continue the struggle in a determined manner and began planning again on the possibilities of reworking the nationalist programme. He decided to personally give shape to a national education scheme which he felt necessary in a drastically altered manner having observed the declining impact of the first attempt.

Probably, for no other programme during his political phase did Sri Aurobindo express his intention to 'personally' initiate action. Attributing the collapse of the movement also to the repression unleashed by the government and the general 'depression' that followed it Sri Aurobindo observed that the idea of national education 'lived on' expressing his hopes that 'it will one day find an adequate form and body'.[39] A number of aspects are compressed in the above statement; they are, first, that national education was an important agenda in the manifesto of the nationalist party founded by Lokmanya Tilak and Sri Aurobindo. Sri Aurobindo gave the credit of laying the foundation of national schools in the 'Mofussil' to the 'enthusiasm of the Nationalist party, the propaganda of its leaders and the ardent self-devotion of little bands of workers who gave their self-sacrifice and enthusiasm...'.[40] To the 'successful organisation of the Bengal National College in Calcutta', he accorded complete

38. Ibid., pp. 32.
39. Ibid., p. 32.
40. Article on National Education, in his English weekly *Karmayogin*, 1 January 1910, *CWSA* vol. 3, 1997, p. 387.

credit of the work to 'its able and enthusiastic Superintendent aided by a body of young and self-sacrificing workers'.[41]

The other aspect that emerges from Sri Aurobindo's statement is that the movement had an enthusiastic beginning and had a number of able men as teachers; this has also been authenticated by Prof. Haridas and Uma Mukherjee in their landmark work on the origins of the national education movement. The intellectual base was growing and was being organised and it saw a number of young scholars, researchers and teachers emerge and cast their lot with the fledgling national education set up. The third point that is evident is the fact that the economic base was rather weak, and Sri Aurobindo hoped to explore the possibilities of giving it a sturdier and lasting base.

The hope that national education 'will one day find an adequate form and body' gives credence to the third point which is that Sri Aurobindo retained a continuous interest in national education; he believed in the necessity of creating a truly national system of education and not a modified copy of the existing colonial system. He realised that it had not been done till then [i.e. when the statement was made in 1946] and that independent India ought to truly give it proper attention, thought and energy. National education, its need, the movement and its future were all central to Sri Aurobindo's public life and action. His contribution and participation in its quest now becomes the central focus of this work.

IV.1. RISE OF THE DEMAND: A SURVEY OF THE EDUCATIONAL SCENE

Between January 1902, when Sir Guru Das penned his note of dissent and November 1905, when the first national school was

41. Ibid. p.387.

declared open at Rangpur, East Bengal, the national education discourse began occupying an animated space among the various discussions that had been generated for greater public awakening by the nationalist thought-leaders of that era.

The colonial administration devised the educational system in India with a clear set of intentions in mind. It had studied its effects on the Indian mind, it had evaluated these effects of an education with alien content and images on the Indian psyche. Some of the most well-known representatives of colonial power and domination in India at times expressed these evaluations in public, such as strangely enough did Lord Curzon on a number of occasions.

Speaking around 1899 of the differences between 'a residential and teaching University such as Oxford and Cambridge' and 'an examining and degree-giving University' such as Calcutta, Curzon observed that the curriculum at the Calcutta University was defective and simply whetted in pupils the hunger for diploma' while sacrificing 'the formation of character upon the altar of cram' and turned the recipients into 'a sort of phonographic automaton'.[42]

Curzon's colonial disdain shone through the comparison, but it had more than a grain of truth especially if we leave aside for the moment the fact that his own administrative predecessors played not a minor role in the entire state of affairs. 'A residential and teaching University of Oxford or Cambridge' said Curzon:

> ... with its venerable buildings, its historic associations, the crowded and healthy competition of its life, its youthful friendships, its virile influence upon character, its *esprit de corps*, cannot, either in Great Britain or in any country, be fairly compared with an examining and degree University such as yours. They are alike in bearing the same name, and in constituting parts of the machinery by which in civilized countries all peoples work for the

42. *Notable Speeches of Lord Curzon,* edited by C.S. Ragunatha Rao, *1905*, p.99.

same ideal, namely, the cultivation of the higher faculties of man. But they are profoundly unlike in the influence they exert upon the pupil, and in the degree to which they affect, not so much his profession, as his character and his life.[43]

The products of a university which is a mere examining and degree university have in them a heightened hunger for diplomas and emerge as something 'better than a sort of phonographic automaton into which have been spoken the ideas and thoughts of other men'.[44] Curzon also saw such an exposure giving rise to a type which was 'half-denationalised' and had 'lost the virtues of his own system, while only assimilating the vices of another'.[45]

In his convocation address on February 17, 1900, Curzon again dwelt on the issue when he said, "We teach you in your Indian Colleges, and we examine you in the Universities upon subjects not merely conveyed to you in a foreign language, but representing foreign ideas and modes of thought. They are like an aerolite discharged into space from a distant planet, or like exotic plants imported from some antipodean clime." Thus, if the object of University education was to mould the individual into 'a finer specimen of a man' then it failed to perform that task.[46] Obviously Curzon advocated 'cautious reform and not wholesale reconstruction' of the existing system.[47] Curzon himself did little to usher in wholesale reform in the Indian education system. Doing that would have defeated the coloniser's purpose of dominating India and of exploiting her. However his

43. Ibid., pp.98, 99.
44. Ibid., p.99.
45. Uma and Haridas Mukherjee, 'Attempts at National Education (1905-1906)' in *Studies in The Bengal Renaissance,* op.cit., pp. 355-56.
46. Uma and Haridas Mukherjee, 'Attempts at National Education (1905-1906)., p. 356.
47. *Notable Speeches of Lord Curzon*, op.cit., 101.

words can be construed as an indictment of the system by Curzon, himself then Governor-General, and a few years later, to be the divider of Bengal. It was an act which suddenly galvanised into action the till then simmering forces of nationalism and gave a huge impetus to the national education movement itself.

IV.2. TECHNICALITIES OF A COLONIAL EDUCATION SYSTEM: AN OVERVIEW

A survey at this stage of the official educational scene provides an insight into the issues that Indian thought-leaders, then spearheading the gradually growing movement for educational reform, were facing and grappling with. The colonial educational structure followed a certain line of development from 1854 onwards since the formulation of the Wood's Education Despatch till 1902, when Lord Curzon set up the Indian Universities Commission. The development during this period was mainly focused on the spread of education rather than the quality. Curzon had, ever since his initial vice-regal phase in India, targeted the area of education; he appeared to want to bring about a certain qualitative change as opposed to the quantitative that was being clamoured for by the 'native' intelligentsia. He also wished to bring about a greater degree of official control over education and looked askance at most of the private attempts then being made, inspired by the national education movement.

Nearly five-odd decades before Curzon, the Wood's Education Despatch clearly saw the spread of colonial education as a means to achieve greater control. The Company's aim in 'spreading' education in India was clear, it was to confer 'upon the natives of India those vast moral and material blessings which flow from the general diffusion of useful knowledge, and which India may, under

Providence, derive from her connexion with England', the aim was to 'raise the moral character of those who partake of its advantages, and so to supply you with servants ...' Promotion of European knowledge in India will advance the material interest of England, while conferring on the natives all the advantages of commerce and wealth will 'secure to us [the British] a large and more certain supply of many articles necessary for our manufactures and extensively consumed by all classes of our population, as well as an almost inexhaustible demand for the produce of British labour'.[48] It was ironical that having destroyed Indian indigenous industries, education and commerce, the British educational aim in India spoke of imparting the advantages of commerce and wealth to Indians! The real motive was to ensure the nurturing of faithful servants and a certain supply of material goods for the prosperity of Britain.

To Macaulay, the ideologue of the fanatical proponents of 'European knowledge' in India, Indian 'medical doctrines' would 'disgrace an English farrier', her 'astronomy would move laughter in girls at an English boarding school' and her history abounded with 'kings thirty feet high and reigns thirty thousand years long, and geography made of seas of treacle and seas of butter' were to be completely cast aside.[49]

Let us revert to Curzon, in a sense a colonial descendent or successor of Macaulay and Wood. In the field of primary education, Curzon's focus was quantitative as well as qualitative and in the area of higher education his focus was a qualitative improvement rather than a quantitative one. As early as 1901, he convened a conference of chief education officers at Simla which set in motion the process of appointing the Indian Universities Commission in

48. Syed Nurullah & J.P.Naik, *History of Education in India: British Period*, 1943, pp.159,160.
49. Ibid., p.106.

1902. In conformity with his temperament of disdain for Indian educators, especially those who clamoured for Indian control of India's education, Curzon did not invite any Indian educationist to the conference. Shunned, the Indian intelligentsia read a hidden motive behind the whole exercise. One may take a look at Curzon's educational work in India during his tenure based on official documents; it will serve the purpose of having a view from the other side. It will also reveal the official educational scenario and opinion surrounding it in Bengal around the time Sri Aurobindo arrived in the province to start work, first as an educationist and then predominantly and directly as a politician, who was deeply concerned with educational issues and programmes.

The two decades from the appointment of the Indian Universities Commission to 1921, when the subject of education finally passed to Indian control – though Indian ministers even then did not have much independent say or scope of action – saw a number of administrative and infrastructural changes in the Indian educational framework. It is certain that many of these were seriously considered or implemented because of the pressure exerted by the first phase of the national education movement between 1906 and 1909.

The movement, though it was short lived, had succeeded in making national education a national issue and a part and parcel of the larger struggle for freedom. Most of the changes that were brought about were of an administrative nature and little was really done to bring about a change in the intellectual content of the curriculum, which is what the national education movement leaders including Sri Aurobindo, demanded.

By 1909 it became clear to Sri Aurobindo that mere infrastructural tinkering would not serve the long-term goal of national regeneration and development, and that is why he opposed the officialised approach and the replication of the existing university model that the national college and council resorted to later. Sri Aurobindo felt that the national council would finally morph into 'a centre of scientific and technical education; [but would] no longer be a workshop in which national spirit and energy are to be forged and shaped'.[50] Around this time, Satish Chandra Mukherjee had also delinked himself from the National College, tendering his resignation in 1908 and continuing only with the work of his magazine, *The Dawn*, till November 1913, after which it ceased to appear.[51] With Satish Chandra's disassociation, not only the principal pillar but the inspiring and organising soul of the national education movement withdrew.

The two decades, from the official point of view, were beneficial ones for educational reorganisation. Compared to the Victorian Era, this period saw much larger finances, and a more active role on the part of the government which had earlier adopted a laissez-faire attitude *vis-à-vis* education; there were 'vigorous attempts at qualitative improvement' in all 'types of educational institutions', an almost unprecedented expansion 'in almost all branches of education, also the growth of a revolutionary as well as mass national movement demanding national emancipation became

---

50. *CWSA* vol.8, p.265, the observation was made in an article that appeared in the Karmayogin issue of Saturday, 19th October, 1909 under the title '*Apostasy of the National Council.*' Sri Aurobindo criticised the Council's directives that all schools must abjure 'all connection with politics as part of the duty of a "National" school'. Sri Aurobindo called it a 'National Risley Circular' and pointed out that this completed the divorce of the national education experiment with the national movement.
51. *Origins of the National Education Movement*, op .cit., Life-Sketch of Satish Chandra Mukherjee, p. 200.

one the major factors that made the rulers sit up and take serious note of education and educational reform.[52]

---

52. J.P.Naik & Syed Nurullah, *A Student's History of Education in India-(1800–1973),* p.239, 6th revised ed. Macmillan, New Delhi, 1974. A shorter version of a larger work based on primary sources, such as government educational records, minutes etc. J.P.Naik (1907–1981), well-known educationist who worked in the area of educational research, planning and policymaking for four decades was 'the largest single influence in originating and promoting Indian educational research, in institutionalising educational innovations and reforms, and also in educational planning and policy-making'. For a brief critical analysis of Naik's life educational thought and role in the Indian educational field see e.g. A.R. Kamat's article in PROSPECTS: *the quarterly review of education,* vol. XXIV, no.1/2, 1994, page 203–16, UNESCO, International Bureau of Education, Paris. Syed Nurullah, distinguished educationist rose to become the Pro-Vice Chancellor of the Aligarh Muslim University. The authors in their *History of Modern Indian Education* have shown, and it is relevant to our discussion on colonial education, based on a number of reports and statistics that a 'fairly efficient and indigenous education system [was in operation] in many parts of [India] before and at the time of the British conquest. The authors have described its strong and weak points and have emphasised that the modern Western educational system introduced by Macaulay and Wood, instead of utilising the traditional system, simply ignored it much to the detriment of mass education. It could have been continued and strengthened by modernising its content and organisation. Some of the British rulers also belatedly realised the value of indigenous education at the time of the Education Commission of 1882. By that time, however, irreparable damage had been done and the old system was dying out' [Kamat, PROSPECTS]. This is the issue that Mahatma Gandhi repeatedly from the 1930s onwards when it came to discussing national education and Indian educational scenario under the British. The decay of the indigenous system and its replacement by a British model of education completely divorced education from life and surrounding and snapped the organic link that had hitherto

The national movement and the vigorous educational debate that it had generated saw the participation of some of the leading minds of the epoch. This generated pressure on the colonial government too.

The British Indian government, during this period, sanctioned regular central grants to education and the surpluses were allotted to the provinces for expenditure in education. 'The earliest of these grants was sanctioned by Lord Curzon and the policy was kept up by his successors'. Between 1902 and 1918–19, the grants allotted were about Rs.500 lakhs non-recurring and about Rs.300 lakhs recurring. Such large central grants were previously unknown in the history of Indian education and were greatly responsible for the expansion and improvement of educational infrastructure that was then being undertaken.[53]

The other issue which Curzon set in motion was a more active role for the State in matters of education. 'Prior to 1902, the State played a minor role in education, the doctrine of State-withdrawal from direct educational enterprise held the field, and the State did little more than pay grant-in-aid to private institutions and in return, exercise some control over them,.[54] The shift in this approach began from 1902 onwards. Under Curzon, the state-withdrawal policy was officially given up, the inspecting system was strengthened, attempts were initiated to set up model institutions and the inspection and surveys of till then largely unmonitored private institutions were also stepped up. As a result of the new policies the State began, along with playing a more active role in educational matters, to

---

existed. It is this aspect that Sri Aurobindo too emphasised, in his early educational thoughts & writings – the omission of the impact of the environment and society in the education of the individual...

53. Naik & Nurullah, op.cit., pp. 239, 240.
54. Ibid., pp. 240-41.

assert the right to '*control private enterprise' in education as tightly as possible.*[55] Among the many issues that influenced this stance was the fact that official India began to realise with trepidation, that political consciousness among the people was spreading. 'The growing political consciousness among the educated people made the British officials feel a little concerned. They had hoped that the men and women who came out of British schools and colleges' would profess a lifelong loyalty to Britain for her 'services to India. But what they now found was that the average educated man became a discontented critic of British rule'.[56] The colonial administrators began to scrutinise this aspect and felt that a greater state control over education had to be asserted. The need was felt for an increase in monitoring and controlling of private institutions, especially those under Indian control. These, many argued, were 'breeding sedition'.[57]

The desire for greater control of education, was thus, '*only partly educational but mainly political*' and the nationalist opinion vigorously opposed such a move.[58]

Between 1902 and 1905, Curzon made a number of disparaging remarks against the Indian intellectual prowess and capacity. This further inflamed nationalist passions. The essential conflict between a section of the nationalist intelligentsia and Curzon was political and it went on simultaneously on a number of fronts, education being an important one. The nationalists demanded the 'early Indianisation of the Education Department; adoption of Indian languages as media of instruction; the teaching of history from the Indian viewpoint as against that of the imperialist power;

55. Ibid., p.241.
56. Ibid.
57. Ibid.
58. Ibid.

the development of a feeling of patriotism among the students of schools and colleges'[59] etc.

The enumeration of these points miss out on the essential spirit of the demand which wanted a deeper change of the whole system and a comprehensive transformation of the whole intellectual content. But they at least point out the major political demands in education. Most of the principal thought-leaders of the national educational movement such as Satish Chandra, his young scholar-followers, Sri Aurobindo, Sister Nivedita, later Mahatma Gandhi, who articulated his thoughts on education in his *'Hind-Swaraj'* in 1909, and Rabindranath Tagore who was always radical in his approach to institutionalised education, having distanced himself from the national education experiment when he saw it getting institutionalised, spoke of a fundamental change in the education system. Not just change but a complete transmutation which ought to be based on stronger and more lasting intellectual and spiritual foundations. A mere surface cosmetic change, they felt, would not take the movement much forward nor allow it to have a lasting impact on the people's mind and on the nation's psyche.

The growth of national education was seen as a 'revolt against the intellectual domination of the West'.[60] What were the issues in education which Curzon felt needed attention and which he set up as the mandate for the Universities Commission? Some of these were: a) the feeling that the recommendations of the Indian Education Commission of 1882 were becoming less relevant in the present environment i.e. in 1902, that it was mainly concerned with quantitative improvement whereas what was needed now, according to Curzon, was qualitative improvement; b) the replacement of

---

59. Ibid., p. 247.
60. Ibid..

the policy of laissez-faire and expansion with that of control and improvement. Curzon argued that, it was this laissez-faire policy of the government which was responsible for the poor standards of most of the private institutions which had become more of 'coaching institutions for examinations than educational centres in the proper sense of the word'[61]; c) the continuance of British dominance in all superior posts of education[62]; d) the exclusion

---

61. It is interesting to note that the effects of the colonial education system as put into operation in an organised manner from 1854 onwards and which remained focused on the passing of examinations may have played a leading role in converting educational institutions to mainly coaching centres for passing examinations.
62. This was obviously reversed when Sir Asutosh Mookerjee (1864–1924) was appointed the Vice-Chancellor of Calcutta University and remained in the post till 1914. He reformed the institution from a mere examining body to a centre of teaching; within the limited framework that he functioned in, Sir Asutosh succeeded to a great extent in reforming the system and in accommodating to an extent the nationalist demands in the field of education. Making an assessment of Asutosh Mookerjee's transformation of Calcutta University, Dr Syama Prasad Mookerjee writes, 'His monumental achievement was the transformation of the Calcutta University from a merely examining body to one of the greatest teaching universities in the East, manned by and controlled mainly by Indian scholars. It was here that his broad statesmanship, his remarkable powers of organisation, his versatility, his administrative skills, his love for national culture and his courage and tact came into full play.' One of Sir Asutosh's greatest achievements in the field of education, observed Dr Mookerjee, 'was to give Bengali its due place in the University studies. The principle of adopting the mother-tongue as the medium of instruction was adopted after a prolonged discussion and controversy. Bengali was included as a subject for study and research in the highest University examinations, and the scheme for a systematic publication of important works in Bengali and other languages was taken up'. Sri Asutosh not only encouraged study and research 'in the Indian and other languages classical

of politics from schools – especially at the secondary schools and colleges which were believed to have been most affected; and e) the raising of the standard of English.[63]

On most of these, Indian opinion stood opposed to that of the Viceroy's. The Indian opinion questioned the wisdom of placing the qualitative over the quantitative arguing that while such an approach might suit England where expansion of education had already been carried out but was irrelevant to India where expansion had never been undertaken in the right manner. It also pointed out that the official attempt to 'control and improve secondary and collegiate education' was politically motivated and was going to be undertaken with the aim of trying to subvert the growth of national feelings in the mind of young Indians. The expansion proposals at the primary level was felt to be too meagre, instead they called for the speedy Indianisation of the Education Department. The Indian opinion demanded that modern Indian languages be adopted as the media of instruction and the exaggerated importance given to English be reduced and finally, that education must develop love and patriotism for the motherland and not loyalty to the British.[64]

Curzon accorded priority to educational reform and on January

and modern, in Literature, Philosophy, History, Religions, Art and Archaeology, but also in Economic, Commerce, Science...' See e.g. Syama Prasad Mookerjee, *Sir Asutosh Mookerjee: Creator of the Modern Calcutta University*, Kolkata: Sutradhar, 2021). Since Asutosh was Vice-Chancellor of the Calcutta University from the period of Sri Aurobindo's arrival in Bengal and remained so through the period when Sri Aurobindo was writing on education in the *Karmayogin*, we may assume that he read some of the articles of the journal. It would be interesting for some future scholar to undertake a comparative study of the changes that Sir Asutosh brought about in the Calcutta University system with Sri Aurobindo's educational thoughts and call for reform during that period.

63. Naik & Nurullah, op.cit. p. 248.
64. Ibid., p. 249.

27, 1902, appointed the Indian Universities Commission to 'inquire into the condition and prospects of the universities established in British India and to consider and report upon proposals of improving their constitution and working.'[65] The Commission submitted its report in the same year. But there were some inherent limitations to the mandate of the Commission. It curtailed its capacity to cover all areas of educational reform and to suggest a systemic revamping; the area of secondary education was also excluded from the purview of the Commission. It could not thus deal with the educational problems in its entirety and could not address the fundamental question of what type of university organisation was to be ultimately developed in India. It also failed to propose the kind of transitional arrangement that would be suited for this phase in order to lead the country to this 'predetermined goal in the shortest possible time'.[66]

What were some of the recommendations of the Commission: the Commission adopted the model of the London University as modified by the Act of 1898. Accordingly, it proposed that every university ought to be a teaching university, that a college should be well staffed and equipped for it to be granted full privilege, that teachers must be closely associated with the governing of the university, the supreme governing body of the university called in India, as in London, the Senate, ought not to be too large.[67] This clearly showed that the Commission examined Indian conditions against the backdrop of educational issues then being discussed and debated in London; it did not contain any discussion of the fundamental problems of the university organisation in India.[68]

The nationalist educators accused Curzon's 'unstable head'

65. Ibid., p. 250.
66. Ibid., p. 251.
67. Ibid., p. 250.
68. Ibid., p. 251.

of working to root out Indian education altogether. Referred to as an 'amusing egotist' one of whose 'idiosyncrasies is that he thinks himself to be an Educational Reformer'[69], Curzon was accused of trying to 'destroy the indigenous colleges that have grown up all over India'.[70] The 'native' intelligentsia took up the issue, severely indicting the recommendations of the Commission and blamed the Viceroy himself. The majority report of the Commission was seen merely 'as a lengthy exposition of Lord Curzon's expressed ideas and utterly subversive of the existing system of higher education in India'.[71] When the report of the Commission appeared in June 1902 along with Sir Guru Das's note of dissent, it created a stir among the Indian intelligentsia and was criticised by almost all leading Indian newspapers and journals of the day. As soon as the report of the Commission was published, 'a public meeting was held at the Town Hall in Calcutta protesting against its recommendations'. The meeting was attended by students in large numbers showing that 'young Bengal was no longer prepared to take things lying down but was trying to raise its head'.[72] Even those 'native' men of distinction who were chosen sometimes as Members of the Legislative Councils, expressed their bewilderment and agony over the recommendations. Mahendra Lal Sircar (1833–1904) 'the foremost native scientist in India and the most senior member of the Senate of the Calcutta University' for example, lamented:

> ... We are enjoying under the rule of this nation more liberty, more freedom of thought and action, than we ever enjoyed under our own. But alas, that I

69. J.C. O'Donnell, *The Failure of Lord Curzon: A Study in "Imperialism"*, 1903, p.65.
70. Ibid., p.66.
71. Ibid.
72. Paramananda Dutt, *Memoirs of Motilal Ghose*, Calcutta: Amrita Bazar Patrika, 1935, p.137.

should live to see this liberty ominously being threatened in a matter, which has been the greatest blessing under British rule! ...I cannot but observe, and it breaks my heart to do so, that the recommendations of the Commission seem to me to strike at the root of general education and to discourage the study of science.[73]

Raja Pyari Mohan Mukherjee for instance, called upon 'every well-wisher of the country to avail himself of all constitutional means to get those recommendations set aside'. Norendra Nath Sen, Editor of the influential *Indian Mirror*, commented that the 'recommendations of the Universities Commission may spell life to a few, but they mean death to countless aspirants after not only fame and fortune, but for very subsistence.'[74] Another 'most capable educationist himself the Principal of a very successful indigenous college', Surendra Nath Banerjea, condemned the crudity of the new policy in a 'very moderate language'. 'With all possible respect for these gentlemen', wrote Surendra Nath in pages of his *Bengalee:*

... We are bound to say that they proceeded as if they had a *tabula rasa* upon which they might inscribe anything they pleased. The great middle class of England are wealthy, and can afford the heavy educational expenses of the Public School and of the University. The middle class in India are poor, and for reasons, which it is needless to enquire into, are poorer now than they were fifty years ago. To transplant the English system into their midst, without reference to existing conditions and the totally different circumstances of the two countries, would be a piece of political unwisdom, which we trust the present rulers of India will permit us not to associate with their names.[75]

Satish Chandra too began a systematic attack of the Commission's recommendations in the column of the leading nationalist daily *Amrita Bazar Patrika*, and launched a detailed criticism of the 'Present System of University Education in India'.

73. J.C. O'Donnell, *The Failure of Lord Curzon.*, p.67.
74. Ibid., pp.67, 68.
75. Ibid., p.68.

Satish Chandra formulated 'a Scheme of Reform' of the system in the pages of his, by now well-established magazine, *The Dawn.* He did not just stop at mere theoretical criticism but took the initiative of establishing, in July 1902, an education society and named it the Dawn Society.

With the intent of remedying the 'defects and deficiencies of the existing system of University education, the Dawn Society aimed to be 'an institution for the cultivation of patriotic and nationalistic impulses'.[76] Writing sometime in 1904 in *The Dawn* magazine, Satish Chandra dwelt on the need for inculcating a spirit of unity which would grow from the awareness of the richness and diversity of the nation and generate an empathy towards fellow Indians. Education, Satish Chandra argued, ought to focus on imparting and inculcating these. The existing education system was incapable of doing it, and a future system, which is what the newly founded Dawn Society would ultimately aim at creating, would be capable of realising that objective. The lack of knowledge of India by Indians, lamented Satish Chandra, was a serious lacuna of the present education system:

> At the present-day, we Indians, have hardly any real or extensive knowledge about India, its people .... We know almost nothing of the actual condition of the teeming masses in the different provinces, of their social manners and customs, their languages, means of livelihood, religion, education, or general character ... and where there prevails this widespread ignorance about each other's concerns in a community it is idle to expect that there should be an effective bond of sympathy or unity, among its members. All our present unity is because of our living under a common administration, which, however, in our case is not a growth from within but a structure imposed from without. Hence this sort of force such as is likely to grow among us from a more intimate acquaintance with each other's actual wants and conditions

76. *Origins of the National Education Movement*, op.cit., pp. 14, 15.

in life.[77]

Satish Chandra also spoke of the 'spiritual foundation' of Indian nationalism and referred to the essence of true unity as opposed to a forced unity. Since Satish Chandra felt that sufficient thought was not being given to the growth of this perspective, he emphasised that the Dawn Society in its varied activities should also focus on the cultural progress of the Indian mind.

Since its inception the Society began by holding two weekly classes – the General Training Class and the Moral and Religious Training Class. Satish Chandra himself conducted the former every Sunday and he lectured on wide-ranging subjects, and 'discussions were conducted on a comparative basis, Eastern ideals and institutions being thrown in relief side by side with western ideals and institutions'. Whatever the subject of discussion, Satish Chandra always drew attention to 'man's moral values, self-sacrifice and patriotism'. The Moral and Religious Training class at the Society was conducted by one Pandit Nilkantha Goswami who explained the Gita to the youth in a simple manner giving them the essence of the deep spiritual thought contained in its verses.[78]

Between July 1902 and July 1905, the Dawn Society had attracted around 500 students; in a sense the Society prepared the initial ground for the movement of national education to gather steam around October-November 1905.[79] The inputs by the Society and its organisation were instrumental in giving the support required for the movement to gather momentum. The data and experiences of

77. Haridas Mukherjee, 'Satis Chandra Mukherjee and National Education', in *In Search of Our Nationalist Roots for a Philosophy of Education,* 2005, pp. 132–135.

78. Ibid.

79. *Origins of the National Education Movement, op.cit.* pp. 40–41.

Satish Chandra's organisation proved useful when considerations were being made to give the national education movement a mass dimension. In creating the narrative of national education Satish Chandra Mukherjee and his Dawn Society unarguably played a crucial role

The next outcome was the Indian Universities Act of 1904 which was passed on the basis of the Report of the Universities Commission of 1902. Among the changes suggested by the Act was the 'enlargement of the functions of the university', making the size of the Senate 'manageable', provisions for 'stricter conditions for the affiliation of colleges to a university', emphasis 'that all affiliated colleges should be periodically inspected by the Syndicate in order to see that a proper standard of efficiency is being maintained', the requirement of Government approval for 'affiliation and disaffiliation of colleges', and the introduction of the provision of election of Fellows etc.[80]

Indian opinion received the Universities Act 'with a violent outburst of indignation'. Among the main areas of Indian opposition to the Act were the following issues: it was believed that the provision for the University to become a teaching centre would not be implemented in right earnest, regarding the election of Fellows it was felt that the seats marked for election were too few and that the professors who were the real stakeholders of the University were kept away from participation in the election, the small number of Fellows fixed by the Act was seen to be a ploy to 'create a majority for Europeans in the constitution of Indian Universities', stricter provisions for college affiliations were also seen negatively because it was seen in the light of the argument that the government was trying to control education. All provisions of the Act that gave

80. Naik & Nurullah, op.cit. p. 253.

'more powers to the Government in the administration of the Universities'[81] was opposed, since they were seen to be the outer manifestations of an innate tendency for imperialist domination of the national mind.

What needs to be examined is Curzon's attempt to ensure Governmental control of private enterprises in education, especially in the secondary section where his Government tried to ensure that improvement took place simultaneously with the increase of greater control. The Government tried to control private educational enterprises through a number of measures. Between 1882 and 1902, the two decades in focus, the colonial Government, as per the earlier recommendations of the Indian Education Commission, followed the policy of regulating only those institutions which asked for grants-in-aid and allowed those that did not ask for financial assistance to develop freely according to their ideas. These two decades, therefore, saw some structured guidelines for aided institutions and no serious effort made to regulate the unaided ones. Though it must be mentioned that the system of revenue for education which was one of the bases on which India's indigenous education network subsisted, was decimated by the colonial administration. The policy of not regulating unaided educational institutions was altered and it was stated that all private institutions, aided or unaided, must be brought under the purview of Government control. The Government Resolution of 1904 clearly explained this policy thus:

> Whether these schools are managed by public authority or by private persons, and whether they received aid from public funds or not, the Government is bound in the interests of the community to see that the education provided in them is sound. It must, for example, satisfy itself in each case that a secondary school is actually wanted; that its financial

81. Ibid., p. 253–54.

stability is assured; that its managing body, where there is one, is properly constituted; that it teaches the proper subjects up to a proper standard; that due provision has been made for the instruction, health, recreation, and discipline of pupils; that the teachers are suitable as regards character, number, and qualifications; and that the fees to be paid will not involve such competition with any existing schools as will be unfair and injurious to the interests of education. Such are the conditions upon which alone schools should be eligible to receive grants-in-aid or to send up pupils to compete or, or receive pupils in enjoyment of, Government scholarship; and schools complying with them will be ranked as 'recognised' schools.[82]

The provisions for control, as is evident from the resolution, were rather elaborate and took into consideration almost all administrative aspects. The rider for recognition at the end ensured that most private educational enterprises veered round to acceding to governmental control and to seeking official recognition. This ensured their pupils a reasonably safe academic path and a secured future in terms of jobs which they saw the national education institutions incapable of ensuring. It was perhaps this aspect of the Act that slowed down the growth of the national education movement, limited its sweep, prevented its influence from percolating to all sections of society and finally made many of its institutions compromise and turn into stereotyped educational institutions, with no urge to bring about change or innovation in the Indian education system.

The Indian Universities Act of 1904 made all universities frame a regulation for recognition of schools which desired to present pupils for matriculation examinations under universities. These regulations 'laid down the conditions which must be fulfilled by a *recognised* secondary school' and prevented the appearing, in such examinations, of candidates from the *unrecognised* category of institutions. The benefits of recognition were enlarged so as to

82. Ibid., p. 258–59.

make the seeking of recognition appealing to private institutions. It was laid down that Departmental recognition will entitle an institution to 'receive a grant-in-aid from Government, send pupils for Government examinations including Government technical schools'. The grant-in-aid to recognised private schools was increased. Those private institutions wanting recognition would value them because of the advantages it gave in terms of grants-in-aid and for the purpose of being allowed to avail of the matriculation examination scheme.

But because there remained a large number of private institutions which were not overtly bothered about recognition or grants-in-aid and therefore did not pursue the path of seeking recognition, a devise had to be planned in order to subjugate these schools into the controlling framework. This was done 'by prohibiting automatic transfers of pupils from unrecognised to recognised schools'. The Director of Public Instruction (D.P.I.) Madras, for example, noted around 1902–07 the benefits of such a move, "The rule was quite effective for the purpose," he observed. "It closed to the pupils of the unrecognised schools, admission to a recognised school and consequently to the Matriculation and Upper Secondary Examination, and under present conditions no secondary school which does not lead to one or other of these examinations can hope to succeed."[83]

This control-seeking effort drawn up with a larger plan in mind was one of *the* most important interventions which stunted the growth of national education institutions that grew out of the larger Swadeshi movement in Bengal and elsewhere, and were affiliated to it. Under these stringent regulations, the nascent national schools which grew out of the national education movement could not respectfully survive because the terms and benefits of affiliation

83. Ibid., p. 261.

that the National Council of Education offered could never have matched those of the State. They proved thus less attractive to the majority of the populace who were seeking a secured future rather an uncertain one offered by a nationalist educational dispensation.

In the area of primary education, Curzon emphasized '*expansion* side by side with *improvement*.' Curzon felt that expansion in the area of primary education had been slow and its requirement was therefore urgent. He also identified the inadequacy of grants as the principal reason for this slow expansion and sanctioned 'large non-recurring grants to primary education' as well as recurring grants. This policy led to a large increase in primary schools and pupils. Between 1901–2 and 1911–12, the number of recognised primary schools went up from 93,604 to 1,18,262 as against 82,916, in 1881–82 and the number of pupils in the above schools increased from 30,76,671 in 1901–02 to 48,06,736, as against 20,61,541 in 1881–82; the full effects of Curzon's policies were noticeable by 1911–12.[84]

Government-recognised schools remained throughout the preferred institution for the large majority of Indians, especially during the period when the national education movement had been initiated.[85] Among the agendas of Curzon's reform for education, especially at the primary level, was the introduction of a more structured training for primary teachers, a revision of curricula which he wanted to be enriched according to the State's understanding of the needs of the pupil – the desire to include agriculture as a subject at the primary level in the rural areas, the

84. Ibid., pp. 262–63.
85. This re-schooling of the Indian society was taking place after the effective decimation of the indigenous Indian system of education had been effectuated by the colonial power. The indigenous system had a wide ambit which included pupils from all strata and class of society.

desire to see the kindergarten method become more common and the universalisation of physical education etc. It would also be interesting to see what his ideas were, on moral education and training. The issue of religious education was discussed at the Simla Conference; the tradition that State schools must remain secular was well established. The Education Commission of 1882–83 had prescribed a 'moral primer or textbook' at the college level. Curzon brushed this aside as inadequate, "If pupils can cram Euclid," he said, "there is nothing to prevent them from cramming ethics." The Conference therefore examined the question of how an education system that was secular could realise moral and spiritual values. Curzon's Resolution on Educational Policy (1904) noted:

> ... In Government institutions the instruction is, and must continue to be, exclusively secular. In such cases the remedy for the evil tendencies ... is to be sought, not so much in any formal methods of teaching conduct by means of moral textbooks or primers of personal ethics, as in the influence of carefully selected and trained teachers, the maintenance of a high standard of discipline, the institution of well-managed hostels, the proper selection of textbooks, such as biographies, which teach by example, and above all in the association of teachers and pupils in the common interests of their daily life.[86]

The indigenous model of value and moral education remained overlooked. In their efforts to supplant the indigenous education system which they considered to be undemocratic and obsolete, the colonial planners did not as much as pay causal heed to models in it on which other frameworks could be grafted.[87]

86. Ibid., pp. 264–66.
87. Joseph Bara of the Educational Records Research Unit (ERRU), Jawaharlal Nehru University, in his *Colonialism and Educational Fragmentation in India* puts up a resolute argument regarding the indigenous system of Indian education. Bara argues it was far more socially mobile and democratic than was projected or assumed to be by the colonisers. Among a number of points he makes in the

The nationalist Indian criticism of the Act of 1904 was stringent and continued to gather momentum which would finally culminate in the formation of the National Council of Education and the founding of the National College. The regular critics were the journals and newspapers representing nationalist opinions. Annie Besant, in an article published in *The Dawn* in January 1906, asked Indians to take the 'question of education into their hands'. She felt that this had become necessary 'in consequence of the late University Act' which was likely to render higher education 'very,

---

essay, is the one on the pre-colonial Indian education-system not being devoid of value-based morals. He quotes F. Keay's 'A History of Education in India and Pakistan' to support his argument that value-based morals were 'nurtured and practiced by the general literate population mainly in the family, and passed on from generation to generation.' He also points out that M. Elphinstone (1779–1859, Scottish statesman and historian, later Governor of Bombay, associated actively with administration in India, especially the educational aspect) favoured the rehabilitation of those morals and values which he found prevalent in the then Indian society, he felt that nothing extraneous could or ought to be done to improve the morals of the people 'except by improving their education ... there exist in the Hindu languages many tales and fables that would be generally read and that would circulate sound morals. There must be religious books tending more directly to the same end. If many of these were printed and distributed cheaply or gratuitously, the effect would without doubt be great and beneficial ....' [Source: *The Contested Terrain-Perspectives on Education in India*, op.cit.] Elphinstone may have been assailed by the educated upper-class Indian intelligentsia, including a section of his own countrymen, for taking recourse to obscurantism but it does show that this aspect of the indigenous system existed and, if developed or modified to suit the age, could have been an adequate vehicle, at least for a while, for the imparting of moral-value education. A similar case was built up much later by Nivedita and Coomaraswamy who pointed out the educational and integrative uses of the Indian epics.

very costly' and would thus exclude from its purview 'the very class that demands it most urgently' and would 'shut the doors of the University to many brilliant students in India who would do their country very good services'.[88]

It was the iconic Motilal Ghose (1847–1922), founder-editor of the *Amrita Bazar Patrika*, a nationalist associate of Sri Aurobindo, 'one of the guiding spirits of the agitation against the Partition of Bengal'[89] who voiced the overall nationalist Indian opinion towards this Act. Ghose's *Amrita Bazar Patrika* carried a series of articles which criticised Curzon's attempt to control Indian education. In an analysis in the *Amrita Bazar Patrika*, Ghose observed that first of all the whole Act was based on the realisation that the growth of education led to the growth of political consciousness and therefore the educational system itself had to be revamped. The Act, Ghose argued 'was designed to check unofficial control of education. [But] It led, on the contrary, to the officialisation of the whole educational machinery' and the drastic reduction of the native influences. The other point that Ghose made was that the educational policy enumerated by the Act, 'was not intended to give to the young students any useful or solid knowledge, whether scientific, technical or literary'. "Even before 1904," complained Ghose, "the textbooks taught in the schools had been too numerous for the young students, but their numbers had been [now] practically increased ... by doing away with a specified course for the Entrance Examination so far as English was concerned. The pass mark in English under the new Act was raised from 33 per cent to 37 per cent." This heightening of standards, Ghose observed, was meant to act as 'a brake upon high percentage of passes and to arrest the rapid expansion of higher education.' According to him, when the

88. *Origins of the National Education Movement*, op.cit. pp. 15, 16.
89. Paramananda Dutt, *Memoirs of Motilal Ghose*, op.cit., p.160.

pass mark was 33 percent, 50 percent of the appearing candidates faced elimination, but now that it was raised to 37, he was certain that about 80 or 90 percent would face the same fate. He feared that in the higher examinations, the rates of failures also would be correspondingly higher. The portals of higher education thus was to be effectively closed to Indian aspirations, the number of those failing in the entrance examinations would annually increase and 'our country will be filled with tens of thousands of half-educated men belonging to respectable classes, who will either be useless or dangerous members of the society'.[90]

This is how the educational scenario unfolded during the Curzonian period in India. The momentous partition of Bengal was to follow a year later and would further galvanise the nationalist sentiments and give lead to a movement which would have education as one of its cornerstones. It would inspire the founding of the first national school in 1905, the National College in 1906, and would finally bring Sri Aurobindo to the province to give shape to a number of nationalist policies and programmes that were to be implemented in the course of the country's struggle for freedom.

IV.3. THE AGENDA OF NATIONAL EDUCATION: THE POLITICAL FILLIP TO AN INTELLECTUAL DEMAND

Sri Aurobindo came to Bengal in 1906 having made the decision of relinquishing his post at the Baroda State Service. He came to observe the development of political movements and programmes that had been initiated, post the partition of Bengal in 1905.

The major developments on the national education front that had taken place prior to Sri Aurobindo's arrival in Bengal are worth noting because each of them pushed the movement further towards

90. *Origins of the National Education Movement*, op.cit., pp. 16, 17.

greater strength. The Swadeshi movement was gaining momentum and the 'students proved to be the chief props and pillars of the *Swadeshi* and Boycott movement from the beginning.' Many of them prompted by the leaders took part and gave lead to many of the movements of the Swadeshi period.[91] The students community, in fact, 'learned to impose upon themselves self-denying ordinances, such as fasting or going about barefoot on special days, attending political meetings, joining processions and singing national and patriotic songs in the public streets and meeting places in violation of official orders.' The more they were persecuted, the more 'it whetted their appetite for freedom.'[92]

The young scholars who had gathered around Satish Chandra Mukherjee also resolved to boycott the M.A. examinations of the Government controlled Calcutta University and they gave a lead to the agitation for boycotting the 'officialised University'.[93] The Government took serious note of these developments and realized that the leaders' principal intention was to get the students actively on their side in this movement against partition. Large numbers of students both in the city of Calcutta and in the *moffussil* took the oath of Swadeshi and Boycott. The students' active participation in the movement helped to broad-base the twin concepts of Swadeshi and Boycott.

The Government decided to weaken this support through the Carlyle Circular – a circular issued over the signature of the Officiating Chief Secretary to the Government of Bengal, R.W. Carlyle. The Circular which first appeared on October 22, 1905 in the Statesman, warned that students involving themselves in political agitation and activity in institutions 'assisted or countenanced by

91. R.C. Majumdar, *History of the Freedom Movement* Vol.-II, 1997, p. 60.
92. Paramananda Dutt, *Memoirs of Motilal Ghose,* op.cit., p.156.
93. *Origins of the National Education Movement*, op.cit., p. 19.

the Government' shall face disciplinary action and the schools and colleges 'concerned will forfeit their grants-in-aid and the privilege of competing for scholarship holders, and the University will be asked to disaffiliate' these institutions. It also directed authorities who were unable to sanitise their respective institutions they were to immediately submit a report to the District Magistrate attaching a list of the disruptive boys. The district superintendents of police were directed to instruct their local police stations to report any misconduct of boys in the nature of political agitation or participation.[94] The nationalist opinion burst out on this issue. It saw this as a first step at strangulating the movement, curbing the basic freedom of students and in trying to take control by force, and through intimidation, of young minds which had begun questioning publicly the status quo of colonial rule in India.

This gave a fillip to the political movement and the demand for establishing an independent system of education began to be voiced in numerous public meetings that were regularly convened to condemn the circular. On October 24, 1905, a large public meeting was held in Calcutta where a number of Sri Aurobindo's political associates such as Bipin Chandra Pal and Shyam Sundar Chakravarty (1869–1932) among others, addressed the gathering and demanded the repealing of the offensive circular and the initiation of a movement that would start a national education system. Hemendra Prasad Ghose (1876–1962), another political associate of Sri Aurobindo, who would later assist him on the *Bande Mataram* editorial board pleaded, in a letter addressed to an English daily, that the teaching of boys must be undertaken without government help and that serious consideration ought to be given to the founding of a national University. This was followed by the now famous 'general

94. Ibid., pp. 22–24.

meeting' to protest the issuance of the circular on 27th October, with Tagore in the Chair and attended by a galaxy of nationalist leaders, among them Satish Chandra Mukherjee and Krishna Kumar Mitra (1852–1936), Sri Aurobindo's maternal uncle, and a leading nationalist of his era, whose journal *Sanjibani* was one of the most popular voices of nationalism and of the downtrodden. Also present were Bipin Chandra Pal and Monoranjan Guhathakurta (1858–1919), a close political co-worker of Sri Aurobindo and proprietor of the Bengali nationalist newspaper *Navasakti*, which Sri Aurobindo planned to revive just before his arrest in 1908. Manoranjan was one of the financiers of the revolutionary party whose son bore the brunt of police brutality during the break-up of the Barisal Provincial Conference in April 1906.

A number of Sri Aurobindo's political associates were part of the national education demand since its inception. Sri Aurobindo was *au courant* with the educational issues then being discussed and debated in the province though he did not a play an active role in their propagation as yet. The general meeting was followed by the first open act of educational defiance when, in protest against a circular which prohibited the students of the Rangpur Zilla School [East Bengal] to participate in 'boycotting, picketing' and under whose provision the defiant students were fined and expelled, the students of the Zilla school and their sympathisers decided to act independently and boycotted the school.

In Calcutta meanwhile, opinion was being mobilised to extend moral support to the struggling students of Rangpur. A students' meeting attended by Satish Chandra, Manoranjan Guhathakurta, Hemendra Prasad Ghose and others resolved to form the Anti-Circular Society. Sachindra Prasad Basu, a 4th year student of the City College, moved the resolution for the establishment of the

Society which would have Krishna Kumar Mitra as treasurer and his son Sukumar Mitra (1885–1973), who acted as Sri Aurobindo's messenger during the nationalist phase, and was among those who would later organise his ship journey to Pondicherry, was to be its assistant secretary. Sachindra Prasad along with other student co-workers rushed to Rangpur and on November 7, 1905, the people of Rangpur, led by eminent citizens, convened a public conference which decided to organise the education of the Rangpur students and to start a national institution on national lines to impart education. As a result, the Rangpur National School was started on November 8, 1905, the first national school to begin functioning openly.[95] The first milestone in the political demand for educational reform had been achieved.

A review of these major historical events which lent weight to the demand for a national education system is relevant to understand the link between national education and Sri Aurobindo's championing of the issue as a political programme in his overall scheme of nationalist action. It is evident from Sri Aurobindo's writings on education that he did not merely see it as a political programme that would add weight to political demands but as an important area that schemes of national reconstruction would have to take into account and work out.

That Sri Aurobindo was keenly observing and formulating his stands and thoughts on political issues in Bengal is clear from a number of articles written by him, most of them incomplete and unpublished, on the political issues of the day, that have come to light. A look at these writings from 1904 to 1906, though they do not contain any direct reference to the educational demand, show that Sri Aurobindo was indeed closely observing events in Bengal during

95. *Origins of the National Education Movement*, pp. 24–29.

the time of the partition.[96] It was during this period that the national education movement also gained momentum.

At first, Sri Aurobindo did not play a direct role in initiating the demand for national education; his service under the Baroda State made him an observer and an occasional participant in Bengal politics and prevented him from active and open action. As mentioned earlier, initiating Jatindranath Banerji and directing his brother and fellow revolutionary Barindra Kumar Ghose to set up a revolutionary group in Bengal and visiting the province periodically to assess the progress of his programmes was all that Sri Aurobindo could do for a while. His observations and study at Baroda enabled him to plan and prepare possible courses of action to be made applicable in future to the political movement in other provinces. His espousal later of a philosophy of national education and his talks and writings on the issue indicate that he intended to give an entirely different turn to the educational discourse in the country and had realised that unless a movement for a thorough change of the educational system was initiated no meaningful and lasting impact of education would be felt. However, his preoccupation with politics, his incarceration, his almost single-handed effort at reviving nationalist politics post his acquittal in the Alipore Bomb case in 1909, and his eventual departure for Pondicherry left him with little time to focus on creating such a movement. It was left to others – such as Mahatma Gandhi and Rabindranath Tagore – to

96. The series, entitled 'Unity', started off with an 'open letter to those who despair of their country'. Another article, written 'during the early stage of the agitation against the partition of Bengal' around 1904, dwelt on 'The Proposed Reconstruction of Bengal – Partition or Annihilation?' Sri Aurobindo argued that [Curzon was] 'a vain man, loving praise and sensitive to dislike and censure ... [and that] he [was] a statesman of unusual genius who is following a subtle and daring policy in which immense issues hang ...'

keep the educational problem and the demand for a new system highlighted throughout the struggle for freedom. In being one of the most articulate voices on national education during the Swadeshi period and early nationalist phase, Sri Aurobindo contributed in laying the foundations of the national education discourse. His interventions gave a major fillip to the movement itself and to the creation of its narrative.

IV.4. DEBATE OF IDEAS – ANALYSING INDIAN EDUCATION: BIPIN CHANDRA PAL AND SATISH CHANDRA MUKHERJEE

Satish Chandra Mukherjee and Bipin Chandra Pal, both Sri Aurobindo's contemporaries in Bengal, remained largely neglected figures in the nationalist educational discourse and historiography. Sri Aurobindo worked briefly, but closely, with both. The inclusion of some key aspects of their educational thoughts will enrich the content of our discussion and enable us to develop an idea of the prevailing approaches to education in Bengal just before Sri Aurobindo's sojourn in that province.

As we have seen, the demand for a review of the existing system of colonial education and suggestions for reforms in it had already begun to be voiced before Sri Aurobindo came to Bengal to actively participate in politics.

One of the most effective, systematic, erudite and discerning voices in support of this demand was that of Satish Chandra Mukherjee's. It would be relevant, therefore, to focus in some measure, on Satish Chandra's educational thought of this period. No discussion on the nationalist educational demand can be complete without adequately taking into account Satish Chandra's role in underscoring and accentuating that demand.

A reading of some of Satish Chandra's writings on education reveals that he had begun early to study the system and diagnosing the ills affecting it. Early on, Satish Chandra ensured that his journal became a forum for freely and extensively discussing new thoughts on education, attacking cogently the existing system and suggesting reforms in it. His *Catuspathi* days in the 1890s were characterised by the attempt at reviving the dynamic and defining aspects of the Hindu education system. His belief that there existed perennial principles in the classical Hindu educational discourse that could be successfully implemented in the educational system of his time to make it truly suited to the Indian character, temperament and requirements, and make it intelligible to the vast majority, drove him into becoming active on that front.

In fact, this belief had influenced Satish Chandra to start a parallel and alternative educational institution It was perhaps the first of its kind which experimented with an alternative model. Tagore was to start his educational experiments a few years later. The early issues of *The Dawn* magazine mostly contained articles on Indian philosophy and scriptures; it reflected Satish Chandra's quest of trying to reinterpret a number of ancient concepts in modern light. Satish Chandra strove to integrate classical Indian educational concepts and aspects of indigenous educational structures to the educational scenario and the demand of his times.

Satish Chandra firmly believed that the dimensions of classical Indian education-thought needed to be reintegrated under present conditions. As early as 1898, we see him comparing the **'Principles of University Education in the East and the West'**. The Hindu and the Western ideal of education, he argued, seemed 'to differ as poles asunder'. While the Hindu ideal insisted on the development of the intellect 'as a means to an end, the end being the development of the higher, spiritual nature of man' in the West even though education is a means to an end, the end there is 'greater worldly comfort, greater worldly prospects, acquisition of wealth and power'.[97] Satish Chandra spoke of this as the fundamental difference between the two. The ancient sages of India made 'all-conduct part of an all-comprehensive scheme of education' this was the 'spiritual discipline known as Karma-yoga (work-discipline)'. In support of his point, Satish Chandra cited from Dr. Bhandarkar's[98] convocation address as Vice-Chancellor of Bombay University, which succinctly defined the complete goal of education in the ancient Indian context. Bhandarkar referred to a saying of the ancient Indian sage Patanjali, that 'a man who does not store up wealth [who retains only so much as can be contained in a jar], who is not greedy, and who disinterestedly and without any further object acquires proficiency in some branch of learning', and spoke of the key concept of education in the classical Indian tradition thus, '*The idea, therefore, is that he that devotes himself to the pursuit of knowledge or truth for its own sake and disdains mere worldly prosperity is a man of education and culture*'.[99]

Satish Chandra agreed with this formulation and insisted, in his article, on reviving the core ideals of ancient Indian education. His

97. 'Principles of University Education in the East and the West', in *The Dawn*, September, 1898, vol.2, op.cit., p. 214.
98. Ramakrishna Gopal Bhandarkar (R.G.Bhandarkar) (1837–1925) Orientalist, scholar, social reformer. Was Professor of Sanskrit at the Deccan College, Poona and appointed Vice-Chancellor of Bombay University in 1893. He made pioneering contributions to the study of Sanskrit and Indian antiquities, his elementary books of Sanskrit were in wide use, his lectures on philology and books on the history of the Deccan were widely read and remained authoritative sources for a long time. Recipient of a number of awards, Bhandarkar sent a paper to the International Congress of Orientalists in London in 1876 and attended the Vienna session in 1886, where he made valuable contributions. [Source: S.P. Sen ed., *Dictionary of National Biography, Vol.1*, 1972.]
99. *The Dawn*, September, 1898, op. cit., p. 214, italics in the original.

article is important because it not only tried to discuss the positive aspects of an indigenous Indian system of education but also made a brief survey of existing University systems in Europe and of their key objectives. Satish Chandra's article also reproduced a long passage from Michael Foster's[100] address at the John Hopkins University, where Foster discussed some ideas and methods followed at the Cambridge University. By pointing at this lecture, Satish Chandra wanted to indicate deficiencies that were inherent to the Indian universities system.

Talking of training the mind, Satish Chandra observed that 'all mental discipline subordinates itself to requirements of the age', which for this age was a race 'for greater worldly enjoyment, greater worldly power'. He argued that though the development of the dimension of aesthetics of life – the development of the ability to appreciate expressions of beauty in art – is a legitimate objective in 'all higher education', it seemed to be hardly an important objective with 'most men in the West'. And where this appreciation is present, there is also present an element of 'a suspicion', a questioning on whether the development of this appreciation leads one to true enjoyment as compared to the enjoyment felt by 'those whose thoughts are so earth-bound, so prosaic...' [101]

Indian universities, Satish Chandra castigated, are 'copies of copies' because English universities were in themselves bad copies and therefore Universities in India suffered a 'double taint' – first, because they were 'bad imitations' and second, because the originals themselves required reorientation and further perfection

100. Sir Michael Foster (1836–1907) British physiologist, who played a key role in the development of the Cambridge biological school. Foster also represented the University of London in Parliament.

101. *The Dawn*, September, 1898, op. cit., pp. 214–15.

before they would be capable of absorbing the 'true functions of education', which was the aim of developing '*not* a lordly animal with a thousand *wants* (which must always be distinguished from *activities*) and tossed at every turn by the angry gusts of passion, but the evolution of a higher nature in man which lifts him up to the level of a god.'[102] Since Indian universities did not even remotely profess such an objective that was inspired by India's own cultural tradition and educational heritage, Satish Chandra felt the absence of a sound intellectual and philosophical base in the system of education in India and saw its adverse impact on the Indian mind accelerating.

Comparing Universities of Germany and of England, Satish Chandra pointed out that German universities were far 'ahead of their other continental rivals', the reasons being that these produced 'greater original work' had 'greater freedom of teaching, greater freedom of learning, a wider keener, fresher intellectual atmosphere' compared to English universities.[103] He traced the similarities of the German system with the indigenous Indian education system of *tols*

102. Ibid., p. 215.

103. English universities in India and the colleges under their affiliations during this period, and even later to a great extent, were examining bodies and coaching centres and the principal complaint against these bodies by Indian education reformers was that they did not encourage sufficient initiative, new research and originality. Satish Chandra himself was to write later [starting from April, 1902 in *The Dawn*] a detailed exposition on what ailed the university system in India and would suggest possible reforms. We have not tried and attempted to get other views on systems of universities in the West — supporting or contrary – because our intention here is to simply read Satish Chandra's analysis of the educational problem, nevertheless it is to be observed that in *The Dawn*, as well as in other journals of the period, regular articles did appear comparing the western universities and their poor replicas in India.

or *catuspathies*. Original work, rather than results in a competitive examination, received appreciation and paved the way to 'a higher social position' under this system. According to him, original work in such a system was possible because the learner was placed under the influence of teachers who 'devoted their lives to the cause of education' and lived ascetic lives dedicated whole-heartedly to the 'cause of higher individual and collective life.'

Satish Chandra also spoke of another fundamental difference between the ideal of ancient Hindu education and Western education. The teacher – *Acarya,* in the Indian context – symbolised the spirit of self-sacrifice; he did not charge the students for the knowledge he imparted and instead bore the expense of their education 'out of his own pocket'. It was this ideal of disinterestedness, of self-sacrifice and dedication to a cause that attracted learners to the *Acarya*, and they in turn lived under the tutelage of the master, willingly submitted to the system that he drew up for them, and served him one-pointedly.[104]

The whole of life itself, with all its activities included, was part of the process of learning. The householder, *grhasta*, aware of the sacrifice and dedication of the *Acarya*, supported him in his mission by ensuring that 'his home was always full of the necessaries of life which were always left at the throng of pupils by whom he was surrounded even as a father by his dutiful children'. Satish Chandra referred to the existence of an organic link between the community and the system of schooling. The system of education did not function in isolation from the community but was sustained by it.[105] It was this organic link which made the education imparted,

104. *The Dawn*, September, 1898 op. cit., p. 215.

105. Educational records of the colonial administration prove that the community sustained the pre-British indigenous system of education in India. [See. *Political Agenda of Education*, op. cit.,] The teacher under

this system had the liberty to formulate his own teaching material and the space to implement it according to local needs and conditions. The system of instruction in basic skills was widely prevalent in India before the 'colonial control of the economy was established'. Teachers were revered. William Adam's schools survey of Bengal in 1835 revealed that the 'teacher exercised autonomy in choosing what was worth teaching and in deciding how to teach it'. The curriculum usually comprised of an 'acquaintance with culturally significance texts, and the learning of skills' that were perceived to be useful to the village society. [Krishna Kumar, Origins of the Textbook Culture in *What is Worth Teaching*, 3rd ed., 2004, p. 27.] The organic link and teacher's autonomy were two crucial aspects that made education then relevant and meaningful. It may be concluded that Satish Chandra was not off the mark when he described the indigenous Indian education system being supported by the community and encouraging original work because of teachers who had the freedom to function and who had dedicated their life to the cause of education. Dharampal who based his study of pre-British indigenous education in India on primary archival sources observes in his pioneering work (cited above) *The Beautiful Tree: Indigenous Indian Education in the Eighteenth Century*, that education in the traditional institutions of the *pathshalas, madrassahs, gurukulas* 'were kept alive by revenue contributions by the community including illiterate peasants' and was termed as *shiksha*, and included the ideas of *prajna, shil* and *samadhi*. He referred to these institutions as 'watering holes of the culture of traditional communities' and argued that the term 'school' for these institutions do not really convey the role that they actually played in Indian society. [Dharampal, op. cit., pp. 17, 18.] Discussing the fiscal arrangement that could make such a widespread network of schools possible in the pre-British period, Dharampal points to the existence of a 'sophisticated operative fiscal arrangement of the pre-British Indian polity'. This fiscal arrangement, he argued, had for long assigned a substantial portion of the revenue for a variety of public works. According to him the arrangement 'seems to have stayed more or less intact through all the previous political turmoils' and thus made sustenance and functioning of such an educational network possible. It was the colonial system's introduction of a centralisation of revenue and politics that led to the eventual collapse of such an

meaningful to the learners. Speaking on 'Women in India' in California on January 18, 1900, for instance, Swami Vivekananda spoke of 'revenue from land, in Hindu traditional system, being used to maintain a physician, a village school master'.[106] The existence of such a system has been discussed with supporting historical evidences in earlier sections.

Discussing briefly the education system in France, Satish Chandra observed that the 'higher University education' in that country suffers because of its being clubbed with 'professional or civil service training or equipment.' He divided French educational institutions in two sectors, one, the *Academies*, which 'fulfils the functions of a true university', that is, encourages original research and innovative teaching, and the other the 'so-called Universities' that are in reality Government institutions, 'that prepare and test candidates' in order to fill various administrative departments and posts.[107]

On the other hand Indian Universities, Satish Chandra observed, had been successfully fulfilling the 'functions of Government Institutions' by preparing candidates for Government service and 'facilitating the work of the administration of the country'.[108] But such a stage, Satish Chandra argued, was reaching its end and it was

arrangement and the subsequent decay in the socio-economic life and in the education system of the country. [Dharampal, op. cit., p. 21] This perception, based on primary records, again supports Satish Chandra's position that Indian education was supported by the community. It is interesting to note here that basing himself on primary documents and records, Dharampal demonstrated the existence in India in the 1800s, of a wide-spread, well-established indigenous public schooling system, and the absence of such a system in British society of that period.

106. *CWSV. vol.*8, p.68.
107. *The Dawn*, September, 1898 op. cit., p. 216.
108. Ibid.

becoming imperative for Universities themselves to realise the need for a reorientation, and the need to prepare themselves to play their true roles.

Having established a 'line of demarcation between the Western and Eastern methods of education', Satish Chandra highlighted the peculiarities of University education at Cambridge by referring to Michael Foster's passage which discussed Cambridge University, life of the past and the present. In showcasing this passage, Satish Chandra probably tried to elucidate features that made a university the centre of learning and life – features which he felt the Indian version of the British system sorely lacked. He wanted to tell the colonial educationists that they did not practice in India what they preached back home. The recognition of the training in the University as 'a preparation for practical life' was one of the features that struck Foster most, both among students and teachers. The dominant occupations of the early social period in England influenced the founding of three faculties – the faculties of theology, law and medicine. And the conviction that 'teaching should be an earnest preparation for practical life' was firmly held by the teachers. The lack of such a perception in the colonial set-up in India was what Satish Chandra tried to put forth by quoting this part.[109]

The other striking features of the University, as Foster observed, was the realisation that 'the work of the University consisted not in the mere acquisition of knowledge, but in the training of the mind.' The objective was to train the pupil's mind in thinking and 'in

---

109. *The Dawn*, September, 1898 op. cit., p. 217. The Historical Register of the University of Oxford 1220–1888, Oxford, 1888 also indicates that Civil Law, Medicine, Divinity were among the first professorships to be created in 1546 [Source: Dharampal, op. cit., p. 11, a chronological list of professorships created from 1546 onwards at Oxford University]

arriving at conclusions'. Even the concept of examination then had a different connotation, the concept of a written examination and use of paper was absent. The present system assigns two examiners for hundred students; the earlier system assigned nine to each student. The examiners had, what could be termed as discussions rounds with students, they 'went in with him and out with him until they satisfied themselves that he knew something, and had gathered something from what had been told to him'. The final test consisted of putting the student on the 'stool', that is to make him debate in public and to draw out his 'stock of knowledge', especially to assess his ability to use it and to demonstrate 'that his mind had been trained' simultaneously with his exercise of gathering 'a certain number of facts'.[110]

Satish Chandra's reason for referring to this analysis becomes evident in his next arguments. The present universities in India, he pointed out, were exhausting themselves in solely preparing students for examinations, examinations which mostly consisted in testing pieces of information that had been loaded onto the learner's mind – just for the sake of success – through the instrument of memory and not genuine understanding.

Another feature that was present in the old system according to Foster and as cited by Satish Chandra, was the 'spirit of inquiry'; 'a spirit of free inquiry' prevailed even though the knowledge available was limited. The 'long-drawn-out discussions' that the scholars indulged in were an 'expression of their love of inquiry'. Nationalist educators complained that this spirit of inquiry was not encouraged by the colonial official Indian education mechanism. In a number of his later analyses of the colonial Indian education system, Satish Chandra would repeatedly emphasise this issue. The final 'striking'

110. *The Dawn*, September 1898, op. cit., p. 218.

feature that Foster enumerated was that of the university being 'an open home for all those who wished for learning', anyone who displayed a 'promise of benefiting for the instruction given' there was welcomed and nurtured.[111] Merely an interest in learning was sufficient for enrolment.

Thus the features that were at the foundation of the university system in England – the recognition that education must be an earnest preparation for practical life, that the work of the universities was not mere information gathering but the training of the pupil's mind, so that it could analyse and arrive at conclusions, the concept of examination being based on debates and discussion, the encouraging and nurturing of a spirit of free inquiry and the acceptance of all those who evinced a wish for learning – were conspicuously absent or intentionally discouraged in the colonial version of that education.

Perhaps George Birdwood's encouraging letter of this period – the one cited earlier – convinced Satish Chandra of the relevance and immediacy of the position he had taken, '... you will never assimilate and receive real nourishment from any alien culture imposed on you under the compulsion of the drill-sergeant's cane', Birdwood had written to Satish Chandra in his letter of September 9, 1898. He encouraged a reverting to the study of classical Sanskrit, Greek and Latin 'as essential items in every college curriculum' and interestingly suggested the leaving of English literature 'for private reading'.[112]

Satish Chandra provided space to the contents of Birdwood's letter in his magazine and kept alive the issues in an exchange through January and February 1900. In an article entitled 'Sir George Birdwood on the Need for Higher Sanskrit and Vernacular

111. Ibid.

112. *The Dawn*, June, 1899, op. cit., pp. 326–28.

Education in India'[113] Satish Chandra summarises the contents of Birdwood's letter citing passages where the latter urged India not to surrender her extant 'literary and artistic and philosophical and religious' – in a word her 'spiritual culture', and instead to strengthen it and 'extend its influence'. In his letter, Birdwood argued that India would necessarily be exposed to modifying influences of the West which may prove to be of 'real' and 'lasting good' to her but that these influences could not be imposed upon her unilaterally as was being done through the 'Government schools and the not less official Indian Universities'. One point that touched Satish Chandra in Birdwood's arguments, was his exhortation for maintaining India's personality, because 'it was representative of a unique highly developed type of civilisation that can still command the admiration of the world' and for maintaining of the 'historical personality of the Hindus'. These were important criteria. Birdwood felt that these could be done through the revival of 'classical Sanskrit and literature of the literary *Prakrts*, such as Mahratti and Tamil as essential items in every college curriculum in India'.[114] But he also believed that Sanskrit being a dead language kept alive only through dialects that owe their origin to the language, could not effectively work towards this preservation. The 'still living arts' of India instead, could become a 'far more efficacious rallying centre for the revival of the indigenous and traditional culture of the Hindus' and thus work towards preserving the Indian personality.

The aim therefore of the whole effort must be, as Satish Chandra summarised it, for modern India to:

> Fix its eyes more especially on all that is *living* of its ancient past, all that having proceeded from the pure spring of ancient culture, still preserves its

---

113. *The Dawn*, January, 1900, p. 167.

114. Ibid., p. 168.

indigenous character and stamps on the present Hindu race as a distinctive personality of a strictly beneficent type.[115]

This remark summarises the whole effort and aim of Satish Chandra's early educational endeavour.

Satish Chandra's letter in answer to Birdwood's, indicated his thinking on the 'educational problem in India' then. It will be relevant to cite certain passages from his reply. Satish Chandra agreed with Birdwood's expressions of delight at 'every symptom of the spontaneous revival of the indigenous and traditionary, literary and artistic and philosophical and religious life of India – India of the Hindus' and felt an equality of sentiments on this count. But he noted that 'our schools and colleges, *such as they are and have been*, are getting to be a growing hindrance'[116] to this act of spontaneous revival. He provided an interesting insight – it seemed to him that these existing institutions have 'outlived their initial stage of usefulness'; and that if they were to be of help in the 'future evolution' of the country, 'they would have to be remodeled on, or informed by a principle, the keynote of which would be a greater help by the people themselves along lines suited to a natural, peaceful, indigenous growth,' and also aided largely by 'responsible men in authority'.[117]

These seem to be some of the keynotes of Satish Chandra's views and indicated his future educational action. To Satish Chandra, the contentious issues and ones that really created an imbalance, was the fact that Indian schools and colleges were under the control of government officials who with the 'best of motives' desired to stamp the influence of a culture with which they were familiar 'at a high speed' upon the Indian mind and way of life. That process, Satish Chandra argued, was not evolutionary; it was 'not a growth from

115. Ibid., p. 169.
116. Ibid., pp. 169–70.
117. Ibid., p. 170.

within ourselves' but rather a unilateral imposition from without. He suggests therefore a line of reform that must be initiated for a permanent improvement of this structure and for a good that would be 'stable' 'enduring' and 'lasting'.[118]

The other impediment towards developing an indigenous system of education was the fact that Indian universities were being 'more and more governed' by a section of countrymen who were themselves products of this enforced culturisation and were unable to envisage anything different. When a 'more progressive road' was to be taken, and a 'larger foresight' was required, such countrymen, Satish Chandra saw were incapable of taking this initiative. In the present system, Satish Chandra saw 'little of life either in the teachers, or the students, or the University Fellow' due largely to this enforcement of culture. Everything moved because of a certain momentum, there was life, but it was a life which could not 'work out its salvation' because the 'culture has been imposed' and the activity it generated thus was an 'artificial, delusive' one which must eventually disappear.[119]

This enforcement of culture created an artificial life and representative activity and produced men who were incapable of undertaking any original experiment for the progress of the race. Satish Chandra was careful to point out that he does not 'deprecate high English Education' but he advocated its infusion with a 'higher informing spirit', that could only come about by pursuing the comparative method and by the growth of 'a critical spirit'. The method to be pursed was to take 'nothing of English life or civilisation' on trust, the spirit of approach to these would have to be of 'truthfulness and fairness' and would have to be understood and 'appreciated in constant reference to the civilisation and culture of India's past', which Satish Chandra saw to be still providing the

118. Ibid.

119. Ibid., pp. 170-71.

'motive power for further evolution'. It was such a meaning that he had in mind when he spoke of 'awakening a purer and higher thought' amongst his countrymen.[120] The critical and comparative approach was missing in Indian education and Satish Chandra realised that unless this was rectified, further degradation could not be inhibited, and a comprehensive regeneration was near impossible.

Satish Chandra kept the debate on educational matters alive through the pages of *The Dawn*, even though metaphysical and philosophical matters also occupied greater space in its columns. He encouraged various personalities to air their views on different aspects of education, Indian and Western, reflecting his quest for an alternative system.

The Dawn issue of September 1900 carried an article on the '**The System of Teaching in Indian Colleges.**' It adopted a comparative approach of the system followed in Oxford and Cambridge with the one followed in India. The comparative was the preferred approach of narrative building since a comparison revealed the extent of distortion and dilution that took place in the Indian application of the British system of education. Some of the features that were highlighted and compared were similar to those discussed earlier by Satish Chandra himself.

The writer, Atul Chandra Chatterjee (1874–1955)[121], talks of his first-hand experience of the system in England and complained that 'even brilliant and promising graduates of foreign universities' 'sink in the slough of routine and examinations and are heard no more' when they migrate to India. Chatterjee also discussed the large and heterogeneous nature of classes in India where no attempt is made 'at individual teaching' and where the 'lecture merely consists of the

120. Ibid., p. 171.

121. Perhaps the diplomat, scholar, ICS, who served as India High Commissioner to the UK, author of *New India, A Short History of India, Notes on the Industries of the United Provinces.*

paraphrasing of one of the textbooks, line by line ...'[122]

Some major afflictions of the Indian system – inordinate reliance on and domination of the textbook, unwieldy classes where there was a uniform treatment of a heterogeneous group, and the absence of research and serious study – were discussed in great detail by Chatterjee. Over the years, with the progress of the educational debate, Satish Chandra wrote detailed papers on various aspects of educational reform and re-organisation. A look at these articles reveals that *The Dawn* did indeed place the entire educational debate on a serious level. It showed that the nationalist education demand always based itself on a sound intellectual base and was not a mere reflexive and revivalist action.

The series on '**The System of Classification of Boys in Indian Schools: A Scheme of Reform**' in the January 1901 issue of *The Dawn* reflected Satish Chandra's ingenuity and also expressed his futuristic perceptions. This series showed that Satish Chandra was not merely concerned with the reform of higher education in India but also advocated the restructuring of school education. The acute problem was that 'under the present system ... of school instruction ... boys of widely unequal merit and attainment in very branch of study [were] herded together and treated as an homogeneous whole and placed under the tuition of one teacher at a time during the different hours of the day'. This, Satish Chandra, argued, led the teachers to 'gradually cease to take a living interest in their work from a sense of the helplessness of their position' while the students 'silently deteriorate or are prevented from rising to the full height of their powers ...'

Satish Chandra suggested a reform of such a system. The business of his paper was to examine one branch of school-instruction, to see whether it was feasible to 'classify boys into forms or groups for the purposes of most efficient teaching'. He

122. *The Dawn*, September 1900, vol.4, pp. 31–37.

found the classification of boys into classes, defective and pointed out that his remedies 'will be in the nature of *adjustments*, leading to greater economy [of energy], instead of waste', as is presently seen of the energy that is spent on school-work by the tutor and the learner. His suggestions 'would not necessitate any addition to the tutorial staff, and would generally lead to a better *organisation* of ... educational institutions.'[123] Such an intricate examination of the existing education and detailed debate on its structural reformation had scarcely been taken up before.

In March 1901, Satish Chandra started his widely discussed series on '**Education and Examination**' with a review of Max-Muller's views on education which revisited 'on the eve of some great constitutional changes' that were about to be initiated in the Calcutta University. Quoting the English historian E.A. Freeman (1823–1892) on examination being an evil that made 'men read not for the attainment of knowledge, but for the object of passing the examination ...' Satish Chandra spoke of the central theme of his discussion in this series:

> True educational reform in India must principally consist in manning our Indian colleges with original workers and investigators as professors and lecturers, giving them free scope or full liberty to teach according to the best of their lights, or in other words, giving them as much of independent discretion as possible in the work of teaching. And having got together the right sort of men, the genuine scholars, the true thinkers, the true workers and investigators, the function of testing or examining candidates, of rightly appraising their work must be left completely in their hands ...'

Attention must also be paid to the 'recruiting of a body of men on adequate pay who will be able to set a very high standard of teaching in India and will not degenerate into mere crammers or

123. *The Dawn*, January, 1901, pp. 189–90.

amateurs'.[124] The national education institution that Satish Chandra organised would have such a body of scholars dedicated to setting a high standard of teaching and research in the country beyond the routine of examinations. These scholars would also be encouraged to produce original research work, taking into account the living influences of the Indian past.

Satish Chandra's early writings reflected his thinking on remedying the existing system, his later actions indicated that he realised the urgent need of an alternative system which would work out the remedies in education that he envisaged. The gradual growth of the nationalist education demand culminating in the formation of the Bengal National College in 1906, gave Satish Chandra that opportunity. It is to him, therefore, that one must look as one of the initiators of the early nationalist education discourse in India, one who not only identified and analysed the symptoms but also suggested remedies. It was largely due to Satish Chandra Mukherjee's efforts that the early debate on Indian education assumed a greater intellectual and a more thorough technical texture and substance. He was of one of those dynamic thought-leaders and educators who laid the intellectual foundation for the quest of a philosophy of national education.

IV.5. BIPIN CHANDRA PAL: AN EDUCATION FOR A 'NEW INDIA'

During 1901 and 1902, Bipin Chandra Pal was still a political moderate. On his return to India from England, he launched the English weekly *New India*, its first issue appearing on August 12, 1901. Launched initially as a vehicle for transmitting and encouraging cultural thoughts and debates, *New India* quickly assumed a wide readership and 'transformed into a mighty mouthpiece of resurgent

---

124. *The Dawn*, March, 1901, p. 235.

Indian Nationalism'[125] when it began discussing the major socio-political issues of the day.

During the first two years of its existence, between 1901 and 1902, the paper focused on, and vigorously debated, economic and educational issues. The inaugural issue which stated the weekly's policies, perceptions and areas of focus spoke of the economic problem as the 'most pressing and important' of all the 'perplexing problems that confront New India' and of the educational problem as next in importance to the economic.

Setting the tone for the analysis of educational issues, Pal succinctly observed in his first issue that, 'the present system of education is bad, but the cure for bad education is not *no* education, but *good* education'. He enumerated the fundamental defects of the existing system of education and spoke of two of them, namely that 1) It is not a national [system], and 2) that it is not a rational system ...' A flawed economic policy, he argued, was 'undermining the material basis' of the country and an 'irrational educational policy has been emasculating the intellectual and moral life of the nation'.

New India, Pal stated, while taking into account the importance of political, social and religious issues confronting the nation, would make persistent agitation on present day economic and educational problems its 'speciality'.[126] Satish Chandra's *The Dawn* had already begun highlighting the educational problems and together the two journals began building a formidable case for reforming and restructuring the Indian education system. 1901–1902 were the years when the Indian Universities' Commission was at work, and this

---

125. Haridas and Uma Mukherjee, *Bipin Chandra Pal and India's Struggle for Swaraj,* op.cit.,, pp. 17–18. Also see e.g. R.C. Majumdar, *History of the Freedom Movement of India, vol.2*, op.cit., pp. 139, 140 for an analysis of Pal's conversion from moderatism to extremism.
126. *New India*, August 12, 1901, Ibid., p. 18.

coincided with the first two years of *New India's* existence. It was during these years that Pal wrote a number of articles on economic and educational problems and advanced not only well-structured criticisms in them but also placed 'positive lines, of reform and reconstruction'.[127]

A survey of some articles in *New India* reveals that Pal did not overtly concern himself with direct political issues during that phase and that wherever he thought it necessary he appreciated and praised the government's efforts, especially on education reform. His criticisms were of course direct and bold. This was to be his approach till the disclosure of the Bengal partition plan. The revelation of this plan transformed Pal into a political extremist and one of the chief thinkers of the nationalist group.[128]

An examination of portions of the *New India* articles on education reveal Pal's grip of educational matters. Pal, like the editor of *The Dawn,* encouraged others to write in his paper on educational issues. Thus we see, in his 'Weekly Record & Review of Modern Thought and Life', as he termed the *New India's* mission, Prof. S.C. Mahalanobis[129] write a sketch of the Edinburgh University. Talking of the integrality of physical education in the scheme of English education, the author observed that 'British University life without athletics would indeed be *Hamlet* without the Prince.' The author spoke of the social and collective aspect of the British scheme of education by showcasing the role of the Students' Union in the University. The institution of the students' union was a

---

127. Ibid., p. 20.
128. *New India,* August 12, 1901, pp. 21–28.
129. Prof. S.C. Mahalanobis (1867–1953) had returned to India from England in 1900 and had joined the Presidency College as Head of the Department of Biology. In 1898, Prof. Mahalanobis was with the Physiology Department of Cardiff University.

lively arena for debate, intellectual exchange and expansion. The students were in-charge of its activities and administration. The Union building was a 'great varsity' institution. The building was usually a 'magnificent one provided with a splendid dining room, a commodious debating hall, smoking room, news room, library, baths, gymnasium, billiard room'. 'The management of the Union is vested in the hands of a committee of students.'[130] It may be recalled that Sri Aurobindo was active in the Baroda College Union activities and had done much to enliven the intellectual atmosphere of the body.[131]

The theme of Indian Universities being mostly examining bodies was highlighted in the article. Comparing the Calcutta University as patterned nearly on the London model, Prof. Mahalanobis argued that the 'Scottish universities' instead 'are not merely examining bodies but teaching institutions' which have, 'along with the German Universities, fully retained the medieval synthetic type'.

The Scottish universities, observed Prof. Mahalanobis, basing himself on his first-hand experiences in one of them, 'are not satisfied with merely stamping a number of students with the "hall-mark" of examination, but there the student owed his intellectual life to the cherishing, nourishing and fostering care of his alma mater. Whereas the Calcutta University, patterned after the University of London, 'requires of a student to be taught according to the standard of the *test.* [Thus] consequently, it matters very little whether a student is well trained or not, so long as he is well *informed.*' [Therefore] 'the *result*' of the examination' continued to remain 'the pole-star, in view of which [the entire] educational argosy is steered'.

---

130. Prof. S.C. Mahalanobis, *Sketches of Edinburgh University, New India,* August 26, 1901. *New India* Files, Microfilm Copies, National Library of India, Kolkata.

131. Peter Heehs, *Sri Aurobindo —A Brief Biography*, 2005, p. 23.

'Unfortunately', lamented Prof. Mahalanobis, 'our present system of education demands of the student, the maximum amount of work in a minimum time' and it was this quick-fix demand that was giving rise to the cry for 'something of the "'put-a-penny-in-the-slot" nature that will save time and bother. This [was] provided by the elaborate machinery of cram. And behold the result!' Prof. Mahalanobis concluded the piece with a light-hearted remark which nevertheless pointed at a deeper truth which reflected the predicament of teaching in the Indian system. "A friend once remarked" he recalled, "that some students were 'like safety matches': The latter ignited 'only on the box', whereas the former shone only on examination papers. I am afraid the safety-match students are steadily growing in number."[132] Excerpts from such articles are useful to set in perspective the discussion of dominant educational matters that preoccupied some of the leading academic minds of this period under review. It appears from such an analysis that Bipin Chandra Pal, like Satish Chandra Mukherjee during that period, encouraged and invited a wide-ranging debate on educational matters.

In the September 9, 1901, issue of *New India*, Pal discussed the Viceroy's [Curzon] speech delivered at the Simla conference on education reform and brought out deficiencies in it. The stupendously lengthy speech with its variety of topics covered and issues analysed failed to clarify the real intention of the Government *vis-à-vis* educational reform. Pal touched upon some of the issues that had ignited debate after the speech.

The perception that the Government sought to centralise the whole system of education and thus preclude the growth and consolidation of the indigenous educational initiative was the foremost charge against the official reform initiative. It was also the one that generated the most vocal opposition. 'The general

132. *New India*, August 26, 1901, op. cit.

feeling has been', wrote Pal, giving voice to that perception, 'that the Viceroy proposes to centralise the educational agencies more completely than they had hitherto been, and to leave little or no room for the free and unrestricted development of national ideals of education, in the school system of the country whether aided, or unaided, by Government grants'. Curzon's speech, according to Pal , did nothing to remove such misgivings. In fact, it was this attempt at centralising that created much apprehension and generated protest. The proposal of appointing a Director-General of Education was seen 'as the main move' in this direction. The other steps that would make the official element supreme in educational matters were 'the reorganisation of the Provincial Textbook Committees' and 'the power of absolute control over the selection of textbooks [to be] vested in the Director of Public Instruction'.

Pal opposed these. He spoke of the Director of Public Instruction as being 'generally innocent of all knowledge of the language, traditions, and the thought life of the people' and it was this that raised serious misgivings on the genuineness of the reforms. They were looked upon by the Indian public as attempts at 'thought-breeding', seen as the core aim of the colonial administration to be worked out through education.

Pal also boldly wrote on the necessity of broad-basing governance: "No Government, in our times, however autocratic, can feel itself secure unless it is broad-based upon the will of the governed. This basis may be found in two ways – by suiting official actions to the feelings and opinions of the people, or by training these feelings and opinions to be in consonance with official ideas and ideals." The general feeling in the country, Pal concluded, was that the educational reforms aimed at carrying out the second experiment – that of training of people's feelings and opinions to be in consonance with official ideas and ideals. The legitimacy of the reforms, therefore, was suspect from the start itself.[133]

In his meticulous analysis of Indian education, Pal also analysed numerous dimensions of the revised scheme of education in an article entitled, '**The Revised Scheme of Primary Education in Bengal**'. Interestingly, Pal supported the revised scheme, provided an insightful summary of the 'salient points', analysed its positive features, as he saw them, and made suggestions how to fulfill the lacunas as he read them.

Pal identified the object of the new scheme of 'Primary and Middle Vernacular Education' to be that of training and improving 'the intelligence of the young whatever may be their future course of technical instruction or occupation life'. The primary was not to 'impart technical instruction or to prepare boys for learning any particular trade or profession'.[134]

With such an aim the new scheme had been based on a twin principle '(1) "the recognition and stimulation of the child's spontaneous activity," and (2) "the complete and harmonious development of the child's faculties."' The child's education, argued Pal, must therefore start with developing the 'senses and powers of observation' and with the training 'of the hand and the eye', and to continue to the 'strengthening of the memory and the reasoning powers'. Besides this training of mental faculties, provisions must exist for a 'healthy physical training which is necessary to the growth of the young'.[135] Keeping these objectives in mind, Pal explained, certain changes had been proposed to be incorporated into the new scheme, they were (1) the introduction of the Kindergarten scheme suited to Indian conditions which Pal recognised as an useful

133. *New India,* September 9, 1901.
134. *New India,* November 4, 1901.
135. Ibid.

addition for 'training through senses in the infant stage', '(2) a well organised scheme of object lessons embracing sensible properties e.g. colours, form, weight, size, and phenomena of the sky and the atmosphere, action of metals, growth of plants etc' up to the Upper primary stage, '(3) the science of everyday life or simpler and more fundamental facts of Botany and Natural History' for both boys and girls, and for girls the subject of Domestic Economy would find a place. The additional subject for urban boys at this stage was to be physics and chemistry and agriculture with 'gardens-attached to the classes' for rural boys, '(4) drawing for training the hand eye'; (5) action songs in the infant stages, drills and gymnastics for boys in the higher stages replaced by drills and calisthenics for girls, for furthering physical growth [it is interesting to note that provisions have been made for girls to continue with some form of physical education as well]. Sixth was the provision for manual training of pupils – needle work for girls and manual training for boys, which was to include such work as 'paper and clay modeling and simple wicker-work for teaching the use of tools and appliances'. Manual training however was to be optional. Reading and writing – including the reading and writing of vernacular documents useful for court and zamindari work – was to remain, and arithmetic and mental arithmetic '(European as well as Indian) retain the same place in the new as in the old curriculum'.

History, Geography, literature and Grammar had been 'slightly' and 'considerably' reduced so as to 'make room for the object lessons and the Science primers'. Keeping in mind the necessity of serving the needs of 'emotional culture' in the young, 'Moral lessons and Poetry' was to be included in Literature [it is again to be noted that Moral lessons was not treated as a separate subject but was instead clubbed together with poetry and included in literature.

Such an attitude may have appeared to be incomprehensible to the Indian mind which gave great importance to the Moral element in education. Pal, however, did not comment, at least in the article, on such a provision.]

The scheme emphasised the importance of 'objective lessons' and intended that 'every subject should be taught as much as possible by means of object lessons.' Keeping to this, lessons would be taught in a certain manner such as 'geography lessons should be taught by visible illustrations and by modeling in sand and clay, of rivers, mountains, plains, &c. and tales from history are to be graphically told and illustrated by striking pictures or when possible, by magic lantern slides'. These would help to 'powerfully foster the child's imagination and representative faculty'. Pal concluded the summary with his support for the ideas in the reforms, 'it must be admitted' he concluded, that these reforms are a 'decided improvement upon the existing system, and is along the lines of the most advanced systems of Primary instruction in the Western countries [and] if intelligently and faithfully carried out, it is sure to lead to both the deepening and broadening of elementary instruction in this country'.[136]

In the following issue of *New India,* November 11, 1901, Pal articulated his views on the revised scheme of education that he had summarised earlier. Commenting on the reform committee's method of training through the senses in the lower stages, Pal observed that what was needed instead is 'not training *through* (sic) but first and foremost the training *of* the senses, [for] this alone can ensure habits of accuracy, delicacy, discrimination, and acquisition of skill in the use of each sense, without which the training through sense would inevitably degenerate into mere exercise of the

136. Ibid.

memory'.[137]

His suggestions on how to implement this method was that 'greater attention be paid to the training of the eye, the ear, the touch, the smell and the taste'. The eye should be trained through object lessons and should develop the practice of 'forming accurate judgments of distance in regard to objects on the horizons, of measure and size, of degrees of light or luster, marking shades of colour and varieties of form'. The ear should be trained to be capable of catching 'the time and the pitch of a sound'; the skin and muscles should be trained to be able to give 'approximate measurements of temperature, as well as degrees of pressure, force and weight'. Pal however, noted that for such training, teachers with greater capacity and ability would be required.

The importance of manual training in Pal's early educational discussions is evident in his insistence on making it compulsory, 'enlightened public opinion in no part of Bengal would oppose this measure' [of making manual training compulsory]. He called the argument that mandatory manual training would be opposed by the people as a mythical one and pointed instead to the fact that a number of technical schools and institutions in Bengal had already introduced obligatory manual training.

Referring to the 'Sibpore Engineering College' Pal observed that a thorough manual training was given in such institutions and that 'youths of all castes and of the most respectable families are found' in these. In his opinion, therefore, 'to make manual training optional would be really to give up half the benefits of the new scheme. The senses are intended to lead to active movement, and the training of the senses must always be incomplete without manual practice in wielding the simpler and common tools and implements'. Pal recognised that 'the advanced European system

137. *New India,* November 11, 1901.

of manual training' would be too expensive to be implemented under Indian conditions but nevertheless, 'it would surely be easy to devise methods of manual training based on the highest modern principles and adapted to Indian conditions'.[138]

Pal continued the series containing his observations and suggestions on the reforms in the next weekly issue of the *New India*. He examined its other dimensions, starting with the teaching of history. Narration and illustration, according to Pal, must have primacy in the teaching of history and if history is to truly enliven the pupil, 'historical lessons' should be 'taught with the help of profuse illustrations, and consequently the History Reader [pupil's manual for history] must be carefully illustrated', 'special care should be taken to encourage the boys and girls to narrate what they read graphically, not from memory, in the words of the book, but simply as they narrate stories that they have heard, or describe scenes and incidents which they have seen'.[139]

Such an approach, Pal argued, would automatically discount the role of memory and foster instead understanding and originality of self-expression.[140] The illustrations in the History Reader therefore, Pal pointed out, required to be significantly altered in order to make an impact, and must not only

include portraits of the principal actors, but what is far more important, they

138. Ibid.

139. *New India*, November 18, 1901.

140. This is reminiscent of the experiment to teach subjects in an alternative method undertaken by the legendary Indian educator and Gandhian, Gijubhai Badheka (1885–1939), see e.g. his *Divasvapna* (Trans), rpt. 2006, pp. 44–47, for an alternative method of teaching history mainly through narration of stories. The experiment that Gijubhai undertook succeeded, and pupils did eventually study history with renewed interest.

must contain representations of the life and manners of the age to which the stories refer, reproduction of the coins they used, the dress they put on, the arms and weapons they fought with, as also of the cities they lived in, and the houses they built up. Besides these, along with the portraits of the kings and warriors and statesman, striking scenes and situations in their lives should, so far as possible, be placed before the juvenile reader through suitable illustrations.[141]

Pal wished to make the study of history organic and living, through which the young mind can establish a living contact with the nation's past and civilisational achievements and in the process gain a certain amount of self-confidence and certitude vis-à-vis the nation, its people and future.

Similarly, the teaching of geography had to try to create a lively interest in the pupil, the scheme proposed to use visible illustrations and modeling in sand and clay, of hill and valley etc., and along with these, as Pal suggested, to include illustrations of the 'neighbourhoods of the schools, with which the students must be made to acquaint themselves by long and repeated walks, taken with their teacher' and through which they might also develop the habit of observation. The Geography Reader, Pal suggested, must also 'contain some account of the economic product of the district', 'some statement of the internal trade of the province as well as ... external and foreign trade'.[142] The pupil needed to know first his surrounding and province, develop a thorough knowledge of the region along with gaining knowledge of the far flung areas. The similarity of this suggestion with Sri Aurobindo's third educational principle, which calls for working 'from the near to the far, from that which is to that which shall be ...'[143] cannot be missed.

Commenting on the agriculture for rural areas mentioned in

141. *New India,* November 18, 1901.

142. Ibid.

143. *CWSA* vol.1, op. cit., pp. 384, 385.

the scheme, Pal suggested that it should not be merely confined to a garden attached to the class but must include, in the more advanced stages, 'actual field-work and excursions [and that] the teaching should have direct reference to the actual conditions of cultivation in the different districts' and also to the 'more obvious and feasible opportunities of improvement in these conditions'.

On the subject of Science of Everyday life, which Pal considered to have been rightly included by the reform committee in the scheme of education, he suggested a few additions which are usually 'acquired by people in early life or not acquired at all.' Pal enumerates these as:

> (a) Naming and identifying the commoner plants, flowers and fruits, – with some reference to their properties; (b) Naming and identifying the more important orders, general and species of Natural History, with the help of zoological charts, and with special reference to *fauna* of the immediate neighbourhood of the schools, (c) Naming and identifying the principal planets and stars with periods of rising and setting, with special observations of the sun and the moon; (d) Naming and identifying the principal metals and alloys; (e) Naming and identifying the principal rocks, with geological charts showing the stratification of rocks; and (f) Observation as to the more obvious signs of the weather, as also the changes of the seasons, and where there are opportunities of doing so, observations of the fluctuations of the tides with reference to the moon's quarter.[144]

An acquisition of this elementary and useful knowledge would better equip the pupil in his everyday living and give him an empirical and practical orientation. It also indicated the minuteness with which Pal had actually studied the reforms and applied his mind to the possibilities of further improving them, and of making them responsive and relevant to the circumstances, environment and need of his country and his people.

An important omission that Pal identified in the scheme was

144. *New India,* November 18, 1901.

the exclusion of the training and cultivation of the vocal organs, 'the Committee have either ignored it altogether, or have, considering the present condition of the country, thought any plan for the culture of the vocal powers as unpractical'. Pal found it difficult to see reason for this exclusion and appealed to at least introduce this as an optional subject and supported the conferring of 'special prizes to the pupil and bonuses to the teachers' for its encouragement 'so that the new scheme might bring us at least one step nearer to the regular introduction of singing into primary schools for boys as well as girls, as they have in European countries'. Such a 'sad waste' of human faculty should not be permitted, Pal argued, in any civilised community.[145]

As we have seen, Pal was alive to the fact that the implementation of the revised scheme of education would require a new method of training teachers. He raised this point in the following issues of his paper and identified the present 'teaching staff' to be the first great difficulty to be overcome in the process of implementing this new teacher's training scheme. The present staff 'in charge of [the] Primary and Middle School are admittedly unfitted for the work', he observed and in order to have 'even a tolerably qualified staff of teachers', additional money would have to be expended which for the present seemed to him to be 'almost prohibitive.'

For Pal, the alternate was 'to try and train the existing staff in the secret of the new methods by the help of Manuals specially prepared for the purpose'.[146] Pal also suggested a restructuring or rewriting of the existing teachers training manual. Such an effort, he argued, would be within financial bounds while greatly serving the attempt of making the teachers have a new orientation. Great care, however, would have to be taken to prepare these manuals;

---

145. *New India,* November 18, 1901, op. cit.

146. *New India,* November 25, 1901.

the Government would have to realise that there were none in, and practically few outside the services who could be entrusted with this delicate task. Pal also enumerated the qualifications necessary for such a work, they were of a 'twofold character – namely, a thorough grasp of the fundamental principles underlying the new scheme on the one hand, joined to a thorough mastery of the details of the different systems wherein these principles are being sought to be embodied in the advanced educational methods of European countries, and a clear and deep insight into the peculiarities of life and thought in Bengal in relation to the realities of which the new plan will have to be worked out on the other'.[147]

The formation of an expert committee for drawing up these manuals appeared to him to be a possible way which could be adopted, and he suggested the method of forming such a committee and its possible composition. The Director of Public Instruction, he suggested, may be allowed to nominate 'two of the most competent men ... from among the officers of his Department' and supplied two names which he felt would be of invaluable assistance in the Committee's functions, 'we can, confidently name two gentlemen who could render invaluable assistance ... in this matter. They are Principal Brajendranath Seal of the Victoria College, Cooch Behar, and Babu Rabindranath Tagore, the leading Bengali author who adds to his unrivalled qualifications as a master of the language in which the Manual will have to be compiled, considerable practical experience of the system of sense-training which he tried to work out in the education of some of the members of his own family'.

These two Indian educational and literary stalwarts were considered, by Pal, to be the persons best suited because of their deep understanding and study of indigenous conditions and because of their direct involvement with education in the country.

147. Ibid.

The Committee thus, could comprise two officers of the State Education Department, these two external experts and the Director as the President, 'a Committee thus constituted will ... be able to get up the best Manual for teachers under the new scheme'. Trying to work out any other plan and entrusting the whole work to a 'single individual' would, Pal argued, 'court total failure'.[148]

The procedure of selecting textbooks under the new scheme, Pal pointed out, was bound to face serious difficulty. He realised that the responsibility of textbook selection had devolved in incompetent hands, whose only qualification was that they were on the right side of officialdom. Pal's trenchant critique of this approach was that:

> the duty of providing textbooks for our vernacular schools have drifted into the hands of a class of people, who as a body, must be declared to be half-educated at the best, and whose success has hitherto to a large measure depended upon, not the intrinsic merit of their productions, but upon the strength of their heels to dance attendance upon the gods who preside so long over the work of making selections, or on the degree of their consanguinity or the measure of their personal and private friendship with the Members of the Text Book Committee.

The Committee itself was not competent to 'select the sort of books that are wanted for a satisfactory working out of the new scheme', thus it would be in the healthy interest of the scheme itself, if the selection of the textbooks could be left to some independent body – the suggested Committee for Teacher's Manual preparation could also be entrusted with the task of textbook selection.[149] Pal was keen on indigenous voices being heard in the formulation of the education syllabus. This would ensure the successful implementation of the new scheme which appeared to him to have merits and to be in tune with the latest educational methods

---

148. Ibid.
149. Ibid.

followed worldwide.

The December 2, 1901, issue of the *New India* sees Pal indicting the High School system in India as one which was in a bad shape and merited the 'severest condemnation that could be passed on any educational scheme'.[150] Pal saw it as a system of not mere cram and rote but one that was 'positively injurious to the brain and seriously [arrested] the growth of the mind as well as of the body. It [injured] the eyesight, [produced] weakness of the brain and the nerves, [reduced] length of life, [atrophied] the mental faculties with the exception of the memory, and [made] the latter a receptacle of second-hand colourless images and meaningless abstractions'. The newly-devised method for the primary and middle schools, he felt, 'will be a distinct boon to the very large number of boys, especially the upper and middle classes of society who, as a rule, do not go to any Primary or Middle school, but go directly to a High School'.[151]

In the following weekly issue of *New India*, Pal formulated his observations in support of the need for technical training and pointed to the infrastructural deficiencies in promoting such training. He mentioned the problem of the large number of 'young people whose circumstances do not permit them to go in for a full University course' and of those 'who cannot even go into the University at all' and who thus have no other opportunities or avenues that would make them self-reliant. He complained that there was 'practically no provision for learning any suitable trade or business; and in the absence of these provisions, the smattering of general education which they receive in the Primary, Middle, or High Schools simply involves a waste of energy, and lets loose on society an army of half-educated people without any training or purpose or profession for their future life, [as a result] they drift into

150. *New India,* December 2, 1901.

151. Ibid.

every kind of places for which they have no fitness'.[152]

This was the 'greatest evil of the present educational system' in the country, and it could only be remedied 'by a scheme of technical or professional training sufficiently comprehensive to permit the filiations of every grade and stage of education with it ...', Pal signed off.[153]

1902 saw Bipin Chandra Pal continue his examination of educational themes. In the May 19, 1902, issue of *New India*, Pal took up the cause of '**Higher Education for Women**' and articulated his conception of the modern ideal of women's education. In the article, Pal took on those, Mrs. Annie Besant included among them, who, he said, view 'education almost exclusively from the social standpoint'. The individual in their view existed only 'for the society ... and consequently the object of all education' for them was to fit the individual 'for the due discharge of their functions as parts of the social machine'. Pal placed his ideal of modern education in contrast with what he termed the ancient Hindu ideal of education which was to mainly educate women to 'make them immeasurably more useful as the wives and mothers they will be', that is, making them ready to dutifully just serve or live out their social functions and duties.[154] Such an ideal, Pal believed?, was not in consonance with modern requirements – 'it is not in consonance with modern conception of nature, man, and society. The object of all education in the modern view, is self-realisation, this self being considered as a *person*, that [has] very definite personal ends. Every individual, in this view is an end unto himself or herself, and not a mere tool for the realisation of others' ends, whether civic or social. The education of women, as much as that of men, must therefore aim

152. *New India*, December 9, 1901.

153. Ibid.

154. *New India*, May 19, 1902.

at something higher than mere fitting them up as efficient organs of the social whole'.

But Pal was careful to point out that the personal aim of education should not be in conflict with the 'highest interest of society'. The individual is intimately related to society, and in pursuance of his social aims, the individual develops an 'organic and living relation with the universal system of ends' and thus, Pal argued, this harmony was essential. There had to be a harmony and synthesis between the personal ends of the individual and the ends of his 'particular class, community', nation and the whole universe. Pal differentiated between private and personal ends in education, the former, he argued, reeked of selfishness and would therefore be untenable and suicidal in the long run. He sympathetically defined the contours and aims of a personal education, one perceives in it a comprehensive scheme for the individual's personal growth – social, ethical, spiritual. Pal spoke of personal education as involving:

> (1) the education of the senses, that is the powers of observation; (2) education of the imaginative faculty, the object is to free the mind from the immediate and the present interest, by relating it to the past and the future, and to correct merely subjective notions by objective verifications or realisation; (3) education of the emotions, with a view to raise the mere feelings into sentiments, and to train the mind to the contemplation and enjoyment of the ideals of life – intellectual, aesthetic and ethical; (4) education of the social instincts of sympathy or altruism with a view to create enthusiasm for one's own nation or for humanity; (5) education of the will, to train the individual in habits of self-control, of subordinating the appetites and desires to ideals and principles, and thus to develop a life of deliberative self-control; (6) education of the faculties of reason, the development of the sense of the categories and relations, and the training of the mind to habits of systematic thinking; and (7) education of the spiritual faculty, the education of the sense of the unseen, and the training of the mind to a perpetual consciousness of the presence of the Eternal within and without.

These were the contours of 'personal education' and Pal expressed hope that proponents of the predominantly social aspect of education would recognize the absolute necessity of such an education to be imparted to women.[155] The ingenuity of Pal's educational thought finds expression through these writings; the approach is not a didactic but rather a deeply suggestive one. His expression of a spiritual education has a universal appeal. Such a perspective on personal education was absent from the colonial system of instruction, the apprehension that its existence would further crystallise the individual personality may have proved too strong for such inclusions to be made into the system.

Pal's progress towards greater radicalisation began accelerating from 1902 onwards. In an article in August that year, on '**The Cause of High Education in India**', he spoke of the unnational character of the present educational system as the 'central evil'.[156] Pal's analysis of the whole aspect and the originality of his reading of this problem is almost metaphysical. Pal accepted the universality of the mind, the drive towards unity inherent in man's evolution but also pointed to the diversity of expression that he felt was a necessity and required preservation and nurturing.

One finds in this piece clear indications of the major problems of education in India. "Though the mind is one", Pal argued, "the vehicle through which this mind works and expresses itself are many and diverse, owing to diversities of structure and environments of different peoples, resulting in variations in experience and associations. And all true education is imparted through real experience." This real-experience education was what was missing from the present-day education. Education through real experience simply 'seeks to place the individual minds in living contact with the

155. Ibid.

156. *New India,* August 7, 1902.

experience of the race. National and historical associations are the vehicles of these experiences. All education must work, therefore, through these national associations, which alone can have any reality to youthful and inexperienced minds'.

The prevailing education system lacked such an approach. He argued, "The system of education so long prevalent in this country has, however, always failed to do this. It is English associations, British sceneries, European experiences, that have been used so long as the main instruments of education in India. It has therefore never been a *national* [sic] system."[157]

This was one of the central arguments on which, as we have seen, the whole nationalist educational discourse and demand concentrated and revolved. The habit of citing foreign examples and settings 'created a divorce' between the mental and practical life, it 'caused a wide breach between what one was taught to think and what one saw, heard, felt and lived'. This divorce Pal called the 'root-evil' in the present education, and it 'is in the power of no foreign government, however beneficent, to bridge this breach. This can only be done by indigenous educational agencies, absolutely unfettered by official guidance or official control'.[158]

The 'right method of reform would, therefore, be', insisted Pal, 'for [the] alien Government ... to gradually withdraw from the position of supreme controlling authority in the matter of the education of the people. Where the Government pays for the maintenance of schools, they must, no doubt, exercise absolute control over the expenditure, and see that the money is used for legitimate purposes; but except this financial control, all else should be left to the people themselves.'[159]

---

157. *New India,* May 19, 1902.
158. *New India,* August 7, 1902.
159. Ibid.

In 1902, Pal did not call for a total cessation of control. He asked for monitoring of the financial aspect to remain, in case of aided institutions but even there, the rest – syllabus formulation and structuring, textbook selection and preparation etc. – must be left to the people.

The divorce of education from the realities of everyday life and of its surrounding, and the strict centralisation and official control of education which discouraged all indigenous initiatives, were the principal issues which would dominate the educational discourse in the capital of the Indian empire at the beginning of last century. The first demand of the nationalist education discourse was to render the education system national, by giving it over to indigenous control. This was seen as the first step towards creating a national system of education that would be responsive to national needs and would also largely create future responses and necessities.

The two nationalist thinkers and leaders – giants in their respective fields of action – who have been analysed in some detail, exerted a major influence in shaping the early nationalist discourse on education and on nationalism. Both were associates of Sri Aurobindo during the latter's active political life in Bengal.

Referring to Satish Chandra Mukherjee and to his defining role in laying the foundation of the National College and the national education movement in Bengal, Sri Aurobindo said that the former was one 'who had given his life' to the work of organising the movement and was the one 'who had really organised the National College in Calcutta'. Talking of the nobility and depth of Satish Chandra's personality, Sri Aurobindo observed that although 'he lives in the world, [he] lives like a sannyasin ...'[160] It was to Satish Chandra

160. Sri Aurobindo, *Speeches,* op. cit., p.23. The speech entitled *'Present Situation'* was delivered at a public meeting at Mahajan Wadi, Bombay on January 19, 1908. The text was published later in the weekly edition of the *Bande Mataram* on 23rd February.

that the burden of shouldering the additional responsibilities of the National College fell when Sri Aurobindo was forced to take repeated leave for political reasons. This task Satish Chandra carried out with utmost dexterity and devotion. Interestingly, Satish Chandra's association with Sri Aurobindo, though brief, was not limited only to the educational field, and at the risk of digression here into the arena of political philosophy – which cannot be altogether avoided while discussing Sri Aurobindo's early nationalist activities – we need to take a look at this nearly forgotten aspect.

When Sri Aurobindo started in his *Bande Mataram*, the 'Doctrine of Passive Resistance', enunciating the 'New Thought' in Indian politics between April and May 1907, Satish Chandra's was the first article to appear in the paper in defence of the 'New Thought'.[161] Some contemporary papers – *Hindu Patriot* among them – had begun haranguing the Extremists as people who talked nonsense, who had no policy and who, behaving like maniacs, were reducing 'the chance of self-government to the people to a shadow'. Leaders such as Pandit Motilal Nehru (1861–1931) observed, while presiding over the U.P. Provincial Conference held at Allahabad, that the new school of thought that had arisen in India had 'evolved out of the depths of despair'. Satish Chandra emphatically refuted this with a resounding 'No'. He saw the new thought and spirit not as the product of 'any passing wave of feeling' but as 'something very vital and life-giving'. Articulating the keynotes of the New Thought by defining what it was not, Satish Chandra wrote, "it [was] *not* the offspring of a spirit of revenge, it [was] *not* the advocating of mere measures of coercion and retaliation, [and] it [was] *not* a

161. Satish Chandra Mukherjee's article in the 'New Thought' series – 'The Essence of the New Movement – The Extremist's Position Defined' in Haridas & Uma Mukherjee, *Sri Aurobindo and The New Thought in Indian Politics*, 1997, p. 12.

mere suggestion of despair."[162] In an eloquent defence of the new movement, he observed:

> New Thought proclaims from the housetop that India has a right to live in history as a separate nation with a destiny and a mission all her own .... The New Thought holds and declares, as a fundamental axiom of political philosophy, that the countenance of foreign *predominance* or overlordship in any shape or form, political, industrial, intellectual, social or religious, is fatal to the continuance and growth of self-conscious life among a people subject to such overlordship.[163]

And therefore the vital question, argued Satish Chandra, that the New Thought puts to the Indian people was whether India shall be permitted to have 'an independent destiny which she shall be at liberty to work out in her own way' or whether she shall forever be yoked to 'the chariot-wheels of superior Power' and receive alien dictates as to how she should live and grow. This crucial question the New Thought sought to address, and for this it had formulated a mass action programme that had as its core components 'the Swadeshi Movement, the Boycott Movement (both in its industrial and political aspects) and the new Education Movement'. These were, according to this new thinking, the 'natural and legitimate outcome of the desire of the Indian peoples to assert and vindicate their inalienable right to achieve their own salvation – to work out their own ideals, in their own way'.[164]

Satish Chandra demonstrated a perceptive understanding of Sri Aurobindo's political philosophy at that time. He was one the best exponents of that political philosophy during that era and did much through this one article to spread its tenets among a wider intellectual circle of the province and the country. This 'sannyasin'

162. *Sri Aurobindo and The New Thought in Indian Politics* , pp. 13, 14.
163. Ibid.
164. Ibid., pp. 14, 15.

thus displayed a remarkable capacity to both organise national education as well as explicate political themes and philosophies. The following assessment of Satish Chandra by his biographers perhaps aptly describes his whole outlook and contribution:

> ... Although never an extremist political leader like Bipin Chandra or Aurobindo, yet Satischandra was an exponent of radical ideologies in the educational sphere and in the cultural realm. As a thinker, his natural affiliations were more with Rabindranath than either with Bipin Chandra or with Aurobindo for each of whom he had, however, an abiding respect. But the essence of nationalism which Satischandra had been preaching through *The Dawn* during all these years, from 1904, was comparable in deeper spiritual quality with the spirit of nationalism as preached by Aurobindo in the *Bande Mataram*.'[165]

A discussion of Sri Aurobindo's contribution to the Indian nationalist movement can never achieve integrality if one chooses to omit Satish Chandra and his role in the origin and growth of the national education movement in Bengal.

Sri Aurobindo looked upon Bipin Chandra Pal as 'perhaps the best and the most original political thinker in the country, an excellent writer and a magnificent orator'.[166] To recall, it was with Pal that Sri Aurobindo went on a tour of East Bengal after the breaking up of the Barisal Conference in1906, and surveyed first-hand the political and social condition of the province. This was also the beginning of Sri Aurobindo's close association with the 'forward group in the Congress' of which Pal was already an established ideologue. It was from Pal, who had by then begun 'expounding a policy of self-help and non-cooperation'[167] that Sri Aurobindo received the invitation to join the *Bande Mataram* that the former had launched. In a sense it was Pal who provided, to a certain

165. *The Origins of the National Education Movement*, op.cit., p. 72.
166. *On Himself*, op. cit., p.27.
167. Ibid., p.28.

extent, the platform Sri Aurobindo needed 'for starting the public propaganda necessary for his revolutionary purpose'.[168] Without this timely offer, the issue of mass mobilization through propaganda may have been delayed.

Pal, on his part, was among the first of the influential Bengal leaders to recognise Sri Aurobindo's genius and his necessity in the movement. In a masterly analysis of Sri Aurobindo's personality and contribution to the advanced nationalist movement, Pal movingly described him as the 'youngest in age among those who stand in the forefront of the Nationalist propaganda in India' but 'superior to them all' in 'endowment, education, and character' who 'seems distinctly marked out by Providence to play in the future of [the] movement a part not given to any of his colleagues and contemporaries'.[169]

Assessing his role in transforming *Bande Mataram* into a fiery organ of revolutionary nationalism, Pal writes:

> ... The hand of the master was in it from the very beginning. Its bold attitude, its vigorous thinking, its clear ideas, its chaste and powerful diction, its scorching sarcasm and refined witticism, were unsurpassed by any journal in the country, either Indian or Anglo-Indian. It at once raised the tone of every Bengali paper, and compelled the admiration of even hostile Anglo-Indian editors. Morning after morning, not only Calcutta but the educated community in almost every part of the country, eagerly awaited its vigorous pronouncements on the stirring questions of the day .... Long extracts from it commenced to be reproduced week after week even in the exclusive columns of the "*Times*" in London. It was a force in the country which none dared to ignore, however much they might fear or hate it, and Aravinda was the leading spirit, the central figure, in the new journal.[170]

---

168. Ibid.
169. Bipin Chandra Pal, 'Indian Nationalism: Its Principles and Personalities', 1918 cited in Manoj Das, op. cit., p.185 and Sumit Sarkar, *The Swadeshi Movement in Bengal (1903–1908)*, 1973, p.171.
170. Ibid., p.200.

Discussing the growth of the national education movement and of the formation of the National College, and the political challenges that the fledgling institution faced which led to the curtailment of Sri Aurobindo's powers in it, Pal emphatically noted that had 'Aravinda' 'been given a free hand in the new National College [in Calcutta], that institution would have opened an altogether new chapter not only in the history of modern education in India, but perhaps in the whole world'. But the spirit that generally guided the functioning of the National Council, according to Pal, was '[a] timid, temporizing spirit', this was 'galling to the reformer and the man with new visions and large ideas' and thus made it 'almost impossible for Aravinda to throw himself heart and soul into his educational work in Calcutta. His place in the National College, though he was its nominal Principal, was not really that of an organiser and initiator, but simply a teacher of language and history, even as it had been in the Maharaja's College at Baroda'.[171]

Pal was the only leader to state unequivocally, Sri Aurobindo's uneasy situation in the National Council and College. Sri Aurobindo too, in his later political writings indicated why the National Council could not make the impact it was originally meant to, and how, because of its hesitant approach to education re-organisation, it dislocated itself from the larger nationalist movement.

By this compromise, it diluted core objectives and its zeal for charting out a new path. This eventually deprived it of its earlier 'patriotic appeal'. Sri Aurobindo's argument when he speaks of the movement's dislocation from the larger nationalist movement is in consonance with the view which argues that had the leaders and the policy makers of the Council firmly aligned themselves with the 'radical political currents of the age', the movement could

171. Ibid., pp.198, 199.

have retained a greater degree of appeal.[172] Sri Aurobindo's was a trenchant attitude when he discussed the National Council's succumbing before the colonial machinery.

Anyway, the opportunities that were denied to Sri Aurobindo in the National College, Pal wrote, were given to him by the *Bande Mataram* and 'from a tutor of a few youths he ... became the teacher of a whole nation'. Sri Aurobindo hailed Pal as the 'Prophet of Nationalism' who, as the speaker of a 'God-given message', stood 'before India as the exponent of the spiritual force' of the nationalist movement, 'its pure 'Indianity', its high devotion to principle ...' and as the 'voice of the Gospel of Nationalism'.[173]

We shall not delve? into an analysis of the National Council's failures and shortcomings; it does not directly form part of this discussion, and can be treated in as much as it helps us comprehend Sri Aurobindo's dissatisfaction with its efforts and aims. One thing, however, that must elicit our attention in Pal's tribute to Sri Aurobindo, is a succinct observation that he made on national education. One perceives in it the now radical nationalist boldly enumerating the ills of the colonial education system.

Discussing the old education policy that existed prior to the Curzonian educational reforms, Pal argued that the old one 'had given birth to wide-spread disaffection' and the new education policy aimed to cure this evil by attempting to 'manufacture loyal citizens – men who would be eternally content to remain loyal to the autocratic government in their country, without any desire for free citizenship'.

Pal saw the national education movement as 'the people's reply to this official policy'. Attacking the 'officially-controlled' education, Pal called it 'shallow' 'rootless', which 'imparted the shadow, but not

---

172. Ibid., pp.170-171.

173. Sri Aurobindo, March 10, 1908, *Bande Mataram*, 1997, pp.742, 743.

the substance, of modern culture to the youths of the nation'. He perceived it as 'artificial' because it was 'foreign in both spirit and form [and] led to a fearful waste of youthful time and energy by imposing the necessity of learning a foreign language, to receive instructions through its medium in all higher branches of study'.

The system, Pal told his readers, was controlled by an unresponsive alien bureaucracy who exercised control over it 'in the interest, mainly, of their own political position, and only secondarily in those of real intellectual life of the pupil. It was excessively literary, and detrimental to the industrial and economical life of the country. The movement of National Education was [therefore] started to counteract these evils of the officially controlled system of public instruction'.[174]

There is truth to the perception highlighted by Pal's biographers that 'between [them] Aurobindo, Bipinchandra and Brahmabandhab [Upadhyay] ... created a new Nationalist Movement and philosophy in the country to which Rabindranath supplied the genius of his poetic Muse. Before this, there was certainly politics, but there was no ideal of composite nationalism ...'[175] which was the special contribution of the new school of politics in Bengal.

Thus Pal, one of the most original political thinkers of his times, gave vent early to his ideas of a new system of education and became a front ranking leader not only of the nationalist movement but also of the national education movement. Between them, Satish Chandra Mukherjee and Bipin Chandra Pal, helped shape the national education discourse not merely out of an emotional reaction to a colonial question but as an attempt at a

174. Bipin Chandra Pal, *Indian Nationalism: Its Principles and Personalities*, op. cit., p.195.

175. Dr. S.C. Roy, The Story of My Times (Calcutta, 1934) cited in *The Origins of The National Education Movement,* op. cit., p. 72.

deeper national self-searching. Their contribution to the quest for a philosophy of national education did much to evolve a cohesive thinking on the issue, and provided an intellectual mooring as well as a philosophical foundation to the whole quest. Their initiation of a debate of the educational question prepared the stage for the movement to take-off later on a wider scale and attracted to it some of the best young minds of the period. The nationalist education discourse thus started shaping up before Sri Aurobindo's arrival in Bengal; he would make it an integral part of the political demand and would give it a deeper philosophical turn.

Our *tour d'horizon* of the beginnings of the national educational demand, of the evolution of Sri Aurobindo's early educational thinking, of the position of the colonial government on educational issues of the day, of the early nationalist or indigenous responses to these positions must end here. It is a survey and a discussion which has revealed to us that Sri Aurobindo was preoccupied with the Indian educational question ever since his early years in India, and though he was not prolific in writing on education, as he was on other issues, he did dwell on it considerably and systematically formulated his educational thought.

It was his philosophy of national education which argued for a complete overhaul of the system of education then prevalent in the country. It also revealed Sri Aurobindo's 'constant preoccupation with the problems of right education in the context of national resurgence'. These early education thoughts of his contained the 'germs of the Aurobindonian conception of integral education'.[176] We shall next read and discuss some of Sri Aurobindo's educational formulations, expositions and ideas in greater detail and attempt to ferret out certain salient features that provide signposts in the quest for a philosophy of national education.

---

176. K.R. Srinivasa Iyengar, op. cit., p. 353.

IV.6. NATIONAL EDUCATION: ITS CONTINUITY IN SRI AUROBINDO'S THOUGHT AND IN THE NATIONAL MOVEMENT

A point, however repetitive, must be made here in support of the stand that national education was an important segment of Sri Aurobindo's thought, not only as a political concept and programme, but more fundamentally as an imperative for national reconstruction. It is also meant to argue that even though Sri Aurobindo spent a brief period in direct service of the national education movement and wrote less on the subject in comparison to his writings on other subjects, the subject of national education nevertheless remained in his scheme of thought and he continued considering its organisation to be of great importance in the scheme of national development and national regeneration.

Most of these early experiments, however, did not have a sustained continuity; they ceased either because their founders further evolved their ideas and restructured their experiment as in the case of Tagore and Satish Chandra, or because they did not receive the requisite time to keep up the continuity as in the case of Brahmabandhab Upadhyay. But each one, whatever their conceptual shortcoming, contributed to the evolution of the concept of national education as a potent force in the nationalist struggle and to the awakening of the mass consciousness.

It is therefore important not to minimise or ignore their contribution. A word on the decline of national schools may be made here. They collapsed as discussed earlier, due to administrative repression especially after revolutionary nationalism came to the fore. The colonial government saw national schools as a hotbed of seditious activities and platforms for spreading disaffection among the younger generation. This led the colonial intelligence department to undertake a detailed surveillance of national schools and the activities of their teachers and students. It is interesting to note the minute details of the activities of the national schools that were recorded and how on a number of occasions connections of teachers and students with Sri Aurobindo and his brand of politics was sought to be established, so that these could be blacklisted as seditious and potential threats to the order of the day.[177]

The other reason for the eventual collapse of the movement was that a large number of people, especially the well-to-do urban elite stayed away from these schools and continued to be part of the official university system since the national schools, they felt, did not hold out bright prospects in the professional field and their students risked being discriminated against by the administration.

Paucity of funds and its unequal distribution, the fast pace of setting up schools, at times without adequate administrative infrastructure, also contributed to the eventual decline of these institutions. But nevertheless the contribution of the national education movement to the overall character of the freedom struggle is immense; it was one of the factors that generated a rapid awareness of the need for freedom, for self-confidence and self-reliance. It also contributed, along with other factors and movements, to the broad-basing of the freedom struggle and of bringing into its mainstream a large number of youth, not all of whom lost out on their education and careers .

A number of them went on to become established authorities in their respective fields of study and research as is evident from the cases of Dr. Radha Kumud Mookerjee (1880–1963), Prof. Benoy Kumar Sarkar (1887–1949) and Dr. Radhakamal Mukherjee (1889–1968), to name a few and in one province. It is known that the national education experiment gradually spread to other provinces,

177. Sumit Sarkar, op.cit., pp.176–77.

especially in areas where the new party – i.e. the nationalist party – began gaining ground, provinces such as Maharashtra, Punjab and the Madras Presidency. Between 1906 and 1909, the national education movement made rapid progress outside Bengal particularly in the district of Berar, and in the Presidencies of Bombay and Madras.[178]

This showed first, that the urgency of the need for education controlled by Indians and responsive to the Indian mind and conditions was felt by a cross section, and was not limited to the sphere of elitist deliberations and two, that the nationalist movement, as initiated by Sri Aurobindo, assumed a pan-Indian dimension and was not confined merely within the precincts of Bengal.[179]

The national education movement and its principal representative organisation catered to the depressed sections of society. At least it tried to reach out to them and attempted to bring about a qualitative change in their circumstances, especially in their educational status. A record of this effort is made by none other than Radhakamal Mukherjee, one of the early and prolific young scholars at the National College and later to be one of the most prolific economist and social scientists of his age, who had initiated the 'Adult Education Movement'. In his memoirs, *India: the Dawn of a New Era*, Mukherjee recollected how he had written a 'Primer for Adult Education – The *Siksha Prachar*' which had an introduction 'from the pen of Prafulla Chandra Roy and was distributed in thousands to all adult schools of Bengal'. Radhakamal also recalled that he was the pioneer 'in setting up Night Schools in the slums of Calcutta. [And that] these were established especially

178. R.C. Majumdar, *History of the Freedom Movement in India vol.2*, op.cit., p. 83.
179. Radhakamal Mukherjee, *India: the Dawn of a New Era*, 1997, pp.68–69.

in the depressed caste quarters. To liquidate illiteracy, remove untouchability and ameliorate the condition of the poverty-stricken mass'. Interestingly, Radhakamal also noted that a quarter of a century later, when he visited the 'Working Man's Training Institution established by the Calcutta Corporation in Mechuabazar', he was 'dumb-founded to find that the Head Master of the institution was the same Chamar boy Fagua, whom I taught the three R's on my lap in the Night School in 1906 and whom Ramesh Chandra Roy had treated for beriberi during an epidemic'.[180] Surely a re-evaluation of the position that the national education movement suffered from an upper-class bias is called for in the light of observations such as the above.

Awareness grew with youthful minds internalising the truth that national education was an indispensable programme along with Swadeshi, Boycott and Swaraj, for expediting national emancipation. It cannot be said that the education movement collapsed; its outward edifice might have disappeared with only traces left behind but the debate it generated continued long after its light had dimmed. The national education movement and discourse firmly planted in the national psyche the realisation that apart from indigenous industries, an elaborate system of education that could be truly called national and would suit and express India's temperamental requirement needed to be evolved for India to be truly emancipated from foreign domination. A national education would also direct her mind towards a true de-colonisation and place her firmly on the path towards self-reliance and original thinking.

It was because the spirit of national education remained alive that one saw stalwarts of the freedom movement and the cultural discourse continuously deliberating on the need for creating edifices, starting new experiments which would continue

180. Ibid.

the journey of discovering and creating systems which would embody the need and demand for national education. One saw this throughout Tagore's life and in the life and actions of Lala Lajpat Rai who wrote extensively on the demands and forms of a national education.

While spending the First World War years exiled in the United States, Rai studied in great detail, the American education system and copiously wrote on education. He wrote on the *Problems of National Education in India,* apart from contributing a series of articles on the issue in the celebrated journal *Modern Review* which was published from Calcutta. It is interesting to note how, amidst the eddy of nationalist politics, these front- ranking leaders found time to contemplate on the topic of national education, and draw up an alternative line of thinking in education for people and their movement to work with. We saw this in Lokmanya Tilak who resolutely propagated the idea, we witnessed it in Sister Nivedita who wrote a number of papers on the theme and who gave it an almost revered place in her scheme of national regeneration, we observed it in that pioneering interpreter of Indian culture who, too, had his period of Swadeshi activism, Ananda Coomaraswamy.[181]

181. Tagore, Sister Nivedita and Ananda Coomaraswamy were invited to deliver lectures at the newly formed National College. Coomaraswamy delivered two extension lectures between 18th and 20th August 1909 at the National College, the first one having Tagore in the Chair. While describing national education and its urgency, Coomaraswamy criticised the university education system because it ignored the 'traditional culture of the land and [because it was] modeled on the lines of the ancient English University system' which had come about when modern advances in Europe had not taken place etc. vide. *The Origins of the National Education Movement*, op.cit., pp. 145–48. It may be also mentioned that in his *Essays in National Idealism*, Coomaraswamy devoted chapters to the educational question in India.

Coomaraswamy was among the first few, along with Sri Aurobindo, to highlight the necessity of a cultural education as an indispensable necessity to free the Indian mind, making it conscious of its innate qualities. In line with that aspiration and assertion, 'Mahamana' Pandit Madan Mohan Malaviya established the University at Benares in 1916 with cooperation from leading personalities of the day, including Mrs. Annie Besant and Satish Chandra Mukherjee, who had by then withdrawn to Benares. In fact Malaviya had worked at his pet project of establishing a Hindu University at Benares from 1905 onwards. He was clear that the University he wished to establish would be different from the existing universities which were mainly examining universities. The university he envisaged was to be a teaching, examining and a residential university, and would try and realise 'the ideal of the University life as it was known in the past in India, and it is known in the advanced countries of the West ...'.[182] The principal educational objectives of Malaviya's proposed university were: 'To promote the study of the Hindu Shastras and of Sanskrit literature generally, as a means of preserving and popularising ... the best thought and culture of the Hindus, and all that was good and great in the ancient civilisation in India'; two, 'to promote learning and research generally in arts and science in all branches; three, 'to advance and diffuse such scientific, technical and professional knowledge, combined with the necessary practical training, as is best calculated to help in promoting indigenous industries and in developing the material resources of the country'; and four, 'to promote the building up of character in youth by making religion and ethics an integral part of education'.[183]

The inspiration of the national education philosophy of the first phase of the national education movement is clearly visible

182. Madan Mohan Malaviya, *Speeches and Writings*, 1919, p.237.

183. Ibid., p.238.

in Malaviya's objective clause. Undoubtedly inspired by the past experiments and quest of the national education movement, Mahatma Gandhi evolved his Basic Education programme for India in the 1930s. A continuity of thought and action was therefore maintained albeit in different forms and under different circumstances.[184] We perceive it consistently in Sri Aurobindo's

184. One of the major items in Mahatma Gandhi's boycott programme during the Non-Cooperation movement in 1920–21was the call for boycotting government schools and colleges; no other item of boycott had as much success as this one. This may be termed as the second phase of the national education movement A large number of 'national schools' were established numbering 1,200; as many as 80,000 students 'got enrolled in them'. This period 1920–21also saw the founding of national education institutions under Gandhiji's leadership such as the Gujarat Vidyapith, the Kashi Vidyapith, under the tutelage of scholar and educationist, Dr. Bhagawan Das (1869–1958), and the Jamia Millia Islamia, under the stewardship of eminent nationalist educationist, Dr. Zakir Hussain (1897–1969), who introduced a number of educational reforms in India, and Dr. K.G. Sayiddin (who as Member of the Kothari Commission on Education for National Development-1964–66, received a message from the Mother, defining the term 'Integral Education' (vide. Footnote-6 in Indrani Sanyal, 'What is it to be Educated in the Light of Sri Aurobindo's Philosophy', op. cit.) These institutions managed to survive under extreme adversity and functioned as symbols of the educational demand of the national movement. When asked why the agitation against the Bengal partition failed [rather it would be correct to ask why the national education movement during the partition movement failed to sustain itself with dynamic vigour] Gandhiji put forward the reasons as, 1) the students had not been withdrawn from classes and 2) the leaders continued to send their children to colleges. He termed the attending of government schools and colleges sinful. [Amrik Singh, 'Education and the National Movement' in *The Contested Terrain – Perspectives on Education in India*, op.cit.]. Though the educational movement reignited by Mahatma Gandhi petered out after a short period – especially when he abandoned the non-cooperation movement which seemed to be

actions too, who, after arriving in Bengal, was the first one to present a cohesive programme for the nationalist struggle at different levels. In Sri Aurobindo's programme, reaching out to the masses would become an important component and the evolution of a national system of education would develop into a programme of supreme importance.

Sri Aurobindo realised that unless the Indian mind was freed from the shackles of the colonial thought process, political emancipation would have no meaning. By 1906, the demand for national education had grown in Bengal, especially after the government's irrational handling of the students protest by trying to tame the students' wave through paper circulars and repressions. It gathered further momentum after the 1902 University Commission. It was to this demand for national education that Sri Aurobindo gave a shape – he channelised and gradually transformed it into a dynamo that became one of the sustaining powers of the nationalist mass movement.

Satish Chandra Mukherjee and the National College became beacons of the national education movement. At a time when the movement was in its infancy and was growing, they represented the

the organic lifeline of the education movement – it showed that the educational demand remained as an undercurrent throughout the national movement. Mahatma Gandhi did not cease to take interest in education and continued to highlight the educational plight of the country in a sustained manner. The reasons for the inability of the second educational agitation to take off on wider scale are similar to those of the first national education movement, both failed to attract a majority of their countrymen, both faced a sustained pressure from the official machinery. But they succeeded in leaving behind at least some institutions which kept the flag of national education aloft – the second movement especially. In that sense, the first, even in spirit, gave momentum to the second, and both played their parts in voicing and shaping the educational dimension of the Indian struggle for freedom.

light of hope for all those who wanted to start national educational institutions. It was Sri Aurobindo who put national education on to the political arena as an instrument of political action. He brought the national education discourse to the masses and revealed the way of emancipation through education on a mass scale. This aspect of Sri Aurobindo's political programme is often overlooked, he is mentioned as being the first principal of the National College who resigned from it due to his greater involvement in the political movement. While this is true and his contribution to the National College is gratefully acknowledged and mentioned in laudatory terms, it is also often understood by this that after relinquishing his charge at the College, Sri Aurobindo ceased to further champion the cause of national education and was only occupied with the currents of 'revolutionary terrorism'.

It is true that after a while, Sri Aurobindo did not have time to spare for the College's administrative and teaching work, and could not devote sufficient attention to nurture the institution to achieve its larger goal because his hands were full with the editorial work of *Bande Mataram* ... Sri Aurobindo was increasingly preoccupied with giving concrete political shape to his new programme, which would have Swaraj, Boycott, Swadeshi and National Education as its 'four planks' (*chatus-sutri*).[185] This left him with little time to focus on the shaping of the National College as one of the first major institution that grew out of the national education movement. Yet for Sri Aurobindo, National Education was to become an instrument to awaken the masses and to educate them on the needs of freedom. But he did not use it merely as an instrument of political rhetoric to arouse the masses; instead he believed that a national

---

185. K.R. Srinivasa Iyengar, op. cit., p. 228.

education structure on a wide scale ought to be built first. Most of the provinces and districts in which nationalists had influence had started national schools.

Eventually, Sri Aurobindo envisaged that a radically new system of national education needed to be evolved. It needed to be not merely a replica of the existing colonial university system under Indian control pursuing the same cycle of subjects, textbooks, evaluation and examination. He believed that a complete overhaul was necessary if national education was to succeed as a movement and positively affect the Indian character.

At the same time as the movement advanced, he realised its problems and the deficiencies that were preventing it from assuming a wider sway, and highlighted them, critiquing the attitudes that he felt projected the old mindset, especially that of imitating the colonial structure, and appending the term 'national' to institutions which continued to be essentially colonial in outlook and function.

A careful reading of Sri Aurobindo's political writings and speeches during 1906–1910 will reveal that ever since his arrival in Bengal, Sri Aurobindo projected, among other issues, the need for national education, and began working towards making it an inalienable part of the political discourse. Even after his resignation from the National College, Sri Aurobindo continued working for widening the ambit of the national education movement and encouraged and assisted the establishing of several national schools. While returning from the deliberations of the Surat Congress 1907, Sri Aurobindo toured the Bombay Presidency, which had already been converted due to the efforts of Tilak and other leaders into a stronghold of the nationalists, and delivered speeches on the situation in the country, and the programme of the new nationalist party.

In almost every speech, Sri Aurobindo dwelt on national education. At the Pabna [East Bengal] Educational Conference in February 1908, just two months before his arrest in the Alipore Bomb Case, attended by about 10,000 men, Sri Aurobindo moved the resolution on national education, and Rabindranath Tagore delivered a 'stirring speech' on the subject. At the district conference that followed, Sri Aurobindo 'explained the aims and ideals of national education'.[186] As late as 1909--1910, just before his departure for Pondicherry, Sri Aurobindo started writing a series to discuss 'some preliminary ideas' on a national system of education in his newly-launched English weekly, *Karmayogin*, and 'almost' outlined 'a philosophy of National education for India'.[187]

The thread thus never snapped, the contemplation on education continued and even in Pondicherry, Sri Aurobindo wrote a Preface on National Education in the last two issues of his journal of philosophy, culture and socio-political thought, *Arya,* between 1920 and 1921. In this series, Sri Aurobindo involved the idea nearly two decades after he had begun working on it. The journal was discontinued, the series could never be completed, but it demonstrated that Sri Aurobindo had concrete ideas on the issue of national education, and the fact that he had given the subject due attention over the years, proved how serious an aspect of national development he considered it to be.

From 1920 onwards, while being absorbed in his Yoga, Sri Aurobindo was preoccupied with the thought of how India was to organise her freedom. It may have been such a preoccupation

---

186. R.C. Majumdar, op.cit., pp. 78, 79.

187. K.R. Srinivasa Iyengar, op. cit., p. 250.

that had led him to start a series on national education. He must have considered an area that was critical to national development. As late as 1946, while dictating a general note on his political life, Sri Aurobindo mentioned that national education was another programme in the political plan that he chalked out and to which he attached much importance. In 1949, a year before his passing, he wrote a series on the importance of physical education in the national, individual and yogic life, and the importance of cultivating the body in the Indian as well Western classical traditions, for the inaugural issues of the Bulletin of the Department of Physical Education of the Ashram.

In the beginning of 1951, when the Mother contemplated the setting up of an university in the name of Sri Aurobindo, she revealed that 'one of the most recent forms under which Sri Aurobindo conceived of the development of his work was to establish at Pondicherry an International University Centre, open to students from all over the world'.[188] We see in this, the thread of national education continuing nearly five decades after Sri Aurobindo had started working on it. From a system of education for the nation, his thoughts had evolved towards creating a system of education open to all seekers of knowledge from across the world.

Though he wrote very little on education in comparison to his contributions of epic proportions in the fields of philosophy, metaphysics, socio-political thought, lingustics, and literature, Sri Aurobindo continued to be in touch with the subject, and the Centre of Education became, after the Ashram itself, the second most important outward manifestation of his integral philosophy. It continues to be an important contributing factor to the ongoing

---

188. *Collected Works of the Mother* (CWM) vol. 12, 1978, p. 111.

discourse on national education and its need and shape in the Indian context. National education and its quest looked at from this aspect assumes a centrality in Sri Aurobindo's philosophy as well as in his life.

5

Sri Aurobindo and the Demand and Need for a National Education System

Political and Ideational

"

There are times in a nation's history when Providence places before it one work, one aim, to which everything else is, however high and noble in itself, has to be sacrificed. Such a time has now arrived for our motherland when nothing is dearer than her service, when everything else is to be directed to that end. If you will study, study for her sake; train yourselves body and mind soul for her service. You will earn your living that you may live for her sake. You will go abroad to foreign lands that you may bring back knowledge with which you may do service to her. Work that she may prosper. Suffer that she may rejoice. All is contained in that one single advice.

– Sri Aurobindo, Advice to National College Students

V.1. INTRODUCTION

While looking at the educational question championed by Sri Aurobindo during the phase in which he was politically active, we discern a distinct division in the tone, tenor and substance of that demand. In his initial educational articulation, Sri Aurobindo's primary focus was on its political dimension. He repeatedly highlighted the deficiencies and the corrugating influences of the colonial education system on young minds and on their aspirations.

As one of those who saw national education as a people's aspiration, Sri Aurobindo spoke on the topic almost everywhere that he travelled. He sought to define the term 'national education', trying to shape its narrative, so that people at large could grasp its meaning and substance. Peoples' support and participation was imperative for the movement's success. Sri Aurobindo knew that unless people supported such an endeavour in large numbers through sheer strength of participation, such an experiment would be incapable of taking off on a national scale. The nationalists, as we have discussed, kept the national education question at the forefront of their political demands and sought to radicalise its political discourse.

The second approach to the question that interests us is the one formulated and adopted by Sri Aurobindo from 1909 onwards, when after his acquittal in the Alipore Conspiracy case, he launched two weeklies *Karmayogin* in English, 'A Weekly Review of National Religion, Literature, Science, Philosophy' (June 1909) and *Dharma* in Bengali (August 1909). As one of his biographers notes, "Sri Aurobindo came out of prison on May 6, 1909, and launched the *Karmayogin* on 19th June. Clearly, he didn't allow the grass to grow under his feet. Speeches, consultations, exhortations – his mere presence – and now this weekly paper!"[1]

The *Karmayogin* would be the broadcaster, among other things, of his educational philosophy. It was not meant to be a mere weekly commenting on the political issues of the day, that phase was over with the closure of *Bande Mataram. The Karmayogin* would initiate a new direction and discourse on various national issues. It would attempt to bring about a certain originality of perception and integration in the diverse strands of national thought and urges that were being thrown up and would move 'far beyond the confines of contemporary politics'.[2] Current events would be noticed in 'only as they evidence, help, affect or resist the growth of national life and the development of the soul of the nation'.[3] A mere varied activity in diverse areas 'might prove to be activity at cross-purposes, and instead of strengthening the nation might actually weaken it and give its movement a wrong or even a backward direction'.[4] The *Karmayogin* came to assist in the integration of this diverse action, 'to give voice and definiteness to the deeper aspiration' that was 'forming obscurely within the national consciousness'[5] and to unite its energies in a mighty process of national regeneration by evolving a distinct national goal. Sri Aurobindo inspiringly spelt out the actual goal of Nationalism – "To recover Indian thought, Indian

---

1. K.R. Srinivasa Iyengar, op.cit., p.346.
2. Peter Heehs, *Sri Aurobindo: A Brief Biography*, op. cit., pp. 61–62.
3. Sri Aurobindo, 'Ourselves' *Karmayogin, 19 June, 1909* in *CWSA* vol.8, op.cit., p.22.
4. K.R.Srinivasa Iyengar, op.cit., pp. 336, 337.
5. Ibid., pp. 18, 19.

character, Indian perceptions, Indian energy, Indian greatness, and to solve the problems that perplex the world in an Indian spirit and from the Indian standpoint, this, in our view, is the mission of Nationalism"[6], and in *Karmayogin* aimed to catalyse and articulate its ideational contours, "We have to return to the fountainheads of our ancient religion, philosophy, art and literature, and pour the revivifying influences of our immemorial Aryan spirit and ideals into our political and economic development. This is the ideal the *Karmayogin* holds before it...".[7]

Education was an essential part of that regeneration, but the approach to it would not be, in keeping with the spirit of the *Karmayogin*, to simply demand its reforms, restructuring and reorganising but to try and explore and evolve a deeper perspective to the whole issue. The emphasis would be on the mental and spiritual growth of the learner. The political rhetoric would be absent[8], the pointed accusatory tone aimed at the colonial dispensation's educational control would be subdued, and instead a more fundamentally philosophical analysis of the whole problem of education would be formulated. The subject of art and its importance in a system of national education and in the national

---

6. 'National Resurgence' in SriAurobindo, *On Nationalism*, 1996, p.470.
7. Ibid., Interestingly, the *Karmayogin* soon became popular and was in wide demand outside Bengal also, primarily on Maharashtra and Madras. (Manoj Das, *Life & Times of the Mahayogi*, op.cit., p.621.
8. During this phase (1909–1910) Sri Aurobindo would continue to 'place the nationalist ideal before the country' but he now 'conceived this ideal in less purely political terms...' than before. [*CWSA* vol.8, op. cit., p. 469] His biographer noted, "The bureaucracy couldn't appreciate the shift in emphasis implied in the change from the *Bande Mataram* to the *Karmayogin*. Perhaps a trap – a subtle and dangerous trap – was suspected in the change itself." (K.R.Srinivas Iyengar, op.cit., p.346.

life would be taken up, and the issue of the 'Brahmacharya-Yoga axis in education'[9] would be analysed and established. This series would explore the different dimensions of the Indian educational question against India's civilisational rubric.

That attention to education was given at a time when the political scenario for the nationalists was far from favourable, and when tremendous pressure was being brought on them to capitulate and disband, is indicative of the importance that Sri Aurobindo gave to national education and of its imperativeness in his scheme of national regeneration.

On his acquittal, Sri Aurobindo was the 'only important Bengali Extremist, indeed the only Extremist with a countrywide reputation, in a position to lead a party that had become completely disorganised, demoralised and inactive'. He was quickly drawn back into politics.[10] Sri Aurobindo's close political associates such as Tilak, Bipin Pal and Lala Lajpat Rai, Krishna Kumar Mitra, and others were either deported or had gone into self-imposed exile to the West. Tilak was deported to Mandalay for a six-year rigorous imprisonment. 'Everywhere there was depression and hopelessness, though the feeling against the foreign rule had not abated. It had, on the contrary, increased by repression'.[11] Sri Aurobindo described the atmosphere as he found it, on his release:

> The whole aspect of the country altered; most of the Nationalist leaders were in jail or in self-imposed exile and there was a general discouragement and depression, though the feeling in the country had not ceased, but was only suppressed and was growing by its suppression. He determined to continue the struggle; he held weekly meetings in Calcutta, but the attendance which had numbered formerly thousands full of enthusiasm,

---

9. K.R.Srinivasa Iyengar, op. cit., p.353.
10. Peter Heehs, *Sri Aurobindo: a Brief Biography*, op.cit., p.62.
11. A.B. Purani, *The Life of Sri Aurobindo*, op.cit., p.124.

was now only of hundreds and had no longer the same force and life.[12]

But we shall first start here with reading some of Sri Aurobindo's key political writings and utterances on the educational question. We shall begin with his arrival in Bengal and the shaping of the national education discourse after he had openly joined politics. Many of his utterances and writings on education during this phase deal primarily with the technicality of the national education demand as a political programme, and do not contain defining or philosophical aspects. We shall try and avoid analysing these, mainly because a study of these lies strictly in the realm of pure nationalist politics, and would have to be seen in the backdrop of other essential political demands and would thus suck us deep into the vortex of early nationalist politics, *vis-à-vis* the Moderates and the Extremists, their programmes, maneuvers, manipulations, failures, and triumphs.

Though an exciting proposition, we may risk getting diverted from the quest of educational philosophy and get bogged down instead into the nitty-gritty of constitutional demands, resolutions, and committee politics. A surface survey of the political demand of national education and the nationalist efforts at upholding the issue would therefore serve our purpose. It would be absurd to deny the fact that both national education and national politics were intertwined at a crucial phase of the Indian struggle, but to simply look at this political demand would divert us from its philosophical formulations.

During his discussion of national education as a political demand, and when Sri Aurobindo talked only of national education, we see him providing nearly always a philosophical underpinning

12. *Autobiographical Notes*, op.cit., p.61.

to his thoughts and arguments. We shall try and attempt to trace that philosophical reinforcement in the political formulation of education, and thereby try to expand our understanding of this quest for a philosophy of national education.

V.2. SRI AUROBINDO'S POLITICAL DEMAND FOR A NATIONAL EDUCATION

Sri Aurobindo arrived in Calcutta sometime in March 1906. By then the Swadeshi movement 'had been in progress for seven months'.[13] Thousands had emerged to participate in the movement that saw the whole province thrown in the throes of a convulsion. The Government tried to mow down the movement through drastic extra legal measures and intimidations. Its target were Swadeshi leaders and students who provided the much-needed energy and momentum to the whole exercise of boycott of foreign goods and in popularising and implanting the idea.

The administrations of both Bengals had issued a number of prohibitive ordinances; among them was one that debarred students from participating in demonstrations. The revolt against this ordinance saw the setting up of the first national school, and imparted the momentum for national education to emerge as a movement.

As we discussed earlier in the work, all these had happened by November 1905. To display solidarity with the first national school that had been established in the East-Bengal district of Rangpur,[14]

13. Peter Heehs, op. cit., p. 39.
14. It would be relevant to point out that Sri Aurobindo spent the first five years of his childhood at Rangpur. Sri Aurobindo's father K.D.Ghose's first posting after return from England was at Rangpur. Dr. K.D.Ghose was appointed as the station's medical officer in 1871, and became popular with his involvement in the town's welfare activities. He was

the Calcutta nationalist leaders assembled at a mass meeting in the evening of November 9, 1905, with Subodh Chandra Mallik (1879–1920) in the chair. Sri Aurobindo's close collaborator, brother-in-arms, acolyte and principal financier of the advanced nationalist and revolutionary group, Subodh Mallik had first met Sri Aurobindo around 1904, at the house of C.C. Dutt who was then posted as the District Judge of Thane in the Bombay Presidency. Sri Aurobindo 'found in him [Subodh Mallik] a friend and collaborator in the country's cause' and Mallik extended the hand of support and was 'instrumental in Sri Aurobindo's coming to Calcutta to lead the national movement'.[15] Sri Aurobindo was to become 'the central guiding spirit of the Malliks' and they in turn 'gave him wholehearted financial and other assistance in order to realise his objectives'.[16]

In 1904, Mallik founded the 'Academy Club'; the building which housed this club was also a well-known haunt of nationalists such

---

also elected to the Town Committee in 1876 and in 1877, 'his medical and official interests came together to produce the biggest triumph of his career'. In December that year, he launched the works for cutting a canal, 'that still bears his name: The K.D.Canal'. Work on the canal began apparently to fulfil a major recommendation that Dr. Ghose had made six years earlier while submitting a report on the sanitation of Rangpur. The town lying on the Gangetic delta was 'swampy and malaria-ridden' and Dr. Ghose saw the cutting of a major canal as a way out of the problem. 'In recommending drainage, Dr. Ghose showed himself to be near the cutting edge of medical technology. The theory that mosquitoes carried the disease was not confirmed until 1898'. [Archival Notes in *Sri Aurobindo Archives and Research, Vol.14, No.1, April 1990*, pp. 105–108] Dr. Ghose was to become Vice-Chairman of the Rangpur Municipality. A field apart from education, we have include it here to indicate Rangpur's link with Sri Aurobindo's life.

15. Sisir Kumar Mitra, op.cit., pp. 74, 75.
16. Amalendu De, *Raja Subodh Chandra Mallik and His Times*, 1996, p.54.

as Satish Chandra Mukherjee and Brahmabandhab Upadhyay. Other well-known nationalists were also boarders in this building which had a mess on its first floor. Mallik's Club became, 'the meeting ground of leading writers, politicians, lawyers, and other distinguished men'. Bipin Chandra, Brahmabandhab Upadhyay, C.R.Das, Vivekananda's younger brother, Bhupendra Nath Datta, and others regularly joined Subodh Chandra in the evening at the Academy Club. Sri Aurobindo 'also joined them when he visited Calcutta.... The Academy became a platform of the extremists, and in time made significant contributions to the growth and extension of the spirit of Swadeshi in Bengal'.[17]

It was through his presidential address in that mass meeting that Subodh Mallik, then all but 26 years old, altered altogether the course of the national education movement. Terming the system of western education applied to India a 'bastard system', Mallik said that he had known both the education systems, this one, 'as well as the natural type of it in the West' and rejoiced that at last it had been realised that 'our salvation must be worked out by ourselves in spite of dangers and difficulties that may at present appear' insurmountable. The Government's attitude towards the students' issue was an 'eye opener' Mallik said, and it had become evident that the attempt at controlling education would gradually become 'a dangerous weapon' in the hands of that very Government. Mallik's remedy thus, was as drastic as his youthful energy, a 'secure career of national progress will be impossible for us unless we take the same [the weapon of educational control] away from their [Government's] hands'.[18] Quoting Mazzini on education, an association he must have imbibed from Sri Aurobindo, his

17. Ibid., p.55.
18. Ibid., pp. 59, 60.

newfound mentor in nationalist politics, Mallik spoke of how education for 'mere personal use' becomes 'an agent of tyranny and corruption' whereas an education 'consecrated to aid the progress of all' becomes a 'means of civilisation and liberty'.

Speaking of the predicament of Indian education under the colonial regime, Subodh Chandra said that 'ideas of nationality, self-respect, and the higher attributes which ennoble a man, have no place in it' and that the first task thus must be to reverse that trend and 'put education on a sound basis'.[19] He was ashamed, he told the massive gathering, that he was forced to address them in English, "I am ashamed to own that I am one of the products of the present de-nationalised system of education, who can better express themselves in the foreign tongue than their own."[20]

His following announcement gave a mighty and timely impetus to the founding of the National College. Reflecting the spirit and dynamism of youth, Subodh Chandra called for making sacrifices to keep up the momentum that had picked up because of the recent students' action:

> The great demand is that of sacrifice. If I may say so, the next and the last essential is sacrifice in the present crisis. Let us make a beginning here today. The students are already stinting themselves of their comforts in order to contribute their humble mite to the National University Fund. Their example has not been, but is bound to evoke universal response. For my part, to show sympathy with their laudable efforts, I most humbly beg to place at the disposal of the promoters of this cause my humble contribution of a lakh of rupees. I am not, gentlemen, a wealthy man. I can ill afford the luxury of making such a gift. But the call of the Mother is clear, and we must respond, be we great or small.[21]

---

19. Ibid., p.61.
20. Ibid., p.60.
21. Ibid.

An interval of thunderous applause was followed by the conferring on him of the honorific of 'Raja' (King) by those present.[22] Earlier Subodh Chandra had confided to one his nationalist colleagues that 'that this is the opportune moment for imparting national education to our boys. If you can establish such a college, I shall donate one lakh rupees'.[23]

Among those present were some of Sri Aurobindo's close nationalist collaborators, Bipin Chandra Pal, Manoranjan Guha Thakurta, and C.R.Das, later to become his defence council in the Alipore Trial. The munificent offer, however, came with the stipulation that 'Aurobindo Ghose' then at Baroda 'should be given a post of professor in the [National] College with a salary of Rs. 150'.[24] The rider was accepted and the arrangement thus made it possible for Sri Aurobindo to eventually come to Bengal and to implement the programmes of nationalist action that he had drawn up for the last few years unnoticed in distant Baroda.

Satish Chandra Mukherjee, had by then sounded the bugle on the need for organising a 'National University'. In an article in the January 1906 issue of his now-metamorphosed *The Dawn and Dawn Society's Magazine*, he elaborated on 'A Scheme of National Collegiate Education for the Proposed National University for Bengal'[25] with the 'Quickening of the national life of the people'

22. Ibid.
23. Ibid., p.59.
24. Sri Aurobindo, *On Himself*, p.28.
25. It is said that Satish Chandra Mukherjee met Sri Aurobindo while the latter was on a visit to Bengal from Baroda and suggested, in course of a discussion on national education, that Sri Aurobindo join the Dawn Society. Sri Aurobindo answered, "Nobody can relate to the concept of national education with a name like Dawn Society; they will have no interest. We need a national university. We have to build up a National Council of Education." (Manoj Das, *Sri Aurobindo: Life and Times of the Mahayogi*, op.cit., p.231,)

as its object and ideal. The ideal would be attained 'positively, by seeking to draw inspiration by a proper study of both the West and the East, and of India in particular' and 'negatively, by setting our faces against imitation of the West, or the tendency to welcome fashions imported from the West'.[26]

The proposed University not only accepted the system of granting certificates or degrees in subjects by the University, but would also attempt to chart out an alternative path by proposing that, even while adhering to this degree-granting system, the subjects, courses of study, and examinations be so arranged and conducted, that 'the whole atmosphere about a College or University ... be such that the thought, attention and energy of the student become naturally more drawn to and fixed upon the supreme value of the life that he is living as a student in his College or University, and less upon the external mark of proficiency and culture, in the shape of a Degree or a Certificate that may ultimately be conferred on'.

In the proposed National College, the scheme pointed out, certificates or degrees would not be artificial ones symbolising surface accomplishment; instead they would 'stand for something intrinsically higher in the life and character and thought of a student than what is involved in the possession of Degree which leaves such life and character and thought all but untouched or which improves or elevates them in an indirect, or collateral or subsidiary manner'.[27]

In his proposed National University scheme, Satish Chandra delineated a detailed method enumerating various schemes of studies and examinations that may be followed in order to achieve such an objective. His concluding arguments on 'two

26. *The Dawn and Dawn Society's Magazine*, January 1906, *The Dawn and Dawn Society's Magazine*, vol.9, 1907, p. 137.
27. *The Dawn and Dawn Society's Magazine*, January 1906, p.138.

ways of establishing' a National University indicated the direction the national education movement could chose to follow, and the experiments it could decided to undertake. Their significance lies in the fact that even before the movement had assumed an organised character, Satish Chandra foresaw, quite rightly, two possible models of implementing the national education plan.

The first possible way was to 'establish a particular type of Model College at a central place, *i.e.* impart a particular type of teaching to a limited number of pupils and seek to influence the surrounding educational life of the people by the example of superior teaching'. Satish Chandra argued that was a 'slow and laborious process' but hoped that if graduates of the Model College 'proved to be men of real force of character and also of superior abilities, they would in course of time be able to leaven the mass, and gradually, by the influence of such a College, educational institutions of the type represented by [it] would grow up and might in course of time actually replace, to a very large extent, the existing educational institutions affiliated to the official University'.

The Model College would have to withstand the pressures of organised education as represented by the colonial Government, and until the network of such colleges spread throughout the country, it would not gain sufficient credibility. A struggle was bound to ensue between the entrenched official system and new system which would seek to challenge the official supremacy. To survive in such a struggle, the Model College would have to 'look less to the severity of the tests it imposes upon the candidates aspiring after its Degrees and Certificates than to the manner in which it is able to inspire their lives with a spirit and ideal which would be at once pre-eminently national and modern'. [28]

---

28. *The Dawn and Dawn Society's Magazine*, January 1906, p.143.

The second way proposed by Satish Chandra for organising the National University was to 'foster the spirit of *self-reliance* evinced by' institutions 'who have severed connection with the Official University and started what they have called National Institutions'; Satish Chandra meant the newly-founded national school at Rangpur and Dacca. The primary task in this second way was to direct attention to the 'spirit of independence, or the desire to govern themselves in matters educational without the leading strings of Government'.[29] Where the desire for 'independent management of its own educational interests is not acutely present', no National University could find acceptance or root.

The way forward for fruition of such a project would therefore be to support the newly-established national schools, and these, if 'properly taken in hand and developed along right lines, may supply the needed impulse for new institutions to grow on independent lines supplanting old one; or the impulse may result in many of the existing institutions catching the contagion and following their lead'. Satish Chandra saw no reason why the second method of action could not be applied and did not agree that it was 'altogether out of the range of practical politics'.[30]

The nationalist leaders, Sri Aurobindo among them, who formed the advanced nationalist group in the struggle for freedom, appear to have chosen the second line of action. It was perhaps driven and inspired by Sri Aurobindo's political stance which saw the necessity of involving the masses in the struggle for liberation in order to broad-base the movement. The second method suggested for establishing a National University seemed to take that criterion into consideration as well, and allowed for a certain organic and spontaneous action in developing a national education network.

---

29. Ibid.

30. Ibid., pp. 143, 144.

Such were the broad contours of the educational discussions prior to the convening of the meeting to form the governing body of the national college.

'On March 11, 1906, just days after his arrival in Calcutta' Sri Aurobindo attended the meeting convened to inaugurate the National Council of Education.[31] The conference convened at 4 p.m. saw some of the leading lights of Bengal participate in the deliberations. It considered the report of the Ways and Means Committee that had been set up to scrutinise the scheme of a National Council of Education submitted to it by a 'Provisional Education Committee' formed in November 1905. 'A provisional body of trustees had already been formed consisting of Raja Peary Mohan Mukherjee (1840–1924), Subodh Chandra Mallik' and others, 'to receive donations and subscriptions and build up funds for the National Council of Education'. That evening, the conference constituted the National Council of Education with 92 members, 'representing virtually the cream of contemporary Bengali society'.[32]

The name, 'Mr. Arabinda Ghose', figured sixty-third in the list of the luminaries. The object of the Council was declared, in the now famous words, to be that of imparting education, 'Literary as well as Scientific and Technical – on National Lines and exclusively under National Control, not in opposition to, but standing apart from, the existing systems of Primary, Secondary and University Education'. It defined the term 'Education on National Lines' as implying among other things '1.a) Imparting of Education ordinarily through the medium of the Vernaculars, English being compulsory subject', b) The preparation of suitable text-books, especially in the Vernaculars

---

31. Peter Heehs, *op. cit.,* p. 39.
32. Dr. Amitabha Mukherjee, *Fifty Years of National Education: The Story of An Experiment 1906–1956*, 1992, pp.35, 36.

and '2. Promoting of Physical and Moral Education and providing for denominational Religious Education out of funds specifically contributed for that purpose and inspiring students with a genuine love for, and a real desire to serve, their country…'.[33] The Council was to be conferred with the power to 'establish in Calcutta and elsewhere … educational institutions for the imparting of such education'.[34]

Sri Aurobindo attended subsequent meetings of the Council's Executive Committee and signed some of the minutes of these meetings. It appears from these minutes that 'he himself was appointed as paper-setter of examinations in English, a member of the faculty of Arts, a lecturer in English etc'.[35] But before he could formally assume his responsibilities at the College, Sri Aurobindo had to officially terminate his association with the Baroda College. He went to Baroda in June and 'on the nineteenth, took one year's leave without pay'.[36] He never returned to Baroda.

It is unnecessary to go into the details of the conference; such a detailing has been admirably undertaken in well-known studies and works. What must be pointed out here however, is that the National Council fell short of calling for an altogether fresh line of educational action which would challenge the established order of the day. The 'not in opposition to' indicated the real stance of the experiment and pointed to the fact that political moderates were in control of the body. The sharp division on this question among the leaders

---

33. 'Inauguration of the National Council of Education in Bengal' in *The Dawn and Dawn Society's Magazine*, op. cit., March, 1906. The article in the magazine gave in detail the proceedings of the conference and the resolutions it passed.
34. *Sri Aurobindo Archives and Research, Vol.3, No.1, April 1979*, pp. 118–119.
35. Ibid.
36. Ibid.

had already exposed itself, and groups 'could easily be identified as extreme and moderate'. The moderates while agreeing to expose the inadequacies of the prevailing official education system were not in favour of totally boycotting the system. The other group called for setting up a totally different system of education which would be completely under national control and evolve along national lines and function under a 'complete educational autarchy'.[37]

Sri Aurobindo summed up the positions best when he wrote that differences between the two groups were most acute over the issues of adopting the policies of Boycott and National Education – 'National Education is regarded by one school as an educational experiment to be carried on side by side with Government education, and by the other, as a great national cause, the progress of which is to culminate in a truly national system replacing or absorbing the Government schools and colleges'.[38]

A political analysis of these demands and differences does not need a detailed analysis as that would divert us again into the realm of various theoretical divisions and political differences that surfaced at that time. It would suffice for our purpose to point out that a moderate and cautious approach to National Education went against Sri Aurobindo's approach. It fell far short of his demands of complete restructuring in all spheres of national activity which included the educational. Sri Aurobindo clearly indicated such a line of thinking in his later articles on education. The times were perhaps too volatile, and those conducting the experiment, the first of its kind to be undertaken in an organised manner, were perhaps too unsure of its viability and eventual acceptance, and therefore thought it prudent not to openly court official displeasure and bureaucratic wrath.

---

37. *Raja Subodh Chandra Mallik and His Times,* op. cit., pp.69, 70.
38. Sri Aurobindo, August 22, 1906, *Bande Mataram,* op.cit., pp. 222, 223.

But this attitude militated against Sri Aurobindo's policy. Ever the political radical and the political pragmatist, Sri Aurobindo knew that a hesitant approach to the reorganisation of national education would perpetually keep the attempt subdued under the official system, allowing it to eventually swamp it beyond recognition. Indeed, it 'soon became evident that the moderate-dominated Council, afraid of giving undue offense to the British, was willing to make only tinkering changes in the syllabus in the name of national education'. Sri Aurobindo is himself on record, in his articles, especially later in the *Karmayogin*, to have expressed such a view. He 'regretted the Council's timidity but did not think it profitable to oppose it'[39] as that would have unnecessarily hampered the progress of the experiment. Moreover he did not have time to do that because of his growing preoccupation with direct and dynamic nationalist political action.

V.3. EDUCATIONAL ISSUES IN POLITICAL FORUMS

The Bengal Provincial Conference held in the East Bengal district of Barisal in April 1906 must have been the first political conference Sri Aurobindo openly attended in Bengal after his Baroda stay. As has been briefly described, all the senior Calcutta leaders were present at this conference which was widely reported and talked about in nationalist circles. The Conference saw the display of a brazen spirit of defiance by nationalist workers against the colonial administrative ukases, and witnessed the colonial administration resort to extreme repression and arbitrariness in face of an organised and peaceful disobedience of their draconian laws. A record of the description of the Conference dramatically writes of it thus:

The first day of the Bengali calendar year 1313 will ever remain a Red Letter Day in the history of Bengal, the day fixed for the first session of

39. Peter Heehs, op. cit., p.40.

the Barisal Provincial Conference. That was the memorable day when the streets of Barisal were turned red with the blood of patriotic sons of Bengal ... It was a day of all days. The day dawned with thousands of patriots rising from bed with one solemn purpose to attend the Conference and offer worship to Mother India.[40]

The Barisal Provincial Conference was also perhaps the first such Conference which 'saw a warm response from people of different walks of life'. Earlier such meets would be supported primarily by the 'educated middle class.'[41]

Our interest in the Barisal Provincial Conference is, as we have stated earlier, because of Sri Aurobindo's participation in it 'mainly as an observer ... associated with the [Bipin Chandra] Pal faction',[42] who was in 'the front row of three persons in the procession' when it was 'dispersed by the police charge'.[43] Some aspects of the proceedings of the conference is also of interest because of what was said in them on the topic of national education. Because Sri Aurobindo witnessed and participated in these proceedings, it makes it necessary and interesting to examine these. It also help us understand the issue of national education as he saw it then being discussed and debated.

Aswini Kumar Dutta (1856–1923) one of the tallest nationalist leaders of Barisal who made the district the epicentre of the *Swadeshi* movement through his incessant educational and political

---

40. Yatindrakumar Ghosh, *Bengal Provincial Conference 1905 & 1906*, (1956) 2007, p.115.
41. K.L. Chattopadhyay 'Bengal Provincial Conference at Barisal, 14th & 15th April, 1906' in: *Proceedings of the Indian History Congress*, 1979, Vol. 40 (1979), pp. 581–586
42. Peter Heehs, op. cit.
43. *On Himself*, op. cit., p.46.

activities[44], was the Chairman of the Reception Committee and in his

44. Aswini Kumar Dutta was closely associated with Sri Aurobindo during the nationalist movement and especially supported initiatives for setting up national schools. A highly revered leader, Aswini Kumar was one of the few Swadeshi leaders who commanded a mass base. He was among the nine Bengali leaders who were deported under the draconian Regulation III of 1818 that authorised the 'Government to place a person under confinement as a State-prisoner without any trial'. Subodh Chandra Mallik, Manoranjan Guha Thakurta, and Syam Sundar Chakravarti, were among other close nationalist associates of Sri Aurobindo to be included among the nine deportees. In his public speech delivered at Jhalakati in the Bakarganj district of East Bengal (the town of Barisal was the headquarters of the district which was then at times referred to as the Barisal district) on June 19, 1909, Sri Aurobindo openly and vehemently criticised this act and spoke of those leaders incarcerated under it. Paying his tribute to Aswini Kumar, Sri Aurobindo movingly said, "When I come to this soil of Bakarganj, which has been made sacred and ever memorable in the history of this country, I come to no ordinary place. When I come to Barisal, I come to a chosen temple of the Mother, I come to a scared *pithasthan* [pilgrim spot] of the national spirit, I come to the birth-place and field of work of Aswini Kumar Dutta ...'[Sri Aurobindo, *Speeches*, op.cit., pp. 91–100.] Sri Aurobindo also referred to Aswini Kumar's educational experiment through the celebrated Brajamohan (BM) College in the latter's home district of Barisal. BM College and its allied institutions had become models to be emulated for the new national education institutions. Aswini Kumar had succeeded in developing through these chains of institution, a large network of nationalist youth, who not only excelled in academics, but who were repeatedly called and relied upon for community work of all kinds, and demonstrated an independent spirit of self-reliance, unity and inclusiveness. Describing the work of the young students Sri Aurobindo observed that 'when epidemic broke out, when cholera appeared in all its virulence, the young men of the Barisal Brajamohan College went out in bands. They nursed the sick, they took charge of those who had been abandoned, they took up in their arms those whom they found lying on the roadside. They were not deterred in those moments by the prejudice of caste or by the

address spoke pointedly on certain aspects of national education. The basic thrust of Dutta's educational argument was that alien minds were incapable of understanding and training Indians; they could not appreciate the needs of indigenous growth and would only serve to disconnect young Indians from their national milieu.

In the course of his address, Aswini Kumar identified three areas that would gradually evolve into some of the principal pillars of the new nationalist movement – they were, 'National Education, creation and development of Indigenous Industries and the foundation of Arbitration Committees and such other Institutions as would, by self-help, promote the general welfare of the people' these would form the 'ground-work of the structure' of the new nation.[45]

---

difference of creed. The orthodox Brahmin took up in his bosom and nursed the Mahommedan and the Namasudra. They did not mind the epidemic or fear to catch the contagion. They took up and nursed them as brother nurses brother, and thus they rescued many from the grasp of death .... While ordinary colleges under the control of the Government were mere soulless machines where they cram a few packets of useless knowledge into the brain of the student, Aswini Kumar breathed his lofty and noble soul into the Brajamohan College, and made it an engine indeed out of which men were turned in, in which hearts and souls were formed. He breathed his noble qualities into the young men who grew up in the cherishing warmth and sunlight of his influence. He made his college an institution which in the essentials of education was a model for any educational institution in the world ....' [*Sri Aurobindo, Speeches*, op.cit., 2005, pp. 120–21]. R.C.Majumdar writes of how Barisal 'under the leadership of Aswini Kumar Dutta, who was revered by the local people almost as a saint, proved to be the strongest centre of Swadeshi and Boycott movements .... The Swadeshi and Boycott movements had tremendous success in the whole district'. (*History of the Freedom Movement in India*, vol.2, op.cit., p.86.)

45. Yatindrakumar Ghosh, *Bengal Provincial Conference 1905 & 1906*, (1956) 2007, p.124.

Aswini Kumar did not completely deny what he saw as the benefits of an 'exotic' education. It had, he said 'revived in us the thought of rising above the interests of individuals and families and to think of national concerns; it has impressed on us that no nation by servile dependence on another can achieve the end of its existence'. Such an education 'exposed to us our defects and revealed to us the general principles on which the growth of a nation depends'.[46] But those principles had to be 'adapted to the modes of our national being' through 'our own efforts' and until that was done 'we can never expect to rise or even to hold our own, the little we have in the competition of the world'.

There was a fundamental difference between the occidental and the oriental mind, habits and perception, and the present system of education, argued Aswini Kumar, 'does not seem to take this into account' and the boys were not trained in anything Indian – history and traditions. It was impossible for those charged with educational dissemination to be able to 'dive down into the depths of our national heart in which lie imbedded ... beneath the slime of ages, precious truths that were propounded by the Hindu Rishis and Mahomedan Saints of old'.[47]

The moral and spiritual education of the race was neglected precisely because those responsible for imparting it were themselves ignorant of the indigenous traditions and wisdom. The present educationists did not possess, observed Aswini Kumar, the acumen or depth to recover those precious truths and 'utilise them in the practical up-building of the old fabric in a new form'.

Aswini Kumar's suggestions were similar to Satish Chandra Mukherjee's *Dawn* experiment. He argued that western acquisitions would have to be integrated with Indian traditions and this would

46. Ibid.

47. Ibid., pp. 124, 125.

become the bedrock of the new system, which could then be spread among the people. The old fabric, traditions, indigenous cultural and spiritual wisdom have to be 'drawn out and cemented with our acquisitions from the West by our own exertions and this compounded material must be placed at the door of every individual, every family, every society and every community of our Mother-land ...'.[48]

Referring to a leading nationalist leader's perception that the nation minus a national education is deprived of a 'moral existence', and that it is on a moral existence that a 'national conscience is formed', Aswini Kumar supported the efforts of organising a system of national education in the country. He did not utter these words out of mere political compulsion; his by then well-established and successful experiment of the Brajamohan Institution, had convinced him of certain basic components and prerequisites needed for a successful, comprehensive, and a truly national education.

In his Presidential Address, Abdul Rasul (1872–1917) alluded to the need for educating the masses if permanent success was to be achieved by the 'National Movement.' In his speech—which did not discuss the philosophical underpinnings of national education as much as Aswini Kumar's did, but which dilated instead on the practical and technical sides of the whole issue—Rasul identified 'want of education' as the cause for 'our lagging behind other nations .... It is a reflection on the British rule in India that what it could not accomplish in the field of education in 150 years, the Japanese have done for Japan within less than 40 years'.[49]

Rasul expressed wholehearted support for the newly-inaugurated National Council of Education, especially its attempt to 'establish industrial and technical schools all over the country

48. Ibid.
49. Ibid., p. 142.

to teach [Indian] youths how to make, with small capital, the necessaries of life which' were, till then, imported from foreign countries. Continuous and wide support would hasten the process of building a 'full-fledged University' which would impart education along national lines, which would inspire students 'with a genuine love for, and real desire to serve their country'.

For the Swadeshi Movement 'to have a permanent hold on the hearts of the people' such an education was needed.[50] The masses, when educated on national lines, will not need coaxing to believe and follow Swadeshi methods and programmes; 'they will understand their own responsibilities', achieve a certain widening of perspective and feel that 'as a nation they will have to play an important part on the stage of the world', and the adherence to the Swadeshi cause will then appear spontaneously 'from within'. The new education, under national control, will serve to generate awareness among the mass as to the state of their degradation and humiliation, and to make them realise that 'though they were treated in such a degrading manner at present, that they too had a great civilisational past'.

Rasul's emotional exhortation demonstrated his complete identification with the cause of national education. He did not call for a compartmentalised educational programme, but rather one that was varied and inclusive, "We have a glorious past and we must make our future as glorious [and] henceforth, to educate the masses on national lines must be the sacred duty of every educated citizen." In the eventuality of the Government rejecting the National Council's certificates and degrees, Rasul called upon the capitalists, zamindars, and the mercantile class to come forward, and engage in suitably employing those newly trained students.[51] The resolution

---

50. Ibid., p.143.
51. Ibid.

on National Education was the third one to be passed on the second day of the proceedings and was 'unanimously adopted'.[52] The demand thus for a national education system was politically established and mainstreamed.

Sri Aurobindo's reaction to the proceedings and to the priority he conferred on national education can be judged from his observations on it in the August 22, 1906, issue of the newly launched *Bande Mataram*. The article entitled 'National Education and the Congress' referred to a tussle between two groups within the Congress, professing divergent paths and views for achieving national liberation. Sri Aurobindo wrote that 'National Education received the seal of approbation from united Bengal at the Barisal Conference. It should be the aim [therefore] of the nationalists to elicit from the Congress this year [to be held in Calcutta in December 1906] a solemn expression of the national will, recognising the new movement and recommending it to all India'. Had the Congress 'not been hopelessly out of date in its form and spirit', Sri Aurobindo hit out, 'it would, by this time, have organised itself for work, with a department for the organisation of National Education on a basis of voluntary self-taxation figuring prominently in its list of national duties'.[53]

However, Sri Aurobindo saw the unanimous acceptance of the national education resolution as a major triumph for nationalist forces and, buoyed by this acceptance, he pushed for the inclusion of the complete nationalist programme in the annual Congress meet that was to follow in winter. He had already forethought the creation of a department that could implement national education on a large scale but understood that the Congress as a body was then incapable

52. Ibid., p. 152.

53. Sri Aurobindo, August 22, 1906, *Bande Mataram,* op. cit., p. 134.

of working out such a plan. To Sri Aurobindo the demand of national education made as part of a political programme indicated that the movement had gained dynamism and a momentum. He saw that the call given at Barisal for disseminating education on national lines to the masses, the call for it to reach every doorstep, could be worked out if it found inclusion as a programme of national action. In order to do that, it had to be pushed so that it found acceptance within the Congress structure,which was then gearing up for its first transmuting pangs.

V.4. IN THE NATIONAL COUNCIL AND THE NATIONAL COLLEGE

The National Council started functioning on 15th August, 1906, the 34th birthday of its first principal, Sri Aurobindo. He had returned to Calcutta around July 1906. A meeting was convened on 11th August to discuss 'the question of the appointment of [the] Principal. It was resolved that Mr. Aravinda Ghose be requested to act as professor in charge of the college and school, and all matters relating to study be put under his control, and that all questions of Executive management be made under the control of the Supdt'.[54] [Satish Chandra Mukherjee].

On 14th August, an inaugural ceremony of the Bengal National College and School was held at the Calcutta Town Hall. Among the speakers were Sir Guru Das Banerji and the national poet Rabindranath Tagore. Both spoke on national education and of its centrality in a scheme of national regeneration. Presumably, the first Principal-designate of the College was also present on the occasion and must have silently witnessed the events. Sir Guru Das spoke on the various facets of national education especially the concept of education on national lines. An education on national lines should

---

54. *Sri Aurobindo Archives and Research, April 1979,* op. cit., p. 119.

not be 'limited by considerations of nationality, but should proceed upon a cosmopolitan basis', and the National Council accepting such an approach has expressly provided for 'the incorporation of the best assimilable ideals of Western life and thought with our own'. This process of assimilation, Guru Das argued, was 'desirable [only] in the later stages of mental growth' but a compulsion to assimilate such ideals at an early stage of growth, any attempt at coercion 'will retard instead of accelerating the healthy development of the mind'.[55] Guru Das also defined the approach that ought to be taken, and stated that the National Council had decided to follow it. 'Every student, when commencing his school education, brings with him, in addition to his outfit of language, the importance of which should be separately considered, his stock of thoughts and sentiments, the gifts of his nation, which the teacher, instead of ignoring and hastily displacing, should try to utilise and gradually improve'. He saw the refusal to accept this 'elementary principle', as one of the 'main reasons why the existing system of English education in this country has failed to produce satisfactory results'. With his long experience of education in the country, he had correctly stated the core issue, but was also being cautious in the words he chose and reiterated the point that the newly inaugurated system intended to function apart from, and not in opposition to, the existing system.[56]

Tagore spoke in Bengali symbolising the one core demand of national education – instruction in the mother tongue. Tagore spoke of the race's lost capacity of believing that its welfare and progress depended on it. Talking of the English proverb 'where there is a will there is a way', he said, "we refused to believe that a collective will to action could show the way forward, we perhaps also willed but

---

55. *The Dawn and Dawn Society's Magazine, September, 1906*, op. cit., pp. 27–28.
56. Ibid., p.28.

continuously believed that to show the way was beyond our means, it was not in our hands or control. But events of today [setting up the National Council and subsequently the national College] show that will is the principal motivating and creative power, and such a will has entered the Bengali race, Bengalis have at last received something worthwhile after a long and fallow period."

Calling upon the students to enter the '*swadesher bidyamandir*' [the nation's temple of learning] with an exalted spirit, Tagore asked them to dedicate themselves to it in a spirit of worship, dedication, and surrender. He exhorted them to experience the living entity that this institution truly was, and to dedicate themselves unreservedly to its wellbeing.

Tagore's oration was perhaps the only one that addressed the students and expounded on their role and deeper responsibilities *vis-à-vis* the new institution. It was not delivered as a sermon but made with a direct appeal to the young students' minds and hearts. The poet's words came out as a genuine appeal which articulated the spiritual vision of the students' link with the newly founded educational institution.

Defining true education, Tagore said that it was an education which, instead of overwhelming the individual, liberated him. The education imparted for so long had made people helpless; it was learnt by rote and was thought to be the ultimate and had failed to develop the capacity of original thinking and research. The poet was hopeful that the new direction in education would at last free India from the suffocating clasp of an alien education system, and would allow it to graduate to a liberated state which knowledge truly engenders. Tagore's appeal was for a national self-discovery and self-realisation through the means of a new education. And this process demanded a great deal of sacrifice from students as well as the organisers of the new movement. Tagore's involvement with the national education movement from the early phase was fundamental and life-giving. He kept up the spirit of educational revolt and breathed into it a poetic fervour that gave a new life and a new direction to its early phase.[57] R.C.Majumdar, spoke of the effects of Rabindranath Tagore and Sri Aurobindo on *Swadeshi* thus – 'One cannot ignore the fact that the writers and nationalists like Rabindranath and Arabinda [Sri Aurobindo], and their followers, are entitled to the chief credit for changing the Swadeshi into a genuine national movement which swept the whole country ...'. From the creation of the nationalist education narrative to imparting it an ideational contour, both Tagore and Sri Aurobindo played a crucial and defining role. It was due to Sri Aurobindo's push that national education became a principal pillar of the nationalist movement.

Sri Aurobindo's association with the National College was a brief one. We shall briefly state the association before getting on with trying to read his views on national education articulated during his first phase of political activism. Sri Aurobindo's involvement with *Bande Mataram* began in the first week of August 1906, that is, just before the opening of the National College. Right from its inception the journal demanded more and more of Sri Aurobindo's attention and therefore '[a]t an early period he left the organisation of the College to the educationist Satish Mukherji and plunged fully into politics'.[58] He continued to officiate 'as Principal and taught regularly at the College for a full year ... in 1907 (as also in 1908), he

57. Ibid., pp.47–53. For a brief survey of Tagore's involvement with the National Education Movement, see eg. Haridas and Uma Mukherjee, 'Jatiya Shiksha Andolone Rabindranath' in *Swadeshi Andolon and Banglar Nabayug*, 2004.
58. *On Himself*, op. cit., p.43.

[was] listed in College literature as a member of the departments of Indian History and Geography, English History, Political Science (European Systems), French and German, and English. Most of his time seems to have been devoted to the teaching of History. The Fifth and Seventh Standard examinations in History for 1906 and 1907 were set by him'.[59] It is interesting to examine the details of the question paper in the following:

Fifth Standard Examination, 1907.
HISTORY.
Full marks-50.

Paper set by-ARAVINDA GHOSE, Esq., B.A. (CANTAB.).

Examiners-BABUPRASANNA KUMAR BOSE, M.A.
PANDEYA UMAPATI DATTA SARMA, B.A.

GROUP A.
(Candidates are required to answer not more than one question of Group A).

1. Give some idea of the effect of the Black Death on the condition of the labouring classes in England in the 14th century.
2. What was the mercantile system? Narrate the steps by which it was replaced by a system of Free Trade.
3. Describe the policy of Aurangzeb and its effects on the permanence of the Mogul Empire.
4. Describe the organization of the Mahratta power under the Peshwas and state its advantages and defects.

---

59. *Sri Aurobindo Archives and Research, April 1979*, op. cit., p. 119.

GROUP B.

(Candidates are required to answer not more than two questions of Group B).

1. Describe the model Parliament of Edward I.
2. Describe briefly the part which Henry VIII took in the Reformation in England.
3. Write a short account of the career of the elder Pitt.
4. State the causes which led up to the American War of Independence.
5. State what you know of any two of the following:– (1) The Gunpowder Plot; (2) The Treaty of Utrecht; (3) The Massacre of Glencoe; (4) The Darien Scheme.

GROUP C.

(Only three questions to be answered).

1. State briefly what you know of the following: – Chandragupta, Adisur, Shankaracharya.
2. Describe the conquests of Alauddin Khilji.
3. Give some account of the origin of the Bahamani kingdom and its final break-up.
4. Narrate briefly the career of Hyder Ali.
5. Name the states and principalities annexed by Lord Dalhousie and give the reasons alleged for annexation in each case.[60]

When the *Bande Mataram* sedition case was brought against him in August 1907, Sri Aurobindo 'resigned his post in order not to embarrass the College authorities'.[61] It was during this period that 'an Interesting Ceremony [took place] at The Bengal National

60. *Sri Aurobindo Archives and Research, April 1979*, op. cit., p. 115.
61. *On Himself*, op. cit., p. 43.

College'. On 22nd August, the students and teachers of the Bengal National College converged and:

> expressed their heartfelt appreciation of the eminent qualities as a teacher, of Srijut Aurobindo Ghose, their late beloved Principal, and recorded their deep regret at his resignation on August 2, 1907, of the high office which he had filled with such conspicuous ability and at so much personal sacrifice to himself during the first year of the existence of the college.[62]

They further 'expressed their heartfelt sympathy with him in his present troubles in connection with his prosecution on the alleged charge of editing and publishing certain seditious articles in the *Bande Mataram*'. It was resolved on the occasion 'that a photograph of [him] be taken to be hung up in the college hall'.[63]

Accordingly, the next day [August 23, 1907] the Principal 'was invited to come over to the college premises to be photographed. When the boys of the college and school came up to their beloved principal one by one, bowed at his feet and garlanded him, it was a sight for the gods to see! ... After the photographs were taken, Srijukta Ghose was entertained by the boys to a sumptuous lunch in the Hindu style. The teachers then requested him on behalf of the boys to speak to them a few words of advice.'[64]

What followed was Sri Aurobindo's celebrated speech as advice given to students of the National College. It articulated the soul, the essential aim and purpose of national education as Sri Aurobindo saw it:

> When we established this college and left other occupations, other chances of life, to devote our lives to this institution, we did so because we hoped to

---

62. *The Dawn and Dawn Society's Magazine, September, 1907, vol. 11,* op. cit., p. 24
63. Ibid.
64. Ibid., pp. 24, 25.

see in it the foundation, the nucleus, of nation, of the new India which is to begin its career after this night of sorrow and trouble, on that day of glory and greatness when India will work for the world.

This was the essential nature and aim of national education, it was to lay the foundation of a new India and that had to be done adopting completely new directions and lines. Therefore:

What we want here is not merely to give you a little information, not merely to open to you careers for earning a livelihood, but to build up sons for the motherland to work and to suffer for her.

That was the essential objective in starting the College.[65] The aim of uplifting the Motherland, that was the principal spirit which national education had to give rise, it had to be a dedicated existence liberated from the pangs and restrains of the ego:

When I come back, I wish to see some of you becoming rich, rich not for yourselves, but that you may enrich the mother with your riches. I wish to see some of you becoming great, great not for your own sake, not that you may satisfy your own vanity, but great for her, to make India great, to enable her to stand up with head erect among the nations of the earth, as she did in days of yore when the world looked up to her for light'. Even those who were to 'remain poor and obscure' would have to devoted that very state of existence to motherland, there was no space for self-regarding pity and sympathy.[66]

The thing most dear and most urgent was the service of the motherland – this urgency, national education had to convey to the young minds under its tutelage:

There are times in a nation's history when Providence places before it one work, one aim, to which everything else, however high and noble in itself, has to be sacrificed. Such a time has now arrived

65. Ibid., p. 25.
66. Ibid., p. 26.

for our motherland when nothing is dearer than her service, when everything else is to be directed to that end. If you will study, study for her sake; train yourselves body and mind and soul for her service. You will earn your living that you may live for her sake. You will go abroad to foreign lands that you may bring back knowledge with which you may do service to her. Work that she may prosper. Suffer that she may rejoice.[67]

All was contained in that one single advice which was to inspire generations of Indian youth.[68] The alienation, the divorce from the mother country brought about by a foreign and artificial education system was to be erased by the mighty influence of a national and Indianised education. An education that would primarily attempt to relocate and re-link that disconnected bridge. This speech serves as an indicator, of how Sri Aurobindo perceived the essence of national education in India's national resurgence.

On being acquitted of the charge of sedition, Sri Aurobindo was 'reappointed to the Chair of History and Political Science. However, his political responsibilities prevented him from taking any further part in college activities. In fact after the 'Bande Mataram case, Sri Aurobindo became the recognised leader of Nationalism in Bengal' and led the party at several provincial conferences and addressed large public meetings.[69]

Finally, when he was arrested in connection with the Alipore Bomb Case, the National College authorities resolved 'that in view of the serious charges pending against him, Mr. Arabinda Ghose be asked as early as possible to resign his membership of the Council

---

67. *The Dawn and Dawn Society's Magazine, September, 1907*, p. 26.
68. Radhakamal Mukherjee who was present in that meeting at the College recalled how the last sentence still rang in his years even after six decades. (*India: the dawn of a new era*, op.cit., p.82.)
69. *Autobiographical Notes*, op.cit, p.59.

and of the Executive Committee, and his appointment as a lecturer in History'.[70] Thus, during the 'Alipore case he resigned finally at the request of the College authorities'[71] on May 23, 1908, Sri Aurobindo's formal association with the National Council of Education ended. Satish Chandra Mukherjee would also end his association with the National College in December 1908, when on the ground of ill-health, 'he tendered resignation to his office [and] addressed himself wholeheartedly [for the next five years] to the *Dawn* magazine which he continued to run till November 1913'.[72] Thus, within a span of seven months the Bengal National College was deprived of the guidance and mentoring of two of its most valued organisers and inspirers. Its revolutionary embers were finally doused. The head-priests of the quest for a philosophy of national education had withdrawn.

A number of factors and the overall political atmosphere led to the gradual petering out of the first institutions, especially the National Council of Education and the Bengal National College. Benoy Kumar Sarkar recollected how in the course of a few years, 'Bengal National College found itself with empty benches and automatically ceased to exist' and by '1916–1917, not a student cared to come for a literary and scientific instruction along national lines'. Its off-shoot which had separated following a vigorous debate, 'The Bengal Technical Institute and the Society for the Promotion of Technical Education' survived, since it was looked upon as an institution based on the 'bread-and-butter' philosophy.[73]

The pre-eminent early historian duo of the national education movement and of early nationalist era, Uma and Haridas Mukherjee,

70. *Sri Aurobindo Archives and Research, April, 1979*, op. cit., p. 120.
71. *On Himself*, op. cit., p. 43.
72. 'Life – Sketch of Satis Chandra Mukherjee' in *Origin of the National Education Movement*, op.cit., p.200.
73. Ibid., p.172.

analysing the eventual dissolution of the first experiments of national education, have argued that since the national education movement was primarily a political movement, 'it flourished only in the hectic days of the Swadeshi Movement', and as soon as the 'first flushes of enthusiasm for political struggle subsided, there was a corresponding flagging of the emotional urge for national education'.[74]

We must also remember that the years between 1907 and 1910 were years in which the colonial government had unleashed intense repression. The Indian language press was gagged, prosecution of the Indian newspapers and journals became a regular affair with the passing of a number of Press Acts, the Seditious Meetings Bill (1907), and the Criminal Law Amendment Act (1908) made it very difficult for the nationalists to organise public movements and protest, deportations of leading nationalist from all over the country and the British Indian government's act of balancing the Moderates through granting of concessions and reforms, served to weaken the movement and dampen the initial zeal. The years 1906 and 1907 saw intense tussle between the nationalist press and the colonial administration – 'a large number of prosecutions were launched against the members of the press in Bengal and Bombay, Punjab and the United Provinces, Madras and the Central Provinces, and many persons were sentenced to long terms of imprisonment', wrote Lajpat Rai.[75] 'In this background of repression and governmental tyranny' the National Council of Education 'could not maintain its early evolutionary fire'. Between 1908 and 1910, apprehending a clampdown from the colonial government, leaders of the National Council of Education, 'as seasoned

74. Ibid.

75. Lajpat Rai, *Young India: An Interpretation & a History of the Nationalist Movement from Within,* 1916, p.180.

real-politikers, had to tone down their spirit of boycott with the authorities'.[76]

In 1908, for instance, the Council issued a circular to the national schools under its jurisdiction in various districts of the province, directing the schools 'not to associate themselves with non-literary bodies and not even to participate in the Boycott and Swadeshi meetings'. The movement which had emerged out of political agitations displayed a 'moderatist climb-down' from its 'original spirit of independence' which had inspired the formation of its institutions in the early days.[77] The movement, its institutions and philosophy did not receive sufficient scope and milieu to work out its experiments.

Lala Lajpat Rai, analysing the predicament of the national education movement and Sri Aurobindo's disassociation from it, wrote about how he was told by one who had worked with 'Arabinda Ghosh' at the National Council of Education, that Sri Aurobindo could not support the Council's 'non-political attitude', he could 'not appreciate their needless dread' of offending official susceptibilities.[78] His position thus, argued Rai, as 'the nominal head of the National College, controlled by men' who 'differed from him in their political views and opinions, became almost from the very beginning anomalous'.[79] Rai found this 'rather unfortunate' because he saw Arabinda Ghosh as having 'received the best modern education that any man of his country and generation could expect to have' and having taught in Baroda', having knowledge of the 'most advanced principles of pedagogy' and if it could be successfully

76. *Origin of the National Education Movement*, op.cit., pp.172,173.
77. Ibid.
78. Lajpat Rai, *Young India: An Interpretation & a History of the Nationalist Movement from Within*, op.cit., p.173
79. Ibid.

'worked into a thoroughly national system of education in India':

> He [Sri Aurobindo] knew that the foundations of national independence and national greatness must be laid in a strong and advanced system of national education ... politics meant to him much more than is ordinarily meant by the term. It was not a game of expediency, but a 'school of human character' which acted and reacted on the life of the nation. 'Education could no more be divorced from politics', in his opinion, 'than it could be divorced from religion and morals. Any system of education that helps such isolation and division between the various organic relations of life is mediaeval and not modern.[80]

The 'monied leaders of the National Council of Education movement' Rai lamented, were not ready to accept 'Arabinda's' principles, they feared that a possible official opposition when roused would 'make their work absolutely impossible'. They suffered from a 'real dread of the bureaucracy' which they were not willing to defy. Rai saw it as a flawed argument; 'experience has shown that they were quite mistaken if they thought that they could develop their scheme of education without rousing the fears and the bitterest opposition of the bureaucracy, even after declaring the non-political character of their scheme'.[81]

Another crucial factor was the challenge of livelihood and of acceptance faced by students who passed out of national education institutions. S.C Roy, closely associated with the movement, and himself a scholar at the National Council, recollected:

> True, the students who had come to these schools and colleges knew, and were prepared to forego, the chances of the security of Government service and service under the European merchants in the country, but they did not

80. Ibid., pp.173, 174.
81. Ibid., p.174.

know, at the same time, what they would do after they had come out of their educational institutions. The insecurity of the future for the students of the national schools coupled with the unprovoked oppression of the police, gradually induced our students to fall out of the scheme of national education and quietly and clandestinely almost go back to the Government services or service in merchant office.[82]

Roy also described the attitude of the general public to the students who graduated from national schools and colleges as one of 'contemptuous negligence'. These students would not be recognised, Roy recollected, 'as educated' and would sometimes even be denied the 'privileges of educated men'. This collective behaviour was also a factor which was 'greatly instrumental in ultimately detracting from the attractions' of national education institutions and national education as a whole. 'This fundamentally prejudiced psychological atmosphere was what we found it so difficult to fight', Roy rued.[83]

The disassociation of Sri Aurobindo, along with the other factors also contributed to its eventual slow-down and dissolution. The British colonialists clearly saw that the spread of the national education movement and the stabilisation of its institutions would create a generation of scholar-student activists who would be effective in challenging the ideational status quo and in spreading the Indic and the nationalist narrative in education, research, and industry and therefore, made an all out effort to throttle the experiment and arrest the movement. Though the early institutions dissolved, and there appeared to be a reversal, the ideas generated by the national education movement and its thought-leaders continued to float and found eventual expression in a number of educational institutions and ideas in the course of the next few decades. National education

82. *Origin of the National Education Movement*, op.cit., p.172.

83. Ibid., pp. 173, 174.

remained a central idea, a principal dimension, and a fundamental field of action in the larger struggle for India's freedom. In fact, post-independence too, its fundamental ideas and postulates continued to drive and influence the educational discourse.

6

Political Delineation of a National Education for India through Writings, Speeches, Recollections

"

Swadeshi in Education does not mean teaching by Indian professors only or even management by Indians only. It means an education suited to the temperament and needs of the people fitted to build up a nation equipped for life under modern conditions and absolutely controlled by Indians.

– **Sri Aurobindo, *Bande Mataram***

The past is our foundation, the present our material, the future our aim and summit. Each must have its due and natural place in a national system of education.

– **Sri Aurobindo, *Bande Mataram***

It is not the objective of National Education to make somebody else carry him on his shoulders. The student must support himself and not look helplessly to others. Self-reliance is the basic principle we diligently try to impart to a student.

– **Sri Aurobindo, *Speeches***

Let us continue with the exploration of national education as a political demand. Looking back at the year which gave him an exposure to the national education issue in the province's politics as witnessed at Barisal, Sri Aurobindo wrote a lengthy editorial 'The Old Year' in the *Bande Mataram* on the Bengali New Year's Day of April 16, 1907, surveying major world events indicating the lessons that the Indian struggle could take from them. In its brief existence the *Bande Mataram* had made a wide impact and had come to be looked upon as the principal platform of the Nationalist Party; the first historians of the early nationalist phase commenting on *Bande Mataram* wrote, 'The life of *Bande Mataram* as an Extremist organ was a short-lived one (August 1906–October 1908) ... But during the brief period of its existence, it effected a profound revolution in Indian politics, in the thoughts and feelings of the Indian people'.[1] Celebrated historian and thought-leader, Radha Kumud Mookerjee, who was associated with Sri Aurobindo in the National Council of Education and the Bengal National College, writes of *Bande Mataram* and Sri Aurobindo, 'the editorials he [Sri Aurobindo] contributed to this daily were read with avidity all over the country in the days when such literature was rather rare'. For Mookerjee, Sri Aurobindo's articles in the *Bande Mataram*, constituted 'a most original first-hand source for the history of the freedom movement in India'.[2] To us, it will give an insight into the political narrative of

1. Haridas Mukherjee, Uma Mukherjee, *Sri Aurobindo & the New Thought in Indian Politics*, 1964, p.xxvii.
2. Radha Kumud Mookerjee in his foreword to Haridas Mukherjee, Uma Mukherjee, *Sri Aurobindo & the New Thought in Indian Politics,* ibid.

the national education movement and demand, as it was articulated through Sri Aurobindo's pen.

Sri Aurobindo's *Bande Mataram* editorial looked at the old year, discussed various developments and also analysed the struggle or attempt at national education in other countries, which came in for scrutiny. Lyrically describing the times as those when 'the great Mother, the Adya Shakti, has resolved to take the nations into her hand and shape them anew', Sri Aurobindo spoke of these as 'periods of destruction and energetic creation' and that those participating in struggles for liberation and self-determination were 'assisting ... at the birth of a new Asia and the modernisation of the East'.[3]

Sri Aurobindo particularly analysed all attempts that were being made towards national modernisation, development, and unity, and described efforts at creating a national system of education wherever he saw such an effort being in progress. It also demonstrated that for nations desirous of self-organisation, the agenda of national education was a vital one and was taken up in right earnest. Looking at the Far East in the last twelve months, Sri Aurobindo spoke of the rapid progress China had made, 'within these twelve months, China has been educating, training, and arming herself with a speed of which the outside world has a very meagre conception', and among other things 'she has pushed forward the work of revolutionising her system of education and bringing it into line with modern requirements'.[4]

The 'most remarkable feature of the past year', Sri Aurobindo observed, was the 'awakening of the Mahomedan world' and drew attention to the experiments in national development initiated by the Amir Habibullah Khan (1872–1919), and observed that the 'inception of a great scheme of National Education' would eventually

3. Sri Aurobindo, April 16, 1907, *Bande Mataram,* op. cit., pp. 259–263.
4. Ibid., p. 260.

'lay the basis of State, strong in itself, organised on modern lines and equipped with scientific knowledge and training'.[5]

---

5. Ibid., p. 261. Amir Habibullah who visited India in 1907 had initiated a grand programme of national modernisation in Afghanistan and through it, sought to bring about national unity in the country. His efforts covered all areas of national development including education. His attempts in the area of educational modernisation laid 'the foundation for Afghanistan's modern education system. Habibya College, the first secondary school – an all-boys school – was founded in 1904. Initially, the school offered courses in mathematics, geography, callisthenics, English and Urdu'. To this were added courses in education, drawing, history, public health etc. The first public library in Afghanistan was also established around this time. Most of the teachers in the college were Muslims from India. At the time of Habibullah's ascension to the throne, the Afghan illiteracy rates were 98%. [Rameen Moshref, *The Life and Times of Amir Habibullah Khan*, accessed at: http://www.afghan-web.com/bios/detail/dhabib.html on 3.10.2010]. Sri Aurobindo's mention of the Amir can be understood from the fact that his visit had caught the attention of the revolutionaries, this is evident from an article in the radically nationalist *Jugantar*, 'Amirer Bharat Paridarshan' [Amir's India Visit], February 17, 1907. Amir Habibullah was the first free king to visit India .... It discussed how European, Western powers were vying with each other to take greater hold of Asia, they were also greedily looking towards China. It spoke of the situation as an existential struggle between Europe and Asia, a game of life and death, any civilisation not capable of self-defence will perish. Afghanistan was involved in discovering methods of that self-defence. The Amir's intention, the *Jugantar* said, was to perhaps to make the Indians aware of the need for such a self-defence, self-preservation and of the way this could be acheived, and perhaps that is why he has asked the Muslims to work with their Hindu brothers to realise this goal. The enemy of both Hindus and Musalmans is the same, they are faced with the same problem, and they have to come together for the same mission – that is to win Swaraj for Indians. [English rendition from the original Bengali]. [Anshuman Bandyopadhyay

The rapid growth of the Nationalist Party and its spread in other parts of the country was the other crucial progress made. The third satisfying feature of the year had 'been the growth of National Education'. The Bengal National College had become 'an established fact' and was 'rapidly increasing in numbers and [had] begun to build the foundations of a better system of education'. The 'Barisal outrage' had encouraged other schools to come up in quick succession in other districts and this appeared to be a 'no mean record for a single year' and 'most of these schools have grown up in the great centre of Nationalism, East Bengal'.[6]

All in all, the record of the nationalist advance was a satisfying one as Sri Aurobindo noted, and one of the direct fallout of the rising nationalist tide was the founding of national schools in greater numbers all over the province.

Sri Aurobindo argued that the principal objective of National Education was to inculcate and develop a spirit of self-reliance among the youth of India. He spoke of it during his public talks on national education and it impelled him to encourage and support the establishment of national schools in greater numbers.

A few incidents and recollections illustrate Sri Aurobindo's working within the structure of the newly-established national education machinery, apart from their sheer biographical interest; it would be useful to have a look at them.

One of Sri Aurobindo's pupils at the National College recalled his days in the College – 'When I reached there [in the class]I saw

---

ed. *Agnijuger Agnikatha-'Jugantar' 1906–1908,* 2001]. The nationalists' interest in Habibullah was because of his attempts to modernise his country educationally, socially, and militarily, displaying a spirit of freedom and self-reliance, a spirit that the revolutionaries would have themselves preferred to emulate.

6. Sri Aurobindo, April 16, 1907, *Bande Mataram,*, pp. 262, 262.

in the middle hall a young man of placid appearance. He was clad in a shirt and a *chaddar* (upper cloth)'. On that day the Principal, Sri Aurobindo,was addressing the students and the teachers alike, and the topic was not purely educational. He was speaking instead on the need for developing a spirit of self-reliance in youth which, he argued, was one of the primary tasks of national education.

> He [Sri Aurobindo] spoke of a sad accident that had happened. A student of the Calcutta University had fallen from the verandah of the first floor of a University Building and lost his consciousness. A crowd immediately collected there, but all it could do was to look on helplessly and wring their hands. None thought of rendering any active help. Just at that time, an Englishman was driving by. He noticed the boy, lying unconscious, picked him up in his car, and took him straight to the Campbell Medical College for first aid. Relating the accident, Sri Aurobindo compared the character of the Indians with that of the Europeans, and observed that it was their devotion to duty which had made the Europeans masters of the world'. The national character thus could achieve unbounded strength if it could unite 'that titanic power of practical work ... with the spirituality of India'.[7]

Perhaps to inculcate or reignite that trait, 'devotion to duty', leading to an all-round self-reliance was the ultimate aim of national education.

Pramathanath Mukhopadhyay (later Swami Pratyagatmananda) (1880--1973),[8] Sri Aurobindo's colleague in the National College and

---

7. Reminiscences of Balai Dev Sharma in *Galpa Bharati*, [Beng era] 1357 trans. in Rishabchand, *Sri Aurobindo: His Life Unique*, 2007, pp. 225–226.
8. A scholar and saint, Swami Pratyagatmananda had a number of original works to his credit. In his long quest of over six decades he tried to work out a synthesis between science and spirituality. His well known works are *Approaches to Truth, Metaphysics of Physics, Science and Sadhana* (6 Vols.) etc. [*Samsad Bengali Biographical Dictionary, vol.1*, p. 297.] For a detailed analysis of one aspect of Swami Pratyagatmananda's thought with that of Sri Aurobindo's see

among the first group of scholars to join the institution, has recorded his recollections of that period. The Swami gave an insight from his perspective as a philosopher and metaphysician. Recollecting Sri Aurobindo's association with the National College, he observed that 'when he [Sri Aurobindo] started his work in the heaving politics of Bengal, it was the blazing, fiery aspect of Rudra that stood out in front. But those who associated with him in the National College saw his serene figure, glowing with a mellow luster. These two aspects were fused into one in Sri Aurobindo as in the third eye of Shiva'. Swami Pratyagatmananda saw in Sri Aurobindo a fusion of the 'Jnana Yogi and Karma Yogi', a 'Purna Yogi'.[9]

The 'fiery aspect' of the Principal's national education activism expressed itself during his forceful protest against the Risley Circular of 1907, which debarred students from even discussing issues that were political in nature. It directed the 'managing bodies of all schools and colleges to rusticate students who attended political meetings, sang *Bande Mataram* or took part in demonstrations, processions and picketing'.[10]

Sri Aurobindo attacked the arbitrary circular as preventing education from carrying out its sacred duty of inculcating the spirit of patriotism in young minds and showed how the Government was trying to meddle in educational issues so as to arrest the growing strength of the national education movement. The notorious circular proclaimed that 'school students are not even to attend political meetings nor school teachers to teach them patriotism'. This was done because 'at that age the mind is soft and impressionable

eg. Indrani Sanyal, 'History as Applied Metaphysics' in Indrani Sanyal and Krishna Roy eds. *Sri Aurobindo and His Contemporary Thinkers*, 2007, pp. 165–178.]

9. *K.R.Srinivasa Iyengar,* op. cit., pp. 252, 253.
10. Radhakamal Mukerjee, op.cit, p.57.

and what is seen and heard, sinks deep and tends to crystallise not merely into fixed ideas, but into *character*'.[11]

Unnerved by the rapid growth of national educational institutions the colonial government went all out to suppress these. One reads in this article, Sri Aurobindo's perception of the importance and the method of developing universal qualities such as patriotism, benevolence, discipline, courage etc. which intrinsically link young minds with the soil of their birth. Drawing a parallel with the earlier Carlyle Circular that forbade students from participating in political meetings that were especially linked to Swadeshi and Boycott, Sri Aurobindo spoke of the former as a 'local experiment hastily adopted to meet an urgent difficulty and dropped as soon as it was found difficult to work', while the present circular was aimed at 'striking at the very root of the Swadeshi movement'.[12] He saw the Circular as 'a desperate attempt of the bureaucracy not only to recover and confirm its hold on the student population, and through them on the future, but to make that hold far more stringent, rigid, ineffugable than it ever was in the past'. The Government did not care 'if certain academical ideas of liberalism or nationalism are imparted to the young by their teachers, but they desire to stop the active habit of patriotism in the young; for they know well that a mere intellectual habit untranslated into action is of no value in after life.[13]

Drawing an interesting parallel in his argument, Sri Aurobindo referred to Bushido[14], the Japanese Samurai's code of honour and

11. Sri Aurobindo, 'The True Meaning of the Risley Circular' May 28, 1907, *Bande Mataram,* op. cit., p.380.
12. Sri Aurobindo, 'The True Meaning of the Risley Circular' May 28, 1907, p. 377.
13. Ibid., pp. 378–79.
14. The Bushido code in Japan was a national symbol of a fierce spirit of independence as well as sacrifice. The following: rectitude,

morals. Referring to Bushido as a living part of Japanese society Sri

courage, benevolence, respect, honesty, honour, loyalty – were the seven principal virtues of this code and it is evident why a subject nation aspiring to freedom would give a premium on these virtues in order to attract and prepare workers for political work and action. The Japanese diplomat and statesman, Inazo Nitobe (1862–1933), popularised and imparted a certain degree of contemporaneity in the Bushido code through his widely read *Bushido: The Soul of Japan* (1899). Originally written in English for a Western audience, it was the first major work on Japanese culture with special reference to the Samurai Ethics. In 1905, within six years of its first publication, the book become so popular that a tenth revised edition had to be launched in 1905. Writing a preface to that edition, Inazo observed that the book had already been translated into *Marathi*, German, Bohemian, Polish, and the Norwegian, French and Chinese were in the process or being contemplated. Inazo was flattered that President Roosevelt had read the treatise and had distributed copies to his friends as well. It may be assumed that Sri Aurobindo and his revolutionary colleagues must have also seen the book. Because of its popularity and its demand for translation, the book must have gained wide circulation among a certain section of the Indian public. Since it was basically a code for warriors we may also assume that Tilak, one of the leading proponents of revolutionary politics, may have encouraged its Marathi translation in order to ensure a wider dissemination. Stating his objective, Inazo pointed out that his attempt was firstly to relate the 'origin and sources of our chivalry; *secondly*, its character and teaching; *thirdly*, its influence among the masses; and, *fourthly*, the continuity and permanence of its influence'. Among the sections he proposed to dwell at great length was the second aspect which, he said, would interest students of 'International Ethics and Comparative Ethology' in the Japanese way of thought and action. What is of interest to us is the term Bushido as defined by Inazo, which will also help us understand why such a code attracted the early Indian political radicals; '*Bu-shi-do* means literally Military-Knight-Ways – the ways which fighting nobles should observe in their daily life as well as in their vocation; in a word, the "Precepts of Knighthood," *the noblesse oblige* of the warrior

Aurobindo argued that when the Japanese teach Bushido to the boys, they 'do not rest content with lectures or a moral catechism; they make them practise Bushido and govern every thought and action of their life by the Bushido ideal'. This practical way was the 'only way of inculcating a quality into a nation, by instilling it practically into the minds of its youth at school and college until it becomes an ingrained, inherent, inherited national quality. This is what we have to do with the modern ideal of patriotism in India'.[15]

Young minds would have to be filled from childhood 'with the idea of the country, and present them with that idea at every turn and make their whole young life a lesson in the practice of the virtues which afterwards go to make the patriot and the citizen'. The new education wished to make patriots and citizens, and if this could not be done, the desire to create an 'Indian nation' might as well be given up. Without exposure to such a discipline, 'nationalism, patriotism, regeneration' were to remain 'mere words and ideas

---

class .... Bushido, is the code of moral principles which the knights were required or instructed to observe. It is not a written code; at best it consists of a few maxims handed down from mouth to mouth or coming from the pen of some well-known warrior or savant. More frequently it is a code unuttered and unwritten, possessing all the more the powerful sanction of veritable deed, and of a law written on the fleshy tablets of the heart. It was founded not on the creation of one brain, however able, or on the life of a single personage, however renowned. It was an organic growth of decades and centuries of military career. It, perhaps, fills the same position in the history of ethics that the English Constitution does in political history ...' [Inazo Nitobe, *Bushido: The Soul of Japan*, 1905, p. 10.] Sri Aurobindo, as we have seen, had definite plans for organising a nationwide armed insurrection after an extended period of preparation, [see eg. *On Himself*, op. cit., pp. 21– 22] the inculcation of the Bushido spirit and code therefore in young minds keeping that objective in focus would have, according to him, definitely assisted in that preparation.

15. *Bande Mataram*, p.379.

which can never become a part of the very soul of the nation, and never, therefore, a great realised fact. Mere academical teaching of patriotism [was] of no avail'.[16]

Therefore, the students were welcomed to actively associate with political meetings, were encouraged to practice Swadeshi, and engage in work and programmes as volunteers, and develop that deeper bond with the nation. To submit to restriction on this matter was, Sri Aurobindo cautioned, tantamount to committing 'national suicide'. One does not fail to note two interesting points in this article. Referring to students' participation in politics, Sri Aurobindo suggested in the same article that when Indian nationality becomes a reality, 'and the present unnatural conditions have been remedied', then the 'active participation [of students in politics] may be brought under restriction and regulation; for then, the inherited habit of patriotism, the atmosphere of a free country and the practice and teaching of the Bushido virtues within the limits of home and school life will be sufficient'.[17] The other aspect pertains to the teacher's role in this whole exercise of identification and patriotism – 'a teacher may by his personal influence and teachings so surround the minds of his students with the idea of the country, of work for the country, of living and dying for the country, that this will become the dominant idea of their minds and, if associated with any kind of patriotic discipline or teaching in action, the dominant note in their character'.[18] We still appear to be grappling with these two issues and continue to look for ways and methods to satisfactorily work them out. Developing of patriotism, heroic spirit, and the spirit of sacrifice was, in Sri Aurobindo's vision, one of the principal tasks of national education. The official system

16. Ibid.
17. Ibid., p. 380.
18. Ibid.

which tried to arrest this development was to be resisted. The fiery side of the Principal's personality was thus seen when advocating such a stand.

Discussing 'Swadeshi in Education', in an aside, Sri Aurobindo referred to the attempt to practise 'Swadeshi Education under the official Universities', as was being done then by some well-known institutions, and argued that it was bound to fail. He countered the view that Swadeshi in Education could be realised as soon as one involved Indian teachers in the process without trying to alter the scenario in which the institution still remained under the tutelage of the official University. His definition of the term was clear:

> Swadeshi in Education does not mean teaching by Indian professors only, or even management by Indians only. It means an education suited to the temperament and needs of the people fitted to build up a nation equipped for life under modern conditions and absolutely controlled by Indians.[19]

When talking of national education during this period (1906 to 1908), Sri Aurobindo invariably clubbed the issue with other agendas of the nationalist programme, and therefore, one does not find a sustained attempt at developing its philosophy and theme. National education was a principal pillar of the Nationalist Party's political progamme, and through the columns of *Bande Mataram*, its political necessity needed to be articulated and popularized. Sri Aurobindo's speeches and writings during this phase mostly articulate the political narrative and disseminate it across the country. A few of these writings and speeches contain passages and observations that provide a window into Sri Aurobindo's conception of national education, its broad framework and mandate, and its relevance to the nation. We continue with trying to read and sift these from his early political writings and speeches.

---

19. Sri Aurobindo, 'Swadeshi in Education', July 13, 1907, *Bande Mataram*, op. cit., p. 480.

The Congress split at Surat was a watershed moment in the early phase of the freedom struggle.[20] Sri Aurobindo had already written about 1907 being 'a turning-point of our destinies', and called upon nationalist delegates to join the session great strength, 'do not imagine that the session at the Surat Congress will be as the sessions of other years. Let us fear to miss by absenting ourselves the chance of helping to put in one of the keystones of the house we are building for our Mother's dwelling in the future, the house of her salvation, the house of Swaraj.[21]

For a while the Nationalists of the younger generation 'had been discontented with the Congress. They had been drawn into the Congress movement by the immense prestige of its first leaders', but gradually they felt alienated by its ineffectiveness. The Congress was best described by one *Bharadvaj* – obviously a *nom-de-plume* – in an article entitled, 'Wanted – a Real National Congress', written for the widely-read *The Modern Review*, edited by that iconic nationalist intellectual polymath Ramananda Chattopadhyay (1865–1943). *Bharadvaj* described the Congress thus:

> So far as its influence over the Government is concerned, it may be regarded as next to a nonentity. As a resort of professional men making holiday

---

20. See for instance: *CWSA* vol.6-7, Sri Aurobindo, *On Himself*, 1995, Manoj Das, *Life and Times of the Mahayogi*, 2020, Manoj Das, *Sri Aurobindo in the First Decade of the Twentieth Century*, 2003, R.C.Majumdar, *History of the Freedom Movement in India, vol.2*, 1997, K.R.Srinivas Iyengar, *Sri Aurobindo: a Biography and a History*, 1985, Peter Heehs, *The Bomb in Bengal: the Rise of Revolutionary Terrorism in India 1900–1910*, 1993, Prithwindra Mukherjee, *The Intellectual Roots of India's Freedom Struggle (1893–1918)*, 2017, Biman Bihari Majumdar, *Indian Political Associations and Reform of Legislature (1818–1917)*, 1959, Haridas Mukherjee & Uma Mukherjee, *Sri Aurobindo and the New Thought in Indian Politics*, 1964. et.al.
21. *CWSA* vol.7, pp.787, 788.

excursions from different parts of the country and seeking social intercourse and exchange of thought with their countrymen from other parts, it undoubtedly serves a useful purpose; but it can fulfil this purpose without assuming so high-sounding a name as it bears. If the so-called Indian National Congress is ever to deserve its name, it must take into its hands the guidance and control of some of the really important concerns of the country.[22]

Historian K.M. Pannikar wrote of how the Congress's 'eloquence that seemed unmeaning' to these younger generation Nationalists, 'it's faith in words, its party-wrangles, these could not satisfy the more thoughtful: it's holiday aspect, it's unwieldy frame, irritated the more earnest. Discontent soon became open revolt'. There were men within the Congress 'who had lost faith in petitions, resolutions and deputations, who were not content to leave all initiative to the Government, who would no longer consent to approach the Government as political mendicants or as worshipful suppliants. Their hour had come'.[23]

Events were leading to a showdown – a few days prior to the Surat Conference, the nationalists met separately in the outskirts of Surat. Tilak addressed the conference and Sri Aurobindo presided over it. 'Entrance to the Nationalist Conference was conditioned upon personal declaration of being a "Nationalist", while the Conference itself passed resolutions on total boycott and complete independence'.[24] The Moderates on the other hand, had intended to push through mild resolutions. The 'mild formulation' of the draft resolutions to be passed at the Surat Congress on Swadeshi, Boycott and National Education, 'signified the Congress' rebuke

22.. *The Modern Review*, January 1908, vol.III, No.1, Calcutta, pp.39,40.

23. K.M.Pannikar, *Indian Nationalism: Its Origin, History and Ideals*, 1920, pp. 48, 49.

24. Daniel Argov, *Moderates and Extremists in the Indian Nationalist Movement* (1883–1920), Bombay: Asia Publishing House, 1967, p.132.

to the ideas of the extremists and its determination to appease the Government'.[25] For instance, the resolution on Swadeshi, that Moderates intended to push through, 'replaced the crucial clause "even at some sacrifice" by "preference where possible"; the Boycott resolution omitted the term "Boycott Movement", and the resolution on National Education excluded the words "education on national lines and under national control"'.[26]

Addressing the nationalist delegates on the day after the split at Surat, Tilak spoke of how the Moderates were insisting on taking the Congress backwards and compromise on the gains made at the Calcutta Congress the previous years. Tilak told the delegates:

> The way in which it had been proposed to go back on the resolutions of last year [1906] in regard to Self-Government, Boycott, Swadeshi and National Education, on the ground they did not appeal themselves to the Secretary of State, the London *Times* and the Anglo-Indian papers and officials, was a deliberate insult to the whole Congress, and no one, however eminently placed, had any right to drag back the Congress. The Bombay Moderates wanted the Congress to move a little backwards, to be within the safe line of the boundary, so as not to displease the Government.[27]

It has been argued that 'although the extremist' Nationalists Conference posed a consolidated front, it contained two distinct groups; one led by Tilak, who repudiated any intentions to cause a split in the Congress, the other led by Aurobindo Ghosh, who sought to capture the Congress or wreck it'.[28] Indeed the first attempt to organise the advanced young section within the Congress, 'men of extremer views' was made by Sri Aurobindo, who in 1906, 'persuaded this group in Bengal to take public position as a party, proclaim Tilak as their leader and enter into a contest with Moderate leaders

25. Ibid., p.133.
26. Ibid.
27. Bal Gangadhar Tilak: *His Writings and Speeches*, 1922, p.384.
28. Ibid., pp.132, 133.

for the control of the Congress and of public opinion and action in the country'.[29]

In fact, earlier Congress leaders 'had no clear vision of a political future for India'. All that they did, Pannikar argued, was to 'respectfully present to 'the present power' a few complaints and did not see their way to very much more. Neither the official classes nor the Congress leaders were prepared for the New Party's bold demand – 'Swa Raj at once!' When it was made, it staggered them. A blind drift, guided by an inscrutable Providence – *that* was the Moderate vision of India's political life. What chance had it against the energy that lived alertly 'Swa Raj, at once'?[30]

On the Congress split at Surat, Sri Aurobindo later made his famous comment:

> History very seldom records the things that were decisive but took place behind the veil; it records the show in the front of the curtain. Very few people know that it was I (without consulting Tilak) who gave the order that led to the breaking of the Congress and was responsible for the refusal to join the new-fangled Moderate Convention which were the two decisive happenings in Surat. Even my action in giving the movement in Bengal its militant turn, or founding the revolutionary movement is very little known.[31]

The Congress split at Surat, R.C. Majumdar observed, was a 'great landmark in the history of the Congress, as it practically ended the first phase of that great national organization'.[32] Amalendu De, Subodh Mallik's biographer writes, "Surat signalised the end of Moderatism in Indian political life and accentuated the 'forward programme' of the New Party."[33] British journalist and author

---

29. Sri Aurobindo, *On Himself*, op.cit., p.45
30. K.M.Pannikar, *Indian Nationalism: Its Origin, History and Ideals*, op.cit., pp.64, 65.
31. Ibid., p.49.
32. Manoj Das, op.it., p.352.
33. Amalendu De, *Raja Subodh Chandra Mallik and His Times*, op.cit., p.122.

Henry Nevinson who had covered Surat, gives us a description of events after the split. It is useful to read Nevinson's description here, in order to understand the mood and the milieu in which Sri Aurobindo delivered his speeches and articulated his political stance, and also spoke on national education. The afternoon after the split the Extremists held a convention:

> In the large courtyard of a private house, they met in silent crowds. Grave and silent – I think, without saying a single word – Mr. Arabindo Ghose took the Chair, and sat unmoved, with far-off eyes, as one who gazes at futurity. In clear, short sentences, without eloquence or passion, Mr. Tilak spoke till the stars shone and someone kindled a lantern at his side. He reviewed the situation ... He had no wish to destroy the Congress, for its prestige was useful; but a new spirit had entered Indian affairs, and unless the Congress was permeated with the new spirit it had better die – it was dead already. By the new spirit he meant self-confidence and self-assertion, contrasted with the old methods of petitions for rights, appeals for justice, and other forms of mendicancy which the British Government answered with elusive promises, and the Anglo-Indians with scorn .... On that note of deep and perhaps irreconcilable divergence, the twenty third Indian National Congress ended.[34]

All present felt, reported Nevinson, that the 'Congress would never be the same again ... a new spirit, a different and difficult spirit, had indeed arisen in the country'. Nevinson returned with the Congress leaders in the train and at each station the Moderate leaders were shouted down, 'not a cheer, not a single cry of "Jai!" That was on a Sunday, and on the Wednesday before, no cheering, no garlands had seemed enough. It had been roses, roses all the way'.[35]

Author and historian Manoj Das, referring to Surat as a 'landmark in the history of the nation', writes of the 'surging popular

34. Henry Nevinson, op.cit., p.260.
35. Ibid., p.262.

disgust with those who had taken for granted their monopoly of the nation's leadership'. He argues that it was the first time ever that a 'prominent part of the population, a large number of youths – students in particular – and the Middle Class, including its lower strata, were growing irresistibly attracted to the goal of freedom'.[36] It shaped the peoples' conviction 'that they must be liberated from a foreign rule'.[37]

Both Lokmanya Tilak and Sri Aurobindo decisively contributed towards widening and broadening the Congress movement by wresting it out of the control of the clique of moderates, opening its gates to the masses. It is on and with the masses, that the Congress could survive and lead the struggle for Swaraj. The leaders of the Nationalist Party were marked out from the Moderates even in the physical manners that followed. Tilak for instance, writes Swadeshi publisher and journalist G.A.Natesan (1873–1948), who was present at the Surat Congress during Congress session, loved 'to dwell in tents and even uncomfortable lodgings with his many friends and followers, declining many a kind friend's offer to put him in better and more luxurious mansions. Born of the people, bred up among them, he lived to labour for them and it may be said of him, that he was perhaps one of the few politicians who realised that there could be no political advancement in this country unless the heart of the masses was touched'.[38]

To R.C.Majumdar, it was Tilak who 'brought political philosophy in India from heaven to earth, from the Council Hall or the Congress *mandap* to the street and the market', one who carried 'the gospel of

36. Manoj Das, op.cit., p.353.
37. Ibid.
38. S.V.Bapat, *Reminiscences & Anecdotes of Lokmanya Tilak*, Poona, 1928, p.38.

self-help and political agitation to the masses'.[39] As Tilak's foremost biographer Dhananjay Keer put it, 'he [Tilak] resolved to connect the poverty of the peasants with the patriotism of the middle classes, to create a powerful public opinion in support of their grievances, and to make them feel confident that they would someday be able to regain the power to govern themselves'.[40] The best description of Tilak's mass politics is from Sri Aurobindo himself, who wrote in a tribute to him:

> The Congress movement was for a long time purely occidental in its mind, character and methods, confined to the English-educated few, founded on the political rights and interests of the people read in the light of English history and European ideals, but with no roots either in the past of the country or in the inner spirit of the nation. Mr. Tilak was the first political leader to break through the routine of its somewhat academical methods, to bridge the gulf between the present and the past, and to restore continuity to the political life of the nation. He developed a language and a spirit, and he used methods which Indianised the movement and brought into it the masses.[41]

Sri Aurobindo, for instance, always travelled third class. On their way to Surat, Barindra Ghose, recollected how Sri Aurobindo sat in the third class compartment of the Congress Special 'packed to the full of Congress delegates' while 'J. Ghosal, the Congress secretary of the moderate party, was travelling in a first class compartment in perfect European clothes and style'.[42] Commenting on the contrasting styles of the journey to Surat, Barindra wrote:

---

39. R.C.,Majumdar, 'The Genesis of Extremism' in *Studies in the Bengal Renaissance*, op.cit., pp. 167, 168.
40. Dhananjay Keer, *Lokmanya Tilak – Father of Our Freedom Struggle*, 1959, p.105.
41. *CWSA* vol.1, p.645.
42. Barindra Kumar Ghose's reminiscences cited in *Sri Aurobindo & the Freedom of India*, 1995, 2012, p.113.

Aurobindo, the new idol of the nation, was hardly known then by his face, and at every small and big station a frantic crowd rushed about on the station platform looking for him in the first and second class carriages, while all the time Aurobindo sat unobserved in a third class compartment. By the time this fact became known, and he was found out, the train was about to start. In these days of style, luxury, and easy leadership, no one could imagine that Aurobindo – nurtured and educated in England and a high official of His Highness the Gaekwad's service, who could leap into an all-India fame in such a short time – would dream of travelling third class. J. Ghosal felt small in contrast and tried again and again to invite Aurobindo into his first class carriage and keep him there to save his face.[43]

Tilak and Sri Aurobindo and their band of political followers and workers represented 'the new generation of politicians' who came to the 'forefront of our public life, proclaimed in a clear voice that high-sounding liberal professions mouthed by British statesmen, Liberal or Conservative, are a mere snare which Indians need beware'. They urged people 'to shake off that hypnotic spell of British rule in India and to cultivate the virtues of self-reliance instead of helplessly depending on Britain for their salvation'.[44] The events at Surat clearly demonstrated that the time had come for these ideas of freedom to express themselves, and that expression would be based henceforth on the strength and the participation of masses of India.

After the Surat Congress, Sri Aurobindo toured western India and Maharashtra. These visits were spontaneously organised for Sri Aurobindo, while he was on his way to back Calcutta, in places which were nationalist strongholds. 'From Bombay to Nasik, Dhulia, Amraoti, Nagpur – centres of Maharashtrian culture which Tilak had persuaded Sri Aurobindo to visit – and everywhere a spontaneous welcome, and everywhere a memorable

43. Ibid.

44. *Sri Aurobindo and the New Thought in Indian Politics*, op.cit., p.xix.

speech or two' was how Sri Aurobindo's biographer described it.[45]

In most of these places, Sri Aurobindo spoke on the nationalist ideology, the prevailing political climate which led to the split of the Congress and, more importantly for us, he spoke on the effort of national education especially undertaken in Bengal. Sri Aurobindo spoke of this as a major effort of the newly formed nationalist bloc which was being initiated keeping in mind that future generations of a future independent India would have to be trained to learn to handle and shape *Swaraj*. For the nationalist group, National Education was an article of faith; they had opposed any attempts to dilute its objectives and its centrality along with Swadeshi and Boycott in the new political programme that they had suggested.

We also come across one of his public speeches, during this phase, which deals exclusively with national education. It seems to be his longest recorded oral exposition of the theme in public and was delivered at Bombay on January 15, 1908. In this public address, Sri Aurobindo not only dwelt on the definition and philosophy of national education, and articulated his thoughts on the concept of nation, nationality and its defining aspects, but also gave examples on the way the programmes of national education were being implemented in Bengal. One also perceives, while going through this speech, that the methods pursued by some national schools were futuristic and revolutionary. And were being implemented with the aim of creating a generation of dedicated citizens who would help sustain and organise freedom when it would eventually come.

Sri Aurobindo began his public address by acknowledging the fact that the concept of national education is yet to percolate widely in the areas of Bombay, whereas in Bengal it was taken as a 'given

45. K.R. Srinivasa Iyengar, op.cit., p.280.

fact', even though there were people for and against such an idea and attempt. In Bengal, the concept of national required no explanation or discussion for people to be convinced.[46]

Sri Aurobindo also briefly dwelt on the differences in perceptions of national education between nationalists and moderates. The nationalists had, he insisted, expressly included the word '*national*' in the resolutions that they had influenced and got passed in the Congress, but the moderates failed to appreciate its import and changed the wording and talked instead of an 'independent system of education',[47] so as not to offend official sensibilities. But this nomenclature, Sri Aurobindo argued, did not convey what is meant by 'national education'. It gave an idea of the political tussle over education, one position wanted a complete break with the official system of education and the other wanted the perpetuation of the official system and only a nominal Indian attempt that would, in no way, challenge or oppose the former. Sri Aurobindo's political dissections of the situation were only limited to the first part of the speech, the rest dealt with the experiment of national education as it was undertaken in Bengal.

Many, especially those who believed that India is not a nation, ask, Sri Aurobindo told the massive gathering, 'why do we have to qualify the term "education" by calling it "national"'? According to the thinking of these people, India is not a nation, because of the

---

46. Sri Aurobindo, *Speeches*, op.cit., p.11. 'The speech was delivered on January 15, 1908, in Girgaum, Bombay. A translation in Marathi was published in the *Kesari* [B.G. Tilak's celebrated nationalist paper] 21 January. This was retranslated into English by a police agent and published in the Bombay Native Paper Report (a police intelligence report) in 1908.' The text analysed here has been retranslated from a Marathi report by the editors of this edition of Sri Aurobindo's speeches.
47. Sri Aurobindo, *Speeches*, op.cit., p. 12.

existence of thousands of castes and subcastes, sects and subsects, 'any number of religious creeds with differences of opinion and practice; [and thus] in that case the use of the word "national" in the Indian situation becomes meaningless'. These 'people do not really understand what is meant by a nation', Sri Aurobindo countered this typically skeptical moderate opinion, and dilated on unity, why India is a nation and why the term "national" was applicable to the new education system'.[48] While others argue, Sri Aurobindo observed, that 'although India is a vast country geographically, still it cannot be termed a nation', to him, 'by its very geography the country appears to be quite distinct from other countries, and that itself gives it a certain national character'. He compared this physical structure to that of Italy, which was separate from its surrounding, and in 'thirty years became an independent nation'. He dilated on his and the nationalist perception of the composition of India, 'the inner and outer body of India, the customs, culture, and religion of its people, have an independent character different from those of the rest of the world. It has its foundations in the ancient past'.[49]

The imparting of national education implied 'that we need not throw away our traditional background and introduce completely new ideas and ideals'.[50] At a time when the movement for a cultural self-recovery was gaining momentum, these words defined the basic approach and philosophy of the national education movement, which based itself on a convergence of India's cultural and spiritual past. Sri Aurobindo argued that there existed a system of national education in the country in the past, and that such a system was driven by a philosophy which saw the nation as a living and pulsating entity. The Indian vision said that what is in the 'individual

48. Ibid.
49. Ibid., pp. 12, 13.
50. Ibid., p.13.

is also in the universal [and that] a nation is a living entity, full of consciousness; it is not something made up or fabricated'.[51]

The nationalists and their politics were shaped by this definition of a nation. This is what differentiated them, set them apart from the rung of elites who had until then controlled the Congress. Sri Aurobindo saw the projection of such an understanding of the nation among young minds encouraging the growth of a sense of unity, self-reliance and fraternity. One of the central efforts of the national education movement was aimed at creating this sense of organic bonding with the nation while the official system deliberately discouraged it. A detailed reading of Sri Aurobindo's address gives an insight into his thinking on fundamental themes at a time when nationalist politics was shaping, and its leaders, struggling to strike roots, were actively spreading its tenets. In a sense, these articulations indicate the shape and the direction of the philosophy of nationalism.

Sri Aurobindo drew a parallel between the nation and the individual. The individual, he observed, constituted of three parts, 'three types of body, gross, subtle and causal'; similarly the nation too, possessed three bodies and according to Indian philosophy 'it is not only the outward appearance, the gross body (*sthula-sarira*), that makes a complete man. All three bodies have to be taken into account' only then is it possible to develop some understanding of the man.[52] This applied to the nation too, Sri Aurobindo said, describing the nation's physical form. '[To] think about our nation,' says Sri Aurobindo:

> ... is first to think about our physical motherland. Stretching from the Himalayas in the north to Kanyakumari in the south, its boundaries are formed by the seas on the east and west. Ganga, Jamuna, Narmada, Krishna,

---

51. Ibid.
52. Ibid., p.13.

Godavari, flow here [India] unceasingly; here are ancient cities, tall and imposing temples, artistically designed palatial homes. Such is the part of this earth we call India.[53]

Such is the picture that comes into one's mind, he pointed out, while contemplating the physical form of India, and this 'is the gross body of our nation'. The physical is followed by the 'subtle' (*suksma-deha*), and Sri Aurobindo described it interestingly, '[thirty-three] crores of people live on this land with their joys and sorrows, their good and bad desires: they are all part of its subtle body'.[54]

Speaking of the causal body, he spoke of dimensions of the country which 'undergo changes in course of time' and 'yet they remain in the body, in seed-state, as permanent as the atom; they are always present there and, being the origin, it is out of them that the future takes shape. This is the causal body (*karana-deha*) of the nation'.[55]

Continuing with his comparison of the individual and the nation, Sri Aurobindo argued, that when one thought of an individual, one did not simply think of his present condition, but also of his past and his future, the same process applied to the country, 'when we speak of the rivers, mountains and cities of our country, we have in mind not only the present' and what is referred to 'is a history of five thousand years'. Describing how the country's past lights up the present imagination, Sri Aurobindo argued that when one spoke of 'Delhi and Agra, does not the image of Delhi as it was during Emperor Akbar's time [also] stand before your mind's eye?' While talking of the nation, therefore, Sri Aurobindo suggested, one should also remember 'our ancestors ... then Shivaji, Asoka, and Akbar at once become an integral part of our nationhood'. And this

53. Ibid.
54. Ibid.
55. Ibid., pp. 12–13.

was not limited to these warrior historical figures, but included the esoteric wisdom imparting ancient Rishis.[56]

Contributions of all personalities and characters from the past who have contributed to national growth and unity, ought to be recalled and integrated in an evolving national memory that would eventually facilitate the growth of a consolidated nationhood. This was an extremely vital aspect in course of the evolution of the freedom struggle especially in its early phase.

The new national schools, driven by the spirit of national education, Sri Aurobindo argued, attempted to work for this integration of the past with the nation's present; he saw this as essential for national progress and unity. He spoke of the habit of remembering national ancestors, and of how it was an integral part of Japanese culture and society, 'the Japanese people never forget their ancestors who offered their lives as a sacrifice for the sake of their country. This sense of sacrifice was always present in the Japanese blood; they never neglected to remember the sacrifices their ancestors made for sake of country.[57] It is this spirit

56. Sri Aurobindo, *Speeches*, op.cit., p. 14.
57. Indian nationalists, especially the extremists, during the first decade of the last century, continuously referred to Japanese social, political, and educational methods. This was especially *de rigueur* after the Russo-Japanese war between February 1904 and September 1905. As discussed earlier in the work, though a conflict forced by Imperial ambitions, the repeated Japanese victories against the established Czarist Empire pointed towards the tilting of balance in the Asian continent, announcing the rise of an Asian power on the world scene. Indian nationalists, especially those of the advanced group led by Sri Aurobindo and others, were deeply influenced by this emergence. It held before them future possibilities for India. They treated this as a pointer for India and they believed that through the revolutionary movement they had initiated in the country, similar preparation and results would be obtained. They advocated the need for emulating

of remembering and emulating ones' ancestors that Indians ought

them in all their national activities and systems. Hence, one observes in Sri Aurobindo's political speeches and his early political writings, numerous references to Japan. On the effects of the Japanese victory on the Indian youth, Scottish evangelist J.N.Farquhar (1861–1929) in his *Modern Religious Movements in India* (1914), writes, "The educated Indian now regards himself as a full-grown man, the equal in every respect of the cultured European, not to be set aside as an Asiatic, or as a member of a dark race. He claims the right of thinking his own thoughts .... This adult self-confidence was immeasurably strengthened by the victory of Japan over Russia. Every Asiatic felt himself recreated by that great event. To all the Asiatic lands it was a crisis in race-history, the moment when the age-old flood of European aggression was turned back. The exultation which every Indian felt over the victory lifted the national spirit to its height and gave a new note of strength to the period." The concept of ancestor-worship is an intrinsic part of Japanese life and society. It was seen to bind and integrate the nation. In its pursuance, the Japanese kept alive a perennial source of national inspiration. Sri Aurbindo referred to this source of inspiration which, in the Indian context, he felt, ought to translate into aspirations of unity and self-reliance. Nobushige Hozumi (1856--1926), Japanese statesman and legal expert of the Meiji period and sometime professor of German law and of comparative law at Tokyo Imperial University, and one of those enlisted to draft Japan's Civil Code of 1898, in his opus '*Ancestor Worship & Japanese Law*' [Tokyo, 1901] observed that ancestor worship 'was the primeval religion of the country from the earliest time of our history which dates back more than two thousand five hundred years; and it is universally practiced by the people at the present moment ... neither the introduction of Chinese civilisation, the spread of Buddhism nor the influence of European civilisation have done anything to shake the firm-rooted custom of the people'. The Chinese philosopher, Shiu-Ki, in his *Book of House-Ceremonies*, speaking on the origins of ancestor-worship observed that 'the object of worship is nothing else than performing all that is dictated by a feeling of true love and respect'. Professor Kurita of the Tokyo Imperial University in his work, *The Rituals of Worship*, made an

to evoke, giving rise to the emotions of unity and nationalism. And therefore, Sri Aurobindo argued, whatever one did today, must be done with the spirit of repaying one's debt to one's ancestors. Generations which would come, needed to see, as 'an organic component of one's nation', the nationalists' vision of an Indian nation that ought to be shaped and internalised along these lines.

---

observation on ancestor-worship – ' Who, endowed with life in this world, has not a mind to honour his parents? Who, honouring his parents, does not reverence his ancestors? Who, honouring parents and reverencing ancestors, is not prompted to follow the dictates of affectionate sentiment by offering sacrifices to their spirits? This is the outcome of the faculty of intelligence that is implanted in human nature, and through it arose the ceremonies of offering sacrifices to the spirits from the Age of the Gods'. Ancestor-worship formed an integral part of Japanese as well as Chinese society; Confucius in his Book of *Medium* had indicated the way and the process's integrality when he observed, 'it is the highest filial piety to serve the departed as they would serve the present'. It would be interesting to delve briefly into certain concepts of the Japanese ancestor-worship because Sri Aurobindo, in a public speech, laid special emphasis on this aspect, and indicated its utility not only in a national system of education but also in the national life at that time. Three kinds of ancestor-worship are followed, 'namely the worship of the First Imperial Ancestor by the people, the worship of the patron god of the locality, which ... [are] the remains of the clan-ancestors by clansmen, and the worship of family-ancestors by the members of the household'. In every Shinto household is found a second 'god-shelf or *Kamidana*, which is dedicated exclusively to the worship of the ancestors of the house', the first shelf is dedicated to the First Imperial Ancestor. On this second shelf 'are placed cenotaphs bearing the names of the ancestors, their ages, and the dates of their death. These memorial tablets are called "*Mitama-shiro*" which means "representatives of souls," and they are usually placed in small boxes shaped like Shinto shrines. Offerings of rice, sake, fish, sakaki-tree and lamps are made on this second shelf as on the first...' [Hozumi, op. cit.,]

It would generate 'a wide and engaging vision of our nation and nationalism'.[58]

The new nationalism and vision of nation that national education would propagate and help instill in young minds, would be an all- encompassing nationalism. These two words, 'wide' and 'engaging', fundamentally define the nationalism that Sri Aurobindo stood for. It was only with such a vision of the nation and nationalism and a matching action that India would be capable of producing 'great philosophers, statesman, warriors and commanders', and move towards self-reliance and self-respect. The educational vision of national education sought to comprehensively, and not selectively, reinterpret and present and interpret the Indian past in order to instill a sense of nationalism that would push towards national unity. Sri Aurobindo told his Maharashtrian audience that national education had caught the imagination of a section of society in Bengal because 'we have kept before us this grand idea of the nation' while 'formulating the concept of National Education" [59]

Interestingly, instead of touching the surface of the subject, the teacher in Sri Aurobindo was reflected in this address. How was this vision of nation and nationalism imparted to learners under the national education system? This speech, in fact, comes across as laying down, in the words of Sri Aurobindo, a sort of broad-pedagogical philosophy.

'Let us see' he said, 'how the details have been worked out in consonance with this lofty and noble concept' of the nation and taking up the 'simple subject of geography as an illustration', dilated on it in some detail. Hitherto, the subject was being taught in a mechanical and unimaginative manner in Government and private schools. Students are generally 'told about such-and-such a

---

58. Sri Aurobindo, *Speeches,* p.14.
59. Ibid.

country with so many districts, with their District Officers and so forth'.[60] But in the Bengal national schools, the approach itself was organic. While teaching geography, inspired by the ideas of national education, the children were first told 'that India is our Motherland'. In this way, they are made aware of the gross body of the nation. They are told about 'our rivers, Ganga, Jamuna, Narmada, etc., and what these rivers mean, not merely where they flow'.[61]

It is an interesting point on the ideology and practice of national education; an education does not become national merely by listing national rivers as opposed to those of a foreign land. For it to be truly different and relevant it needed to demonstrate and elaborate the organic and the civilisational link that the river retained with the land, and this link would do well to also include the mythical and metaphysical bond that these rivers had forged over millennia with the land of their origin and flow. And when the ideas of the land were taught to the children in the national schools, when the children were taught about the western Indian region of Maharashtra, 'we describe the land in which Shivaji lived', the organic link and past achievements is established in order to instill connectivity with the nation's past and future. 'Speaking about Punjab,' Sri Aurobindo pointed out, 'we tell the children about the Punjab of Ranjit Singh. Speaking about the geography of the Himalayas' the children are taught about how the 'land of the Himalayas has become holy because of its Rishis'.[62] The whole attempt was to present the physical features of India as something more than a mere landmass and to establish a spiritual link between the land and the civilisation that it has nurtured and nourished. The geography of other nations is also taught by the national schools

60. Ibid., pp. 14, 15.
61. Ibid., p. 15.
62. Ibid., p.15.

but what is imparted is their 'importance in the context of our country'.[63] This too was an innovative approach of the national education system.

The teaching of history by national schools also attempted to strike an alternative path. The nationalist stand was that 'true history' could never really be taught following the colonial education method of teaching. It was not important in national schools, Sri Aurobindo said, to remember 'how many kings have ruled the country, which king came to power in which year and how long his reign lasted or the date when the Battle of Plassey was fought'. In short, the importance of dates and chronology was secondary, what was of primary importance was the understanding of how the nation was formed, how the various people evolved a distinct identity and temperament.[64]

---

63. Ibid. In a letter written to a friend in Madras, Sister Nivedita spoke of the need to also study the geography and history of other countries, while undertaking an intense study of one's own history. 'Remember', she wrote, 'it is the national sense *in* the world-sense that we have to achieve.' (CWSV, vol.4, p.398)
64. The writing of history saw intense debate before and during the national education movement. The re-writing of Indian history from the Indian-Indic perspectives was seen to be fundamental to re-creating the Indian nationalist narrative. The young scholars who were involved with the national education and its institutions especially in Bengal, were copious in their research output. In a seminal, but less discussed, essay that he wrote sometime in 1903, Rabindranath Tagore discussed the problem of Indian historiography and history-writing in some detail. He spoke of those countries being fortunate which 'find the everlasting image of their land in their own history'. For Tagore, it was history which served as 'the introduction to one's own country during one's childhood itself'. But in India, Tagore lamented, it was just the opposite, 'it is the history of our country that has kept our own land obscured to us. From the invasion of Mahmud to the arrogant imperial declaration of Lord Curzon, all

Philosophy was also taught keeping in mind the aim of the national education movement. The students are told of the greatness of the Indian systems of philosophy. Sri Aurobindo lamented that in Government schools, the 'degree-holders know of what Schopenhauer has to say, but they have hardly any knowledge of the spiritual foundations of our own thought'. The national education sought to reverse this cloistered approach. But the greater and more

---

the historical annals till yesterday, are only a mass of strange mist for Bharatavarsha. These accounts do not give clarity to our vision of our motherland. In fact, these only serve to cloud it. These accounts throw a beam of artificial light on such a spot that, in our own eyes, the very profile of our country is made dark.' Tagore complained that 'by not viewing Bharatavarsha from Bharatavarsha's own perspective, since our very childhood we learn to demean her and in consequence we get demeaned ourselves, while the English boys were taught the glory of their inheritance and developed a pride and sense of heirship to a glorious legacy. We learn that our ancestors did not conquer other countries and did not extend trade and commerce: to make just this fact known is the very purpose of the history of India. What our ancestors did, we do not know; therefore we also do not know what we ought to aim for. Therefore we have to imitate others. Whom should we blame for this? The way we get our education since our very childhood, with every passing day we get increasingly alienated from our own country, till a sense of rebellion against the land of our birth overtakes our mind...' (See, for instance, Rabindranath Tagore, *The History of Bharatvarsha,* accessed at: http://www.ifih.org/TheHistoryofBharatavarsha.htm (14.12.2011). This little-known but seminal text of Tagore's was written in Bhadra 1309 Bengal Era (August 1903). Translated from the original Bengali by Sumita Bhattacharya & Sibesh Bhattacharya. For a detailed discussion on the debate on nationalist history writing see eg: Anirban Ganguly, *Alternate Perceptions of India; Arguing for a Counter Narrative,* Occasional Paper, May 2013: available at: https://www.vifindia.org/sites/default/files/alternate-perceptions-of%20india-arguing-for-a-counter-narrative.pdf)

relevant point that Sri Aurobindo made is that the 'philosophy the students learn in college, they should try to put into practice'. The bases and fundamentals of philosophical knowledge should not be mere theoretical and divorced from everyday life.[65] The learning of philosophy in classrooms must have as one of its results also the amelioration of the individual and his collective activities and of his collective existence. Essentially the approach to the teaching of philosophy in national institutions was that of a philosophy for life and living.

One of the fundamental aims of national education was to instil a sense of greatness in a subject nation. Sri Aurobindo spoke of such a system being in place in ancient times. The National Education programme discarded nothing useful or worthwhile, all past figures who contributed to the shaping of the Indian civilisation and identity shall have a permanent place in it and become integral dimensions and centre of national growth and consolidation. Sri Aurobindo also referred to an essential issue with which nationalist educators grappled, that of Government schools not adopting an approach which would give rise to a sense of nation, unity, and Indianness.

Sri Aurobindo complained that 'in those schools, the tender minds of our students are overburdened with the European way of thinking. But European thought and European way of life are quite different from our thought and our way of life'.[66] It was one of the principal contentions of the new education leaders, and Sri Aurobindo seemed to be very clear on the necessity of accepting dimensions of modernity from the West for national progress. 'It is true', he observed 'that when we speak of the development of our own country, we cannot ignore the progress of modern Europe. In

65. Sri Aurobindo, *Speeches*, p. 16.
66. Ibid.

our reform we must certainly include it; whatever is acceptable must be adapted suitably by us. But we have to guard against damaging our foundation in the process'.

The advances of Western science must be put to use, Sri Aurobindo spoke of the Japanese who implemented the ideas of Western science, but were not 'blind to the achievements of [their] forefathers'. He referred to the ancient Indian Ayurvedic Science as an example; in Government medical colleges, he pointed out, 'students remain unaware' of this ancient science 'though there are many occult and valuable truths behind it, to which the Western system has no access'. Sri Aurobindo also cautioned against the unthinking attitude 'that whatever is ours, is always the best'.[67] This broadly sums up the overall attitude of the nationalist educators on the intensely debated issue of assimilation and rejection *vis-à-vis* Western methods and systems. Satish Chandra Mukherjee was of a similar opinion when it came to these fundamental questions.

One issue which gave a huge impetus to the organising of the national education movement was issuance of circulars preventing students from participating in political activities. While opposing these dictates, the leaders of national education insisted that such activities gave rise in students to a sense of participation in national growth and awakening. The Government obviously stamped such an attitude as seditious while others perceived this as an interference with the students' academic growth and development. Sri Aurobindo insisted that in the 'field of politics we have a lot to learn from the West', especially the democratic system of government. And the National Education system did not isolate students 'from the political field; in fact we give them first-hand experience of the

67. Ibid., p.16.

democratic system of government making them work alongside us'.[68]

Sri Aurobindo insisted on the need for vocational training observing that it led to self-reliance and was thus being diligently imparted in national schools. These were taught along with science and when the students came out of national schools, they did not find it difficult to earn a modest wage. The national education system tried to address this challenge of imparting an education that developed skills, and gave technical training, an education which would, as Vivekananda said 'help the common mass of people to equip themselves for the struggle for life', a real education which would enable one to 'stand on one's legs'.[69]

The whole 'special emphasis' given in a national system of education was on 'creating a future Indian nation'. The propelling thought that drove the effort of National Education, Sri Aurobindo said, was this thought, 'When will this Indian nation occupy a place in the company of other nations? When will it be great among other nations in the world? Our learned and accomplished people must be great as people in other countries are great'.[70] These are the thoughts that impelled the whole idea to action.

Sri Aurobindo also spoke of how the mother-tongue was used in the national schools. 'We give education up to fifth standard in the mother-tongue of the students; teaching the children through English is harmful'. To those who said that the vernaculars 'do not have an adequate vocabulary for teaching certain subjects', Sri Aurobindo's advice was to first experience the method of instruction through the vernacular, and then arrive at an adequate conclusion. In this public meeting at Girgaon, Sri Aurobindo also spoke of the

---

68. Sri Aurobindo, *Speeches*, p.16.
69. *CWSV* vol.7, pp. 147–48.
70. Sri Aurobindo, *Speeches*, op. cit., p. 17.

system followed in the National College, 'the seventh standard in our national schools is equivalent to the intermediate courses conducted by the universities. In our colleges we conduct a four-year course. A college student usually studies a single subject and for that purpose special emphasis is given to the use of the English language', but English in the national education framework retained the status of a second language. [71]

The motto of National Education was self-reliance and Sri Aurobindo concluded this rather long descriptive public speech on the subject by reiterating its basic principle:

> A student must be able to stand on his own. It is not the objective of National Education to make somebody else carry him on his shoulders. The student must support himself and not look helplessly to others. Self-reliance is the basic principle we diligently try to impart to a student.... We [in Bengal] have absolutely no expectation of help from the Government in our endeavour [of establishing national schools and colleges]. On the contrary, with Government support our nationalist enthusiasm will disappear.[72]

The inveterate nationalist in Sri Aurobindo asserted himself when he argued that official help will deprive the movement of its vigour and originality and stem the tide of bold thinking and of courageous experimentation. Sri Aurobindo called for charting out a radically different and bold path for national education. National training for self-reliance was the basic principle of national education. It was also the guiding principle of the national movement, placing the educational dimension as an integral part of the political demand too.

Sri Aurobindo held the view that the national education movement needed to be part of the greater national struggle for freedom so as to be able to derive sustained strength, replenishment,

71. Ibid.
72. Ibid., pp. 16–17.

and direction. A divorce from the latter would, he believed, prove fatal to the education movement. In fact he argued throughout along these lines and emphasised it when he saw the National Council adopting a meek and imitative attitude *vis-à-vis* the official system.

It is the right moment to briefly refer, at this juncture, to another historic speech on the need for national education delivered around the same time in the same geographical location by Sri Aurobindo's close nationalist collaborator and host during these visits, Lokmanya Tilak. In his public address on 'National Education' delivered at Barshi, Solapur, in 1908, Tilak, who had already made contributions to the national education movement in the Deccan,[73] broadly spoke along the lines developed by the national education movement. Addressing what seemed to be a group of potential donors to the cause of national education, Tilak spoke in nearly the same manner as his nationalist comrade in arms. Tilak too, felt that the term 'national education' needed some explanation. Merely developing the capacity to read and write did not constitute education, instead that which gave a 'knowledge of the experience of our ancestors is called education' was how Tilak placed the issue before his listeners.

Defending the need for religious education in a country like India, Tilak linked the absence of it to the growing influence of missionaries 'all over our country' and the lack of pride in one's religion. It is evident that Tilak was much concerned on over the issue of religious education. For Tilak a 'healthy veneration of the old gods and the national heroes would best infuse a true spirit of nationality and patriotism'. Earlier in a series of articles in the *Mahratta*, Tilak had criticised the 'official panacea' of including moral textbooks in Indian schools, for him, in order to make 'Indian

---

73. For a detailed discussion on Tilak's educational initiatives in the pre-Swadeshi days see e.g. D.V.Athalye, *The Life of Lokmanya Tilak*, Published by: Annasahib Chiploonkar, Pune, 1921.

youths more self-reliant and more energetic, they must be taught greater self-respect, and that could only be done by making them respect their religion and their forefathers'. Tilak had argued that an 'excessive and aimless self-debasement may perhaps be a good thing in an ascetic or a philosopher, but it does mischief in practical life'. The youth ought to be injected with this self-respect, yes, perhaps, 'superfluous patriotism may sometime lead to excesses', but would also do some good, at least, Tilak had pointed out, it was better than 'a self-denying abjectness', which only led to 'lethargy and death'. In a sense, the essence of the national education movement, the leitmotif of all the debates that surrounded it and shaped it was in essence this, the need to infuse young India with the spirit of self-reliance and self-respect.[74]

Tilak's speech did not go into great detail about the system, spirit, and method of national education; it was more of a direct discussion of some of its issues and challenges. But it is worth examining since it gives us an insight into the thinking of two of nationalist stalwarts around the same time. The principal points that Tilak raised with his interlocutors was that the colonial government was neglecting 'scientific and mechanical education' and was by design preventing the evolution of a self-reliant India. Colonial education was emasculating Indian youth, Tilak argued:

> The reason of this is that the education which they receive is one-sided. The Government wanted engineers, doctors and clerks. It therefore started such schools which could supply its need. The students therefore who came out of these schools at first were bent upon services. It was the state of things sometime back that after passing three or four classes in school one could easily get on in life, but it has now become absolutely difficult, even to live from hand to mouth. We have therefore become conscious. It has become

74. N.C Kelkar, *Landmarks in Lokmanya's Life*, 1924, p.11.

now almost clear that it is not the fault on our part that even after getting so much education we remain unable to satisfy our bare necessities; but the fault goes direct to the education that we receive.[75]

The colonial government was neglecting education in the villages; it was obstructing villagers from training their children. The national education movement, Tilak said, sought to address these, 'in the end we have come to the conclusion that, for proper education, national schools must be started on all sides'. The private schools that already functioned, Tilak pointed out, were unable to undertake a radical programme 'owing to the fear of losing the grant-in-aid', therefore an effort to start 'our own schools' must be made in a selfless manner.[76]

There were movements in this direction in other parts of the country already and though Maharashtra [was as yet] a little backward, Tilak talked of those dimensions that were to be given primacy in these nationalist institutions: (a) 'religious education will first and foremost engage our attention' – secular education was not sufficient to build up character, a religious education allowed the mind to dwell on high principles and kept 'us away from evil pursuits'. Conscious of the argument prevalent in certain quarters then, that an exposure to religion and religious education 'begets quarrel', Tilak clarified that it was the Hindu religion which 'advocates toleration of other religious beliefs and instructs one to stick to one's own religion', therefore, the religious education that the nationalist schools proposed to impart would teach 'Hinduism to the Hindu', 'Islamism to the Musalmans' and would encourage 'to forgive and forget the differences of other religions'; (b) national schools proposed to 'lighten the load of the study of the foreign

75. Bal Gangadhar Tilak, *His Writings and Speeches*, revised ed., 1919, p.82.
76. Ibid., p. 84.

languages – the compulsion of learning through a foreign language unnecessarily lengthens the process. 'We spend twenty-years or twenty-five years', Tilak argued, 'for the education which we can easily obtain in seven or eight years' if it were acquired through the medium of the vernaculars. Tilak argued that one 'who speaks good English is said, in these days, to have been educated. But a mere knowledge of the language is no true education'. Even during the Mahomedan rule, he contended, there was a requirement to learn Persian but there was no compulsion to the requirement. Therefore to 'save unnecessary waste of time [it was proposed in the national schools] to give education though our own vernaculars'. (c) The national schools would promote 'industrial education' which would give training for the setting up and launching of indigenous industry. Ample scope and resources remained for the setting up of indigenous industries and the gap would be filled up by a well-designed industrial training.

The British government, Tilak pointed out, attended to the immediate needs of sick industries back home, but failed to provide the same attention to languishing industrial ventures in India. A 'large mechanical and scientific laboratory' was in the pipeline and Tilak solicited funds for setting it up, the 'educationists [were] helping with their learning and experience, and [it was upon the] well-to-do to help them with money'. The objective was to empower the future generations to be able to 'earn their bread and be true citizens'. And his final plea was for the imparting of political education. The young learners had to be made aware of the drain that was being enforced on their country by the colonial master. 'Every year', Tilak contended, 'some thirty or forty crores of rupees are drained out of India without any return. We have, therefore, fallen to a wretched state of poverty. These things, if understood in the prime of life, can make such a lasting impression over the hearts of our young men, as it would be impossible in an advanced age'.[77]

Tilak's concluding remarks pointed to a deeper truth of the whole movement and in a sense, also its uniqueness. Because the sort of education aspired for was beyond reach 'for want of self-Government' Tilak argued, 'we should not therefore await the coming of these rights, but we must get up and begin the work'.[78]

Let the Government be displeased —- we hope the Government will never deter us – we must do our duty. If the Government prohibits us from marriages, do we obey it? The same is the case with education. As men do not give up building houses for fear that rats would dig holes, so we should not give up our work for fear of Government displeasure. If perchance any difficulty arises, our young men are to face it. To fear difficulties is to lose manliness. Difficulties do us immense good. They inspire in us courage and prepare us to bear them manly. A nation cannot progress if it meets no difficulties in the way. We do not get this sort of education for want of self-Government. We should not therefore await the coming of these rights, but we must get up and begin the work.[79]

Writing on National Education, a decade later, for Annie Besant, who had asked him to express his views on 'National Education' for her journal *New India,* Tilak wrote:

Where the people and the Government are one, that is, actuated by the same ideals of citizenship, there can arise no conflict or differences of opinion in the matter of National Education. But where the people and the Government have different ideals of citizenship before them, where the governing class wants to keep the people down in spite of their desire to rise to the status of full citizenship in the Empire, there arises the necessity of National Education as distinguished from governmental education. Viewed in this light. National Education is only a branch or a means to the attainment of Self-Government, and those who demand Home Rule for India cannot but

77. Ibid., pp.84–87.
78. Ibid., pp.86–87.
79. Ibid., pp. 88–89.

zealously support a movement for the establishment of National Education in this country.[80]

Sri Aurobindo's other speeches on his way back to Calcutta contain brief references to national education, though often rhetorical and made in the context of nationalist politics, they succinctly convey the objectives of national education as perceived by the nationalists.

In his speech at Dhulia, Maharashtra on January 26, 1908, Sri Aurobindo spoke on 'Swadeshi and Boycott'[81] and discussed it at first politically. The grand objective of national education was the establishment of 'self-government in India'. The approach would be to gradually give up 'schools and colleges under foreign control' because these institutions gave 'us an education which [did] not develop our intellectual capacity. Education in English schools colleges [had] cut us off from our ancient strength .... The education we receive is narrow, meagre and incomplete'. The objective of the movement was to establish an education 'of our own in India'[82], Sri Aurobindo told his audience The educational dimension of the movement, like its other counterpart, is based on Swadeshi – and its aim was to prevent pecuniary, moral, intellectual, and physical ruination of India and to realise this, the ancient Indian system became the natural fountain of inspiration and guidance.[83]

Speaking to a gathering of industrialists and merchants in Nagpur on February 1, 1908, on 'Commercial and Educational

80. Ibid., p.368.
81. Like most of Sri Aurobindo's speeches from this era this one was noted down 'on the spot by a police agent, who later had a fair copy typed'. Though deficient 'in terms of English usage and grammar' the type scripts as well as the first notes were produced as evidence in the Alipore Bomb Trial. [*CWSA* vol.7, Notes & Texts, p. 1175]
82. Sri Aurobindo, *Speeches*, op.cit., p.43.
83. Ibid.

Swarajya', Sri Aurobindo exhorted the indigenous education institutions to inculcate a spirit of self-reliance and faith in young minds. The idea of achieving commercial *swarajya* – commercial and industrial self-sufficiency – would have to be impressed on young minds so that they could prepare themselves accordingly.

Sri Aurobindo spoke of an 'unnecessary parrot-like education' which was wasting away the 'strength and intellect' of the young. He indicted the education that was being imparted as 'poisonous', and having a 'blighting effect on the ideas of political morality and national greatness by creating a hankering in them for the subordinate posts under the Government, in order to earn their livelihood'.[84] The principal aim thus of national education, a truly national education, was to awaken in 'one's mind the highest ideas of national activity, which make one forget oneself and feel that he does not exist separately from his country'. It aimed to kindle in the students a basic and binding sense of being part of a great national march. For this, education had to be imparted along 'national lines' and it had to be under 'national control'. These were the twin defining adage that nationalist educators and thought-leaders kept harping upon. This also drove to push for their inclusion in the resolutions of the Congress resolutions.

Since the gathering consisted of representatives from the field of commerce and industry Sri Aurobindo directly appealed for their support:

> It is not possible to have national education without the help of the rich and the learned men. If the money of the wealthy is utilised in this direction, it will be very well spent. All should work in order to secure a future generation that is sturdy – both physically and mentally.[85]

84. Ibid., p. 64.
85. Ibid., p. 65.

Commercial and educational *Swarajya* would usher in the era of political *Swarajya.*[86] It was these two areas of action that would eventually lay the foundations of a self-reliant and self-sufficient and free India. Sri Aurobindo's emphasis on national education during this tour of the region and his public addresses helped shape its narrative and reinforced its demand.

The Bengal Provincial Conference at Pabna (East Bengal), held in the second week of February 1908, saw an unambiguous resolution on national education being moved. Rabindranath Tagore, by then having poetically articulated the liberty-yearning aspirations of a rising nation, presided over the meet. Disturbed by the developments in Surat, Tagore had expressed dismay at the turn of events, and called for unity among the two factions. In an article written after the split, he had advised the Congress to unite and launch a mass-contact programme, to initiate people in the *mantra of truth.*[87] Initially reluctant to accept the invitation to preside over the Pabna provincial conference, Tagore finally agreed to take the Chair. He was not sure whether he would be able to maintain peace, when there was no peace in the country. In a letter to the eminent litterateur and polymath, Ramendra Sundar Trivedi (1864–1919), the Poet complained of how he was being flooded with anonymous letters from all sides, often abusive in nature, that it was becoming difficult for him to actually decide on which side he must stand. One letter even warned the Poet that if accepted to preside over the Pabna Conference, the events of Surat would be repeated!

In his presidential address at Pabna, Tagore dwelt at length on the need to rejuvenate India's villages and rural life. He dilated on these themes which he had discussed in his earlier essay, 'Swadeshi

86. Ibid., p. 65.

87. Prabhat Kumar Mukhopadhyay, *Rabindra Jibani* [Beng], vol.2, Kolkata: Visva Bharati Publication Dept, 1423 [Beng era] p.221.

Samaj'. He spoke in detail on rural development, implementing 'labour-saving scientific techniques, encouraging the growth of a variety of cottage industry and more. India's life-energy was hidden in her villages, and each section needed to unite to rejuvenate and rekindle that energy. Tagore delivered his address in Bengali. It was the first time that a presidential address was drafted and also read out in Bengali, the habit of speaking in English was broken.[88] Sri Aurobindo's nationalist colleague Hemendra Prasad Ghose, who was part of the nationalist contingent at Pabna along with Subodh Mallik and others, wrote that the Poet 'attempted to steer clear of party politics but could not conceal his sympathy with the Nationalists'.[89]

According to observers and reports at Pabna, amidst the tussle between the Moderates and the Nationalists, national education 'received a further impetus' and the 'resolution adopted ... [had] been a considerable advance upon those adopted at the previous years' conferences by the addition of the phrase "to establish and maintain National Schools throughout the country".' The resolution moved by Sri Aurobindo said:

> ... that in the opinion of this conference, steps should be taken for promoting a system of education, literary, scientific and technical, suited to the requirements of the country *on national lines under national control* and to establish and maintain national schools throughout the country."[90]

Satish Chandra Mukherjee's *The Dawn* and *Dawn Society's Magazine* which, as we have discussed earlier, spearheaded the national education debate reported the proceedings in its April

88. Ibid., pp. 219–224.
89. Amalendu De, *Raja Subodh Chandra Mallik and His Times*, op.cit., p.125.
90. Sri Aurobindo, *Speeches*, op. cit., Appendix – I, p. 150.

1908 issue —'in a short but inspiring speech' the Principal of the Bengal National College, 'Srijukta Aurobindo Ghose, B.A. (Cantab)' said:

> ...that national education was a work which had already been accomplished and was already visible in a concrete shape to the eyes of the people. There was the Bengal National College at Calcutta and there were about 25 secondary National Schools at work in the mofussil [rural areas] under the direction of the National Council of Education. There were besides some three hundred primary National Schools, all seeking the aid of the Council, which in turn should be more liberally supported by the whole of Bengal in order to enable it to do its sacred work. [91]

Sri Aurobindo also briefly criticised the University system in India, the report noted, 'Srijukta Aurobindo Ghose pointed out that the University system was defective in its aims and methods intended only to serve the purposes of the Government, not requirements of the country. It turned out machines for administrative and professional work, not men'. The 'national system of education [on the other hand], intended to create a nation [and] produce men with all their faculties trained, full of patriotism, and mentally, morally, physically the equals of the men of any other nations'.[92]

The official education system taught subservience, and national education taught mastery of self and nation. Sri Aurobindo always made a direct appeal, simply explaining the necessity and the system of national education for the masses to realise its relevance and to develop faith on it as a genuine alternative to the governmental system. This manifested through the founding of a number of national schools, especially in the East Bengal districts where the nationalist organisations had created a remarkable network. Sri

---

91. Ibid., p. 150.
92. Ibid., p. 151.

Aurobindo himself stayed back after the Pabna Conference to found a national school at Pabna.[93]

The idea of a National University was mooted from time to time. It would be relevant to revisit a debate around this time on the National University demand with Sri Aurobindo opposing the move to develop through an external charter. Annie Besant, whose educational thought we have had occasion to examine, reinitiated 'a campaign in favour of national education and in a speech outlined her idea of a National University'.

Discussing her demand, in an editorial in the February 24th, 1908, issue of *Bande Mataram*, entitled 'A National University', Sri Aurobindo supported the idea and expressed his enthusiasm for the growth of the national education movement, but opposed Besant's demand that the Charter for the proposed National University be acquired from England.[94] Sri Aurobindo exuded a great sense of optimism that the movement for a National University was growing and called it:

> ... a seed which is sown and must come to its fruition, because the future demands and the heart of the nation is in accord with the demand ... there may be many errors and false starts, but like a stream gathering volume as it flows, the movement will grow in force and certainty... [95]

At the time of his writing, the movement for establishing national schools was indeed growing but writing about a year later, Sri Aurobindo observed how the national education system and structure, having disjointed itself from the mainstream national movement, lost its formative orientation and initial impetus. [96]

---

93. Amalendu De, op.cit., p.127.
94. *CWSA* vol.7, op.cit., pp. 894.
95. Ibid.
96. See eg. his article, entitled 'National Education' *Karmayogin,* 1 January, 1910. 'It is now apparent,' Sri Aurobindo argued in the article,

Anyway, continuing with his discussion of the attempt at forming national educational institutions, Sri Aurobindo observed that the effort was a longstanding one – 'there have been many attempts before the present movement to rescue education in India from subservience to foreign and petty ends, and to establish colleges and schools maintained and controlled by Indians which would give an education superior to the Government-controlled education'. But the institutions which had started with such an aim gradually became 'monuments of a frustrated idea', having 'fallen to the state of ordinary institutions, replicas of the Government model, without a separate mission or nobler reason for existence'. This happened, he argued, because the promoters of these institutions 'could not understand, or forgot that the first condition of success was independence – an independence jealously preserved and absolute. In other words, there can be no national education without national control'.[97]

This educational independence never manifested itself because the indigenous institutions were chronically dependent on Government largesse. Referring to the Benares Hindu College and the Dayananda Anglo-Vedic College[98], two institutions started by nationalists with India and her civilisation in focus, Sri Aurobindo pointed out that these institutions have secured a 'certain measure of success', they are 'successful institutions, but isolated. They have not developed into centres of a network of schools affiliated to them and forming one corporate body. They have not in themselves

---

'that it was the Nationalist element which by its energy, courage, boldness of thought, readiness to accept the conditions of progress, gave the movement its force and vitality. Wherever that force has been withdrawn, the movement has collapsed'.' [p. 385]

97. *CWSA* vol.7, op. cit., pp. 894–95.
98. Founded in Lahore in 1886 inspired by the ideal of Dayananada Saraswati (1824–1883).

the makings of Universities'.[99] Though they are different in one

99. Lala Lajpat Rai (1865–1928) one of the stalwarts of the nationalist movement and a close collaborator of Sri Aurobindo, 'who raised the cry of "national education" in India as far back as 1883', and who used the cry 'rather effectively for enlisting sympathy and collecting funds for the various institutions' that had begun imparting education along 'nationalist' lines', made similar observations on national education and nationalist education institutions in his seminal, and now largely ignored, *The Problem of National Education in India* [1920]. 'The Mohammedan College at Aligarh', Rai argued, 'the Arya College at Lahore, the Hindu College at Benares, all embodied the "national" ideals of their founders.... Each professed to provide its own kind of national education. The educational facilities provided by these institutions were open to persons of all creeds, denominations, and religions, but the nationalism aimed at was undisguisedly denominational'. What is of relevance to our search is the 'nationalist' content of instruction in these institutions which Sri Aurobindo questions and Rai condones, through an independent study. 'The education imparted in these institutions, as distinguished from the ordinary state-owned schools and colleges,' observes Rai, 'was "national" only in so far as it helped the creation of the denominational atmosphere aimed at by its promulgators'. There was an emphasis on the study of the vernacular and sacred language but the focus 'all the time was on the University course and the University examination. The scheme of studies promulgated by the official Universities was accepted unreservedly .... The principal business of the staffs engaged was to prepare students for University examinations. The results achieved in these examinations were the measure of their success and popularity'. [*The Problems of National Education in India,* op. cit., pp. 16,17, 18] Referring to the Dayananda-Anglo Vedic College at Lahore, to stabilise which he did much, and to which Sri Aurobindo also alluded, Lajpat Rai observed that prior to the forming of the National Council of Education in Bengal, the former was the only institution which could 'even by a stretch of imagination and language, lay any claim to being called "national" in the sense in which the word

sense, in that 'they give religious teaching' which is a 'wholesome

was then understood'. Taking the case of the Fergusson College as Sri Aurobindo did, Rai argued that the College with the 'exception of the spirit of self-sacrifice of its founder, directors, and teachers, had no other claim to be distinguished from the ordinary State Colleges'. The Aligarh College, the Benares College and the Fergusson College [founded in 1885 by the Deccan Education Society and named after Sir James Fergusson, then Governor of Bombay who had donated a princely sum of Rs. 1,200] have had a constant presence of foreigners on the staff and 'have been almost regularly in receipt of State aid, thus subjecting practically the whole of their policy to Government control. Not that that fact necessarily makes them denationalised, but it does reduce their claim to any great distinction from the ordinary State-managed institutions'. [Ibid., pp. 22–23.] Sri Aurobindo alluded to this while enumerating the reasons which prevented an institution from being authentically 'national'. Its dependence on official largesse and as a corollary, the curbing of institutional freedom, emerged as a principal factor. One institution, the Gurukul at Kangri Haridwar, received Lala Lajpat's approbation as having a greater 'claim to being "national" than any of the others mentioned previously [because] it is an institution founded, managed, staffed, and financed by Indians only. In its curriculum it gives the first place to Indian languages .... It takes no notice of the official University courses or the University examination' but this institution too was what Rai termed 'sectarian', in the sense that it was inspired by a certain sectional religious idea or thought. The only effort in his opinion that was 'truly national, was that made by the National Council of Education in Bengal under the impetus of the Swadeshi and the Boycott. The scheme of the National Council was free from [a] sectarian tinge ... it took no notice of denominational nationalism [and] it frankly recognised the necessity of ignoring the official University curriculum on the one hand and State aid on the other. It aimed at national consolidation and national independence'. This was Rai's assessment though, with the advantage of hindsight, Rai accepted that the National Council movement eventually became a 'dilapidated and

departure from the barren official form of education', this [religious instruction] remained only 'one part of education on national lines' and merely its inclusion did not wholly make a system national.[100]

In the editorial, Sri Aurobindo also defined national education and argued that such an aim could only come about when the system was under national control. He spoke of national education as that 'which starting with the past and making full use of the present builds up a great nation.' The agenda was not one of a complete reversal to the past, Sri Aurobindo observed:

> Whoever wishes to cut off the nation from its past, is no friend of our national growth. Whoever fails to take advantage of the present is losing us the battle of life. We must therefore save for India all that she has stored up of knowledge, character and noble thought in her immemorial past. We must acquire for her the best knowledge that Europe can give her and assimilate it to her own peculiar type of national temperament. We must introduce the best methods of teaching humanity has developed, whether modern or ancient. And all these must harmonise into a system which will be impregnated with the spirit of self-reliance so as to build up men and not machines – national men, able men, men fit to carve out a career for themselves by their own brain power and resource, fit to meet the shocks of life and breast the waves of adventure...'[101]

For national education to develop rightly and correctly, it had to be 'on national lines and under national control. This necessity [was] the very essence of its being'.[102]

While he expresses his respect for this 'great orator and organiser', Sri Aurobindo differed on the approach; he pointed out

---

discarded landmark in the educational progress of the country'. [Ibid., pp. 23,24,25, 26] Sri Aurobindo had predicted such a fate for the movement much earlier in 1909.

100. *CWSA* vol.7, op. cit, p. 895.

101. Ibid.

102. Ibid.

that 'a university organised by Mrs. Besant will not be a National University'. Because in 'the first place, the future University must be one built up by the brain and organising power of India's own sons...' and ' secondly, Mrs. Besant [had] forgotten that the basis of a National University has already been laid. The National Council of Education in Bengal [had] already commenced the great work on lines which have only to be filled in'.[103]

Sri Aurobindo charged Mrs. Besant of ignoring the efforts of the Council, and of being desirous of projecting the Benares Hindu College as 'the basis of the National University' and argued that the Benares College shall fail to be the foundation on which the edifice of a National University can be built up because it 'has been obliged to rely on foreign funds and to court Government patronage'. The Dayananda Anglo-Vedic College on this count was 'a more robust growth', for the Arya Samaj has had a 'munificent self-sacrifice' in creating it. It was imperative, therefore, to realise that no 'institution which cannot rely on the people of India for its support and build itself up without official support or patronage, can be considered to have developed its capacity of developing into a National University'.[104]

His final attack through the editorial was on the proposed importation of a Charter from England. 'We are aware,' wrote Sri Aurobindo, 'that she talks of organising the University with the help of Indian talent and keeping it as a preserve for Indian control, but when she asks for a Charter, it is evident that she has not realised what national control implies'. No Government would willingly confer a Charter 'which excludes them from all control'. In other words, a Government Charter shall never allow complete autonomy and control to a National University, and an institution that calls itself

103. Ibid., p. 896.
104. Ibid.

National must necessarily be under national control professing an ideal and aim that is national. A Charter would invariably introduce a possibility of control and once this was 'allowed to overshadow the infant institution, goodbye to its utility, its greatness, its future. It will follow the way of other schools and colleges and become a fruitless idea, a monument of wasted energy and frustrated hopes'.[105]

It was a no-holds-barred repudiation of the idea of any kind of foreign or Governmental aid. Sri Aurobindo opposed the idea, even though it originated from one who had by then [1908] made meaningful contributions to the development of national education in India. Government aid or recognition in any kind and manner, as Sri Aurobindo saw it, would have the built-in possibility of subverting any effort at national education and thus needed to be meticulously avoided for the movement to strike root and spread. He appealed to the commercial and industrial class for support and to the parent body – the National Council of Education – to pay greater attention to the far-flung fledgling national education institutions of all across the province.

One point however remained, and it eventually came to confront the national education movement, it was the issue of Government recognition as a key to meaningful placement in society. As we have seen, the Government-aided and controlled institutions did eventually surpass the indigenous institutions on this count. Sri Aurobindo once again refuted Mrs. Besant's reiteration of the need for a Charter which, she argued, was 'a guarantee for the education which the University undertook to give'. Sri Aurobindo counterpointed it by saying that such a guarantee would pave the way for 'potential State control' and would in the case of the National Council make the institution lose its 'principle of robust independence and faith in its own future...'. Politically, on such

105. Ibid., p.896.

issues such as these, Sri Aurobindo's stand was radical, as his earlier editorial indicated. A new education system first[106] meant liberation from bureaucratic control direct or implied, and a compromise on this front would itself mean a diluted beginning.

The survey of the political demand of education must necessarily conclude here with a few brief references to the demand that Sri Aurobindo made at a later period in 1909 and 1918. Sri Aurobindo's political career had a brief break of one year from May 1908 onwards; the period of incarceration was replete with spiritual experiences and is one of the most well known and widely discussed episodes of his life in politics.

After his release, Sri Aurobindo, 'determined to continue the struggle', attempted to revive the suppressed spirit of nationalism and led again, for a while, the nationalist forces in Bengal. During this period, he was 'not only the Extremists' chief public spokesman but also their principal policy-maker and negotiator'.[107]

In September 1909 he led the nationalist contingent at the Bengal Provincial Conference at Hooghly [West Bengal], considered then to be the 'most important political meeting [of the year] in Bengal'[108] and appended his amendments on various issues to the draft resolutions drawn up by the Moderate Congress leaders. Of particular interest in our quest of trying to understand Sri Aurobindo's political stand on the educational question is resolution (X) Clause (a) of the draft, which gives an idea of the position he wished to be articulated on the issue. The Moderate resolution read:

> That this Conference urges the Government to take immediate action on their circular on free primary education issued about three years ago and invites their attention to the fact that the grants in aid of technical and

106. Ibid., pp. 932–934.
107. Peter Heehs, op. cit., p. 67.
108. Ibid.

scientific education are not at all commensurate with the needs of the country. [109]

The amendment as appended by Sri Aurobindo speaks for itself – the Government could not be urged to facilitate an alternative and responsive national education system. True to his policy of opposing the attitude of mendicancy in national politics, his amendment said:

That in the opinion of this Conference, steps should be taken for promoting a system of education literary, technical and scientific suited to the requirements of the country on national lines and under national control and maintaining national schools throughout the country.[110]

He made it a point to record that 'Clause (a) is omitted.' Clause (b) of the resolution remained unscathed, which it may be assumed to have received his assent; it urged the people *inter alia* to 'take steps to establish educational institutions throughout the country on national lines and under national control'.[111] That the national education movement had to be a people's movement, sustained and popularised by them, was evident to Sri Aurobindo. The Hooghly Conference was crucial. It reflected that the nationalist had gained control of the provincial Congress and yet did not wish to wreck. Sri Aurobindo in fact 'piloted the Hooghly Conference'. The reception committee consisting of the Moderates had framed 'draft resolutions welcoming the reforms granted by the British government', Sri Aurobindo, leading the nationalist cause, was able to, in the 'Subjects Committee defeat the Moderates' resolution, welcome the Reforms and to 'pass his own resolution stigmatising them as utterly inadequate and unreal' and rejected them. It became 'evident for the first time that Nationalism was gaining the ascendant, for it

109. *CWSA* vol.8, *Karmayogin,* op. cit., p.218.

110. Ibid.

111. Ibid., p. 219.

commanded a majority among the delegates'. The 'Moderates were defeat and thought of leaving' the Conference. Sri Aurobindo 'again used his statesmanship and softened the resolutions a little and ordered his party, which was in the majority, not to oppose those resolutions which the Moderates were persuaded to propose'. He did this to 'preserve the political unity of Bengal'. His own partymen were not very happy about this situation, so 'he asked them to absent themselves from the session. When Moderate leaders rose to speak, they were shouted down; Sri Aurobindo intervened, asked the members of the Nationalist group to either be silent or leave, leading to the restoration of order. A bitter senior leader of the Moderates complained that 'the people had refused to listen to their old and tried leaders and clamoured against them, but at the bidding of a young man new to politics they had obeyed in disciplined silence as if a single body'. If demonstrated, that as the most prominent nationalist leader in the country, then, Sri Aurobindo and his nationalists were not only gaining ascendancy, but had taken complete control of the Congress in Bengal.[112]

By 1909, Sri Aurobindo's official connection with the National Council of Education had ceased. Being quite out of sympathy with its ways of functioning and with what, he felt, was its capitulation to and compromise with the official system, Sri Aurobindo spoke out against its deficiencies and shortcomings. He saw the Council's isolation from the mainstream national movement, and the nationalist movement's weakening in general, which had, due to severe repression, been unleashed by the colonial bureaucracy as factors that were affecting the process of strengthening the national education movement. Sri Aurobindo indicated as much in an article [discussed earlier] in the pages of the *Karmayogin* [January 1, 1910] and analysed the failure of the Council to chalk out an alternative

112. See e.g. A.B. Purani, op.cit., pp.126, 127 & Sri Aurobindo, *On Himself*, op,cit., pp.32, 33.

educational path. That national education remained within the ambit of his considerations becomes evident when one sees that eight years into his retirement in Pondicherry (1918), Sri Aurobindo consented to give a message on national education at the request of Annie Besant.

The message appeared in Besant's journal *New India*[113] on April 8 1918, 'under the heading: Messages from Sons of The Motherland to Their Brothers'. Sri Aurobindo's message was the longest among nine, contributed by India's 'leading patriots'.[114] His was a political message on education, 'National Education is, next to Self-Government and along with it, the deepest and the most immediate need of the country…'.[115] Sri Aurobindo argued, indicating how important the whole issue continued to remain with him. Supporting the Home Rule Movement that Mrs. Besant had initiated, Sri Aurobindo saw the Movement and National Education as 'two inseparable ideals' and observed that 'none who follows the one, can fail the other, unless he is entirely wanting either in sincerity or in vision'. Home

---

113. Annie Besant launched two journals, the first, *Commonweal,* a weekly review in 1914 to champion the Home Rule Movement. The ideal that the review set before itself and the issues that it decided to champion are best described in her words: 'Religious Liberty, regarding all religions as ways to God; for National Education, "with an open path from primary schools to the Universities"; for Social Reform, including foreign travel, uplift of the submerged classes, abolition of child-marriage, seclusion of women, colour, bar and caste system'. It was in the same year that she bought a Madras daily and rechristened it *New India* and utilised it to realise the same objectives. The two journals were to form the two weapons with which the battle for Home Rule was waged. They 'bore aloft the banner of Home Rule through the years of the Great Agitation which ended in 1917, when Britain declared her goal to be the establishment of Self-Government in India'. [Theodore Besterman, *Annie Besant: A Modern Prophet*, pp. 199–200, 2003.]
114. *CWSA* vol.1, op.cit., p.772.
115. Ibid., p.411.

Rule would usher in the 'power of self-determination' which in turn would give the 'soul' of the nation the 'space' to grow, the 'strength for the life to raise itself again from darkness and narrow scope into light and nobility'. In other words, Home Rule would strengthen the demand for self-determination and pave the way for an effective and all round national self-expression. But this self-expression could effectively come about only through a system of national education, 'the full soul, rich with the inheritance of the past, the widening gains of the present, and the large potentiality of her future, can only come by a system of National Education'. This self-expression would come about through an imitation or extension of the existing university system plagued by 'radically false principles ... vicious mechanical methods ... dead-alive routine tradition and its narrow and sightless spirit ...' [116] both lines would have to gain momentum simultaneously, with each lending strength to the other. Sri Aurobindo's always emphasised the three upholding dimensions of past, present and future. In his scheme of educational policy or philosophy, each phase contributed and gave force and stability to the next. There was no dilemma about the past's utility in evolving a future system of education, he had indicated this in his series on 'A System of National Education' – the only systematic written exposé of his basic educational thought – when he wrote that 'the past is our foundation, the present our material, the future our aim and summit [and] each must have its due and natural place in a national system of education'.[117]

But in order to calibrate, Sri Aurobindo spoke of the need to imbibe principles of the past rather than its structures. In his two-part incomplete 'Preface on National Education', written over a century ago, for his philosophical journal *Arya* between November and December 1920 and January 1921, Sri Aurobindo argued that one

116. Ibid., p.411.

117. Ibid., p.385.

cannot be satisfied with a mere resuscitation of some past principle, method, and system that may have happened to prevail in India in the past, however great. Such a reversion even if contemplated 'would be a sterile and impossible effort hopelessly inadequate to the pressing demands of the present and the far greater demands of the future'.[118]

Making an appeal in his message for the National Education Week, to rally behind the National Education effort just as the nation veered round to supporting the Home Rule movement, he cautioned however that much more than 'intellectual sanction' for the effort would be needed. The support that would have to be given to the National Education effort would have to exceed and 'be free from all taint of lip-service, passivity, and lethargic —inaction, evil habits born of long political servitude and inertia...'

Mere moral sympathy was not sufficient, 'active support from every individual [was] needed. Workers for the cause, money and means for its sustenance, students for its schools and colleges, are what the movement needs that it may prosper'. Regarding the first requirement – workers for the cause – he was certain they would be

---

118. Ibid., p. 418. In his fundamental and seminal political thesis of 'Integral Humanism', one of the foremost political thinkers of independent India and leader of the Bharatiya Jana Sangh (BJS), Deendayal Upadhyaya also echoed line when he said, referring to the need for a practical programme, 'We have taken due note of our ancient culture, but we are no archaeologists. We have no intention to become the custodians of a vast archaeological museum. Our goal is not merely to protect the culture but to revitalise it so as to make it dynamic and in tune with times. We must ensure that our nation stands firm on this foundation and our society is enabled to live a healthy, progressive, and purposeful life. We shall have to end a number of traditions and set in reforms which are helpful in the development of values and of national unity in our society. We shall remove those traditions which obstruct this process'. (April 25, 1965) Devendra Swarup, edited, *Deendayal Upadhyaya's Integral Humanism: Documents, Interpretations, Comparisons*, 1992, p.60.

emerging; the second requirement – money and means – he argued, would come because the 'habit of giving as well as self-giving for a great public cause is growing...'; but he expressed his skepticism for the third – students for its [national education movement] schools and colleges – Sri Aurobindo realised that it had not been sufficiently satisfactory from the beginning because 'habituated individually always to the customary groove, we prefer the safe and prescribed path, even when it leads nowhere, to the great and effective way, and cannot see our own interest because it presents itself in a new and untried form....'[119]

This was perhaps the one of the most acute shortcomings of the national education movement – an inability to attract in a sustained manner a continuous stream of learners who, reposing confidence in the system, would integrate themselves with it. It was primarily this issue, among a host of others, which ultimately led the movement then, in the first decade and even later, to have a limited national impact. If this non-participation was induced by 'material and prudential considerations' then, argued Sri Aurobindo, 'let it be seen that, even in the vocational sphere, the old system opens only the doors of a few offices and professions overcrowded with applicants, whence the majority must go back disappointed and with empty hands, or be satisfied with a dwarfed life and sordid pittance.... The new education Sri Aurobindo foresaw, developing the capacity to 'open careers which will be at once ways of honourable sufficiency, dignity, and affluence to the individual, and paths of service to the country...'.[120] The official promise of gradual self-government given in 1918 may have given hope for the growth of an all-round national reconstruction – with national education being a major part of it. It made Sri Aurobindo, the eternal as well as the cautious optimist to place hope in the movement's eventual success and spread.

119. *CWSA* vol.1, op.cit., p. 412.

120. Ibid.

7

Deeper Fundamentals of National Education

A Quest Beyond Politics

"

It is not the eighteenth century India, the India which by its moral and intellectual deficiencies gave itself into the keeping of foreigners, that we have to revive, but the spirit, ideals and methods of the ancient and mightier India in a yet more effective form and with a more modern organisation.

– **Sri Aurobindo,**
***The Brain of India*, 1909**

Men have made language, poetry, history, philosophy agents for the training of this side of intellectuality, necessary parts of a liberal education, but the immense educative force of music, painting and sculpture has not been duly recognised. They have been thought to be bypaths of the human mind, beautiful and interesting, but not necessary, therefore intended for the few. Yet the universal impulse to enjoy the beauty and attractiveness of sound, to look at and live among pictures, colours, forms ought to have warned mankind of the superficiality and ignorance of such a view of these eternal and important occupations of human mind.

– **Sri Aurobindo,**
***The National Value of Art*, 1909**

The *Karmayogin* had, as mentioned earlier, a distinct trait. It not only commented on political issues of the day but also focused on subjects such as philosophy, yoga, culture, art, literature, and education. Sri Aurobindo felt that 'the movement [had] drawn back to await a farther and truer impulse', and that it would be worthwhile to focus on other issues of national importance that needed urgent attention.

Not that the *Karmayogin* did not focus on other issues or elicit the attention of the colonial intelligence. J.C. Ker's *Political Trouble in India:1907–1917*, for instance, refers to almost all journalistic ventures that Sri Aurobindo launched, including the *Karmayogin*. The journal had sufficiently unnerved the British government for it to prosecute its printer Monmohan Nath Ghose, who was 'convicted and sentenced to six months' rigorous imprisonment under section 124-A, Indian Penal Code' in June 1910. Following an appeal and a protracted hearing, the 'conviction and sentence were set aside in October, 1910'. Ker noted, 'Arabindo Ghose, however, did not return to Calcutta, and the magazine came to an end'.[1] By then Sri Aurobindo was already six months into his exile in Pondicherry.

It was in the *Karmayogin* that Sri Aurobindo wrote his famous 'An Open Letter to My Countrymen', in which he 'enunciated the main lines along which the Nationalists' would have to continue the work 'in case he was imprisoned'; enunciating his electrifying doctrine of 'no cooperation without control', he called for 'no compromise'. It was 'only if real political, administrative and financial control were

1. J.C.Ker, *Political Trouble in India* (1907-1917), op.cit., p.87.

given to popular ministers in an elected Assembly that he would have anything to with the offers from the British Government'.[2]

Through the summer and autumn of 1909, Sri Aurobindo's 'writings and speeches were among the only significant expressions of nationalist sentiment in the country'. And as 'his influence grew', both the Bengal government and the British government of India 'regarded him with increasing anxiety'. The Chief Secretary of the Bengal Government referred to him as 'the most dangerous of our adversaries now at large'. The Lieutenant Governors of Bengal and Eastern Bengal and Assam concurred with him. Viceroy Lord Minto spoke of him as 'the most dangerous man we have to deal with at present'. The Chief Secretary to the Government of India wrote, "I would not hesitate to deport Arabindo if he cannot be silenced in any other way. If he is allowed to go on, he will very soon have the country ablaze again."[3] All these varied and hectic political, public, and journalistic activities were undertaken by Sri Aurobindo while he was himself deeply immersed in yoga and his *sadhana*.

Directing his mind to other issues of urgent national importance saw Sri Aurobindo write a series, 'The Brain of India', between October 9 and November 13, 1909. Its objective was 'to indicate the nature and psychological ideas of the old system and point out its essential relation of cause and effect to the splendid achievement of our ancestors'.[4] The effort was undertaken in order to instil the principles and spirit of ancient Indian education in the Indian

2. A.B.Purani, The Life of Sri Aurobindo, op.cit., p.127, Sri Aurobindo, *On Himself*, op.cit., p.35.
3. Peter Heehs, *Sri Aurobindo: A Brief Biography*, op.cit., p. 66.
4. *CWSA* vol.1, p. 378. This series of essays ... seems to have been, at least in part, a reply to 'The Bengali Brain and its Misuse', an essay by Dr. P. C. Ray that is mentioned by Sri Aurobindo in his review of *Suprabhat*, edited by Krishna Kumar Mitra's daughter, Kumudini Mitra. (*CWSA*, vol.1, p. 772)

mind and to also argue for their re-examination under the light of current educational problems and issues in India. The articulation, interpretation, and re-interpretation of civilisational India's education principles and ideals were an important mission of the nationalist educators and the leaders of the national education movement. Most of the thought-leaders we have discussed, wrote and spoke copiously along these lines. Many of them saw this as the essence of the struggle for freedom. As Ananda Coomaraswamy, writing in his 'Essays in National Idealism' around this time, argued that the national movement would have no justification if it did not 'carry with it some hope of new manifestation of the Indian genius in relation to the real things of life'. In the unrest that was permeating educated India then, Coomaraswamy read a struggle for 'spiritual and mental freedom from the domination of an alien ideal'; to him, it was not 'so much the material as the moral and spiritual subjection of Indian civilisation that in the end impoverished humanity'. In his thirties, Coomaraswamy was galvanised by the 'upsurge of the national movement' and had come in touch with thought-leaders of the national movement. He also became one of the chief articulators of its ideational dimension.[5] Sri Aurobindo's writings on the subject, during this phase, need to be read against this dimension of the narrative.

The series on 'The Brain of India' saw Sri Aurobindo analyse the Indian practice of *brahmacharya,* its integrality in the scheme of ancient Indian education and its relevance to the present quest. Sri Aurobindo also discussed the ancient educational discipline of Hinduism, its system of separating the constitution of man in 'three principles of nature', and of how the education system then would take into account all three and base its system of training on that consideration. In short, as Sri Aurobindo pointed out, he would

5. Monee Bagchi, *Ananda Coomaraswamy: A Study,* 1960, p. 3

attempt to state as 'succintly as is consistent with clearness, the main psychological principles on which the ancients based their scheme of education'.[6] In our effort to understand the quest for a philosophy of national education, let us briefly examine some of the classical concepts of Indian education as Sri Aurobindo saw them. The Brain of India series briefly offers us that opportunity.

The series, as we have seen, was written as a partial response to P.C. Ray's long essay on 'The Bengali Brain and its Misuse'. Sri Aurobindo's review of Ray's essay also gives an insight into Sri Aurobindo's thinking, his refusal to condemn India's civilisational achievements and to throw away or reject her 'old national culture' in its entirety. Describing Ray as a 'pride to the nation' whose 'deep scientific knowledge, original research and creativeness are one of the most conspicuous instances of that strong, acute and capable Bengali intellect which he [Ray] admits to be inferior to none'. But Ray's analysis, Sri Aurobindo argued, showed 'the unfortunate results of the denationalising influence of our past education that a mind like Dr. Ray's should be without intellectual sympathy for the old national culture, whose inherited tendencies his own character, life, and achievements illustrate in so distinguished a manner. If it had not been for the past which Dr. P.C. Ray condemns, such noble types as the last fifty years of Bengal teems with, would not have been possible'. Describing Ray's article as 'narrow' and 'intolerant', couched in a 'general spirit of self-depreciation and indiscriminate fault-finding' which was a 'characteristic of our people when national hope and energy were at their nadir', Sri Aurobindo argued that such writings which were 'void of the note of hope, encouragement, and energy, will not help a nation to rise but rather depress it and push it back into the past'. While there was a necessity of 'far-reaching changes in the future', it had to be recognised that the 'immediate

6. *CWSA* vol.1, p. 376.

past [was] a period of contraction and the reservation of strength', while 'the future will be a period of expansion and the liberation and expenditure of strength'.[7] Ray's mistake was the same as that committed by 'European writers when they condemned the Middle Ages wholesale because they 'were a period of contraction and not of expansion'.

> That mistake has now been recognised in Europe and justice has been done to that which was praiseworthy as well as to that which was bad in the 'Dark Ages'. We in India are recovering from a similar error and if there are those who go to the opposite extreme and see nothing good outside the mediaeval Hindu culture and forms, the same thing happened in Europe and for the same reason, as a reaction from that very intolerance and sweeping denunciation which are the spirit of Dr. Ray's article. It cannot last any more than it lasted in Europe. Some of the strictures we hold to be too much at secondhand; especially in his criticisms of religion, the writer seems to us to be wandering outside the province in which he can speak with authority. After all one must enter into the spirit of an age and civilisation before one can profitably criticise it, otherwise we miss the meaning of history and falsify its values.[8]

'The Brain of India' needs to be read against the backdrop of this fundamental debate.

VII.1. 'THE BRAIN OF INDIA': PSYCHOLOGICAL PRINCIPLES OF ANCIENT INDIAN EDUCATION

The first instalment of the series looked at the necessity of the Indian mind, especially the Bengali mind, of working towards a widening of its horizons. This was required, Sri Aurobindo averred, because the national as well as the Bengali mind found itself surrounded by a 'new set of circumstances', the reaction to which was a perplexed one. The new circumstances were an obvious allusion

7. Ibid., pp. 567, 568.
8. Ibid., p. 568.

to the fast-paced developments taking place then, both politically and culturally. For such an eventuality, Sri Aurobindo argued, the national mind had to begin preparing itself through a new system of training, and argued that for the 'work of the present, and still more, for the work of the future, it [was] imperatively necessary to create a centre of thought and knowledge which will revolutionise the brain of the nation ...'[9]

The revolutionising of the nation's brain and the evolving of a new centre of thought required 'a new centre of education'. But under the present University system, Sri Aurobindo argued, such a hope was unrealisable. In a severe indictment of the University system, as was his stance during the first phase of political action, he reiterated his criticism of it as one which:

> ... ignores the psychology of man, loads the mind laboriously with numerous little packets of information carefully tied with red tape, and, by the methods used in this loading process, damages or atrophies the faculties and instruments by which man assimilates, creates, and grows in intellect, manhood and energy.[10]

Referring to the National Education experiment as inaugurated in Bengal, Sri Aurobindo conceded that it did succeed to a certain extent in altering a number of these atrophying approaches and methods by seeking 'to enlarge the field of knowledge to which the student was introduced'. It laid an emphasis on 'observation' and 'experiment', and employed 'the natural and easy instrument of the vernacular'. It thus encouraged the habit of thought 'on the subject of study'.[11] These were essential features that were absent in the official system. But this new attempt too, Sri Aurobindo observed, was not free from the taint of old habits, and a number of 'the vicious

---

9. Ibid., p. 367.
10. Ibid., p. 368.
11. Ibid.

methods and ideas employed by the old system were faithfully cherished by the new', because the new too came to be dominated by men who were 'wedded to the old lines'. This eventually cast 'a most unfavourable effect on the integrity of the system in its most progressive features'.[12] These new progressive features thus, did not have scope of adequate expression.

Sri Aurobindo had started openly analysing the systemic defects in the new educational attempt. His principal complaint against the entire effort was that those leading it were still driven by the officially constructed system, and the one thing that was ignored was the 'psychology of the race'. Sri Aurobindo qualified this by saying that a superficial approach to educational reform would never be able to engender into the system an Indianness – 'the mere inclusion of the matter of Indian thought and culture in the field of knowledge does not make a system of education Indian'.[13] This was a significant observation.

A constant debate raged on what could make a system truly Indian and national – it remained a major challenge for the Swadeshi movement itself. According to Sri Aurobindo the approach had to be deeper, but the Bengal National College version of the system was, he pointed out, only 'an improved European system'.[14] Improved, because it did at least focus on Indian subjects and issues, attempted to impart certain moral-spiritual training and tried to perceive the students as seeking minds, instead of seeing them as mere receivers of nuggets of information.

Here too, Sri Aurobindo cautioned against adopting extreme postures in revaluating the indigenous education system. The demand for, and seeking of, an indigenous system of education,

---

12. Ibid., p. 368
13. Ibid.
14. Ibid.

the aspiration for a Swadeshi education should not give rise to an irrational and retrogressive demand. Sri Aurobindo clarified that this retrogression must not seek to revive the 18th-century educational system in Bengal, which in any case he felt could not reflect the modern aspirations of the people and nation then in the throes of the struggle for self-determination. He called it an 'error which [had] to be avoided' and which attracted 'careless minds'. Calling the suggestion which said that 'in order to be National, education must reproduce the features of the old *tol* system of Bengal' a 'reactionary idea', Sri Aurobindo stated that 'it is not eighteenth century India, the India which by its moral and intellectual deficiencies gave itself into the keeping of foreigners' that was to be revived but rather 'the spirit, ideals and methods of the ancient and mightier India in a yet more effective form and with a modern organisation'.[15] Contemplating on

15. Ibid., pp. 368–369. This was said against a tendency during the Swadeshi period that called for a 'total rejection of the West' and a complete fall back on the old '*tol*' system... [Sumit Sarkar, *op.cit.,* p. 155] Such calls emanated from time to time, and Sri Aurobindo did not endorse its complete revival. Two of Sri Aurobindo's contemporaries, whose views we have discussed at various turns in order to make the study broad-based and to give an idea of some of the dominant thoughts on the educational questions of the day, expressed a certain appreciation for the indigenous system especially evident in Bengal. Sister Nivedita, for example, in her discussion on *The Mediaeval University of India* talks of the 'formal and absorbing' organisation of '*Tols* or schools of Sanskrit' with which 'India was netted from end to end, and men would come from the most distant parts to sit at the feet of some renowned teacher ...'. In these centres of learning, students were moved to work year after year ' for pure love of knowledge'. Nivedita described the link that these centres had with the ancient Indian concept of education – it saw learning inspired by the pure and selfless seeking of knowledge and wisdom. She saw the ancient university system of the 15th-century 'Nuddea' [Nadia district of Bengal famous for its Sanskrit teaching schools] come down in

ancient Indian society's capacity to create diversely, Sri Aurobindo

an intact form to the present day and extolled its virtues as heard from an 'older generation'. Nivedita spoke of the routine of the old *tols* revealing a 'marvelously intense and earnest life'. A system where the 'college' of a single teacher was made up of a household of 'some fifty or sixty students, distributed over a number of mud cottages arranged round a central tank'. Describing a tol of 'Vikrampore' [Bikrampore, Dhaka, East Bengal], she described how students from Maharashtra were admitted, indicating the pan-Indian recognition that these educational institutions of Bengal had earned – the 'fame of Bengal logic went far and wide, and all India knew the names of its best teachers'. Nivedita saw them as institutions where 'was lived out the great ideal of Brahmacharya – the celibate student dwelling as a son in his master's house'. [*Complete Works of Sister Nivedita* (*CWSN*) *Vol.2*, 'The Mediaeval University of India' in *Studies from an Eastern Home*, 4th imp., 1999, pp. 341–42–43] Sri Aurobindo, was referring to an earlier period in his articles and therefore displayed no high regard for the efficacy and utility of the *tol* system. Both appealed to the nationalist mind; one saw in the preservation of the indigenous system, as she witnessed it, the possibility of perpetuating certain fundamental Indian principles and the other saw the working out of an entirely new system inspired by principles of the classical Indian education as the way forward for the national education discourse. The other contemporary mind who is also part of our study is Ananda Coomaraswamy, who in his study of education in India, written around the same period (1909), identified the disconnectedness of schools from the Indian life as the 'great tragedy of the present situation'. Schools, [in the colonial set-up] he argued, are not part of Indian life 'as were the *tols* and *maktabs* of the past' and were instead antagonistic to it. [*Essays in National Idealism,* op.cit., p. 99] Implying that the *tols* of old, the indigenous system, was much more connected, supportive, and formed an inseparable part of the Indian life system while the colonial system adopted an adverse stance. He does not extol on the virtues of the *tol* system but simply indicated that they were a part of the Indian life and thus easily adjusted to by the vast populace. All three of them, Sri Aurobindo, Nivedita and Coomaraswamy refused to condemn or reject wholesale these indigenous education structures. They called for their restructuring

wondered as to what could have pushed civilisational India towards

---

and re-stating instead. On the other hand, in his essay 'The Bengali Brain and its Misuse', Acharya Prafulla Chandra Ray unsparingly analysed the *tol* system and the education it imparted. Ray wrote, "It must, however, be borne in mind that while the great promulgator of Smriti (Raghunandana) was ransacking the pages of Manu, Yajnavalkya, Parasara and others and laying down the rigid rules of fasting to be observed by a child-widow of nine years of age and in default thereof holding out the terrors of hell-fire for her ancestors on the paternal and maternal side; while Raghunadha, Gadadhara, Jagadisa and other mighty logicians were engaged in composing glossaries and commentaries on the classical works of logic and were thus adding to the consternation of the pupils of the *tols*; while our astronomers were calculating the omens and prognostications from the cawing of a crow at a particular moment in the south-west quarter; while our pandits were disturbing the peace of the assemblies by acrimonious dispute over the controversy: whether the sound raised by the falling of the palm-fruit accompanied it or was an after effect I say, while the intellectuals of Navadwipa were thus utilising the precious gift of time, in Europe, Galileo, Kepler, Newton and other philosophers were unravelling the mysteries of nature and ushering in a new epoch and thus glorifying the intellect of man." We should, argued Ray, "now pause and reflect whether in these days of keen struggle for existence we should take our admission in the *tols* of Navadwipa and study modern logic and 'Smriti' and consider the learning and wisdom of the civilized world as erroneous and whether the Bengali race is not already threatened with being wiped off the face of the earth for our failure in realising the situation and moving with the spirit of the times." Ray cautioned against the tendency of spurning new scientific knowledge which was vitalising other nations of the world, "If we hug the past and look upon the commentaries of Raghunandana and Kullukabhatta as our infallible guides and spurn with contempt the new ideas and aspirations which are vitalising the other nations of the world, I am afraid the Bengali nation will cease to exist ere long." (Dr Prafulla Chandra Ray, *Essays & Discourses*, Madras: Ganesh & Co, 1918, pp. 182, 183.) We have read Sri Aurobindo's response to his contentions.

such massive and original creations which demonstrated a huge intellectual, physical, and moral energy. What could have been the secret of this 'gigantic intellectuality, spirituality, and superhuman moral force' that permeated the epics, the ancient philosophy, art, sculpture, and architecture of ancient India? What driving energy and vision, Sri Aurobindo asked, could be at the base of the 'incomparable' feats of 'public works and engineering achievements' the industries, scientific outputs, jurisprudence, logic, metaphysics, and social structure?[16] What was it that generated a 'national vitality and endurance', what was it that supported a civilisation that was

16. Sri Aurobindo was to deal extensively with this theme and question later during his early years in Pondicherry period in a series of essays on the Indian renaissance. He thoroughly refuted the allegation of civilisational India's incapacity in material creation and in her world understanding. Describing the European [read Western] narrative of Indian culture and civilisation as one that saw Indian civilisation as dominantly metaphysical with a distinct inclination towards the trait of 'other worldliness' Sri Aurobindo summed up Western reading of Indian capacities. The perception of India that this Western reading came to present, was that of a civilisation with a controlling mind which was primarily 'abstract' 'metaphysical' and 'religious', 'overpowered by the sense of the infinite, not apt for life, dreamy, unpractical, turning away from life and action as Maya.' A phase of Indian quiescence to this view, Sri Aurobindo argued, was followed by a realisation that though 'spirituality [remained] the master-key of the Indian mind' such a spiritual emphasis was not based on a void. The Indian civilisational view, Sri Aurobindo observed, was 'alive to the greatness of material laws and forces' and for an uninterrupted period of 'three thousand years at least' indeed much longer, India created ' abundantly, incessantly, lavishly, with an inexhaustible many-sidedness' creations that included republics, kingdoms, empires, temples, monuments, palaces, public works etc'. All of them empirical and unequivocal signs that the much misjudged Indic civilisation possessed a balanced measure of the metaphysical as well as the physical. [*CWSA* vol. 20, 1997, pp. 6,7,8]

unique in the 'massiveness of its outlines' and the 'perfection of its details?'[17] Sri Aurobindo's answer was that there must have existed a wide and a deep support system of 'a unique discipline involving a perfect education of the soul, mind'.[18] The absence of such a system would have made impossible the achievements of such huge and varied proportions. The key therefore was to look for the 'principle and basis on which the details' of such an education were founded. To look for the secret of the success of the ancient system in the details of the instructions of the old Ashrams and universities as they have percolated to the present age would be an 'error'. Sri Aurobindo was clear that these ancient methods of instructions need not be replicated under modern conditions, but what was far important for him were the principles and guiding ideals that had formed the base of this grand educational edifice which generated such inexhaustible creativity.[19]

Sri Aurobindo analysed next the ancient Indian discipline of *Brahmacharya* which, he argued, provided a strong foundation for 'building up a great intellectual superstructure'. He spoke of its importance and centrality in the ancient Indian educational system as one that preserved the creative energy in the individual and prevented its dissipation and dilution.

Sri Aurobindo opposed the convoluted approach to education which believed that merely 'supplying the student with a large or well-selected mass of information on the various subjects which comprised the best part of human culture at the time'[20] was sufficient to build a foundation. Such an approach did not take into account the student's preparedness to absorb such a mass of information;

---

17. *CWSA* vol.1, p. 369.
18. Ibid.
19. Ibid., p. 369.
20. Ibid.

it did not question whether the student had received an adequate training to be able to absorb this mass of information. The general formula that appeared to emerge from such an approach and one that seemed to have been broadly followed was that the 'school gives the materials, it is for the student to use them'.[21] Such a formula did not seek to unveil before the student the path and method that could be taken to assimilate and put these materials to effective use. It did not question the very utility or usability of the materials given as part of the exercise of educating. Such a formula was based, Sri Aurobindo observed, on a 'fundamental error' – that of considering 'information' to be the 'foundation of intelligence'. "Information", he argued, "cannot be the foundation of intelligence, it can only be part of the material out of which the knower builds the knowledge, the starting-point, the nucleus of fresh discovery and enlarged creation."[22]

One may recall that the habit of believing information-imparting to be the sole aim of education developed with the growth of the centralised examination system and the over dependence on prescribed textbooks to pass those examinations. It was a system that was institutionalised by the colonial version of education imposed in India. An education which functions thus within the confines of the belief that information imparting is its principal aim is 'no education'. It invariably fails to develop the 'various faculties of memory, judgment, imagination, perception, reasoning, which build the edifice of thought and knowledge for the knower …'.[23]

As we have seen in our discussion, the nationalist thought-leaders and educators were vocal in their deprecation of the exclusively examination-oriented system then prevalent. An idea

21. Ibid., p. 369.
22. Ibid., pp. 369, 370.
23. Ibid., p. 370.

can be derived, for instance, from scholar, thinker, polymath and educator, Benoy Kumar Sarkar, Sri Aurobindo's youthful associate in the Bengal national education movement, who was a proponent of the 'inductive-method' of instruction. Sarkar did not believe in the textbook system and insisted 'that what one should learn [was] not books but subjects'. Sarkar argued that students 'should show the results of study not periodically after the lapse of a year or of several months, but every day in session'. Sarkar saw students who prepared for examinations, 'overload' their memory 'with vague general notions so as to have only a superficial knowledge of the subjects'. For him, this system of cramming was further promoted because, 'in the matriculation schools' the students began to 'learn their subjects in a language of which they [had] not at the time acquired a practical knowledge'. Sarkar insisted that the mother-tongue should be the medium of instruction and called for developing the vernaculars.[24]

Ancient Indian education had deeper layers to its educational vision – it focused on man as a part of the universe and did not remain solely concerned with the development of his mind and his store of information. It sought rather to develop the learner as a greater receptacle [*adhara*] of the universal Energy. Sri Aurobindo terms it as an 'infinite energy, Prakriti, Maya or Shakti [that] pervades the world, pours itself into every name and form, and the clod, the plant, the insect, the animal, the man' in their phenomenal existence are 'more or less efficient *adharas* of this Energy'.

The ancient Indian education system focussed on increasing in man the capacity to store this energy. It held the continual improvement of the *adhara* and an increase in its capacity to hold

---

24. Radha Kamal Mukherjee, reviewing Sarkar's Bengali booklet (1912) in the Modern Review of April 1913. (Banesvar Dass edited, *The Social and Economic Ideas of Benoy Kumar Sarkar*, 1940, pp. 8,9.

the infinite Energy to be the essential aim of evolution. And when the *adhara* was perfected and developed itself to the highest level to hold that Energy then was a man judged and recognized as a *siddha* – the perfected soul, the 'fulfilled or perfect man'.

The aim of education in civilisational India was the creation of the perfected man, and in order to realise that perfection, the storehouse of the infinite Energy had to be allowed greater and uninterrupted flow in the individual himself. For this flow to remain perennial, obstructions in the channel of communication between the individual and the universal energy had to be cleared. Extrapolating from this point, Sri Aurobindo argued that if this theory of increasing capacity-building to hold the universal energy was right, then 'the energy at the basis of the operation of intelligence must be' in the individual too, and must be 'capable of greater expansion and richer use'. The perception that 'the more we can increase and enrich the energy, the greater will be the potential range, power, and activity of the functions of our mind and the consequent vigour of our intellectuality and the greatness of our achievement' came across as a sound principle. Ancient Indians thus based their education on this first principle and the 'chief processes which they used for increasing [the] storage of energy, was the practice of *Brahmacharya*'.[25]

The ancient system designated the practice of Brahmacharya as the 'first and most necessary condition of increasing the force within and turning it to such uses as may benefit the possessor or mankind'. *Brahmacharya* thus was the cornerstone of the ancient educational discipline.

A few collated thoughts on the term *Brahmacharya* would put in perspective the centrality of the concept in the ancient Indian

---

25. *CWSA* vol.1, pp. 370, 371.

educational scheme, since a number of thought-leaders and educators have dwelt on it in the course of articulating the narrative of national education. *Brahmacharya* signified the life of abstinence and self control. It was not limited to physical self-control only but possessed a wider connotation which included other areas of human action and reaction which called for restraint and sublimation. It meant a complete control over all the senses, thus even a wave of impure thought became 'a breach of *Brahmacharya*' as was, for example, a reaction through anger as Mahatma Gandhi analysed it, in his July 23, 1938 issue of the *Harijan*.

According to Radha Kumud Mookerjee, himself an outstanding product of the national education movement who formed among the 'core of the teaching staff' and who had already begun making a name for himself through 'research work in ancient Indian history and culture ...'[26], the system of education in ancient India was standardised and fixed, based on certain 'universally accepted ideals and practices connoted by the term *Brahmacharya* which form[ed] the foundation of the entire structure of Hindu thought and life'. The system or framework of studentship in ancient Indian educational system, observed Mookerjee, retained 'universal validity' it did not admit change according to 'age' or 'clime'.[27] The Atharva Veda 'extols' 'exalts' and 'expounds' the fundamental principle system of *Brahmacharya*.[28] Discussing the system of education in ancient India, Mookerji describes how a student had to find his teacher and formally apply for being inducted as a pupil 'I am come for the *Brahmacharya*, I desire to be a *Brahmacharin*.' The teacher on his part, as a sign of acceptance, 'ties the girdle around him [the pupil] gives him the staff into his hand, and explains to him the

26. Vide Sumit Sarkar, op.cit, p. 168.
27. Radhakumud Mookerji, op.cit., *Ancient Indian Education*, p. 67.
28. Ibid., p. 67.

Brahmacharya (the rules of conduct of a religious student) in the following words: 'Thou art a *Brahmacharin*; drink water; perform service; sleep not by day; study the Veda obediently to thy teacher'.[29]

Sri Aurobindo analysed the benefits of the discipline of *Brahmacharya* and how an adherence to the system expanded the foundations of energy of the individual. A brief survey of the material demands of the system would be in order here. The ceremony of initiating the pupil – *Upanayana* – by his selected teacher – *Acharya* – into the world of knowledge and discipline of *Brahmacharya* culminated in the pupil having a second birth, a spiritual birth (*dvija* or twice born). This birth was a psychological transmutation, an unfolding 'of the mind and soul'. The teacher, as it were, while accepting the pupil, initiated the exercise of recreating and remoulding the pupil's whole personality – '*Acharyah antah vidyasarirasya madhye garbham krinute*' (Sayana), 'the teacher recreates the pupil in a new body of learning'. The initiation of the pupil into *Brahmacharya* required him to follow a twofold discipline, external as well as internal. The external enjoined the following of certain specific physical acts and discipline, while the internal (inner) discipline required the pupil to practice and adhere to *Srama* (self-restraint), *Tapas* (practice of penance), *Diksha* (consecration to a life of discipline through prescribed regulations)...' (Sayana).[30]

Thus, in the 'The Scheme of Life and Education in Ancient India', the period of *Brahmacharya* seemed to possess a great centrality. It connoted the pupil's emergence into self-reliance and self-discovery through a rigorous pursuit of knowledge and physical discipline. It was a period that generally lasted for 25 years and the pupil's 'life spent in his professor's house [was designated as the] life of *Brahmacharya*'. The period was a great leveler too – any

29. Ibid., p. 394.
30. Ibid., p. 67.

distinction of class, caste and position was equalised, the newly accepted 'student would be treated equally with his compeers'. The other positive social quality and perception that it evolved was self-reliance – through the process of *bhiksha*, respect for manual labour, by tilling the master's fields, tending to his cattles, etc. The life of *Brahmacharya* was not limited to being merely and solely an academic one that segregated the pupil from his surrounding life and environment. It was a life dedicated to developing an integral and holistic perception of life.[31]

Arguing against the perception that the teacher-student relation was monolithic and hierarchical in ancient India, especially arguing against that perception during the *Brahmacharya* phase, one of the foremost exponents of Sri Aurobindo's philosophy and educational thought, Kireet Joshi, observes that the pupil during the *Brahmacharya* phase and in general, was looked upon as a 'seeker not to be silenced by any dogmatic answers, but to be lifted in higher processes of thought, meditation, and direct experience or realization'. The pupil, the *brahmacharin* was devoted to 'self-control and askesis'; discipline was not imposed and arbitrary, the *brahmacharin* obeyed the 'command of the teacher, knowing very well that the teacher asked nothing arbitrary' and instead indicated the path through which 'self-perfection' was attainable. The pupil and teacher's lives were intertwined, joint – it was a life of 'joint prayer, joint endeavour, of joint conquest of knowledge'. As the student sought for a teacher, so too, the teacher sought pupils. The *Taittiriya Upanishad* portrays the teacher as saying, "May the *Brahmacharins* come unto me. From here and there, may the *Brahmacharins* come unto me." And in fact, for the *brahmacharin*,

31. Vide Swami Ramakrishnananda, *For Thinkers on Education*, 1949, pp. 3,4,5.

'the home of the teacher represented the fabric of life', which was subtly interlinked with the 'educational process' in a such a way that life itself was education and educational activities were not segregated from 'life-experience'.[32] It emerges that the *brahmacharin's* life was a multi-layered one, evolving and developing simultaneously. And throughout this phase the pupil was treated differently at two separate levels – at physical and material he was leveled, co-equalled with his peers from different backgrounds and of varying nature, and at the psycho-spiritual level he was treated with a great finesse so that his nature and his emotions could be positively shaped and trained.

The ancient Hindus, Sri Aurobindo wrote, clearly perceived that the 'source of life and energy is not material but spiritual, [and that] the basis, the foundation on which the life and energy stand and work, is physical'. This distinction between the '*karana*' and '*pratistha*' – 'earth or gross matter is the *pratistha*, Brahman or spirit is the *karana*' – was well recognised by the ancient educators, who thus propounded the raising up of the physical to the spiritual as *brahmacharya*. The interlacing of the two enabled the energy 'which starts from one and produces the other' to enhance and fulfil itself.[33]

The other fundamental view on which Hinduism based its educational discipline, as Sri Aurobindo pointed out, was the one which believed that 'all knowledge is within and has to be evoked by education rather than instilled from outside'.[34] The idea and the practice of imposition was absent in the ancient Hindu educational discourse. The teacher accepted his function as that of an 'observer, helper [and] guide'. The instructional approach of a taskmaster was

32. Kireet Joshi, *Education at Crossroads*, 2007, pp. 126, 127.
33. *CWSA* vol.1, op.cit, pp. 371–372.
34. Ibid., p. 373. This formed the seed expression of what was to be later much discussed as his first principle of teaching (p. 384).

absent. The teacher taught through the 'example of his wisdom and character'.[35]

The other fundamental view of the Hindu system of education, according to Sri Aurobindo, was that which said that man's constitution consisted 'of three principles of nature [the three '*gunas*'] *sattva*[36] (comprehensive), *rajas* (active), *tamas* (passive) which manifest, as 'knowledge, passion, ignorance',[37] and each of these *gunas,* influenced, depending on their predominance, the thoughts and actions of the individual. Sri Aurobindo gave a succinct description of the three principles: '*Tamas* [was] a constitutional dullness or passivity which obscures the knowledge within and creates ignorance, mental inertia, slowness, forgetfulness, disinclination to study, inability to grasp and distinguish', while *Rajas* was 'an undisciplined activity which obscured knowledge by passion, attachment, prejudgment, predilection and wrong ideas'. *Sattva* was 'an illumination which [revealed] the hidden knowledge and [brought] it to the surface where the observation can grasp and the memory record it'.

Adhering to this conception of the three composing principles of man, the main task of the teacher in the education system was thus the 'removal of *tamas,* the disciplining of *rajas* and the

---

35. Joshi, op. cit., p. 126.
36. As per Sri Aurobindo's various expressions of the three terms: *sattva* – clarity, principle of assimilation, equilibrium and harmony [which] translates in quality as good and harmony and happiness and light', *rajas* – 'force of kinesis, translates in quality as struggle and effort, passion and action', *tamas* – 'principle and power of inertia, translates in quality as obscurity and incapacity and inaction.'[M.P. Pandit edited *Glossary of Sanskrit Terms in Sri Aurobindo's Works*, 2002, pp. 53, 63, 64, 70.]
37. *CWSA* vol.1, op. cit., p. 373.

awakening of *sattva*'.[38] The principle of *rajas* was disciplined through an adherence to 'a strict moral discipline which induced a calm, clear, receptive state of mind free from intellectual self-will and pride' and the obscure shadings of passion; it was this discipline, followed by the *brahmacharin* which was the foundation of the morals and culture of ancient India.[39]

The disturbances induced by 'wrong ideas' was attempted to be arrested by a 'strict mental submission to the teacher during the receptive period', in which the 'ascertained knowledge', 'right ideas', was 'explained to him and committed to memory'.[40] *Tamas* was sought to be removed through the discipline of 'moral purity' and through *tapasya* (askesis, austerity of personal will, spiritual austerity). The learner was thus trained to be a 'reservoir of mental force and clarity'.

The teacher had one fundamental task – training the leaner to be 'receptive of illumination from within'. The guiding belief was that knowledge lay within the individual, and the right approach to education would be to liaise that source with the learner.[41] The awakening or facilitating of this illumination was engineered

38. Ibid., pp. 373–374.
39. Ibid., p. 374.
40. Ibid., p. 374.
41. The first principle of Sri Aurobindo's formulation of education comes in here as a relevant corollary. The idea that all knowledge is within and should be evoked through education forms one of the core formulations of his educational theorem and according to it the role of the teacher undergoes a thorough repositioning, as one who is less of an imparter and imposer and more of a helper and guide. I argue that in the formulation of his first educational principle, Sri Aurobindo, as evident from his earlier writings and interpretations in the *Karmayogin* (1909-10), was inspired by classical Indian educational formulations. This emerges especially from the treatment of the ancient discipline in the opuscule under discussion.

through a well-defined method – a 'triple method of repetition, meditation, and discussion'.[42] *Avritti* (repetition) 'was meant to fill the recording part of the mind with *sabda* (word) so that the *artha* (meaning) might of itself rise from within'.[43] This deconstructs assumed theories of the prevalence of an entrenched tradition of rote learning in ancient Indian educational systems. The emphasis on the necessity of giving rise to the *artha* (meaning) was clear and repetition (*avritti*)[44] was useful in only as much as it aided

42. Ibid., p. 374.
43. Ibid.
44. An aside here on the position of memory in the scheme of ancient Indian education would perhaps be relevant. In an analysis of the role of memory in the ancient scheme, Ananda Coomaraswamy argued that the role of repetition in the Indian educational scheme was not for mere memorising but served several purposes and played several training-imparting roles. Coomaraswamy pointed out that repetition trained the concentration. By way of illustration he drew upon the learning of concentration in the 'atmosphere of Hindu culture'. "A part of the *sandhya* or daily prayer of the Hindus," he argued, "consists in the mental repetition of certain prayers (mantras) a certain number of times" (108 times in many cases he says). Though this could easily convert itself into a 'mind-deadening mechanical process' a careful guard was taken against such degeneration and the exercise was turned instead into a 'good practice in concentration'. Counting was insisted upon for it was believed that 'repetition without keeping count leads to mental vacuity' and the keeping of count while repeating was itself a mental gymnastic of no mean measure. "Let anyone", Coomaraswamy challenged his readers in support of that dexterity, "try to repeat any two lines of poetry exactly 108 times, and see whether it does not require mental concentration to do it without failure." Counting along with repetition was not all that there was to the process. Coomaraswamy pointed at certain 'physical practices, especially that of breathing, retaining and expelling the breath, while prayers are repeated a certain number of times' that had to be 'simultaneously followed'. This could certainly not be done 'without

and promoted the rise and assimilation of that meaning. It was a concept which was quite different from the present method of rote learning and memorisation in order to pass through a standardised system of examination, that nationalist educators saw dominating.

Obvious similarities and inspirations are evident in Sri Aurobindo's reference to the triple method of the ancient system and the classical evidences of the same in ancient Indian educational discourse. The ancient Indian system insisted on the need for the learner to understand the deeper underlying meaning of the text in order to internalise them. The first step was the committing of texts to memory. 'There was a method by which the teacher recited the texts. He recited them in the form of metres, pronouncing every letter, syllable, and word according to standardised rules regulating accent and stresses and giving scope to the vibrations of every sound so as to call up its inner sense'. The learner, had to initially follow the method with 'mechanical precision and monotony, like a body of "croaking frogs"'.

But the mastery of the texts was 'only the first step of learning. The more important step was the mastery of meaning', mastery

---

intense attention'. The aim was to throw the whole mind into the effort of worship and not approach the exercise in a 'slovenly fashion'. There had to evolve a *sankalpa* (resolve) to perform the *sandhya* and on a 'strong determination of the mental effort [depended] the efficacy of the worship'. The repetition thus of the name during the prayer had to have the active mind behind it and if the 'mind is not put into the act; it is done mechanically and loses half its value'. [Ananda Coomaraswamy , *Essays in National Idealism*, op.cit., pp. 123, 124] Repetition thus, in ancient Hindu scheme of education, was never an isolated process meant to serve the purpose of retention, in fact the concept of examination and testing itself was also structurally and conceptually different in the ancient context and was nowhere similar to its modern colonially engineered counterpart.

of text – '*akshara-prapti*' had to be followed by '*artha-bodha*', perception of meaning. For one who was a '*kevalapathaka*' (mere crammer) the texts became a burden.[45] Sri Aurobindo emphasised the point that a 'mechanical repetition was not likely to produce' the effect of the word gradually becoming self-evident.[46] A centralised examination system, that was imposed by the colonial education machinery, required students to 'rehearse endlessly the skills of reproduction from memory, summarising, and essay-type writing on any topic. Students were examined on their study of specific texts, not on their understanding of concepts or problems'.[47] The pressure of examinations, as we have argued earlier, and the demands of meritoriously passing them, eventually sidelined the teacher, who became the mere executor of the textbook's will. It vanquished the teacher's capacity to innovate, originate, and enliven the process of learning.[48] Repetition in the classical Indian educational context had a much wider connotation and was not the dominant element useful only for information storing but was looked upon as an important aid for evolving a genuine understanding of the topic, subject, and text discussed.

And how would the focus, the contemplation on the word be effectuated? Along with the *avritti* of the *sabda*, *dhyana* (meditation) 'that clear, still receptivity and that waiting upon the word or thing with the contemplative part of the mind must also

---

45. Radha Kumud Mookerjee, op. cit., *Ancient Indian Education,* 1998, pp. 35, 36.
46. *CWSA* vol.1, op. cit., p. 374.
47. Krishna Kumar, 'Origins of the Textbook Culture' in *What is Worth Teaching*, op.cit., p. 31.
48. For this argument see e.g. Krishna Kumar, *Political Agenda of Education – A Study of Colonialist and Nationalist Ideas*, Sage, New Delhi, 2005.

occur', as Sri Aurobindo delineated it.[49] This was emphasised by the ancient system too. Sri Aurobindo proffered a concrete example on the effect of *dhyana* in the entire process of evoking the meaning. It was an observation that must have remained with him from the Baroda period when he spent long hours of study. 'All of us have felt,' he wrote, 'when studying a language, difficulties which seemed insoluble while grappling with a text, suddenly melt away and a clear understanding arise without assistance from book or teacher after putting away the book from our mind for a brief period.'

He extended the experience to the learning of languages, 'Many of us have experienced also, the strangeness of taking up a language or subject, after a brief discontinuance, to find that we understand it much better than when we took it up, know the meaning of words we had never met before and can explain sentences which, before we discontinued the study, would have baffled our understanding.' Such a manifestation of understanding is possible, Sri Aurobindo observed, 'because the *jnata* or knower within has had his attention called upon the source of knowledge within, in connection with it'. One whose *sattvic* element has been greatly aroused and trained is capable of such an experience.[50] Adhering to his position that the ancients believed knowledge and illumination to be intrinsic, Sri Aurobindo pointed out that they had also drawn up certain methods

49. Or as Ananda Coomaraswamy lyrically put it while discussing memory in education '... all knowledge is founded on knowledge of the self. How is this self to be controlled and focused? Only by the power of concentration, the capacity for fixing the attention of the whole mind for more than a brief moment upon a single aim or thought ...'; as an example, he pointed to the Mahabharata episode in which Arjuna described ' a bird's head, and in that head only the eye.' (Op.cit., pp. 122, 123)
50. *CWSA* vol.1, op. cit., pp. 374–375.

and practice which could empirically demonstrate the validity of that belief.

The ultimate expressions of an advanced *sattvic* development, Sri Aurobindo concluded, is seen when the learner dispenses 'often or habitually with outside aids, the teacher or the textbook, grammar and dictionary and learns a subject largely or wholly from within' but such a possibility visited only the *Yogin* through a 'successful prosecution of the discipline of Yoga'. He was quite frank though that the majority was never expected to rise to this level of self-education.[51]

The result of placing of energies at the 'service of the brain', Sri Aurobindo noted, had far-reaching results. The training of *Brahmacharya* 'not only strengthened the *medha* or grasping power, the *dhi* or subtlety and swiftness of thought-conception, the memory, and creative intellectual force' but also made comprehensive and analytic the 'triple force of memory, invention, [and] judgment'. The range of the mind was greatly enlarged as was strengthened its 'absorbing, storing, and generative mental activities'. This enabled it to accomplish those extraordinary 'feats of memory, various comprehension and versatility of creative work' such as was achieved by only a few 'extraordinary intellects' in the West. In ancient India, these achievements were common. In keeping with the spirit of the age, when a process of self-examination and re-evaluation was in progress, inspired and expedited by the nationalist movement, Sri Aurobindo drew a parallel with Gladstone (1809–1989)[52] who 'was

51. *CWSA* vol.1, op.cit., p. 375. Jugal Kishore Mukherjee cites this as one of the examples of evoking knowledge from within, he refers to this passage and indicates this to be the 'beneficial result of the process' of evocation. Op.cit., p. 12
52. Homer was a constant inspiration for William Gladstone, four times British Prime Minister. In fact, his political biographers have dwelt on this aspect of his life – a near inseparable link and association with

considered to be the possessor of an astonishing memory because he could repeat the whole of Homer's *Iliad*, beginning from any passage suggested to him and flowing on as long as required', but such a capacity, Sri Aurobindo argued, was quite commonplace in ancient India and would be considered by the teachers of old to be a capacity 'neither unusual nor astonishing, but rather petty and limited'.

Sri Aurobindo mentioned how the ordinary, general curriculum of that age had a certain universality – 'it was for every student and not for the exceptional few, and it implied, not a tasting of many subjects after the modern plan, but a thorough mastery of all'.[53] Sri Aurobindo was to go back to this theme in his series on education where he denounced the modern practice of teaching by 'snippets'.[54] Further discussing the achievements of the Indian mind

---

the Homerian world. Amidst his political struggles, he found time to dwell and contemplate on Homer; he was, writes Richard Shannon in his *Gladstone-II: 1865–1898*, 1999) 'nursing a plan to produce a revised edition of his Studies on Homer of 1858'. He started work on this plan in 1867 and would eventually complete it in 1869, his *Juventus Mundi, The Gods and Men of the Heroic Age.* (p.44) In fact such an obsession or release was Homer for Gladstone from his tedium of office, that he once recorded, 'worked 6 ¼ hours on Homeric primer. What a treat!' (p.218) During most of Sri Aurobindo's stay in England, Gladstone dominated the political scene as Prime Minister , his memory feat must have already started becoming part of the lore!

53. *CWSA* vol.1, pp. 376, 377.

54. 'A remarkable feature of modern training', Sri Aurobindo castigated, 'which has been subjected in India to a reduction ad absurdum .... A subject is taught a little at a time, in conjunction with a host of others, with the result that what might be well learnt in a single year is badly learnt in seven and the boy goes out ill-equipped, served with imperfect parcels of knowledge, master of none of the great departments of human knowledge'. In the same piece he accused the National Council of heightening this practice by following the

and genius, Sri Aurobindo referred to the 'original achievements of a Kalidasa accomplishing the highest in every line of poetic creation', paralleled in the arena of philosophy by Shankara in a short life span of thirty-two years' and pointed to the 'universal mastery of all possible spiritual knowledge and experiences of Sri Ramakrishna'. To him, these were instances of pure creative genius, examples of what the Indian mind, in its supreme capacity was essentially capable of. Though these instances were not as 'common as others', in Europe such parallels were 'with a single modern exception, non-existent'. In Europe, the excelling has been in 'one field of a single intellectual province or at most in two' whereas in India it was the 'greatest who have been the most versatile and passed from one field of achievement to another' with easy and unfaltering mastery.

This many-sided genius of the Indian mind was made possible, Sri Aurobindo argued, because of the practice of *brahmacharya*, which 'developed sattva or inner illumination'. This inner illumination made the 'acquisition of knowledge' and all other intellectual operations and performances 'easy, spontaneous, swift, decisive and comparatively unfatiguing to body or brain'. Thus, Sri Aurobindo argued, in conclusion, that it was finally *brahmacharya* and *sattwic* development that held the secret of ancient Indian 'intellectual achievement', it were these which, in effect, 'created the brain of India'.

Having thus discussed the psychological principles of ancient Indian education, Sri Aurobindo took up the problems and questions of education of that era. While he accepted the common complaint that students 'are too heavily burdened with many subjects and

---

method at the start and the middle and then without sufficient preparation exposing the learner to 'grandiose specialism at the top'. (*CWSA* vol.1, op. cit., p. 393 (*A System of National Education – Some Preliminary Ideas*).

the studying of many books', Sri Aurobindo also pointed out that the 'range of studies [was] pitifully narrow and the books read miserably few'. The reason for this paradox was that the creation of the base, the foundation was neglected. With the young mind exposed to 'snippet' education, the foundation remained weak and was unable to bear even the 'paltry and meagre edifice of our imparted knowledge'. He followed this up with an indictment of the effects of a colonial education on the Indian mind which was 'still in potentiality what it was', but was being gradually 'damaged, stunted and defaced'. 'The greatness of its innate possibilities [was] hidden by the greatness of its surface deterioration'.[55]

To Sri Aurobindo, one of the chief causes of this deterioration and damage was – as the nationalist educators also consistently argued, and as Sri Aurobindo unceasingly reiterated – 'study in a foreign language which was not even imperfectly mastered at a time when the student was called upon to learn in that impossible medium a variety of alien and unfamiliar subjects'.[56] The vernacular

55. *CWSA* vol.1, p. 377.
56. Sri Aurobindo, we have already seen, had highlighted this issue since his early days in India. In his assessment of Bankim Chandra Chattopadhyay, Sri Aurobindo emphasised the indispensability of an education that was rooted to the learners' surrounding, and of which his vernacular formed an integral part. He also spoke for it in a scheme of national education, insisting that 'one who has mastered his own language, has one very necessity facility for mastering another', [and] with the linguistic faculty unsatisfactorily developed in one's own tongue, to master others is impossible' and therefore the mother-tongue was the 'proper medium of instruction' and the child's initial energies had to be directed towards its mastery. (*CWSA* vol.1, op.cit., p.394). Sri Aurobindo raised this issue as a vital component of the nationalist educational discourse. The continuity of his tilt and support for the vernacular is evident in his '*Preface on National Education*,' written decades later in 1920–21, where he supported the

versus foreign tongue evoked, as we have seen, much emotion and debate. Sri Aurobindo was one among the prominent thought-leaders to have dwelt on this aspect, his perception of this need and its importance in shaping the Indian mind had developed since his return to India.[57]

---

need for learning Sanskrit – he did not see the language as impeding the growth of a scientific temper – through a method that was 'most natural, efficient, and stimulating to the mind'. He saw no necessity to cling 'to any past or present manner of teaching'. But the vital question was, as he saw it, how were Sanskrit and other indigenous languages to be used to 'get to the heart and intimate sense of our own culture and establish a vivid continuity between the still living power of our past and the yet uncreated power of our future'. There was no separation in his approach; it was neither a total reverting to the past nor a complete rupture with it. Instead, the use of indigenous tongues was to serve as a bridge. Sri Aurobindo also included the question of the role that English or for that matter any other foreign language were to play in the new educational outlook. Training in these languages would enable one to 'know helpfully the life, ideas and culture of other countries and establish our right relations with the world around us'. He saw national education as accepting the role of the foreign tongue, a tongue that would not dominate but would facilitate a cultural and ideational exchange. This would be the principle of a 'true national education', one that did not ignore, overlook or refuse 'modern truth and knowledge' while taking along one's own 'foundation', 'being', 'mind' [and] 'spirit'. [*CWSA* vol.1, op.cit., p. 421] The philosophical basis of the national education quest could perhaps be located in these lines, it came years after the storm of political activism had abated in Sri Aurobindo's life.

57 Decades later, the youngest Vice Chancellor of the University of Calcutta and one of leading educationists of modern India, Syama Prasad Mookerjee, continued with this advocacy of the uses of Indian languages, the mother tongue. Syama Prasad called for the mother-tongue to be recognised as the medium of instruction and examination in all subjects other than English. Delivering the Convocation Address at the Patna University in 1937, for instance,

The two contemporary minds with whom we are concerned because of their links to Sri Aurobindo, also saw this necessity and were vocal in the promotion of Indian languages, and realised its indispensability in re-creating the Indian mind. Coomaraswamy, for example, brought out a fundamental problem in Indian education. Though not concerned directly in this instance, to the issue of the medium of instruction through English, Coomaraswamy pointed

---

Syama Prasad dealt at length with the issue. He argued that for more than century, 'education imparted through the medium of English had produced a class of men who were 'unconsciously so denationalised that any proposal for the recognition of the Indian languages as a vehicle of instruction up to the university stage is either ridiculed as impossible, or branded as reactionary'. Syama Prasad firmly pleaded for the vernacular languages driven by a firm conviction that 'the fullest development of the mind of a learner is possible only by this natural approach', to him this process alone could lead to a 'great revival of the glory and richness of the Indian languages'. His tenure as Vice Chancellor of Calcutta University saw a huge push to the promotion of Indian languages and to the use of Bengali. Research scholars were encouraged to write dissertations in Bengali and for the first time, a successful candidate who wrote his thesis in Bengali was awarded the degree of doctor of philosophy. Mookerjee wanted to 'enrich India's national languages for which it was essential to make them the vehicle of instruction and spread of knowledge far and wide in diverse branches through them'. He advocated the provision, in education centres, for the study of important Eastern and Western languages as well. While highly favouring the use of Indian languages as the medium of instruction, Syama Prasad was not a 'blind detractor of English as a language per se. While pleading for a due recognition of our own languages, he recognised that English should remain a compulsory second language and that it should be taught to all, mainly for the purpose of a correct expression of ideas and assimilation of knowledge to be gathered from books written in that great language'. (For a detailed discussion, see eg. Anirban Ganguly, Avadesh Kumar Singh, *Syama Prasad Mookerjee: His Vision of Education*, 2017)

towards a more deep-seated and connected or resultant problem – that of Indian students being instructed by Englishmen who, he argued, could never really be 'true educators of the Indian people', because of their inability to not only inherit India's traditions, but also because of their failure to evolve a 'spirit of perfect reverence for those traditions'.

He spoke of the need for English professors to undertake a rigorous, assiduous, and 'sympathetic study of Indian religious philosophy, Sanskrit or Pali, some vernacular language, Indian history, [including the period when the 'ideals of Indian civilisation' saw expression] art, music, literature and etiquette' in order to enable himself to understand the problems of Indian education. Such a study, Coomaraswamy argued, would develop an understanding in him and would make him less inclined to interfere in the Indian ideals 'for he would either be Indianised at heart, or would have long realised the hopeless divergence between his own and Indian ideals'.[58] The prevailing system did not encourage or allow the undertaking of such a study, and English teachers, he lamented, 'have neither the time nor the inclination to spend ten years, or even two, in such a study of Indian culture'.

To Coomaraswamy, the stark manifestations of such an omission were apparent when, rapidly elevated to positions of power and eminence in the education system in India, these badly trained teachers doggedly attempted to apply solutions best suited to an English environment to the Indian educational issues and problems.[59] Two contemporaries writing around the same time

58. *Essays in National Idealism,* op. cit., p. 100.

59. Ibid., p.101. Coomaraswamy thus saw quite early the imperativeness of taking control of the educational scheme if freedom in the actual sense of the term was to be achieved, 'The control of Indian education,' he foresaw, 'is of so much importance that the necessity of gaining this would alone justify the present endeavours to attain

(1909), highlighted a crucial issue in the nationalist education debate and discussed it from two separate dimensions. One directly referred to the ineligibility of English as the predominant medium of educational instruction in a country where the vernacular continued to make sense to the vast majority, and the other spoke of the disconnected Englishman as a teacher unsuccessfully trying to communicate in, and impose, a foreign medium and system to vastly different Indian conditions and situations.

Sister Nivedita considered the language of a people to be their 'highest and most spiritual' creation. The deepest emotions and aspirations of a nation are expressed through it, 'in this is expressed the soul of nations'. The Indian thought-world, the Indian vision-world, best expressed itself through the vernacular. Nivedita took the debate to the ideational level and saw it as the best means to penetrate and assimilate Indian thought, philosophy, and way of life. 'As one studies an Indian vernacular,' she observed, 'the vastness and distinctiveness of the Indian dream-world continually grows on one. First there are the philosophical ideas which give its tone to dream. Then there is the great gallery of ideal characters of which every Indian child by birth is made a free man ...'[60]

An exposure to this vast repository of traditional Indian knowledge was missed out through a forced foreign medium. In her *Hints on National Education in India,* discussing 'the Place of Foreign Culture in a True Education', Nivedita took a categorical position vis-a-vis the issue of a foreign medium of instruction. In her characteristically vigorous tone, Nivedita argued that a mind which is fed on 'foreign knowledge and ideas' at an initial

political freedom.'(Op. cit., p. 188) The basic argument in favour of control of the education by the nationalist leaders was with this objective – its control would in a sense provide an intellectual shape and direction to the movement.

60. *The Mediaeval University of India,* op. cit., p. 340.

stage is not rooted upon and bound by a 'sense of intimacy', with its own surrounding, tradition and psyche, and becomes like the 'waif brought up in the stranger's home. The waif may behave well and reward his benefactor', but this would be forced from a mental sense of duty rather than love. In words strikingly similar to Sri Aurobindo's in the pages of the *Karmayogin* insisting that the child be engaged first with his surrounding and with the land and soil of his birth and growth, Nivedita observed that 'in a true education, the place of foreign culture is never at the beginning [and] all true development must proceed from the known to the unknown, from the familiar to the unfamiliar, from the near to the far'.[61] The pupil was being disassociated from his life and moorings and therefore the nationalist educators spoke of the vernacular as the best suited medium for Indian students. In fact, all three, Sri Aurobindo, Nivedita, and Coomaraswamy, though trained in the western educational system, clearly saw the debilitating effects of an overdose of the foreign exposure on the Indian mind. Especially the bewildering impact it had on the young Indian, unfamiliar with the urbanised surroundings and ways.

As discussed earlier, during this period Sri Aurobindo had interactions and collaborated with Nivedita. Enunciating his third principle of education, Sri Aurobindo argued for the need to give the child a measured exposure, one that would take him from the 'near to the far, from that which is to that which shall be'. The intrinsic relevance and inseparability in an individual's pattern of growth of his surrounding, nationality, country, sustaining soil, the 'air which he breathes, the sights, sounds [and] habits to which he is accustomed' can never be brushed aside. These form a vital

61. *CWSN* vol.4, 'The Place of Foreign Culture in a True Education' in *Hints on National Education in India*, pp.354–355. The similarity of Sri Aurobindo's approach to this problem is also evident.

part of the child's growth and mental evolution.[62] Interestingly, Coomaraswamy in his essays during the period discussed above also referred to the same issue using similar expressions, and stressed the point that a people's intelligence could be developed 'primarily only by means of education in the national culture'. Coomaraswamy argued that it was essential that one understood first that 'with which [one is] already familiar before it is possible to understand the unfamiliar, and relate it to one's life'. An imitation without understanding, and without relating to one's surrounding, results in vulgarity.[63]

The foreign medium of instruction, the practice of describing foreign scenes and subjects, and the forced imitation it generated, stunted free thinking and imagination and dislocated the young mind from his surroundings. Young Abanindranath Tagore (1871–1951), later to become the leader of the nationalist art movement in Bengal, recalled how in his childhood, while being educated at home he was surrounded 'with pictures of all kinds mostly Victorian' and how his impression of 'rustic cottages' were engendered by English picture books. It was not until his first visit to rural Bengal, where he saw peasant dwellings, 'did he realise how different they were from the ones known to him'.[64] The colonial system through a foreign medium, expression, and imagery, sought to delink the Indian mind from his native life and living. This was the basic point that the three contemporaries under study, deeply concerned with the idea of a national education, were making.

Nivedita's primary concern was that the Indian mind was losing hold on the narrative of its native land. This was mainly

62. *CWSA* vol.1, op.cit.
63. *Essays in National Idealism*, op. cit., p.193.
64. Partha Mitter, *Art and Nationalism in Colonial India: 1850–1922*, 1994, p. 272.

because of the 'unprecedented influx of foreign knowledge and foreign criticism, from the early decades of the nineteenth century onwards'. It was an influx that Nivedita believed, lost to the country 'many a mind and many a character that should have been amongst the noblest of her sons'.[65] The idea was to stem that 'brain drain' and recreate, reignite, and reformulate that cultural identity which was essential to redefining the nation. An education in a foreign medium right from its early stages was seen to impede this process. The challenge was either the unwillingness or inability – both effects of a foreign medium – to develop a deep and intimate understanding of the Indian. It was indispensible to train the Indian mind to at least know what was one's own. For that to happen the familiar, the known had to be first re-introduced in an education that called itself national.

When Nivedita wrote – 'in all directions we find that only when deeply rooted in the familiar, we may safely take up the unfamiliar. In proportion as we rightly analyse the known, rightly distinguishing, even in what is familiar, between the ideal expressed and the form assumed, in that proportion will it open for us the book of the whole world' – she was making a case not only for the promotion of the vernacular, but at a deeper level for retraining the Indian mind to be at ease with Indian traditions. She saw such knowledge and training as an essential pre-requisite if India hoped to reposition herself in the larger global community. To achieve this, it was essential to love what is one's own and more importantly to actually know what is one's own. One who was incapable of doing this or has neglected its practice 'will never be received by any people as anything more than half a man'.[66]

The Indian brain thus, to continue with Sri Aurobindo's

65. *CWSN* vol. 4, op. cit., pp. 358, 359.

66. Ibid., p. 357.

argument, 'in this unnatural process' [that of having to learn a wide variety of unfamiliar subjects in an 'impossible medium'] was crippled by the disuse of judgment, observation, comprehension, and creation', thus developing a habit of un-thinking memorisation. Sri Aurobindo termed it an 'exclusive reliance on the deteriorating relics of the ancient Indian memory'. Thus, Sri Aurobindo lamented, exposed to the methods of colonial education, the Indian mind was 'beggared and degraded' and had to contend with 'snippets and insufficient packets of information instead of being richly stored and powerfully equipped'.[67]

The national education experiment in Bengal, Sri Aurobindo recalled, tried to undo this degenerative evil 'by employing the mother-tongue', attempted to encourage and restore the intellectual functions and also tried to provide 'a richer and more real equipment of information'. But it achieved limited success because the teachers and directors of this new educational experiment were 'minds already vitiated by the old system and not often with the best even of these'. Also, the teachers 'had themselves seldom a perfect grasp of the requirements of the new system'. The educational system, Sri Aurobindo complained, while terming itself national, 'neglected the very foundation of the great achievement of our forefathers and especially the perfection of the instrument of knowledge'.[68] But Sri Aurobindo also clarified that the call for re-examining past educational principles did not mean 'that the actual system of ancient instruction' be restored in its outward features .... Many of them are not suited to modern requirements'. His argument was that the ancient system had certain fundamental principles that remain for all times, and such a discipline could only be replaced by the 'discovery of a still more effective discipline' which the colonial

67. *CWSA* vol.1, op. cit., pp. 377–378.
68. Ibid., op. cit., p. 378.

system was incapable of formulating. How the ideas or discipline of the ancients were to be reapplied to the present Sri Aurobindo did not discuss, perhaps he intended to do it sometime in the future and would have done so had the exigencies of politics and yoga not taken him along a different and uncharted route.

Sri Aurobindo thus explained certain principles of the ancient Indian education system and analysed some of its dominant psychological principles which assigned to the term 'education' a wholly deeper meaning and significance. It was an education that had the development and evolution of the individual at the centre of its schemes. The write-up also made a case for developing people's intelligence 'through the medium of their own national culture'.[69] And in that national culture, India's civilisational principles of education would form an important and intrinsic part. In a sense, the contestation discussed above, was a call to recognise and reapply those principles to present conditions so that the education scenario could be transformed. For Sri Aurobindo, the national education movement and its institutions needed to engage with these principles in order to be able to create a meaningful and genuine system of national education for India. Sri Aurobindo thus argued for, and engaged with, classical Indian educational concepts and principles and was concerned with the possibility of re-applying these to modern conditions and systems.

VII.2. ON RESTORING THE ARTISTIC EMOTION: THE VALUE OF ART IN A SCHEME OF NATIONAL EDUCATION

The other vital subject that Sri Aurobindo addressed in the quest for a philosophy of national education was that of art – the necessity of training in aesthetics and its centrality in a scheme of national education. The researcher, undertaking a study of Sri Aurobindo's

69. *Essays in National Idealism,* op. cit., p. 106.

thoughts and writings especially examining them in the backdrop of the national education movement, has to contend with the fact that Sri Aurobindo tackled a wide number of aspects even while dealing with the educational argument. One saw him dwelling on the political, technical, historical, and philosophical as well as aesthetics of the discourse. A researcher attempting to study his arguments in these, requires certain grounding in each of these fields and I must confess my inability to be able to take up each of these in depth and to do justice. Moreover, an analysis of each of these fields would make the present work unwieldy and protracted. A reading and discussion of each of these may perhaps be undertaken later by the specialists in order to be able to contextualise and interpret Sri Aurobindo's thoughts against the backdrop of the nationalist thought-movement. But nevertheless, Sri Aurobindo's observations on the necessity of an art-training, and of developing the aesthetical dimension and of situating it prominently in the national education scheme deserves a reading however brief and cursory.

Sri Aurobindo's commentaries on 'The National Value of Art' appeared in six installments in his newly created thought–vehicle, '*Karmayogin*', between November and December 1909. The Empire's Asian capital, Calcutta, had by then emerged as the centre of the Nationalist Art Movement and had become a remarkable arena for the growth and evolution of an 'ideology of Swadeshi art'.[70] It was but natural for Sri Aurobindo to turn his attention to this important instrument of national growth and unity. He saw the insistence and inclusion of an art-training in the national education curricula as

---

70. See eg. Elleke Boehmer, *Empire, the National and the Post-Colonial: 1890–1920-Resistance in Interaction*, 2002 and Partha Mitter, *Art and Nationalism in Colonial India: 1850–1922*, op.cit.) for a detailed treatment of the nationalist art movement in India.

essential for re-forging an ideational unity apart from aiding in the training of aesthetic and refinement. While the surface necessity was the rekindling of pride in the Indian forms and techniques of artistic expressions which were marginalised by western artistic methods and techniques which were dominant, the inner much deeper objective was to re-establish a link with the artistic and creative dimensions of the nation. The medium of art was felt to be one of the most credible and reliable instruments towards reviving that link. The Swadeshi art movement and the painters that it produced aimed at re-establishing that civilisational aesthetics and of rekindling that link. Referring to the 'work of modern school of painters in Calcutta' as a 'phase of national awakening', Ananda Coomaraswamy, who was himself an active participant in that phase, spoke of their trying to 'bring back or create a state of society in which the ideals expressed and implied in Indian culture', would be 'more nearly realised'.[71]

VII.3. THE NEED FOR AN ART MOVEMENT AND EDUCATION: ART AS AN AGENT OF NATIONAL UNITY AND AS A RESTORER OF RACIAL ARTISTIC EMOTION

Sri Aurobindo participated in the art movement by speaking for it, and by encouraging its alternative forms of artistic expressions. He supported the nationalist effort to reclaim that field. The other two minds – Nivedita and Coomaraswamy – whose ideas on the national education question we have been examining, were themselves active participants in this nationalist art movement. They were firm believers in art's capacity for forging a new national mind, and in the ineluctability of training in art and aesthetics as part of the new national education.

Sri Aurobindo had indicated earlier in the pages of the

71. Ananda Coomaraswamy, *Swadeshi & Art*, 1910, p. 126.

Karmayogin that a 'national awakening' which works itself out within a narrow or single confine can never be 'vital and enduring'. His contention was that the awakening of the national soul would have manifold forms of expression, of the 'strength and the delight of the expansive spirit within'.[72] Recognising the need for a manifold and new artistic expression, Sri Aurobindo threw his weight behind the Swadeshi art movement, and argued in favour of encouraging the growth of national aesthetics. His support for the new art movement was evident from the pages of the *Karmayogin*, where he highlighted, not only its various facets and its place in the new awakening, but also spoke in support of those attempting to support and disseminate its ideas and expressions.

Sri Aurobindo saw the awakening of the national soul in religion as a precursor to its awakening in a wider sphere of intellectual and cultural activities. He saw the religious awakening taking place, as he lyrically put it referring to Sri Ramakrishna, when 'the flower of the educated youth of Calcutta bowed down at the feet of an illiterate Hindu ascetic, a self-illumined ecstatic and "mystic" without a single trace or touch of the alien thought or education upon him'. Sri Aurobindo saw this as heralding the triumph of the religious soul of India.[73] It was this churning of the religious mind in a new direction which not only revived certain robustness in the faith but also encouraged a wider quest in other areas of national activity and expressions.

Referring to these other activities, Sri Aurobindo saw the need of the religious and political life remoulding the national life in all its dimensions. He saw the influence already at work in the sphere of art and literature and sought to strengthen its impact. In Bengal, *inter alia,* Sri Aurobindo saw the national spirit seeking to 'satisfy

---

72. *CWSA* vol.8, op.cit., 'The Awakening Soul of India, 26 June, 1909', p. 63.
73. Ibid., p. 62.

itself in art, and for the first time since the decline of the Moguls, a new school of national art' of which Abanindranath Tagore was 'the founder and master' developing itself. Still influenced, at times, by foreign 'though Asiatic' elements, the new school was trying to express and work on the basic tenet of Indian art, it was an effort to 'express in form and limit something of that which is formless and illimitable'.[74]

The pages of the *Karmayogin* also carried Sri Aurobindo's appreciations of recent paintings and current techniques of expressions.[75] At the same time, appreciating the efforts of other nationalist journals in consistently doing the same, Sri Aurobindo observed that by featuring prints of Indian paintings produced by the new school in Bengal and by others, they were rendering a vital service to national regeneration.

Talking of the efforts of the *Modern Review*, launched in 1907 by the formidable Ramananda Chatterji (1865–1943) and its sister magazine the Bengali *Prabasi*, Sri Aurobindo observed that these reviews, by reproducing every month some work of art by contemporary Indian painters and by bringing them to thousands who had no opportunity to see the original, were 'restoring the sense of beauty and artistic emotion inborn in our race but almost blotted out by the long reign in our lives of the influence of Anglo-Saxon vulgarity and crude tasteless commercialism'.[76] Implied in the statement was an attack on the official education system which seemed to encourage this tasteless commercialism. Most of the pictures, he saw reproduced belonged to the 'new school of Bengali art' which he saw as the only 'living and original school now

74. Ibid., pp. 63, 64.
75. See eg. his write-ups on art and art appreciation in *CWSA* vol.1, op.cit., pp. 455–464.
76. *CWSA* vol.1, op.cit., p. 455.

developing among us'.

Ramananda Chatterji, a stalwart polymath, who attained an iconic status amongst nationalists, presided over their public meetings. In connection with Sri Aurobindo, Chatterji presided over at least one large public meeting held on June 13, 1909, at Beadon square in North Calcutta. Keeping in mind that this was a phase when the revolutionary nationalists were facing severe administrative repression, Ramananda's presence at the meeting was significant. Referring to his ceaseless promotion of Indianness, Sri Aurobindo called him an 'indefatigable literary and patriotic worker' who was 'well-known to the Bengali public as a clear-minded, sober, and fearless political speaker and writer'. Among the many services Ramananda was rendering to his nation, his latest, 'introducing the masterpieces of the new school of Art to his readers' was, Sri Aurobindo argued, a 'yet more valuable and lasting service to his country'.[77] In fact, Ramananda who had long been in search of an agent that would 'bind the fissiparous languages and cultures of India', saw art as 'a universal language' that offered him that opportunity. The binding through literature was hampered due to the inadequacy of translations and he saw the medium of visual arts as offering that scope. He saw in the revival of 'artistic activity' a 'factor silently making for national unity'.[78]

The championing thus of the new school assumed urgency and reproduction in the pages of his journal, and facilitated and encouraged that silent unifying factor. It can be said that Sri Aurobindo too saw this unifying utility of the art movement and threw his weight behind it. Sister Nivedita, who was a prolific contributor to the *Modern Review* and a close associate of Chatterji, discussed in its pages 'The Function of Art in Shaping Nationality'.

---

77. Ibid., p. 460.
78. Partha Mitter, op.cit., p. 223.

'Art ... is charged,' Nivedita declared in the piece, 'with a spiritual message, in India today, the message of the Nationality'. It had to be thus pursued 'like science, like education, like industry, like trade itself' with the sole objective of "remaking of the Motherland" and for no other aim'.[79] Coomaraswamy was as categorical on the issue, 'nations are made by artists and by poets, not by traders and politicians' he had declared, and it was by becoming artists and poets and by beginning to once more understand 'our own art and poetry', that one could attain the highest ideal of nationality ....'[80]

Among the most underrated and understudied figures in the history of Indian nationalism, Ramananda Chatterji was a formidable influence and was one of the prime shapers of the nationalist cultural and historical narrative. Chatterji was a close associate and friend of Sri Aurobindo's maternal uncle Krishna Kumar Mitra, and during Mitra's internment in 1908, Mukherji looked after his family. For years together, in issue after issue of *Prabasi* and the *Modern Review*, Mukherji reproduced the art works and paintings of the young artists of the Swadeshi art movement. Despite incurring loss, despite facing opposition from certain quarters, he persisted with this and was perhaps the single-most thought-leader of that era to popularise the new school of art.[81]

Abanindra Nath Tagore recollected, how, because of Ramananda Chatterji:

> ... [O]ur paintings reached homes across the country; the popularisation of Indian art was possible because of him, none apart from him could have done this .... He did this with a one-pointed

79. *CWSN vol.3*, p. 14.
80. *Essays in National Idealism*, op. cit., preface pp. i,ii.
81. Shanta Devi, *Bharater Mukti-Sadhak: Ramananda Chattopadhyay O Ardha-Shatabdir Bangla* (Sadhaka of India's Freedom: Ramananda Chattopadhyaya & the Bengal of Five Decades), 2005, p. 151.

focus; he poured his resources, kept trying, generated the discourse on Indian art and the demand among the people for our work. He faced a lot of opposition, I too faced it, our Art Society could not promote it the way he did it. Our work would be over by simply painting and drawing, he would patiently go around, trying to connect and link, he wanted our painting to reach very home, even the home of the poor, he wanted these to be sent abroad, he collected advertisements for us from all across India, which are even now yielding us resources. Had he not done this, who would have supported us young artists and our callow artwork?[82]

A polymath, and one of the most well-known linguists and educationists of modern India, Suniti Kumar Chatterjee, speaking of Ramananda's support in establishing and popularising the new Indian art narrative, remembered the day Ramananda took it upon himself to spread the ideals and expressions of Swadeshi art, and how it opened up a new avenue for the young artists. To Ramananda, recollected Suniti Kumar Chatterjee, every grain and soil of India was precious; that is why he plunged into the effort of spreading and popularising Swadeshi art, and also regularly wrote his widely-read '*Chitra Parichay O Chitra Prasanga*', and enlisted avant-garde art historians and interpreters like O.C. Gangoly (1881–1974) and Sister Nivedita to write for his journal in support of the art movement.[83]

82. Shanta Devi, op.cit., p. 151. (my translation from the original Bengali)
83. Ibid., pp. 151, 152. Sri Aurobindo wrote a review of O.C. Gangoly's popular quarterly journal of Oriental Art, *Rupam* which had just made its appearance. Sri Aurobindo saw in the appearance of *Rupam*, a 'significant indication of the progress that is being made in the revival of the aesthetic mind of India. Assailed and corrupted in a time of cultural decline and arrest of its creative and artistic faculty by an alien aesthesis and ideals antithetic to its own spirit, it is returning to a right view and understanding of its past greatness, and though much way has still to be made before there can be any universal recovery of the artistic eye and taste, the first steps have been taken with some rapidity and firmness and are all in the right

Besides being an important forum for the nationalist cultural debate, the *Modern Review* also saw a sustained discussion on India's educational needs. Ramananda was a staunch proponent of mass and adult education. He argued that the principal segment of our country were those who toiled daily to earn their living, the farmer, tiller, mason, artisan, and that by segregating or omitting them, no country could exist. An education which does not empower and equip the most marginalised and neglected cannot be termed as a national education. Any education which did not express itself through the labour, creation, and talent of its people could not be national.[84] Ramananda Chatterji's contribution to the freedom movement, to the national education and the art movement, and to the overall creation of nationalist narrative, his pan-Indian and global influence, his contribution to shaping the Hindu political narrative, is an area of research that has remained largely untouched..

Sri Aurobindo's interest in art training and his deliberations on its value in a national scheme of education was not a sudden development nor was it isolated from his vision of national regeneration. It formed part of the tradition that had by then (1906–1909) made a space for itself. In the movement for national regeneration, education would play one of the most vital parts; not only would it lead to freedom, it would also prepare the people to organise that freedom. An important component of this regeneration was the restoration of the 'sense of beauty and artistic emotion inborn in [the] race'. This is surely what led Sri Aurobindo to elaborate his thoughts on training in aesthetics for the nation.

The demand for the inclusion of art in the education system had been taken up early by those who were directly involved in

---

direction.' (*CWSA* vol.1, p. 589)

84. Ibid., pp. 271, 272.

reviving the Indian art movement. One Shyamacharan Srimani had already set the pace by producing a slim volume on *The Rise of the Fine Arts and the Artistic Skills of the Aryans* (*Suksasilper utpatti o aryajatir silpacaturi*) as far back as 1874. The work was adjudged an important 'marker in the growth of cultural nationalism', it was the 'first history of art written in Bengali' and was looked upon as an early nationalist work.[85] In fact, Srimani was closely associated with the Hindu Mela in Bengal started by Nabagopal Mitra and Rajnarayan Bose. Srimani taught at the national school, organised exhibitions of 'Indian artware at the Mela' and gave lectures at the Mela forum in 1869 on 'the glory of ancient Indian art' and exhorted the youth 'to revive that glory'.[86]

E.B.Havell (1861–1934), one of the leading lights and voices calling for the revival of Indian art, and one who also encouraged the young Abanindranath – soon to lead the nationalist art movement – to take up the revival of Indian art forms had, as early as 1901, urged the Congress leaders to 'take a broader perspective and integrate art more fully into their national programme'. Pursuing the same agenda, Havell had published an 'Open Letter to Educated Indians' in 1903, castigating them 'for their indifference to their own art'.[87] Coomaraswamy noted how the collaboration between Havell and Abanindranath Tagore 'made possible a great change in the public attitude towards art'. Coomaraswamy described how Abanindranath, 'an Indian painter already of great promise', encouraged by Havell, then Principal of the Calcutta School of Art, 'began to seek inspiration in the seventeenth century' Indian

85. Partha Mitter, op.cit., p. 224.
86. Tapati Guha-Thakurta, 'Recovering the Nation's Art' in Partha Chatterjee edited., *Texts of Power: Emerging Disciplines in Colonial Bengal*, 1995, p. 73.
87. Ibid., p. 251.

paintings, 'which had, till then, been so little appreciated'.[88] Speaking of this new Indian school of painting, Coomaraswamy observed that its works were 'full of refinement and subtlety in colour' and showed 'a real love for all things Indian'. The paintings of the new school were 'lavishly praised, and severely criticised both in India and in England', to Coomaraswamy, this at least showed that were of 'some significance'.[89]

Havell argued in his essays on 'Art and Education in India' (1901), that from a political standpoint it was not 'a small thing that the artistic sentiment of the Indian peoples [was] being extinguished under our [British] rule'. It was an argument that found echo in Sri Aurobindo's writings as well. Havell wanted a whole people to be devoted to art but that possibility he saw being resisted by colonial rule. The reading that 'a people devoted to art are a happy and contented people [and] a people without art are restless and unhappy'[90] compelled him to take a hands-on approach to bring back the arts to the people. Similar to what Sri Aurobindo perceived, Havell too, saw India 'as the only part of the British Empire where the aesthetic sense of the people, in spite of all that British philistinism has done to suppress it, strongly influences their everyday life'.[91] There had to be thus a national effort at restoring

88. Ananda Coomaraswamy, *Art & Swadeshi*, op.cit., p. 127
89. Ibid., p. 130.
90. E.B.Havell, 'Art and Education in India' in *Indian Art, Industry and Education*, 1901, p. 137.
91. E.B.Havell, 'Art and Education in India' in *Indian Art, Industry and Education*, 1901, p. 91. Sri Aurobindo beginning his series on '*The National Value of Art*' similarly argued that in modern times the tendency to'depreciate the value of the beautiful and overstress the value of the useful' is corrected in India – a country and a people subjected to a 'mercenary and soulless education' that had cut it off from all its ancient roots of culture and tradition' – only by the temperament of the people in which the 'stress of imagination,

and preserving that sense. Sri Aurobindo stressed on the necessity of this restoration too. He lamented that the age was 'bent on depriving life of its meaning by turning earth into a sort of glorified antheap', and that the value the ancients attached 'to music, art, and poetry has become almost unintelligible' to it.[92] The nationalist art movement attracted some of the most dynamic minds of the Swadeshi period. The triumvirate comprising of Havell, Nivedita and Coomaraswamy were its ideologues, with Havell furnishing the 'aesthetic', Nivedita providing the 'moral', and Coomaraswamy supplying the 'metaphysical content' to the Swadeshi doctrine of art.[93] Sri Aurobindo by lending his moral support and authority to the aspiration gave it a greater fillip and sanction.

---

emotion, and spiritual delicacy' was 'submerged but not yet destroyed.' [*CWSA* vol.1, op.cit., p.433] In his series on Indian art, while defending Indian culture and discussing the Indian Renaissance much later, Sri Aurobindo referred to Mr. Havell and Dr. Coomaraswamy as among the eminent two who had already done a considerable amount of work to clear away the 'misconceptions about Indian sculpture and painting'. While accepting, that during this period a change in perception of Indian art had set in, Sri Aurobindo felt that the change had not yet gone far enough to develop a 'thorough appreciation of the deepest and most characteristic spirit and inspiration of Indian work' [and that] 'an eye or an effort like Mr. Havell's [was] still rare'. [*The Renaissance in India,* op. cit., pp. 254, 260.] Sri Aurobindo held the ideologues of the nationalist art movement in great esteem and valued their pioneering service towards the awakening of the national artistic soul.

92. *CWSA* vol.1, p.433, According to Coomaraswamy, who discerned the 'essential error in modern Indian education as understood by Government ... and Anglicised Indians: [the] refusal or inability to recognise any responsibility to the past', this break 'in the continuity of the historical tradition [and the inability to understand it anymore would prove to be] fatal to Indian culture'. [*Essays in National Idealism,* op. cit., p. 186]

93. Partha Mitter, op.cit., p. 246.

Sri Aurobindo hoped to work towards the restoration of the aesthetic and artistic emotion in the race. The age and the prevalent approach of education had nearly eradicated that emotion and sense. The education imparted – which was mainly looked upon as a 'passport to jobs' – had, by its neglect of the art or refusal to recognise the possibilities of an Indian art, encouraged this non-comprehension of its national value. Sri Aurobindo perceived that the 'whole of humanity' had reached a stage where it now demands 'not merely the satisfaction of the body, the *anna,* but the satisfaction also of the *prana* and the *citta,* the vital and emotional desires'.[94] The new education would have to recognise that urge and integrate the new schools of art so as to satisfy that larger demand.

Sri Aurobindo identified the 'thought' as the 'highest that man has attained' and it was through the power of thought that man sought to create new situations and break the old society. He described thought as having two discernable aspects, 'two separate sides' – 'judgment or reason, and imagination' – both of which were necessary to 'perfect ideation'.[95] Each of these separate sides manifested a certain aspect of human sphere of activity – the former worked through the areas of science, philosophy, and criticism; the other unveiled itself through art, poetry, and idealism. Sri Aurobindo saw these as undermining the old state of humanity and laying the foundations for the new. While the contributions of science were widely recognised, the 'more subtle and profound' value of the other has been less recognised because of the 'less visible and sensational character of its working'. It was this value that needed to be stressed and upheld.[96] An opening up of these areas,

94. *CWSA* vol.1, op.cit., p. 434.
95. Ibid., p. 436.
96. Ibid., p. 437.

Sri Aurobindo pointed out, would enable the mass-mind to undergo a process of *cittasuddhi* 'or purification of the *citta*, the mind-stuff, from the *prana* full of animal, vital, and emotional disturbances'. For Sri Aurobindo, it was vital for the national education system to direct its focus on the man-making aspect. One does not see him getting into discussing the technicalities of the education system and the areas of reforms required. He was concerned with its deeper psychological and emotional dimensions. This is what led him to enunciate the position that a cultivated eye without a cultivated spirit could not make the 'highest type of man'. The cultivation of the spirit could be brought about precisely through the subjects of language, literature, the Arts, music, painting, sculpture, or the study of philosophy, religion, history, all converging on 'the study and understanding of man through his works and of Nature and man through the interpretative as well as through the analytical faculties'. This was the goal of a 'liberal Education'.[97]

The power of the arts to develop higher faculties, to cultivate the spirit, was clearly recognised by the ideologues of the national education movement. They vigorously discussed the issue and tried to give the subject a place of prominence in the new educational scheme. Invoking the Greek philosophers and the civilisation they ideated, Havell argued that one must realise 'that it is no real education which does not help to develop all the higher imaginative faculties'. They were in agreement that this developing of the higher faculties was being impeded by the governmental education then imparted. 'It is not education,' Havell boldly remarked, 'but the most pernicious pedantry, which uses Western culture to blind the eyes and stop the ears of Indian youth to all that the nature, the art, and the culture of their own country have to teach them'.[98]

97. Ibid., p. 438.

98. *Art and Education in India,* op.cit., pp. 105–108.

Coomaraswamy, for instance, discussing 'Music and Education in India' where he touched upon the necessity and utility of an education in art and culture, similarly invoked Plato and the philosopher's views on the utility and effectivity of music in education which ensured the entry of a harmony 'in the strongest manner into the inward part of the soul'. Coomaraswamy recognised, like his other illustrious contemporaries and co-ideologues, that 'English education, as hitherto imparted and understood in India, has merely ignored the importance of music and art in education'. Unfortunately, there was no educational institution in the country under European guidance where 'Indian music [had] any place whatever in the scheme of education'. And there was no Indian University that recognised Indian music. [99]

That was because, and as Nivedita quoted Havell, 'we, aliens in race, thought and religion, have never taken anything but a dilettante archeological or commercial interest in [Indian art]'. And it's deeper meanings therefore, remained 'hidden from us, and those spiritual longings and desires which come straight from the heart of a people, to find expression in their poetry, music, and their art, strike no chord of sympathy in ours'.[100]

---

99. *Essays in National Idealism,* op. cit., pp. 187–188.
100. *CWSN vol.3,* op.cit., p. 22. Nivedita, on her part, cautioned against the tendency to believe that merely because there still existed 'a living, traditional and national art' in the Indian polity, that there could be the habit to hold on to 'every chance thought and impulse that comes to us artistically, believing that we are divinely inspired in this matter ...'. Just as in the art of logic, so in the field of art, Nivedita advocated a stern and rigorous training in order to develop the right judgment and sense of appreciation. She saw India then going through the 'least hopeful and most chaotic transition' in the field of art. 'European Commercialism' had completely shaken to the roots the race's 'decorative faculty'. If the Indian mind were to emerge from this confusion, a preparation must be initiated by 'building up a great

All of them, Coomaraswamy, Havell, Nivedita, and Sri Aurobindo were to continue to defend this need to re-discover and restate an Indian art. They would continue to argue that India, especially Hindu and Buddhist traditions, supported art and had a magnificent tradition of art, while emphasising the necessity of an art training.[101] The activism and ideas were not confined simply to the days of intense nationalist political action, it was an interest that saw continuous expression.

There was an established effort and Sri Aurobindo, being one of the centres of the nationalist vortex, naturally delved deep into the issue. A gleaning of some of his thoughts in the series provides an interesting insight into his thinking on the issue. Continuing with his discussion on the national value of an art training for the Indian

---

art on a basis of sincere admiration of the truly beautiful for true reasons'. The nationalist art movement and its works such as Havell's, facilitated the growth of the mind's capacity of admiration and of relating 'itself to Indian art'.[Ibid.,] Nivedita was to remain 'a mentor of the Bengali artist [and one of the major moving forces behind their efforts and behind the dissemination of their productions] until her early death' in 1911.[Partha Mitter, op. cit., p. 255]

101. Sri Aurobindo, writing later, devoted four chapters on Indian art in his essays on the Indian renaissance and Havell, in a later work, highlighted the 'ancient Universities of Northern India and their influence on Asiatic Art', discussed the art training given in these ancient institutions and argued that the 'essential faculties of the artist, imagination and memory [given primacy in the Eastern universities] are those which are least considered in the curriculum of modern European academies, where the paraphernalia of the studio are used to make up for the deficiencies in the mental equipment of the student'. [E.B.Havell, *The Ideals of Indian Art,* 1920, p. 41] Naturally, therefore, an art training that ignored the basic tenets of the Indian approach could never restore the aesthetic emotions of the race. What was needed was a different kind of training inspired by the Indian traditions.

mind, Sri Aurobindo spoke of the tendency that ignores art and poetry as mere luxuries of the 'rich and leisurely', with no relevance and necessity to the 'mass of men or useful to life'. To Sri Aurobindo, such a tendency developed largely because the 'luxurious' few held these instruments and the world in their hands during a certain period of human progress.[102] Sri Aurobindo spoke for the subaltern voice. He saw their deprivation, recognised their toil and struggle for existence and demanded that they too must be empowered and enabled to absorb from these subjects. It would, in some measure, mitigate their struggles, ennoble their existence and as a corollary, elevate the national life in a wider way.

Sri Aurobindo also recognised that the 'aesthetic faculties entering into the enjoyment of the world' through the representations of daily life such as 'the beautiful in men and women, in food, in things, in articles of use and articles of pleasure' have done an immense service to elevate man, 'to refine and purge his passions, to ennoble his emotions' and to lead him through the medium of the 'heart and the imagination to the state of the intellectual man'.[103] And that which has elevated man to the intellectual level had to be preserved. The danger of an undeveloped heart and spirit was that it would make man 'intellectually developed, mighty in scientific knowledge and the mastery of gross and subtle nature, using the elements as his servants and the world as his footstool', an 'inferior kind of Asura using the powers of a demigod to satisfy the nature of an animal'.[104] The necessity therefore, of an aesthetic training remained. Sri Aurobindo did not limit the evolution and inclusion of art education as necessary for only the strengthening of national unity; he added to this, his concern for the general 'restoration' of

102. *CWSA* vol.1, op.cit., pp. 438–439.
103. Ibid., p. 439.
104. Ibid.

artistic emotions. He saw the Bengal school of art as capable of creating and restoring this emotion to a great extent nationally.

Elaborating on this and discussing the role of music as part of an aesthetic training in a national system of education, Coomaraswamy also expressed much the same aim. He argued that a 'proper education in music' was generally accepted as 'an invaluable aid in the training of character, [which was] the true aim of education'. The arts, therefore, were to be indispensible aids in the training of character and the cultivation of the spirit. Coomaraswamy extrapolated the link further and set the perspective for a system of aesthetic training in an education that would lead towards self-reliance. He described the primary aim of education in India to be the creation of 'Indian citizens'. The age demanded first a thorough training in Indian citizenship, only then could follow a true citizenship of the world. An immersion in one's roots had to precede any cosmopolitanism, 'no Indian can be a true citizien of the world, except by being first an Indian citizen'.[105] In any case, Coomaraswamy felt, it was 'not the time for cosmopolitanism, it [was] the time when India herself needed Indian citizens'. He saw education in Indian music as an essential part of education in Indian citizenship.[106] Coomaraswamy also spoke of the destruction of the livelihood of instrument artisans, and its economic impact due to the loss of artistic understanding – 'The loss of artistic understanding, more than anything else, has ruined Indian industries and prevents the possibility of their revival'. Coomaraswamy pointed out how the 'neglect of Indian music' had 'taken away the livelihood of the maker of musical instruments, with their hereditary and exquisite skill' and has 'destroyed the livelihood of Indian musicians' while 'fifteen lakhs worth of foreign instruments' was being 'annually

105. *Essays in National Idealism,* op.cit., p. 197.

106. Ibid., pp. 196, 197.

imported from abroad'. Coomaraswamy saw this as a 'double loss', 'material on the one hand' and 'spiritual on the other.'[107]

Havell on his part, staunchly believed in the strength of art to reshape the Indian mind and nationality, and saw a larger role for it in an education that demanded that Indian art, hitherto stifled under official direction and patronage, be set free 'to follow its natural channel'. Once free to develop, Havell argued, it [Indian art] can minister to the spiritual and intellectual needs of India and elevate the 'moral and intellectual faculties' of the Indian students.[108] It was of course, too much to expect that a colonial education system would undertake such liberating measures. The nationalists saw this as the task of the new education they were advocating and thus sought to enshrine art training as an important charter of the new system.

Taking the reader through a gradual analysis of the place and role of aesthetics in human evolution, Sri Aurobindo indicated that one of the highest roles of the artistic sense was the 'direct purifying of the emotions'; he linked the process to that of the Greek *katharsis*. Sri Aurobindo argued that art and poetry had a 'mighty utility' in mitigating the 'pressing claims of the animal in man' and were fields where these claims could be excluded. Emotions, 'working disinterestedly for the satisfaction of the heart and the imagination alone, [could] do the work of *katharsis*, emotional purification' which in the Indian context was *cittasuddhi*, 'the purification of the heart'. It was through such purification that man arrived at a greater fulfillment. Sri Aurobindo argued that if it could be established, as he attempted through his series on the subject, that art and poetry were 'agents' and catalysts towards that end, then their 'supreme importance could be established'. He concluded that these subjects

107. Ibid., p. 5.

108. *Art and Education in India*, op. cit., p. 108.

did that – the purification of emotions – and much more and the habit of looking upon these as mere ornamentations of life reduced them to a secondary rank.

Sri Aurobindo did not limit the utility of the subjects to the promotion of a national unity, he perceived in them a deeper role affecting human conduct and the general psychological, emotional, and spiritual state of being.[109] He perceived in them the capacity to generate a 'sense of the beautiful' in national life.

VII.4. CALL FOR A 'UNIVERSAL PROFICIENCY' IN ART TRAINING: THE DEMOCRATISATION OF AESTHETICS

A detailed reading of each of the ideas on the subject that Sri Aurobindo discusses in the series will, in my opinion, not be necessary for our purpose here. Those which we require for our understanding and reading are the ones that provide fairly accurately his ideas on the place, utility, and role of these subjects in education. Henc, we have been selective in our approach while reading his series on art.

Similar to Coomaraswamy's advocacy of the subject, Sri Aurobindo discussed the role of music in the shaping of a national mentality. He invoked Plato and his Republic in which the thinker 'has dwelt with extraordinary emphasis on the importance of music in education', especially its role in shaping the national character of a people – 'as is the music to which a people is accustomed, so, he [Plato] says in effect, is the character of that people'.[110] And in the same manner, Sri Aurobindo too, saw the importance of painting and sculpture in education. Sri Aurobindo's arguments are relevant to educational systems everywhere. The mind he argued, is 'profoundly influenced by what it sees', and a training of the eyes from childhood 'to the contemplation and understanding of beauty, harmony, and

---

109. *CWSA* vol.1, op.cit., pp. 444–445.

110. Ibid., p. 447.

just arrangement in line and colour, the tastes, habits and character' will capacitate the individual to follow, even later in life, as an adult a 'similar law of beauty, harmony, and just arrangement'.

Sri Aurobindo saw this insistence on developing a 'universal proficiency' in arts in societies such as ancient Greece, 'in certain European ages, in Japan' and in India of a better time. He called for a re-assessment of this ancient tradition and for its revival in the present context. Sri Aurobindo argued that since 'art galleries could not be brought into every home', it would serve the purpose of trying to restore the aesthetic emotion of the race if the 'appointments of our life and furniture of our homes are things of taste and beauty'. Such a situation would perhaps inevitably raise, ennoble, harmonise the habits, thoughts and feelings of the people.[111] This ennobling and harmonisation of emotions could also happen through a regular study 'of beautiful and noble art'. Like poetry, which works towards purifying the heart, spoken of earlier as *cittasuddhi,* painting and sculpture too, do much the same thing in its own manner. It is interesting to read here Sri Aurobindo's analysis of how art – painting, sculpture – train and elevate the emotion.[112]

---

111. Ibid., p. 447.

112 An interesting reference may be given which reveals how Sri Aurobindo himself developed the artistic perspective. Assuaging the lamentations of a disciple, much later he wrote with great humility, 'Don't be desperate about your incapacity as a connoisseur of painting. I was far worse in this respect: knew something about sculpture, but blind to painting. Suddenly, one day in the Alipore jail while meditating, I saw some pictures on the walls of the cell and lo and behold! the artistic eye in me opened and I knew all about painting, except of course the more material side of technique. I don't always know how to express though, because I lack the knowledge of the proper expressions, but that does not stand in the way of a keen and understanding appreciation'.[Sri Aurobindo, *On Himself,* pp.226, 227] The series on art was written a few months after release from prison.

Paintings and sculptures, though they did not possess the movement of poetry and were still, fixed, and were the expressions of only a given moment, used these very attributes to gain a separate value altogether. While poetry 'raises the emotions and gives each its separate delight. Art stills the emotions and teaches them the delight of a restrained and limited satisfaction .... Music deepens the emotions and harmonises them with each other'.[113] Each component of an art and aesthetic education – music, art, poetry – contributed something distinctive to the development of the individual; they are, Sri Aurobindo observed, 'a perfect education for the soul', they keep the individual's emotional tendencies 'purified, self-controlled, deep, and harmonious'. Sri Aurobindo saw these as powerful agents, great civilising, educating and 'edifying forces', if properly used and applied.[114]

Further analysing the effects of an art training and to drive home his point of their efficacy, Sri Aurobindo talked of the 'double character of intellectual activity', divided between the 'imaginative, creative, and sympathetic' on the one side and the 'critical, analytic, and penetrative on the other'. The latter, he saw, as 'best trained' through science, criticism, and observation and the former 'by art, poetry, music, literature, and the sympathetic study of man and his creations'.[115] He saw art as a 'powerful stimulator of sympathetic insight' because it raised images that have to be understood not by analysis but through 'a self-identification with other minds'. Art being 'subtle and delicate' made the mind subtle and delicate, it is 'suggestive' and thus, a mind trained in the appreciation of art 'is quick to catch suggestions'. It is an instrument that opens the individual to ways of deeper self-knowledge.

113. *CWSA* vol.1, op.cit., pp. 447, 448.

114. Ibid., p. 448.

115. Ibid., p. 449.

This supreme value of art was never sufficiently recognised by those who made language, poetry, history, and philosophy, instruments for training the imaginative, sympathetic, and the creative side of intellectuality. They made these, Sri Aurobindo argued, obligatory parts of a liberal education without duly recognising the 'immense educative force of music, painting and sculpture'. They were treated, as he interestingly put it, as 'by-paths' which were interesting and beautiful but not as essential for the vast majority, and thus to be kept confined to a limited few. Yet there persisted an almost 'universal impulse to enjoy the beauty and attractiveness of sound, to look at and live among pictures, colours [and] forms'.[116] But this impulse, Sri Aurobindo observed, was not given adequate recognition and was thus denied proper scope for a greater working. A national art training or education would thus have to base itself first on the recognition of the existence of that impulse.

Arguing that if art were to reach its highest expression the 'Indian tendency' would have to dominate, Sri Aurobindo briefly described the Indian concept and practice of art as manifested in India's civilisational expressions. We see him expounding like his contemporaries Coomaraswamy and Havell, on the metaphysical bases of Indian art through the ages.

In Europe, Sri Aurobindo wrote, it was well recognised that there was this close connection of art with religion. The productions of art in Greece, [Renaissance] Italy and India have mostly given expressions to religious thoughts and have adorned temples and other such instruments of national religion. Sri Aurobindo referred to the aims and ideals of Indian art, dilated on what he meant by a spiritual aspiration and growth, and described the qualities of art as an aid in that growth and quest. His words require to be quoted *in extenso*:

116. Ibid., pp. 449, 450.

This [art giving expression to religious thoughts] was not because Art is necessarily associated with the outwards forms of religion, but because it was in the religion that men's spiritual aspirations centred themselves. Spirituality is a wider thing than formal religion and it is in the service of spirituality that Art reaches its highest self-expression. Spirituality is a single word expressive of three lines of human aspiration towards divine knowledge, divine love and joy, divine strength, and that will be the highest and most perfect Art which, while satisfying the physical requirements of the aesthetic sense, the laws of formal beauty, the emotional demand of humanity, the portrayal of life and the outward reality, as the best of European art satisfies these requirements, reaches beyond them, and expresses inner spiritual truth, the deeper not obvious reality of things, the joy of God in the world and its beauty and desirableness and the manifestation of divine force and energy in phenomenal creation. This is what Indian Art alone attempted thoroughly...'[117]

While doing this, Indian art, Sri Aurobindo pointed out, often dispensed with the more material, but not necessarily unimportant, expressions that European art focused upon. And it was this approach to techniques and expressions of art that has created the two divergent streams of European [read Western] and Asian art. This Asian tendency in art was for a long while imperfectly appreciated by the West, and Sri Aurobindo saw this eventually develop in one 'grandiose flood of artistic self-expression perfecting the aesthetic evolution of humanity'.[118]

There was this distinction made that Indian art did not go so much for naturalism, it attempted to portray something deeper apparently hidden to the common sight. As Nolini Kanta Gupta (1889–1984), close political, literary and spiritual associate of Sri Aurobindo analysed it, the art of the East rejected the 'scheme of

117. Ibid., p. 450.

118. Ibid., p. 451. For a further discussion from the Aurobindonian perspective on the Indian tendency in art see eg. Nolini Kanta Gupta's 'The Standpoint of Indian Art' in *Collected Works of Nolini Kanta Gupta* (*CWNKG vol.1*, 1989, pp. 175–180.

sense-perceptions'. The artist within this fold first sought 'to get a focus within the mind, to discover a psychological stand-point, and from there in accordance with ... conventions of inner vision create a world .... The aim was always to build from within, at the most, from within outwards, but not from without, not even from without inwards...'[119]

The Indian point of view in art was a much discussed and debated issue of the period. What was it? How was it explained? Coomaraswamy delving into the issue, was rich and illustrative in his examples in trying to explain the inner vision of the Indian artist and his practice of contemplating on it. He drew an analogy between the 'methods of the Indian worshipper and the Indian artist'. The true artist, for Coomaraswamy, was one who did 'not "compose" (put-together) his picture but "sees" it'. And his desire is 'to represent his vision in the material terms of light and colour'. To great painters, says Coomaraswamy, these vision come crowding and in a continuous stream, and the painter has to possess the ability to still these, dwell on them, and give them expression, and it is here that his approach is like the worshipper. As the worshipper daily adoring his *Ishta Devatā* – 'the special aspect of divinity that is to him all' – first through the 'recitation of the brief mnemonic *mantram* detailing His [*Ishta Devatā's*] attributes, and then in silent concentration of thought upon the corresponding mental image.[120]

Similar are the mental images that the artist sees, and the process of visualization. Invoking the sage Sukrācārya's *Sukranitisāra*, which contains almost the 'whole philosophy of Indian art', Coomaraswamy argued that the 'method of visualization upon the imager' was enjoined by this particular text, which asked the artist and sculptor to 'establish images in temples by meditation on the deities who are objects of his devotion'. It called upon the artist to enter into

119. *CWNKG vol.1*, p. 175.

120. *Essays in National Idealism*, op. cit., pp. 20, 21.

'*dhyāna yoga* (yoga of contemplation)' and went on to describe the method, elements and characteristics of the image. The objective of Indian art has never been 'mere representation of nature'. And no truly Indian sculpture can be said to have been created direct from living models.

The inability of the West to appreciate and comprehend Indian art and the consequent criticism of its expressions, Coomaraswamy pointed out, stemmed from the habit of trying to look for 'something to recognise' in a work of art. And a failure to identify that something recognisable, and if the 'representation is of something they [the viewer] have not seen, or symbolises some unfamiliar abstract idea' it is seen as 'untrue to nature' and therefore self-condemned.[121]

The Indian tendency in art never had as its object the 'reproductions of the external forms of nature', in fact it 'is essentially religious [and its] conscious aim is the intimation of Divinity'. It is an attempt at expressing this deeper truth through symbolism. *Sukrācārya's* doctrine was quite explicit – 'the aim of the highest art must always be the intimation of the Divinity behind all form, rather than the imitation of the form itself'. Krishna's play with the Gopis is a favourite depiction of Indian art panels but it is always done in 'a spirit of religious idealism, [and] not for the sake of the sensuous imagery itself'.[122] These were the basic issues that were highlighted in order to explain the uniqueness of the Indian approach to art, an approach that was, the ideologues felt, being systematically erased by the dominance of the Western perspective and understanding of art.

But why look at all at the Indian tendency in art? It was because, as Sri Aurobindo argued, this tendency would be a dominating dimension in the new training that the nationalists advocated.

121. Ibid., p. 23.

122. Ibid., pp. 23, 27, 31.

Without the dominance of this tendency in an Indian art training, the whole exercise would never reflect the Indian ethos and psyche. It would merely be the developing of another technique devoid of the Indianness and incapable of expressing the Indian mind and its emotions.

Thus, Sri Aurobindo saw an enormous potential in art as a medium of opening the national life to higher thoughts and expressions. His following observation, perhaps, best illustrates the reason for his deep concern with the subject:

> Art can express eternal truth, it is not limited to the expression of form and appearance. So wonderfully has God made the world that a man using a simple combination of lines, an unpretentious harmony of colours, can raise this apparently insignificant medium to suggest absolute and profound truths with a perfection which language labours with difficulty to reach. What Nature is, what God is, what man is can be triumphantly revealed in stone or on canvas...[123]

This perhaps best explains the Indian approach to art.

In this series, Sri Aurobindo principally discussed the enormous value of art to human evolution. What, then, of its value 'as a factor in education'? Sri Aurobindo's stand was that no nation could afford to neglect 'an element of such high importance', an element that has great importance to the cultural life of the people and to the training of the 'higher intellectual, moral, and aesthetic faculties of the young'.

A system of education that recognised this importance and refused to keep artistic training reserved for the specialist few and introduced it 'as a part of culture', equally in importance as science or literature, would have taken a major step forward in the 'perfection of national education and the diffusion of a broad-based human culture'.[124] Sri Aurobindo thus called for art and the

---

123. *CWSA* vol.1, op. cit., p. 451.

124. Ibid., p. 453.

training of artistic appreciation to be diffused and not limited to the privileged few. He did not argue for art education to be imparted in order to make every man an artist; Sri Aurobindo's emphasis was on a general diffusion of the artistic impulse:

> ... [every man should have] his artistic faculty developed, his taste trained, his sense of beauty and insight into form and colour, made habitually active, correct and sensitive. It is necessary that those who create, whether in great things or small, whether in the unusual masterpieces of art and genius or in the small common things of use that surround a man's daily life, should be habituated to produce and the nation habituated to expect the beautiful in preference to the ugly, the noble in preference to the vulgar, the fine in preference to the crude, the harmonious in preference to the gaudy. A nation surrounded daily by the beautiful, noble, fine and harmonious becomes that which it is habituated to contemplate...[125]

Sri Aurobindo saw art as having a fundamental service to render in a national scheme of education and every man and not the few, would have to be covered by its sweep. It was a demand for the democratisation of a very important aspect of human development in education and it was made when the subaltern was as yet unable to speak.

On this need for surrounding the daily by the beautiful and noble, Ananda Coomaraswamy lamented how that approach was destroyed, 'modern India, Anglicised India, has produced no beauty and romance which are our heritage from the past .... Have you ever thought that India, politically and economically free, subdued by Europe in her inmost soul is scarcely an ideal to be dreamt of, or to live, or die, for? India, vulgarised by modern education, and by the ideals of modern commercialism, will never compensate humanity for India with its knowledge of beauty'.[126] He saw this loss of beauty as indicative of our love for India. He put it somewhat emotionally,

---

125. Ibid.
126. Ananda Coomaraswamy, *Art & Swadeshi*, op.cit., pp. 2,3.

'You see, this loss of beauty in our lives is a proof that we do not love India; for India, above all nations, was beautiful once, and that was not long ago'.[127]

Talking of the effort made by the national education system in Bengal, Sri Aurobindo argued that though a beginning was made in this direction by the importance attached to 'drawing and clay-modelling as elements of manual training', the 'artistic ideal' was missing. The limited understanding and misconception of the true aim of manual training, lack of resources, the eventual dominance of the commercial aim in education, of 'English ideas, English methods and English predilections' rendered the whole effort ineffective.

The formal and the mechanical English method was useless for evoking and training the development of an 'inward vision of the relation and truth of things, an eye quick to note and distinguish, sensitive to design and to harmony in colour',[128] all attributes that were essential manifestations of a sustained artistic training.

However, writing in 1909, Sri Aurobindo saw the revival of a 'truly national Art' as an already accomplished fact producing masterpieces that were comparable to the best work of other countries. The nationalist art movement had gained momentum by then. Sri Aurobindo also criticised, as unpardonable, the continued subsistence of the 'crude formal teaching of English schools and the vulgar commercial aims and methods of the West'. Their persistence indicated that the country was 'yet to evolve a system of education which shall be really national'. For Sri Aurobindo, that task yet remained to be accomplished: alien and unsuitable methods and the 'taint of Occidental ideals' had to be removed from the national mind and nowhere was it more urgent than in the field of education

127. Ibid., p. 4.
128. *CWSA* vol.1, op.cit., p. 454.

which must ultimately become the 'foundation of intellectual and aesthetic renovation'.

It is in this task that the resuscitation of the spirit of old Indian art must be accomplished, the 'dexterity of the Indian hand and the intuitive gaze of the Indian eye must be recovered' and then the whole nation, argued Sri Aurobindo, would see an elevation to the 'high level of the ancient culture' and perhaps even surpass that some day.[129]

129. Ibid.

8

Some Observations and Philosophical Hints on the Effort towards National Education

An Assessment

"

The true basis of education is the study of the human mind, infant, adolescent and adult. Any system of education founded on theories of academical perfection, which ignores the instrument of study, is more likely to hamper and impair intellectual growth than to produce a perfect and perfectly equipped mind. For the educationist has to do, not with dead material like the artist or sculptor, but with an infinitely subtle and sensitive organism. He cannot shape an educational masterpiece out of human wood or stone; he has to work in the elusive substance of mind and respect the limits imposed by the fragile human body.

– **Sri Aurobindo,**
***A System of National Education*, 1910**

Some of the final thoughts that Sri Aurobindo articulated before his departure for Pondicherry were made in the pages of the *Karmayogin*. We have discussed a number of them. Among Sri Aurobindo's final discussion on national education was a severe indictment of the whole effort. By 1910, the effort in reforming the official university system, especially undertaken by its dynamic Vice-Chancellor Asutosh Mukherjee (1864–1924) saw a number of demands that were raised by nationalist educators and thought-leaders of the national education movement being fulfilled.

The introduction of a 'compulsory paper in Bengali, the opening of postgraduate teaching departments, an imaginative emphasis on research', the revision and expansion of subjects like history and the gathering of great talents addressed some of the basic criticisms that the nationalists levelled against the official system.[1] One of Asutosh Mookerjee's 'greatest achievements' was to 'give Bengali its due place in the University studies'. Following a prolonged discussion and controversy, 'the principle of adopting the mother-tongue as the medium of instruction was adopted' and 'Bengali was included as a subject for study and research in the highest University examinations, and the scheme for systematic publication of important works in Bengali and other languages was taken up'.[2]

---

1. Sumit Sarkar, op.cit., p. 170, Susobhan Sarkar, 'The National Council of Education' in *On the Bengal Renaissance*, 2003, p. 127.
2. Syama Prasad Mookerjee, *Sir Asutosh: Creator of the Modern Calcutta University*, op.cit., p. 23.

Asutosh encouraged research in a variety of subjects and insisted on examining these from the Indian perspective. Under him, the Calcutta University eventually 'stood for comparative autonomy, freedom from State control as far as was possible', and the emphasis was also on 'the study of the mother-tongue in an attempt to nationalize education…'.[3] Asutosh argued that all universities in India would have to eventually evolve as centres for 'the cultivation and advancement of knowledge'.[4] To him, this was 'unquestionably the true ideal of a university, and the realisation of this stimulating ideal' was imperative. 'Among the brightest signs of a vigorous university', Asutosh told a convocation of the Calcutta University, was 'its zeal for the advancement of learning, and the true function of a university' was not 'merely the distribution of knowledge, but its acquisition and conservation'. [5] In his opinion, 'the most essential feature of university life' was 'absolute academic freedom'. Education to him was religion, and 'freedom was the very breath of its existence' and the part that universities were called upon or expected to play in the life of a nation, could be 'adequately be fulfilled only in an atmosphere of perfect freedom' – it was this which would keep a university alive. For Asutosh, universities in India would have to evolve into national organisations, 'self-reliant' and 'bound in service to the nation', adapting to the 'manifold and varying needs of the community, from generation to generation'.[6] The changes he introduced in the curriculum were of a 'fundamental character' driven by the conviction that 'a combination of research

---

3. Priya Ranjan Sen, 'Western Education' in *Studies in the Bengal Renaissance*, op.cit., p. 351.
4. Lalitmohan Chatterjee & Syama Prasad Mookerjee, *Representative Indians*, Published by A.C. Dhar, Calcutta: Popular Agency, 1931, p. 115.
5. Ibid., p. 115.
6. Ibid., p. 127.

and teaching was the inalienable basic principle of a university'.[7] He realised that the Indian universities had 'contributed exceedingly little towards the advance and increase of knowledge'.[8]

A variety of educational initiatives were undertaken in Asutosh's tenure. For instance, Special Readership lectures in different subjects 'helped create an atmosphere of research'. Experts from across India and abroad were invited to deliver these. Lectures delivered varied from Buddhism to 'Methods of Western scholarship in the field of ancient Indian research', from mathematics, mechanical physics to theories of Indian rhetoric, from 'astronomies of ancient oriental nations' to 'kinship in early law'. A wide array of thinkers and specialists such as Russian historian Paul Vinogradoff, German Indologist and professor of Sanskrit at Bonn, Hermann Jacobi, British Mathematician Andrew R Forsyth, German Indologist and professor at Gottingen, Hermann Oldenburg, among others, delivered these at regular intervals. 'Dinesh Chandra Sen's lectures on the history of Bengali language and literature marked the beginning of a new line of enquiry'.[9]

Stalwarts such as Brajendra Nath Seal, Upendra Nath Brahmachari also received their doctorate degrees between 1909 and 1910. Each would eventually leave their mark in creating the new Indian narrative in their respective fields. Scientific leaders such as S.P. Agharkar were appointed Rashbehari Ghose Professor of Chemistry, while C.V. Raman, who would attain an iconic status in the history of Indian science, was appointed Palit Professor of Physics by Asutosh. A 'band of brilliant young men began their career as lecturers and as research workers'. Meghnad Saha and Satyendra

7. Narendra Krishna Sinha, *Asutosh Mookerjee: a Biographical Study*, 1966, p. 77.
8. Ibid., p. 78.
9. Ibid., p. 80.

Nath Bose, to name a few, were destined to play defining roles in the world of Science and in shaping India's scientific destiny.[10] A nationalist at heart who genuinely supported and sympathised with the national education movement, and saw the need for Indian educational experiments to survive and grow, Asutosh extended his support to Rabindranath Tagore and his Visva Bharati. He drew up a framework of cooperation between Visva Bharati and Calcutta University, 'maintaining intact the complete academic freedom of Visva Bharati. Although the Indian Universities Act did not make such a cooperation possible'. An arrangement was worked out by Asutosh which ensured that for over three decades Visva Bharati could work as an institution where 'work of a special kind was being accomplished and at the same time its students were being permitted to sit at the examinations of the University of Calcutta'.[11]

The Sadler Commission of 1917, headed by the British educationist Michael Sadler, to look into the state of Indian education was 'profoundly shocked by the state of Indian education'. Following 'an exhaustive enquiry', Sadler and his colleagues of the 'Calcutta University Commission (1917–1919), found the University system of Bengal' to be 'fundamentally defective in almost every aspect'.[12] Asutosh Mookerjee was a member of the Sadler Commission which held that 'many of its findings were his personal contribution'.[13]

The Sadler Commission's observations reflected its shock at the state of Indian education. It expressed its strong sympathy

10. Ibid., pp. 82–85.
11. Syama Prasad Mookerjee, in the Debate on the Visva Bharati Bill, 1st May 1951, Parliament of India.
12. Aparna Basu, *Essays in the History of Indian Education*, 1982, p. 12.
13. Priya Ranjan Sen, 'Western Education', op.cit., p. 351.

with 'the view that one of the greatest needs of India is more education, widely spread throughout the community'. It spoke of the need for 'well-staffed primary schools' which would bring 'a new stimulus to the mass of the population by means of training, liberal in spirit and yet adapted to the conditions under which the vast majority of the pupils must afterward seek livelihood'. The Commission insisted on a comprehensive revamping of secondary education and emphasised the value of 'an all-round development of physique, mind, and character' and also not being forgetful of the 'practical needs of modern life'. It proposed to create technological institutions, professional schools, which would be 'popular in their sympathies, exacting in their standards, many-sided in their courses of study, staffed by able teachers'. It suggested that the chief aim of educational institutions in India should be to 'democratise knowledge'.[14]

The national education movement and the education unrest, and experimentation that it generated, had called for a fundamental change in educational structure and approach. The education movement was a channel of the wider movement for freedom. The nationalist intelligentsia, as discussed, saw this education structure as ineffective and incapable of furthering the movement for national reconstruction. It was seen to be hampering and obstructing the expressions of such an aspiration and action. It was felt to be 'dogmatic in its character, restrictive in its operation, meaninglessly elaborate in its method and wasteful in its results' and not 'animated by any high social ideals or principles of progress'. Patrick Geddes, of whom we have seen earlier, termed such an education as 'miseducation'. It had become evident to the nationalist education thinkers that if the programme of social reconstruction, through

14. *Selected Chapters of the Report of the Calcutta University Commission*, 1919, p. 137.

which India could regain her rightful place among the nations of the world, was to be realised, 'a sound system of national education, Indian in its character and universal in its interests' was 'absolutely essential', and had to 'precede all other reform'.[15]

Asutosh's educational reform and action in the University of Calcutta responded to a number of these issues articulated by the national education movement. Asutosh's biographer, argues, how through a 'gradual process' of 'reconstruction and reform', Asutosh was determined to 'realise his great ideal and fulfil his cherished dream of reviving the glories of Nalanda and Vicramsila – he was bent upon making his alma mater an instrument of the intellectual regeneration of his countrymen', and 'the task that confronted him at once called forth the best qualities of a shrewd and firm administrator, a courageous reformer, a far-seeing statesman and a profound idealist and patriot'.[16] Asutosh worked for the 'Return Movement' in India, as his biographer put it, and laboured to bring about a 'wide ranging Indian Renaissance, an intellectual regeneration through a nation-wide progress of education...'.[17]

Asutosh's dream was, recollected Syama Prasad Mookerjee, 'to make his country intellectually free and pre-eminent, to see education spread from town to town, village to village, home to home, an education that would not denationalise his countrymen, but would combine in it the best elements of Eastern and Western thought...'. [18]

---

15. K.M.Pannikar, *Essays on Education Reconstruction in India*, 1920, pp. 4,8.
16. Probodh Chandra Sinha, *Sir Asutosh Mookerjee: a Study*, 1928, p. 183. See this for a detailed study of Asutosh Mookerjee's life and especially in his educational and public actions.
17. Ibid., p. xx.
18. Syama Prasad, *Sir Asutosh: Creator of the Modern Calcutta University*, op.cit., p. 25.

This reformatory effort, since it was official, did not recognise the demand for a wholly new national education, but it did respond to, and gave a push to Indianise research and open its portals to young Indian nationalist scholars who would, over decades, contribute to shaping the Indian ideational narrative. This was largely and primarily because of the push Asutosh Mookerjee gave it. Our intention here, as stated earlier, is not to enter into a statistical analysis of the physical remnants of the national education movement, but rather to look at its later intellectual understanding and assessment by those leaders who were active in popularising and seeding the idea in the national mind. This leads us to briefly read Sri Aurobindo's reassessment of the whole effort and of the idea of national education itself.

In concluding his observations on the national education effort, Sri Aurobindo wrote in January 1910 that the nationalist element by its energy, courage, and 'boldness of thought' had provided the national education movement with its sustaining base, force, and vitality. Its withdrawal led to the collapse of the movement and the distancing of the new education bodies from the nationalist movement.[19]

After such hectic efforts and such favourable enunciations of a national education system, Sri Aurobindo saw it languish because of its artificial disassociation from its fecundating force which was the larger struggle for freedom. It still lingered because 'certain amount of Nationalist self-devotion [had] entrenched itself in this last stronghold and [held] it against great odds'.[20] Benoy Kumar Sarkar's national educational experiment in Malda, in north Bengal, ran successfully and a number of national schools were established, especially in the eastern districts of Bengal. But these functioned

19. *CWSA* vol.8, op.cit., p. 385.

20. Vide. *Sumit Sarkar,* op.cit., pp. 177–180.

under financial strain and fear of political persecution by the administration. It will be useful to briefly read Sarkar's creative effort at running the national school in Malda. Sarkar founded the Malda Jatiya Shiksa Samiti (Malda National Education Council) in June 1906.[21]

The Malda Council's activity report in 1911 showed that it was active and had 'made fair progress all around'. The arrangement to study scientific subjects had been improved, 'the Primary and Secondary schools managed and controlled' by the Council had 'secured the sympathy of the public', and there was an increase in both students and patrons. The 'Literary Research Department' of the Malda National Education Council had also been able to produce several 'publications of historical, linguistic, and educational importance' and systematic efforts were 'being made to promote research and original investigations' and scholars and fellows were appointed to carry out this work.[22] Interestingly, 'four student-teachers of the schools under the District Council' were 'sent to America to complete their education in the University of Wisconsin'.[23] The National School at Sanihati, in the district of Dhaka, for instance, which was affiliated to the Malda Council, had a well-equipped and functioning carpentry section which well supplied customers in the region. The institution saw steady increase of students and its 'free school for girls' also performed well.[24]

Scientific, technical and ordinary instruction was provided to a large number of students as well. To make education accessible

21. Banesvar Dass, *The Social and Economic Ideas of Benoy Kumar Sarkar*, op.cit., 1940, p. 199.
22. Ibid., p. 200.
23. Ibid.
24. Ibid., pp. 200, 201.

to every home, the Council had also started the 'movement for the establishment of night schools'. For training students in higher education, the Council's scheme of training included, besides a 'comprehensive intellectual culture at home and school, regular practical education through taking part in the organisation of village education'.[25] 'Since its inception, Benoy Sarkar had also inspired the Malda Council to found a literary research department for the study of antiquities, culture, and social and economic institutions of the district'.[26]

Under Sarkar's tutelage, the Council had succeeded in establishing a functioning research department with the involvement of a number of promising scholars, and produced a number of research papers and monographs with a focus on studying Indian antiquities and history from the Indian point of view. Works such as 'The Propagation of Hindu Literature', 'A Scheme for Fostering Indian Vernacular Literature', 'The Lines of Industrial Advance in India', 'Small Industries', 'Bhikshu Pratimoksha', translation of Saundarananda (Buddhist Sanskrit Work), 'Shipping Industry at Gauda', 'Ramavati – the capital of the Pala Kings of Bengal', 'The Hindu University – what it means', were some treatises which were published from this centre.[27] Among the advisers of the research centre were Satish Chandra Mukherjee, C.R. Das, Bepin Chandra Pal, Major B.D. Basu, Rabindranath Tagore, Brajendranath Seal, and Rakha Das Banerji, who would later discover the Indus civilisation, all of them thought-leaders of their era and field.[28] In his copious and prolific intellectual corpus, Sarkar had written much, in his early days defining the aims of

25. Ibid, p. 204.
26. Ibid., p. 201.
27. Ibid., p. 207.
28. Ibid., p. 208.

national education. To Sarkar the objects of national education were:

> On the intellectual side, to enable students to think independently and carry on original researches; on the moral side, to evoke in them a desire of work for work's sake, and also a genuine desire to serve their country even at the sacrifice of their personal interests .... On the material side, to enable them to earn their livelihood by the creation of new openings .... The most striking feature of the new educational movement [was] that the boys [were] taught, even in the college classes, in their mother-tongue .... It saves the learner's time [and] prevents the strain on his health by not requiring unnecessary and undue attention to the difficulties and technicalities of a foreign tongue ... [29]

Finally, as Sarkar pointed out, since the National Education system wanted to 'develop the powers of each student's brain and to draw out his own latent capabilities', it did force on them in Degree classes 'one and the same multiplicity of subjects', it allowed the students to 'choose subjects according to their special aptitudes and inclinations'.[30]

Sarkar saw this new educational approach having the objective of training the student to become a 'discoverer of truths', 'pioneer of learning', and 'morally, organiser of institutions and a leader of men'.[31] But such systematic training in the new educational approach, as had been undertaken by Sarkar's national education council in Malda, could not see successful replication in other parts. The success of this experiment, at least for a while, was largely due to Benoy Sarkar's efforts and his comprehensive and institutional elaboration of the philosophy of national education. In the majority of the cases, the national education institutions suffered

---

29. Banesvar Dass, *The Social and Economic Ideas of Benoy Kumar Sarkar*, p. 470.
30. Ibid.
31. Ibid., p. 267.

from a number of challenges and infirmities, and in the absence of an educational organiser and philosopher such as Sarkar, failed to create a solid foundation. These have been discussed in earlier sections.

Apart from pursuing the old method in its curriculum, Sri Aurobindo counted the 'financial problem' as having created a 'crushing difficulty'.[32] The inability of the technical college, which had separated from the main Council, to lay a sturdy foundation and to mobilise resources, was another indication that people in general were as yet unwilling to acquiesce to an education that was 'divorced from [a] general humanistic training, which is essential to national culture'.[33]

The Council, it appeared to Sri Aurobindo, was willing to grapple with only two problems – the first was 'the problem of supporting National Education without incurring the wrath of the officials' and the second, 'the problem of evading the spirit of the clause which [forbade] it to subject itself to any form of Government control, while observing the letter, so as to prevent the invalidation of its endowments'.[34] The reason for the movement and its physical manifestation, the Council, developing a staid status-quoist tendency was, Sri Aurobindo argued, because of the extrusion due to

32. *CWSA* vol.8, op.cit., pp. 387, 388.
33. Ibid., p. 386. The majority who did not finally opt for the national educational institution were driven by the concern of a career. It would appear that the urge for a humanistic training that the national schools offered was not sufficiently alluring. The national institutions also did not have sufficient time for consolidation. Referring to Sri Aurobindo's observation that the technical college failed to gather momentum because of lack of support indicating that people in general did not accept a training divorced from the humanistic dimension of education.
34. *CWSA* vol.8., p. 388.

fear and other motives, of those, who through an 'active enthusiasm and self-sacrifice created the movement', and the abandoning of it by some who were disgusted to witness the movement degenerate in some incapable hands. Those who still continued with the effort found their chances of success weakened because of this confusion and incapacity at the head-quarters.[35]

Sri Aurobindo believed the deeper psychological reason for the movement's degeneration was because it had disconnected itself from the larger nationalist movement which was basically its sustaining force.[36] If the effort at remedying the situation, of restructuring the Council and of altering its character and of infusing the effort with 'keener blood was seen to be impossible', then, argued Sri Aurobindo, 'some other centre of effort must be created,' which would undertake to grapple with the problems of National Education.

This new centre would have to ensure 'a flow of trained and self-devoted teachers and of books which will guide them in imparting of knowledge on new lines'. It would also have to, eventually, work on the 'reawakening of interest, hope, and enthusiasm in the country', and arrange for 'the provision of the necessary funds to the *mofussil* schools...',[37] while forcing the Council, through pressure of public opinion, to adopt a more 'rational and national system of teaching'. But the first condition of success in this work was the 'reawakening of the national movement all along the line', and this could only be

35. Ibid., p. 386.
36. It was perhaps because, when the time came, the 'National Council did not act with sufficient daring,' restrained by the 'ultra-caution of the Moderates'. The favourable momentum seemed to have passed and a refusal to flow with it had, in a sense, caused an irretrievable setback. [Susobhan Sarkar, *op.cit.,* p. 128] Sri Aurobindo's argument too pointed at losing the advantage of the momentum.
37. *CWSA* vol.8., pp. 388, 389.

done by the reorganising and reinitiating of a 'resolute activity of the Nationalist party', whose principal programme would be the shaping of a nationalist agenda of education.

Around this time, writing a review of an article, *'Shantiniketane Rabindranath'* (Rabindranath in Santiniketan), by the historian, iconographer and later author of *The Development of Hindu Iconograhy*, Jatindranath Banerji, Sri Aurobindo spoke of the 'remarkable educational experiment which this original mind [Tagore] is developing in the quiet shades of Bolpur' and referred to 'the moral training and the method of education followed at Santiniketan' which indicated 'a system far in advance of the National Council of Education which is still tyrannised over by a tradition and method not only European, but also unprogressively European'.[38] These words described his reading of the methods followed by the nodal institution set-up to direct the new education system.

An alternate centre of educational effort which could guide the imparting of knowledge on new lines could not be created, and the reawakening of the national movement could not immediately happen. The Nationalist party too, under severe repression, underwent a period of reassessment and reinvention and was therefore not in a position to launch a nationwide movement or to spearhead the national education movement.[39]

By April 1910, Sri Aurobindo himself would leave the shores of Bengal, ceasing his direct and active participation with political activity of any kind. He thus could not carry forward the new

38. *CWSA* vol.1, p. 566.

39. For an assessment of the political situation in which the nationalists found themselves see eg. *Autobiographical Notes*, op. cit., pp. 60–62, A.B. Purani, *The Life of Sri Aurobindo*, 2006, pp. 124–127, Peter Heehs, *Sri Aurobindo a Brief Biography*, op.cit., pp. 60–66.

direction that he wished to give to the educational movement. Thus by 1910, the national education movement had lost momentum. True, but what then of its philosophy? Were there some ideas, some retrospective thought of its leaders and organisers which could provide a perspective to the direction this course had pursued, or could pursue again? Did the quest for a philosophy of national education cease altogether, or did the ideas generated during this quest continue to inspire and generated debate? A comprehensive or detailed answer to all of these is difficult. The future did not see such a comprehensive and wide-ranging debate on the issue of national education. This first quest, even though it had failed to implement and bring about lasting changes in Indian education had, at least, laid the intellectual and philosophical base for the educational ideas, spawned by the national education movement, to be carried on.

Some of the sternest critics of the national education movement were also some of its leading participants.[40] In their quest to formulate a philosophy of national education the lead participants did not lose the habit of constantly engaging with the ideas that the movement based itself on, or threw up at intervals.

Sri Aurobindo also undertook such a retrospective assessment and reformulation of the nationalist education attempt. For a reading of that, a decadal leap – exceeding our stated time-framework – will have to be taken to November-December 1920 and January 1921, the last days of Sri Aurobindo's philosophical journal '*Arya*'. In the last two numbers of the journal, Sri Aurobindo began a 'Preface on National Education', which gave insights into his rethinking of the theme of national education in India and its future expressions. This series contains, in a concise form, hints on his

40. *Sabyasachi Bhattacharya,* op.cit., p. xxiii.

perceptions of a philosophy of national education and, like most of his other writings on education we have discussed, these too remain incomplete. However, by the time the series was discontinued, they had enumerated a number of key areas in the educational thought. I have deliberately left out of our discussion Sri Aurobindo's series, 'A System of National Education – some preliminary ideas' (written in the *Karmayogin* in 1910). These writings were Sri Aurobindo's final views on national education before retirement and instead of dwelling on them exclusively, I have examined these ideas, along with those of other nationalist educators who were Sri Aurobindo's contemporaries or near contemporaries. They were either originators of the national education movement or its active participants and shapers as well.

I have tried to portray a bit of the background of the age and time when Sri Aurobindo began his early ruminations on education. I have continued to trace Sri Aurobindo's ideas on education, his actions in the field in support of the effort to evolve a national system of education, and through it all I have attempted to sketch an intellectual background of the age which generated the debate and in which the debate saw actualisation. The attempt has been to trace some key thoughts on national education that were articulated by an array of dominant minds of that age. These were thoughts that would give insights into their philosophical approach to the issue of national education, into the world of their educational thought, and would, in general, sketch a contour of the entire quest for a philosophy of national education.

As argued in the introduction, Sri Aurobindo's systematic writings on education which appeared first in the *Karmayogin* in 1910, and were later reprinted in 1924 in an authorised version, have been extensively studied, read, discussed, and analysed by many in the last nearly five decades, especially since the inception of the Centre of Education bearing his name in Pondicherry. I have therefore avoided re-reading them since doing so would not impart anything innovative or original. Some of these treatises have been produced by stalwarts who had themselves been active participants in the educational experiment inspired by Sri Aurobindo's educational vision.[41] A number of these practitioners of Sri Aurobindo's education philosophy have been referred to and explored in the work.

Those looking for an exposition of Sri Aurobindo's educational philosophy may perhaps be disappointed by my approach which has basically tried to study and collate the ideas and the age which shaped and inspired the quest for national education by placing Sri Aurobindo in its centre and at the periphery.

But it would be useful, in conclusion, to have a brief look at Sri Aurobindo's reassessment and reformulation of national education and through these, read some of his philosophical perspectives on the theme.

With the advantage of hindsight and uninterrupted literary and philosophical output, Sri Aurobindo undertook a reassessment of the national education movement. One of the reasons for

---

41. Eg. Pavitra, *Education and the Aim of Human Life*, 1961; Kireet Joshi, Yvonne Artaud, *Exploration in Education – Two Essays*, 1974; Jugal Kishore Mukherjee, *Principles and Goals of Integral Education*, 2005; Nolini Kanta Gupta, *Shikkha O Dikkha* (1926), (translated as *Education and Initiation*, 2003; Norman C. Dowsett, 'The New Approach to Education' in *A New Approach to Education*, 1974; Sanat. K. Banerji, 'The New Approach to Education in India' in *A New Approach to Education*, 1974; K.R. Srinivasa Iyengar, *Sri Aurobindo: a Biography & History*, 1985; *Sri Aurobindo and the Mother on Physical Education*, 1996; The Mother, *Education Part I-III*, 1997–2002; Sri Aurobindo and The Mother on Education, 2006; Indrani Sanyal & Anirban Ganguly, *Education: Philosophy & Practice*, 2011; etc.

undertaking a broad- based discussion of Sri Aurobindo's thoughts on national education was also to argue that Sri Aurobindo did preserve a continuous concern for the theme, idea, and expression of national education. His efforts in the winter of 1920, when he was more than a decade into political retirement, in writing a preface on national education amply proves that position. He must have continuously felt the imperativeness of a concerted definition and action on national education for India's freedom to be attained and to be sustained. That the thought of national education permeated his consciousness, that he continued to see it years later, as an extremely crucial dimension of national regeneration is evident from an isolated paragraph, carrying an editorial title, 'National Education' found in one of his notebooks in Pondicherry around 1916–1918. The thoughts on national education condensed in this one paragraph reveal its centrality in Sri Aurobindo's scheme and vision. Sri Aurobindo speaks of national education as 'an attempt to create and organise' India's 'national culture':

> The whole movement of the national life of India at the present moment may be described in one phrase, – a pressure from within towards self-liberation from all unnatural conditions which obstruct or divert its free and spontaneous development. It is the movement of a stream trying to break open a natural path for its dammed-up waters. This effort takes inevitably many sides and aspects; for in politics and administration, in society, in commerce, in education, this national life finds itself bound up in forms, condemned to move in grooves which give no natural play to the new aspirations, powers, and tendencies which have become its inner impelling motives. *The effort to discover and organise a system of national education is part of this general effort of self-liberation, of self-finding, but perhaps the most central movement of all, in the end, even the most important; for it is this which will give shape to the spirit of the nation at present in a state of rather formless flux. It is in fact no more than a chaotic press of tendencies; a national culture alone can give it form and consistency; and national education is the attempt to create and organise that culture.*"[42]

---

42. *CWSA* vol.1, p. 414. (Italics added).

The national education movement, led by Sri Aurobindo, Lokmanya Tilak, Satish Chandra Mukherjee and a host of other thinkers and educationists and education activists, that we have discussed, generated a wide debate and continued to inspire other experiments. While Rabindranath Tagore's educational experiment grew and demonstrated the possibilities of an education experiment that was inspired and sustained by India's civilisational ethos, Mahatma Gandhi's vision of Basic Education, Pandit Madan Mohan Malaviya's grand educational experiment symbolised by the Banaras Hindu University, educationists and teachers such as Gijubhai Badheka (1885–1939) and his seminal and widely acclaimed educational treatise '*Divasvapna*',[43] and his Bal Mandir, established in 1920, were efforts to express the philosophy of self-reliance, '*Aatmanirbharta*' in education.

Dr Syama Prasad Mookerjee and his prolific contribution to the shaping of the Indian education discourse and the effort of a number of others, all symbolised the carrying forward of the ideals and ideas which were shaped, ideated and articulated by the early quest for a national education. The fundamental arguments of the national education movement, seeking India's educational self-reliance, were permanently engraved in the narrative of India's struggle for freedom. The national education movement that we have studied, with Sri Aurobindo as one of its central figures and leaders, had generated sufficient thought-power to ensure its constant presence in the national mind.

When Mahatma Gandhi launched his first Non-Cooperation movement, and asked students to boycott government schools and colleges, the phase saw an intense reiteration of the ideas that the national education movement had thrown up. Gandhi 'condemned the literary bias of the education system and its divorce from

43. Gijubhai Badheka, *Divasvapna: An Educator's Reverie*, 1990.

manual work. It was with this in mind that he launched his Basic Education or Wardha Scheme, which envisaged free compulsory elementary education in the mother tongue for eight years, with the curriculum organised around manual and productive work'.[44] Following the intense debate at the Wardha Educational Conference in 1937, which produced the blueprint of Basic Education, Gandhi formulated its propositions. The first proposition was reminiscent of the proposition of the national education movement:

> The present system of education does not meet the requirements of the country in any shape or form. English, having been made the medium of instruction in all the higher branches of learning, has created a permanent bar between the highly educated few and the uneducated many. It has prevented knowledge from percolating to the masses. This excessive importance given to English, has cast upon the educated class a burden which has maimed them mentally for life and made them strangers in their own land. The absence of vocational training has made the educated class almost unfit for productive work and has harmed them physically. Money spent on primary education is waste of expenditure, inasmuch as what little is taught is soon forgotten and has little or no value in terms of the villages or cities.[45]

Talking of his Basic Education scheme, Gandhi argued that when he considered the masses of India and the masses as they were situated, 'I could not think of any other type of education. With them work must precede anything else, and the concern of an educationist is to make that work educative'. Every child, observed the Mahatma, must be made to feel that he 'creates something for use and also expands his mind and heart there-through'.[46]

It remains to be explored whether independent India had experimented sufficiently and seriously enough with the Basic

---

44. Aparna Basu, *Essays in the History of Indian Education*, op.cit., p. 13.
45. D.G. Tendulkar, *Mahatma, vol.4*, op.cit., pp. 197,198.
46. Ibid., p. 200.

Education scheme. Why was it that the scheme saw no serious application in the early years and decades after independence? Why was it, that like all other aspects that Gandhi spoke on and symbolised, his Basic Education philosophy and its practice too, was allowed to languish on the margins while being paid profuse lip-tribute. It saw no serious attempt at application and no fundamental effort at integration in free India's educational framework. It was not sufficient for individuals to make successful experiments out of it, what was needed was a wide and practical application of its tenets nationally, in synergy with the latest findings in education, and through it, the creation of an up-to-date, practical, result oriented, responsive and organic system, which would be suited to Indian conditions and requirements.

The immediate decade, post-Independence, did not see a comprehensive discussion or debate on the need to revamp and comprehensively restructure and rearrange Indian education by basing itself on the ideational foundations laid by the national education movement. India's indigenous education institutions and experiments, which survived, were not consulted nor seen as signposts in what should have been an exercise in transforming Indian education after independence.

Nearly two decades after independence, an Indian spiritual leader and educationist lamented that, with the gaining of political freedom, 'the bogey of the clamour for national education vanished. A good many of the so-called national schools' were wound up, and a few well-founded ones 'got themselves absorbed into the educational machinery considered bad, but actively continued in free India'. The system of education 'that seemed injurious due to its coming from unwanted masters' now seemed 'good at the hands of our own people' .... Since the British regime withdrew from the field, the sage lamented, 'the instruments for working out the system expanded enormously in volume, but the quality of the educated remained in woeful decline; while the sense of rights and privileges is on the rise, sense of duty and responsibility was nowhere to be seen ... the poison produced by the defective system remains to be thoroughly eliminated'.[47] In short, as I have argued, a comprehensive, wide-ranging, in-depth, detailed and intensive discussion on how free India's education system needed to be relayed was never encouraged or undertaken.

The University Education Commission (1948–49) headed by the education-philosopher Dr. S. Radhakrishnan undertook a comprehensive review of the state of higher education in India. It spoke of and discussed a plethora of issues from the technical to the philosophical, referring to universities as 'Organs of Civilisations', and argued that 'mighty as are the political changes, far deeper' were 'the fundamental questions' which would be decided by 'what happens in universities'. It spoke of how, under the impact of political change, that is freedom, there had to evolve 'a wider conception of the duties and responsibilities of universities'. Universities in free India, the Radhakrishnan Commission observed:

> ... [H]ave to provide leadership in politics and administration, the professions, industry, and commerce. They have to meet the increasing demand for every type of higher education, literary and scientific, technical and professional. They must enable the country to attain, in as short a time as possible, freedom from want, disease, and ignorance, by the application and development of scientific and technical knowledge. India is rich in natural resources and her people have intelligence and energy and are throbbing with renewed life and vigour. It is for the universities to create knowledge and train minds who would bring together the two, material resources and human energies. If our living standards are to be raised, a radical change of spirit is essential.[48]

---

47. Swami Chidbhavananda, *Indian National Education*, 2009, pp. 2,3.
48. *The Report of the University Education Commission (December 1948–August 1949)*, 1949. p. 33.

It spoke of the aim of education and its institutions in free India to nurture and promote the integrated way of life – *samanvaya*, and argued for the need for a connected curriculum:

> We must obtain through it a sense of perspective, a synoptic vision, a *samanvaya* of the different items of knowledge. Man cannot live by a mass of disconnected information. He has a passion for an ordered intellectual vision of the connections of things. Life is one in all its varied manifestations. We may study the factual relations of the different manifestations but. We must have knowledge of life as a whole. It cannot be a collection of distracting scraps but should be a harmony of patterns. The subjects we study must be taught as parts of a connected curriculum.[49]

It looked at education as an evocation and not as an imposed discipline:

> Like all living organisms the individual grows by the impulse of his own self-development. The natural tendency of the child is to grow into maturity. From complete dependence on others the child has to grow into relative independence. The function of the teacher is to assist the growth by stimulation and guidance. The growth is advanced by the acquisition of knowledge and skills. These later are intended to set free and develop the possibilities of human individuals. Education is not a discipline imposed from above on an apathetic if acquiescent nature. It is a process of leading up the inward nature to its fulfilment. All true development is self-development.[50]

The Radhakrishnan Commission's findings and recommendations needs to be extensively examined and debated since it was the first comprehensive re-look at India's higher education sector post-Independence. It is debatable as to how much of its suggestions were seriously deliberated upon, discussed, and implemented. As Syama Prasad Mookerjee, cautioned, in one of

---

49. Ibid., p.34.
50. *The Report of the University Education Commission* (*December 1948–August 1949*, p. 37.

his most comprehensive education addresses, perhaps his last, delivered to the Delhi University in December 1952, that though the Radhakrishnan Commission had 'submitted a valuable report dwelling on the need for a planned and thorough reorientation of the university administration and teaching' , it was unfortunately, like other Commissions which had reported on Indian education, 'in danger of being pigeonholed on account of want of financial resources'.[51]

Syama Prasad Mookerjee argued that it 'was not through changes only in the external pattern of administrative machinery of universities that we can expect to see the ushering in of a new era of reform and expansion'. The vital needs, Syama Prasad argued, were 'improved methods of teaching and research and abundant facilities, both academic and extra-academic, to the staff and the students for performing their essential duties'. Within a few years after independence, Syama Prasad had argued for the need to appoint a 'University Grants Committee appointed by the central government' which would serve not only the 'central but also the state universities', and composed 'to command the confidence of the universities as well as the public'. Syama Prasad also argued that there was 'a general tendency to believe that grants and control necessarily go together', and that there was a 'need for maintaining the autonomy of the universities and not making them subservient to State on the plea that they receive grants'. [52]

One would do well to ask whether the University Education Commission thought it necessary to ascertain Sri Aurobindo's views on education. In 1948–1949, Sri Aurobindo was still physically living and had relaxed, to a certain extent his vow of seclusion, and

51. 'Convocation Address, University of Delhi, 13 December 1952', in *Syama Prasad Mookerjee: His Vision of Education*, 2017, op.cit.
52. Ibid.

had consented to meet a number of dignitaries in his Ashram in Pondicherry. Could the Commission, during its visit to Madras, not have attempted to seek an audience with Sri Aurobindo in Pondicherry, however brief? As one of the last living leaders of the early phase of India's struggle for freedom – Tilak, Lajpat Rai and Bepin Chandra Pal had long predeceased Sri Aurobindo – and as one of the pre-eminent leaders and ideologues of the national education movement, Sri Aurobindo should have been consulted by the Commission comprising of eminent educationists. Two educationist and thinkers, who were products of, and active participants in the national education movement such as Benoy Kumar Sarkar and Radhakamal Mukherjee, were interviewed by the Commission.

The Commission engaged with the likes of Jadunath Sarkar, Suniti Kumar Chatterji, Nilakanta Sastri, P.V. Kane, D.V. Gundappa, R.C. Majumdar and K.T. Shah, to name some of the best representatives who shaped, in modern times, India's civilisational narrative. Yet, could not the new government of free India ascertain the views and ideas of Sri Aurobindo on how free India's education ought to be reorganised to suit her aspirations as a free country?

That Syama Prasad Mookerjee did not find a place as a Member of the Commission is also ironical. It may be argued that since he was a Minister of the Union cabinet, he could not possibly be included in the Commission. This may have some validity, but the question remains as to whether the Commission, whose Chairman Dr. Radhakrishnan, was a close associate of Dr. Mookerjee's father in the University of Calcutta, engaged with Dr. Mookerjee?

Post-Independence, Syama Prasad Mookerjee continued with his advocacy of the need for a systematic and comprehensive reorganisation of India's education. It is relevant to briefly have a look at some of Dr. Mookerjee's ideas and suggestions since they articulated or reflected the aspirations or possibility of evolving a national education post-Independence. Syama Prasad's thoughts on education, post-Independence, are also significant against the backdrop of the fact that he was an ardent acolyte of Sri Aurobindo and of his political vision, and was especially invited by the Mother to preside over the Sri Aurobindo Memorial Convention, convened in April 1951 in Pondicherry, to establish a university or education centre in Sri Aurobindo's name. That Syama Prasad was invited to lay the foundation of such a university is symbolic and demonstrated the continued quest and aspiration for a national education in a free India.

Syama Prasad Mookerjee's vision of education 'rested on the scaffolding of *kshetra* (region), *rashtra* (nation) and *vishwa* (world). He sought systemic reforms in Bengal's education at the level of region, nation in terms of federal policy of education but without oversighting or glossing over universal ideals'.[53] As he saw *kshetra, rashtra* and *vishwa* in relation to each other, Syama Prasad, 'saw primary, secondary or matriculation and university education not in three segments but as parts of the whole'.[54]

To Syama Prasad the future of university education depended 'vitally on the secondary education'; he argued that 'most of the unsatisfactory features of undergraduate and postgraduate education' had their 'origin in a defective system of secondary education'[55]:

> Education wisely planned and rightly executed will ultimately be the principal factor on which the future peace, progress, and happiness of the Indian people will rest. Primary, Secondary and University education

53. *Syama Prasad Mookerjee: His Vision of Education*, 2017, op.cit, p. xxii.
54. Ibid., p. xxv.
55. Ibid., p. xxv.

– all stages demand a balanced attention from the State and the public. Expansion and not curtailment must be our motto, preservation of equality must be our constant aim.[56]

Free India, Syama Prasad argued, 'must be able to cater to the need of all stages of education as parts of one comprehensive national system'. For him, there 'need not be any conflict amongst primary, secondary, and university stages, nor among literary, scientific, technical, vocational, and agricultural courses of study'. A national system of education, thus, ought to 'conceive of a balanced structure where due' and proper emphasis had to be laid on 'every section so as to maintain its harmony, its strength and solidarity.' And now, after freedom, he argued, universities should be 'conscious of much wider conception of their duties and responsibilities than before'. He saw the need for an adequate and new leadership in professions, commerce, and in industry, in politics and administration. For that 'millions of teachers and workers' would be needed for institutions of various types.[57]

He laid great stress for free India to develop 'research activities of our universities', to ensure that basic sciences must become the common factor and specialisation could be shared region-wise. Syama Prasad called for laying special emphasis and encouraging research in universities on subjects which 'have special relation to the Indian problems of today or to the basic conception of Indian culture and civilization. Indian history, Indian thought and philosophy, Indian art, architecture, music and Indian sociology afford fields for laborious work by hundreds of scholars'.[58] For him, all research, new findings and scientific exploration should be directed to rejuvenating free India. Laying the foundation of the Institute of

56. Ibid., p. xxvi.
57. Ibid., p. 123.
58. Ibid.

Nuclear Physics in Calcutta, Syama Prasad emphasised the need for exploration in the fields of new energy, and of employing these to make India self-sufficient in energy. He spoke of harnessing this energy which places 'in the hands of man a source of power limitless in quantity, transportable to every region of the world and usable for every need of mankind'. India, he pointed out, could not therefore, 'remain a mere spectator in this grand drama of human achievement'.

For Syama Prasad, it was imperative that India remained 'fully alive to the needs of fundamental research on every branch of human knowledge'.[59] He saw the need for a comprehensive technical and skilling programme, he spoke of the need for a 'widespread technological revolution in industry and agriculture'; the main task of universities in free India would be 'to impart a system of education that will not produce a race of unemployables'. [60]

In his vision of education, Syama Prasad had roles fixed for all stakeholders for the rebuilding of a new India. In pursuit of a new India, he called upon Indian universities to not regard themselves 'as exclusive institutions' which would 'exist apart from the currents of the country's life'. They would need to train, he argued, 'their alumni in a worthy manner, saturate them with the lessons of Indian history and civilisations, instil into them unity and reason, strength...'. He never saw higher education delinked from Indian heritage, the pursuit of knowledge in all domains like humanities and sciences and entire humanity.

Syama Prasad could be said to have embodied and represented the ideals and aspirations of the national education movement over the decades. He was its most articulate voice and heir in the early years of India's independence. He was among the few who had

59. Ibid., p. 141.
60. Ibid., pp. 127,128.

had the privilege of having closely interacted with Rabindranath Tagore and with a number of thought-leaders who had represented and shaped the national education discourse. In his articulations on education post-Independence, Syama Prasad represented the continuing quest for a philosophy of national education. His ideal of an educated Indian was one who, 'armed with the knowledge of India's past glory and greatness, her strength and weakness', would 'place before their country a programme of work, which, while loyal to the fundamental traditions of Indian civilization, [would] be adapted to the changing conditions of the modern world'.

With rich experience in the field of education and politics, Syama Prasad Mookerjee could 'perceive that the colonial system of education was incapable of realising these objectives'. Hence it called for an immediate and fundamental reorganisation. Under the colonial education system, as Syama Prasad described it, 'the masses were neglected. Villages were stagnant. Poverty reigned supreme. Elementary education remained in the background' while 'our languages were undernourished ... The aims and purposes of education were inconsistent with national aspiration. Respect for the noblest features of our great culture and civilisation dwindled away due to ignorance and disbelief', and the 'pattern of society based on equality, justice, on contentment and self-sufficiency that true education must foster and strengthen, hardly took shape'.[61]

Such an approach to education would be completely incongruous to the ideals of a new and free India; hence an immediate reorganisation would have to be initiated. For any 'scheme of reorganisation of education, truly national in character', Syama Prasad Mookerjee spelt out 'eight primary conditions' – *asthata siddhanta* on the eve of independence:

61. Ibid., p. 122.

First and foremost, a system of education, consistent with the genius of the people of India and suited to modern life and conditions, cannot be fully achieved unless and until India enjoys a political status which will give her the liberty to decide for herself what constitutes her national needs and how best they can be satisfied .... I am concerned with the supreme fact that the Constitution must give us real and not shadowy rights and powers and enable India to be the mistress of her own destiny. *Secondly*, there must be less of degrading poverty and less of disease and pestilence, now nationwide in extent, which are sapping our vitality and energy and shutting out the inrush of joy, light, and beauty into this land of proud and ancient civilization. *Thirdly*, the State must spend far more adequately and generously on education, in all its grades, than what it has done in the past. All schemes for reconstruction will remain unrealized until this paramount condition is wholeheartedly fulfilled. *Fourthly*, there must be an elaborate system of elementary and secondary education which will form an enduring foundation on which the great structure of university education will be built, shinning like a crown of purposeful achievement drawing inspiration and strength from the abundance of materials which the lowed stages will bring to its doors. *Fifthly*, education at every stage should be as cheap as possible while its quality will be maintained at a high level .... *Sixthly*, let us emphasise that the universities must inspire private benefactors on a much wider scale than they hitherto done .... If our wealthy men who have amassed fortunes, whether through personal efforts or through the accident of birth or otherwise, make up their minds to allot a portion of what they possess for the uplift of their brethren, for the wide diffusion of knowledge and culture, for the alleviation of suffering ... and will inspire the affection and confidence of the masses, whose prosperity and improvement they will thus have helped to stabilize. *Seventhly*, there must be a close and honourable connection between education and trade, industry and commerce, so that men trained in different branches of practical skill and knowledge will have natural scope for their talents .... *Lastly*, the universities must be given the amplest freedom to work out their salvation .... Let each university have a constitution judiciously planned on academic considerations and truly representative in character. Let the men chosen for their administration be of the right type inspired solely by the idea of training youths who will be an asset to the cause of Indian progress.[62]

62. Ibid., pp .xxix, xxx.

In his presidential address at Sri Aurobindo Memorial Convention held at Pondicherry in April 1951, Syama Prasad spoke of the need for such institutions which would impart education through a rooted a rooted vision of India's civilisational achievements, values and ideals. He saw the establishment of such universities, 'where the eternal verities of life will be taught and re-taught to a stricken people' become 'supremely relevant'. Of the proposal to found an university in Sri Aurobindo's name, Syama Prasad told the national gathering of eminent citizens, educationists, thinkers, and political leaders, that this was the task of an international university named after Sri Aurobindo and that it was 'in the fitness of things that along with its sister university at Santiniketan, named after another great Indian, this university should also be located in India where so many peoples and so many cultures have met and found their homes'. The Upanishad had 'expressed this synthesis and harmony by three words —– *Santam, Sivam, Adwaitam*'.[63]

Syama Prasad also insisted that free India's government's policy 'should be to encourage experiments of the type being made here [Pondicherry] so that the work may be carried on without hindrance or difficulty'. He had made the same appeal for Tagore's Santiniketan. He was conscious that these institutions having emerged from a nationalist churning, aspiring to express India's civilisational ethos and aspirations needed a special ambience and support, so that they could successfully carry out their experiment.

To Syama Prasad, Sri Aurobindo was the 'true Indian', who 'appeared out of the pages of our ancient sacred lore, the representative of all their wisdom made dynamic by an awareness of the present spiritual crisis', the 'political fighter and the yogi'

63. Presidential Address at Sri Aurobindo Memorial Convention, Pondicherry, April 25, 1951, in *Syama Prasad Mookerjee: His Vision of Education,* op. cit. p. 116.

whose urge for the 'political liberation of India' and 'patriotism' was tinged with 'a spiritual penumbra,' one who struggled with same abandon for India's political freedom as he had pursued a 'long and patient quest for the freedom of the spirit'.[64]

Indeed in the articulation and formulation of his education vision, Syama Prasad Mookerjee comes across as one of the most fundamental and far-thinking spokespersons and interpreters of the thought-leaders of the national education movement.

64. Ibid., p. 117.

9

A Postscript

Some Aspects of a Philosophy of 'National Education' (1920-21) and an Education for the Indian Century

"

With the same abandon with which he had struggled for India's political freedom, he began his long patient quest for the freedom of the spirit. The two Aurobindo's merged with each other, the political fighter and the yogi. Even then his earlier patriotism was tinged with a spiritual penumbra. He was thus a true Indian.

– Dr Syama Prasad Mookerjee,
Presidential Address,
Sri Aurobindo Memorial Convention,
Pondicherry, 25 April, 1951

The issues that Sri Aurobindo raised in his preface on national education are those which activated the leading minds of the national education movement. A number of them continue to remain contemporaneous. Sister Nivedita summed up best the predicament of national education when she wrote, 'It follows that in national *reconstruction* (sic) there is no other factor so important as education'. The issue then was to define and ideate that education, 'How is this to be made national and nationalising? What is a national education? And conversely, what is un-national? And further what kind of education offers the best preparation for the attempt to solve the national problems? What type of education would be not only national, but also nation-making?'[1] She articulated the entire gamut of the dilemma that opinion leaders of national education had to continuously grapple with. In our survey of the quest, we have come across such questions and have also found answers – at times comprehensive, at times partial – to these fundamental questions generated by the movement.

Sri Aurobindo too, in retrospect addressed some of these fundamental questions while writing his preface on national education. His message on national education given in 1918, which we have discussed, made it clear that he considered education to be a principal factor in national reconstruction. He situated the central problematic of the thought of national education, a problematic that faced its leaders and the institutions they supported and founded.

---

1. *CWSN vol. 4,* op.cit., p. 352.

While the 'necessity and unmixed good of universal education' was recognised and accepted, what seem to confound thinkers and knot the debate was the very concept and definition of education itself – there did not seem to be, Sri Aurobindo observed, an agreement 'on what education is, or practically or ideally should be'. And in a country like India where the spirit of independence was awakening and where long political subjection had 'left the decisive shaping and supreme control of education in the hands of foreigners', this uncertainty over a narrative of what was or could be a national type of education, was bound to introduce an 'atmosphere of great and disconcerting confusion'.[2] There seemed to be an even greater uncertainty on what was meant by national education. The only points of unanimity on the issue, Sri Aurobindo argued, was the fact that the education imparted in 'existing schools and universities [had] been bad in kind, and in addition, denationalising, degrading, and impoverishing to the national mind, soul, and character, because it [was] overshadowed by a foreign hand and [was] foreign in aim, method, substance and spirit'.[3]

This purely negative agreement prevailed especially during the heyday of the movement, but it did not seem to go further or to proffer clearer directions. In absence of such a direction, it was not sufficient, as most experiments had done, to tag the nomenclature 'national' onto a school or college and hand it over to an 'indigenous agency' comprising, ironically, of men trained in the very system that was being denounced, and by modifying the existing curriculum by adding to it a technical dimension, believing that the problem had been solved and the cause of national education served.

This approach was delusional and did not promote the cause of a truly national education. Sri Aurobindo referred to the past

2. *CWSA* vol.1, op.cit., p. 417.

3. Ibid.

experiments of national education as he had witnessed it. He did not dispute its capacity to impart education, but he was unsure on what would make it 'more national'.[4] This was the principal problem of national education clearly stated. It was one of 'surpassing difficulty and it was not easy to discover from what point of thought, or of practice, one [had] to begin'.[5] The quest was to try and evolve an education that would be proper to the 'Indian soul and need and temperament and culture'. It was not something that would merely be faithful to some past principle but would have to take into account more importantly India's future needs.[6]

Sri Aurobindo tackled some of the basic objections against National education, objections that further confused the general understanding of the term. National education as Sri Aurobindo foresaw it, did not mean an 'obscurantist retrogression to the past forms that were once a living frame of our culture but are now dead or dying things'. Sri Aurobindo was explicit on this question when he said:

> The living spirit of the demand for national education no more requires a return to the astronomy and mathematics of Bhaskara or the forms of the system of Nalanda, than the living spirit of Swadeshi a return from railway and motor traction to the ancient chariot and the bullock-cart.[7]

And without condoning, what he terms the prevalence of 'plenty of retrogressive sentimentalism', Sri Aurobindo situated the principles of the past and the dimensions of the future *vis-à-vis* national education:

> It is the spirit, the living and vital issue [of India's past civilisational achievements] that we have to do with, and there the question is not

4. Ibid., pp. 417–18.
5. Ibid.
6. Ibid., pp. 418–19.
7. Ibid., p. 420.

between modernism and antiquity, but between an imported civilisation and the greater possibilities of the Indian mind and nature, not between the present and the past, but between the present and the future. It is not a return to the fifth century but an initiation of the centuries to come, not a reversion but a break forward...'[8]

Sri Aurobindo spoke for the retention of past principles which defined education and gave it a distinct Indic flavour. His call was not for the revival of ancient educational structures, but rather the understanding and reapplication of civilizational India's fundamental educational understandings. These were, as we have discussed in the work, the teacher-learner relationship, the view that the acquiring of self-knowledge was also of unique importance, and that education was not mere information-gathering, that the pupil's self-nature (*svabhava*) and (*svadharma*) had to be taken into account by the education system before devising a method or framework, that the pupil, the learner, was not a mere automaton to be filled in with information but rather an aspiring soul with a special and pre-determined object to fulfil in the course of his life – to modern conditions and demands.

Unfortunately, in independent India, any talk of re-examining and reapplying past civilisational principles to modern needs was seen through the glasses of revivalism, and denigrated by an ideologically vocal section that believed in and propagated the tenets of an anti-religious secularism. Such a denigration and irrational hostility stymied any serious effort at trying to synergise and weave civilisational India's educational principles for creating and shaping her future. Sri Aurobindo's philosophy of national education gave space to the past, not in its forms, but in its principles and fundamentals.

Sri Aurobindo was opposed to the view that one could only live and prosper once the European [read Western] civilisation was

8. *CWSA* vol.1, p. 420.

acquired, and that the role of education was to train people for such an acquisition. Sri Aurobindo argued that Europe herself created her civilisation by acquiring directions and light from various sources during different epochs, and gave each of its major acquisitions a new turn and shape suited to its temperament and spirit, which he identified as Teutonic, Latin, Celtic, and Slavic. Similarly, the nations of Asia, Sri Aurobindo pointed out were not 'bound to accept' [Western civilisation *in toto* without examination], and should do well to take over 'whatever new knowledge or just ideas [it] has to offer, to assimilate them to their [the nation's] own knowledge and culture, their own native temperament and spirit, mind, and social genius and out of that create the civilisation of the future'.[9]

National education, as seen by Sri Aurobindo, negated the implicit idea, 'that the mind is same everywhere and [thus] can everywhere be passed through the same machine and uniformly constructed to order'. It was an idea which had to be challenged and renounced. A national education had to recognise that there were several variations and layers in the individual: the individual's mind and soul had infinite variations, due to its connectedness and link with the mind of the nation and the soul of the people it belonged to, or was part of. These peculiarities and variations had to be taken into account by an education which did not wish to become a 'machine-made fabric'.[10]

9. Ibid., p. 422. Sri Aurobindo anticipated the debate surrounding the issue of cultural subjection. A subjection that comes not merely through the assimilation of an alien culture but rather when through a bounden sense one allows 'one's traditional cast of ideas and sentiments [to be] superseded without comparison or competition by a new cast representing an alien culture which possesses one like a ghost'. [*Swaraj in Ideas*, op. cit., p. 13] For a reading of this theme see e.g. 'Indian Culture and External Influence' in Sri Aurobindo, *The Renaissance in India & Other Essays on Indian Culture*, 2002.

10. *CWSA* vol.1, pp. 422–23.

Sri Aurobindo argued against the mechanisation, standardisation, or commoditisation of education. It was a plea for the recognition that the learner's mind had its own demands, needs, and idiosyncrasies, and could not be put through the rut of uniformity. He had already discussed this while describing his third principle of education (written in 1910), where he had emphasised the need to take into account heredity, surrounding, nationality, country, sustaining soil and air, familiar sights, sounds, and habits as powerful moulding factors which had to be made the starting point of education.[11] An education that truly seeks to mould the individual and develop the powers of his mind and nature ought to take into serious consideration these vital formative factors. A national education concerned with developing the powers of the learner's personality and nature should be not only aware of these traits but should seek ways and methods to actualise and evoke them.

However, the challenge of formulating and articulating the idea of what national education meant, and 'the principle and the form that national education must take in India' remained, and Sri Aurobindo recognised that it presented a formidable difficulty. He saw confusion and failure here because, as he argued, the national mind had lost hold of the 'national spirit and idea' in the field of education, in its cultural life, and as well as in other areas. This prevented the growth of a clear understanding of the national temperament and its needs. The first necessity, therefore, was to develop a clear understanding of education. Sri Aurobindo defined national education thus:

> There are three things which have to be taken into account in a true and living education – the man, the individual in his commonness and in his uniqueness, the nation or people and universal humanity. It follows that that alone will be a true and living education which helps to bring out to

---

11. Ibid., pp. 384–85.

full advantage, makes ready for the full purpose and scope of human life all that is in the individual man, and which at the same time helps him enter into his right relation with the life, mind, and soul of the people to which he belongs and with that great total life, mind, and soul of humanity of which he himself is a unit and his people or nation a living, a separate and yet inseparable member.[12]

Such a definition essentially speaks of an education that would enable the learner to enter into a balanced and synchronised relation with his surroundings and with his national life and mind. This is perhaps a vital indicator in terms of developing a deeper *raison d'être* that ought to inspire any effort at developing a system of national education.

The key to a successful working out of a national education was this, to be able to train the learner to enter into a right relation with these three determining factors of the nation's collective life. Sri Aurobindo did not disconnect the individual from larger humanity. This was to him to be the true aim of an Indian national education. This was also a central truth not only of the definition of national education that Sri Aurobindo sought to evolve, but of his entire philosophy of education. This was the core philosophy of civilisational India's education philosophy. This assumes greater relevance and contemporaneity in a world that is increasingly getting globalised.

The following two concluding observations in his incomplete preface, on the conception and view of man in the Indian tradition provide a defining insight into Sri Aurobindo's formulation of a national education. They demonstrate the difference in his approach to the whole concept. The difference was in perceiving the individual. India's civilisational thought saw man differently; it did not see him solely or exclusively as a reasoning animal developed

12. Ibid., p. 425.

by physical Nature to simply satisfy his ego and vital existence. It did not perceive his education to be merely the training of his mental capacities and a training 'that will fit him to be an efficient, productive, and well disciplined member of the society and State'. Though these were given prominence, they were not considered to be the ultimate aim, or the end. Instead India's true vision of the individual was that of:

> ... a soul, a portion of the Divinity enwrapped in mind and body, a conscious manifestation in Nature of the universal self and spirit. Always she has distinguished and cultivated in him a mental, an intellectual, an ethical, dynamic and practical, an aesthetic and hedonistic, a vital and physical being, but all these have been seen as powers of a soul that manifests through them and grows with their growth... [13]

The adoption of this vision of the learner can then never lead him to be treated as a machine which had to be fed with uniform packets of information and then hammered into some pre-determined shape. Sri Aurobindo's call was for national education to base itself on this vision of the learner and to adopt a radically different stance from the usual routine of education. A national education must encourage and facilitate this growth of the soul. Sri Aurobindo called for a radical shift in the perception of the learner and thus in his education.

This shift was based entirely on India's spiritual and civilisational experience. While stating this Sri Aurobindo, was in fact calling for a new Indian education system to build its superstructure on this unique conception and vision of man. Only then could a radical transformation occur in the vision of education. A system of national education for India, must begin thus, with this root vision and inspiration at its inception. A unique perception of man can help evolve a newer vision for his growth and unfolding.

13. Ibid., pp. 425–26.

In the same vein Indian thought perceived the nation not merely as an armed, efficient, and organised state, but as a 'great communal soul and life that has appeared in the whole and has manifested a nature of its own....'[14] Sri Aurobindo brought to the fore a vision of the cultural conception of humanity, which too, must be in accordance with the thought of India:

... [O]ur cultural conception of humanity must be in accordance with her [India's] ancient vision of the universal manifesting in the human race, evolving through life and mind but with a high ultimate spiritual aim, it must be the idea of the spirit, the soul of humanity advancing through struggle and concert towards oneness, increasing its experience and maintaining a needed diversity through the varied culture and life motives of its many peoples, searching for perfection through the development of the powers of the individual and his progress towards a diviner being and life, but feeling out too though more slowly after a similar perfectibility in the life of the race.[15]

A true education will be that which recognises this spiritual aim of a movement towards oneness and will make itself an instrument to work out this spiritual aim in the individual and in the collectivity.

It must be an education that, for the individual, will make its one central object the growth of the soul and its powers and possibilities, for the nation will keep first in view the preservation, strengthening and enrichment of

14. Ibid., p. 426.
15. Ibid., pp. 426–27. This passage is of course packed with possibilities. Sri Aurobindo anticipated by decades the whole globalisation versus national culture debate. While recognising the fact that there is an inevitable movement towards greater interaction, unity and thus, enculturation between nations and peoples, Sri Aurobindo also stressed the imperative of 'maintaining a needed diversity'. This could come through the recognition of the uniqueness and propensities of the national mind and the national soul. Sri Aurobindo repeatedly examines this dimension in his essays on India's renaissance and culture.

the nation-soul and its Dharma and raise both into powers of the life and ascending mind and soul of humanity. And at no time will it lose sight of man's highest object, the awakening and development of his spiritual being.[16]

Thus ends in an incomplete manner his preface on national education. It could be that the preface formulating the philosophical base of a national system of education would have been followed by greater details of how it could be worked out and in its absence one may at best interpret these ideas and develop an individual perception and understanding.

Perhaps these words did not percolate sufficiently in the psyche and mind of a nation then in the throes of a mass struggle to gain political liberation first. And in this struggle for liberation from a foreign yoke, the deeper issues of subjection could not continuously remain on the surface for a sustained debate and discourse to develop. As we have seen, the efforts towards developing a national education became mostly individual and institutional sagas and rarely did the momentum of the first decade revive in a concerted manner. Whether independent India focused its attention towards developing a national system of education inspired by her cultural and spiritual civilisational experience and principles, and whether she tried to transform the colonial education structure and dissolve the aims of an alien education system, is an open question. Though I have raised some of these questions, it would require an altogether separate discussion.

The early nationalist education discourse was, as I have argued, successful in generating a quest for a philosophy of national education. Even though it did not evolve a concerted philosophy or system of education, the quest did throw up crucial ideas, thoughts, revelations, and formulations on the theme. These continued to survive as pointers that kept the issue alive and the quest ongoing.

16. *CWSA* vol.1, p. 427.

'National education was an idea', it was a search 'for an alternative to the colonial educational system, an alternative to be created by Indian agency from out of elements constituting Indian civilisation'[17] and much more.

As Sri Aurobindo saw it, it had to be based fundamentally on the spiritual – *adhyatmic* – conception of man and on the spiritual vision of life. It was that alone which, he argued, could bring about an integral transmutation of our whole understanding of education, and inspire new formulations and methods. The vision of the great purpose of education was that of helping the 'soul to come forward, to assert its mastery over its instruments, gain experience and grow, and eventually manifest the powers it has set forth in life'.[18] This is what defined Sri Aurobindo's vision of education then, and indicates its relevance. It is thus, in the realm of ideas that the entire quest for a philosophy of national education must be truly judged and not so much in terms of its physical and institutional manifestations.

Sri Aurobindo enriched the discourse and highlighted its centrality in India's quest for selfhood through his continuous personal attention to it, through his discussion of its principal aspects, by providing a certain undeniably deeper philosophical base to the whole discourse. He tried 'to get into the mind of the people a settled will'[19] in support of the need for a national education as he had done in support for political emancipation. Such a settled will for a new education would, he argued, pave the way towards a genuine freedom of the mind, of thoughts, and of ideas.

The quest generated ideas and it inspired a philosophy. In a sense, the quest itself, the ideas it generated were, in themselves, the philosophy and it is these that continue to live and to inspire.

---

17. *Educating the Nation*, op. cit., p. xxiii.
18. *Education and the Aim of Human Life*, op.cit., p. 48.
19. *Autobiographical Notes,* op.cit., p. 255.

Prime Minister Narendra Modi's government unveiled the National Education Policy (NEP) in 2020. It is the 'first education of the 21st century' with the aim to 'address the many growing developmental imperatives' of India. After a long interval of over three decades, India finally has an education policy that is reflective of its aspirations in the 21st century. The NEP was formulated after a wide and comprehensive deliberation, spanning over three years and engaging stakeholders at various levels. Such a comprehensive and fundamental top-down approach in formulating a national education policy has perhaps not been undertaken in the past.

For over three decades, the ideational dimension of India's education remained stagnant. Indeed for a rapidly evolving and diversifying world to think that India, which would have the highest population of youth in the world over the next decade, did not have an educational policy which defined how that power would be trained, directed, and channelised was unthinkable. The core ideas and aims of the NEP reflect the fundamental aspirations and aims of the national education movement. In fact, a close look at its various aspects and tenets and suggestions crystallise and synergise the fundamental educational ideas and a formulation that was expressed by those nationalist thought-leaders we have discussed. It is symbolic and significant that, on the 75th year of India's independence, a renewed and a more essential and fundamental debate on India's educational needs, aspirations, and direction has been generated by Prime Minister Modi's effective actualisation of the educational debate. The NEP speaks of the need to facilitate an educational ambience and framework in which the 'children not only learn but learn how to learn'.

It emphasises the need for a new education that would move 'towards less content and more towards learning how to think critically and solve problems, how to be creative and multi-disciplinary, and how to innovate, adapt, and absorb new material in novel and changing fields'. It refers to a new approach to pedagogy which must evolve to 'make education more experiential, holistic, integrated, discovery-oriented, learner-centred, discussion-based, flexible' and enjoyable. It speaks of a curriculum that must include 'basic arts, crafts, humanities, games, sports and fitness, languages, literature, culture, and values, in addition to science and mathematics, to develop all aspects of the learners' brains and make education more well-rounded, useful, and fulfilling to the learner'. It argues for an education that must focus on character building, 'enable learners to be ethical, rational, compassionate, and caring', while also preparing them 'for a gainful, fulfilling employment'.

The NEP's guiding light has been the 'rich heritage of ancient Indian knowledge', its guiding and formulating philosophy is India's civilisational educational philosophy, in which education did not mean just the acquisition of information or knowledge as 'a preparation for life in this world or life beyond schooling, but for complete realisation and liberation of the self'. It recognises that India of yore was a knowledge society and its educational institutions and universities 'set high standards of multidisciplinary teaching and research', and was home to scholars from across the ancient world as well as from diverse backgrounds. It calls for nurturing and preserving this rich educational legacy and to research and enhance its knowledge and discoveries and to put these to 'new uses through our education system'. The aim is to evolve an integrated and holistic education to help develop the creativity and originality of students and to encourage them to innovate'. This statement of intent and purpose reflected in a capsule, a certain dimension and essence of the entire national education movement.

The upholding and defining tenets or principles of the NEP are:

Flexibility: for learners to choose their learning trajectories, no hard-separation between arts and sciences, between vocational and academics, multi-disciplinarity and holistic, emphasis on conceptual understanding, rather than rote-learning and learning for exams, encourage creative and critical thinking, ethics and constitutional values, life-skills, emphasis, formative assessment of learning rather than the summative assessment with its overweening emphasis on the 'coaching culture', respect for diversity and respect for the local context, full equity and inclusion, resource efficiency, teachers and faculty as the centre and heart of the learning process, ensuring integrity and transparency, autonomisation and good governance of higher education institutions, empowerment, encourage outstanding research, continuous and dynamic policy-making, education as public service and substantial and game-changing investment in a strong, vibrant public education system. It aims to create an education system and ideal which is rooted in and exudes pride for 'India and her rich, diverse, ancient and modern culture and knowledge systems and traditions, and its forward-looking aspirations, to be incorporated where relevant in an accurate manner', an education that would form 'an anchor and source of inspiration for all education...

Among some of the refreshing and far-seeing innovations that the NEP has introduced is the reimagining of vocational training, developing multi-linguism, education in the mother-tongue, founding the National Research Foundation in order to incubate and nurture a robust eco-system of research; it speaks of promoting and developing India into a 'global study destination', an idea which India had civilisationally realised in the past, it pledges to promote intensely, Indian languages, art and culture, preserve India's unique languages, to urgently expand its translation and interpretation efforts, expand institutions and universities studying all classical languages, it talks of instituting the Indian Educational Services (IES), and much more. The changes that it suggests, when worked out systematically and creatively, will indeed lay a new foundation for erecting the edifice of a national education. The entire gamut that defines a national and holistic education, its defining principles and upholding pillars, and its ideational texture can be discerned in the essential draft of the NEP.[20]

In his first address on NEP, on August 7, 2020, Prime Minister Modi told the audience comprising of educationists, education administrators, education policy makers and academics that:

> Every country reforms its education system according to its national values and national goals. The idea is that the country's education system should ensure the future of not only its present, but future generations as well. This is the idea behind India's National Education Policy. The National Education Policy will lay the foundation of the new India, the 21st century India. The National Education Policy focuses on the education and skills needed for the youth of 21st century India.

Modi spoke of how, even though India's education system did not undergo reforms for several years, it resulted in the encouragement of the rat-race mindset rather than promoting values of curiosity and of imagination. Such a mindset saw a climate of competition 'to become a doctor, or an engineer, or a lawyer'; it was imperative to pull education out of that competitive mindset since it was an education which moved on without having undertaken a mapping of interest, ability and demand. How can our youth, Modi asked, 'develop critical and innovative thinking if there [was] no passion for education, philosophy of education and purpose of education?' Modi referred to Rabindranath Tagore whose education ideals inspires and directs the NEP, and recollected Tagore's words, 'The highest education is that which does not merely give information but makes our life in harmony with all existence'. The 'far-reaching

20. *National Education Policy 2020*, Ministry of Education, Government of India.

goal' of the NEP was definitely based on and inspired, by that foundational goal of education, Modi said.

'Does our education policy motivate our youth for a creative, curiosity and commitment-driven life ... from roots to the world, from man to mankind, from past to modernity?', Modi asked. All education policies till now had emphasised on what to think, Modi argued, but the new education policy 'lays stress on how to think. The NEP, therefore, insists on reducing the burden of 'unnecessary syllabus and books'. The need of the hour, Modi observed, was to teach learners through methods that were 'enquiry-based, discovery-based, discussion-based and analysis based'. Modi pointed out how children learnt faster if they were taught through the same language in school as the one he spoke at home and that is why the NEP has spoken of using the mother tongue as the medium of instruction, as far as possible, till class five, so that the learners' foundations are strong and their base strengthened while pursuing higher studies.

One of the path-breaking innovations of the NEP is the option of multiple entry-exits. The student will now have the freedom, Modi indicated, 'to leave a particular course in between and take admission in another course if they wish to. For this, they can take a break from the first course for a certain period of time and join the second course. This is the thought behind getting higher education free of streams'. This will facilitate a constant reskilling and upskilling.

Prime Minister Narendra Modi's observations on the NEP's thrust in reimagining vocational training strikes a deep note – it echoes Mahatma Gandhi's questions on the marginalisation of vocational education in the Indian scheme of education, and also that of the national education movement and its national education institutions, which insisted on undertaking an elaborate vocational and manual training programme. Speaking on the transformative approach to vocational training, so crucial and cardinal an aspect for a country like India, he says:

> We are forced to contemplate how a culturally rich nation like India has been infested by such negative mentality. How the idea of high and low and a mocking stance towards people who engage in labour has crept into our minds. The main reason behind this mentality lies in the fact that education remains disconnected from this strata of society. If you ever visit a village and witness the farmers, labourers working, only then can you understand their contribution towards society and how they have invested their lives to nourish the needs of society. Our generation must learn to respect their labour. In order to achieve this prerogative, we have paid attention to the ideas of student education and dignity of labour in the National Education Policy.

Modi mentioned the NEP's commitment to nurturing talent and technology and to creating an ambience in which Indian talent would discover and develop 'futuristic technology'. This was the first time that futuristic technology was being spoken of with India's education system becoming its cradling centre. Reducing the gap between research and education, facilitating a process of autonomisation of educational institution, as Syama Prasad Mookerjee had repeatedly termed it, education in an atmosphere of freedom, was some of the NEP's fundamental objectives, as Modi articulated it.

The other cardinal dimension which the NEP pledged, which Modi pointed out, was a fresh, renewed and creative focus on the teacher. 'The dignity of teachers has also been emphasised in the national education policy. There is also an effort to make the talent of India remain in India to develop the generations to come. There is a lot of emphasis on teacher training and making teachers constantly update their skills in the National Education Policy. I believe, when a teacher learns, a nation leads', Modi observed.[21] The debate on the teachers' role and centrality in the scheme of national education that had been repeatedly reiterated by the national education, the emasculation of the teacher under the colonial framework into a mere executor of the text book, had come a full circle. The NEP professes to hand back the teacher her true and essential role as envisaged and enjoined in India's civilisational scheme of education.

In articulating the NEP, Prime Minister Modi has indeed reignited the national education debate. The NEP encapsulates and articulates, under present conditions and a present context, the essential aspirations and ideas of the national education movement. It offers scope for a renewed debate; it offers the possibilities of finally and comprehensively reorganising Indian education and to push it forward into formulating a national system of education. It would be an education that would reflect India's cultural and civilisational essence, which would give scope for the full expression of her varied talent and potential, and would certainly propel her towards the status of a great civilisational power. That it comes on the 75th year of India's independence and on the sesquicentennial of Sri Aurobindo's birth is symbolic, and generates hope that by the time India reaches the centennial milestone of her independence, she would have successfully worked out and implemented a unique system of national education which would enable her to shape and direct the 21st century.

Sri Aurobindo had said, a hundred years ago, of India passing through a 'new twilight' which was not 'an evening but a morning *Yuga-sandhya*', which offered infinite possibilities and scope. Presciently speaking, he had then said:

---

21. *English rendering of text of PM's speech at Higher Education Conclave, August 7, 2020, Press Information Bureau, Press Release.*

> India of the ages is not dead nor has she spoken her last creative word; she lives and has still something to do for herself and the human people. And that which must seek now to awake is not an anglicised oriental people, docile pupil of the West and doomed to repeat the cycle of the Occident's success and failure, but still the ancient immemorable Shakti recovering her deepest self, lifting her head higher towards the supreme source of light and strength, and turning to discover the complete meaning and a vaster from of her Dharma.[22]

It is through an emancipatory, liberating, empowering, and creative education, which would irreversibly initiate and accelerate the process of a fundamental cultural self-recovery with the aim of shaping a new India, that the discovery of a vaster *Dharma* can be collectively and nationally made. India in the 21st century must be driven and shaped by such an education vision and philosophy.

22. Sri Aurobindo, *The Renaissance in India & Other Essays on Indian Culture*, 2002.

Bibliography

"

Whoever wishes to cut off the nation from its past, is no friend of our national growth. Whoever fails to take advantage of the present is losing us the battle of life. We must therefore save for India all that she has stored up of knowledge, character and noble thought in her immemorial past. We must acquire for her the best knowledge that Europe can give her and assimilate it to her own peculiar type of national temperament. We must introduce the best methods of teaching humanity has developed, whether modern or ancient. And all these must harmonise into a system which will be impregnated with the spirit of self-reliance so as to build up men and not machines – national men, able men, men fit to carve out a career for themselves by their own brain power and resource, fit to meet the shocks of life and breast the waves of adventure...

– **Sri Aurobindo**

Andrews, C.F., *The Renaissance in India: Its Missionary Aspect*, London: Church Missionary Society, 1912.

Animananda, B., *The Blade: Life & Work of Brahmabandhab Upadhyay*, Kolkata: Roy & Sons [c.1946].

Argov, Daniel, *Moderates & Extremists in the Indian Nationalist Movement: 1883-1920, with Special Reference to Surendranath Banerjea and Lajpat Rai*, Mumbai: Asia Publishing House, 1967.

Athalye, D.V., *The Life of Lokmanya Tilak*, Pune: Annasahib Chiploonkar, 1921.

Atmaprana, Pravrajika, *Sister Nivedita: of Ramakrishna – Vivekananda,* Kolkata: Sister Nivedita Girl's School, 6th edition, 2007.

Aurobindo, Sri, *Autobiographical Notes & Other Writings of Historical Interest*, Pondicherry: Sri Aurobindo Ashram, 2006.

——, *Bankim-Tilak-Dayananda*, Pondicherry: Sri Aurobindo Ashram Publication Dept, (1940), 6th ed. 2006.

——, *Speeches-On Indian Politics & National Education,* Pondicherry: Sri Aurobindo Ashram, 7th imp 2005.

——, *The Renaissance in India & Other Essays on Indian Culture,* Pondicherry: Sri Aurobindo Ashram, 2nd impression, 2002.

——, *Bande Mataram: Early Political Writings*, Pondicherry: Sri Aurobindo Ashram, 5th impression, 1997.

——, *On Nationalism*, Pondicherry: Sri Aurobindo Ashram Publication Dept, 1996.

——, *On Himself*, Pondicherry: Sri Aurobindo Ashram, 5th impression, 1989.

——, *Sri Aurobindo Birth Centenary Library*, vol.30, Pondicherry: Sri Aurobindo Ashram, 1976.

Avinashilingam, T.S., *The Educational Philosophy of Swami Vivekananda,* Coimbatore: Sri Ramakrishna Mission Vidyalaya, 4th edition, 1983.

Badheka, Gijubhai, *Divasvapna* (Trans), New Delhi: National Book Trust, 5th reprint, 2006.

Bagal, J.C. edited, *Bankim Rachanabali, vol.2,* (Kolkata: Sahitya Samsad, 16th imp., [Beng] 1417.

Bagchi, Monee, *Ananda Coomaraswamy: a Study*, Varanasi: Bharata Manisha, 1960, 1st edition.

Balasubramaniam, Uma, *Sayajirao Gaekwad III: the Maharaja of Baroda*, New Delhi: Rupa Publications, 2019.

Bandyopadhyay, Anshuman edited, *Agnijuger Agnikatha-'Jugantar' 1906-1908*, Pondicherry: Sri Aurobindo Ashram Publication Department, 2001.

Banerjee, Gooroodass, *A Few Thoughts on Education*, Kolkata: Thacker Spink & Co, 1904.

Banerjee, Upendranath, *Nirbasiter Atmakatha* (English Translation), *Memoirs of a Revolutionary*, Kolkata: K.L. Chakravarty, circa 1921.

Banerji, Sanat K., 'The New Approach to Education in India' in *A New Approach to Education*, Pondicherry: Sri Aurobindo Society, 1974.

Bapat, S.V. edited, *Reminiscences and Anecdotes of Lokmanya Tilak*, Pune: Kesari Press, 1928.

Bara, Joseph, 'Colonialism and Educational Fragmentation in India' in Sabyasachi Bhattacharya edited, *The Contested Terrain – Perspectives on Education in India*, New Delhi: Orient Longman, 1998.

Basu, Aparna, 'National Education in Bengal: 1905-1912' in Sabyasachi Bhattacharya edited *The Contested Terrain – Perspectives on Education in India*, New Delhi: Orient Longman, 1998.

——, *Essays in the History of Indian Education*, New Delhi: Concept Publishing, 1982.

Basu, Sankari Prasad, *Nivedita Lokmata, vol.2*, Kolkata: Ananda Publisher, 2nd imp. [Beng] 1414.

——, *Swami Vivekananda: Notun Tathya, Notun Alo* (New Information, New Light), Kolkata: Ananda Publishers, (2005), rpt. 2011.

Besant, Annie, *The Birth of a New India: A Collection of Writings and Speeches on Indian Affairs*, Madras: Theosophical Publishing House, 1917.

Besterman, Theodore, *Annie Besant: A Modern Prophet, (1934)*, Kessinger Publications, rpt., 2003.

Bhandarkar, D.R., *B.C. Law Volume – Part-II: articles presented to Dr. B.C. Law*, Poona: Bhandarkar Oriental Research Institute, 1946.

Bhattacharya, K.C., *Swaraj in Ideas*, Kolkata: Jijnasa, 1977.

Bhattacharya, Sabyasachi edited, *The Contested Terrain – Perspectives on Education in India*, New Delhi: Orient Longman, 1998.

Bhattacharya, Sabyasachi, Bara Joseph et al. edited, *Educating the Nation – Documents on the Discourse of National Education in India 1880-1920*, New Delhi: Kanishka Publishers & Educational Records Research Unit (ERRU), Jawaharlal Nehru University, 2003.

Boehmer, Elleke, *Empire, the National and the Post-Colonial: 1890-1920-Resistance in Interaction*, New York: Oxford University Press, 2002.

Bona, Joseph Di edited, *One Teacher, One School: the Adam Reports on Indigenous Education in 19th Century India*, New Delhi: Biblia Impex, 1983.

Bose, Nemai Sadhan, *Indian Awakening & Bengal*, Kolkata: Firma KLM, reprint 1990.

Buckland, C.E., *Bengal under the Lieutenant Governors: being a narrative of the principal events and public measure during their period of office from 1854 to 1898, vol.2*, Calcutta: S.K. Lahiri & Co, 1901.

Chatterjee, Lalitmohan & Syama Prasad Mookerjee, *Representative Indians*, Published by A.C. Dhar, Calcutta: Popular Agency, 1931.

Chatterjee, Ramananda edited, *The Golden Book of Tagore*, Kolkata: The Golden Book Committee, 1931.

Chidbhavananda, Swami, *Indian National Education*, Tirupparaithurai: Sri Ramakrishna Tapovanam, 7th ed. 2009.

Chirol, Valentine, *Indian Unrest*, London: Macmillan & Co, 1910.

Complete Works of Sister Nivedita (*CWSN*), vol.4, 'The Place of the Kindergarten in Indian Schools', Kolkata: Advaita Ashrama, 1996.

Complete Works of Swami Vivekananda (*CWSV*), vol.2, Kolkata: Advaita Ashrama, 29th impression, 2009.

Coomaraswamy, Ananda, *Swadeshi & Art*, Madras: Ganesh & Co, 1910.

——, *Essays in National Idealism*, Madras: G.A. Natesan & Co, 1909.

CWSN vol.2, 'The Mediaeval University of India' in *Studies from an Eastern Home*, Kolkata: Advaita Ashrama, 4th impression, 1999.

CWSN vol.3, Kolkata: Advaita Ashrama, 4th impression, 2000.

CWSN, vol.1, Kolkata: Advaita Ashrama, 5th impression, 2006.

CWSV, vol.3, Kolkata: Advaita Ashrama, 21st impression, 2008.

CWSV, vol.4, Kolkata: Advaita Ashrama, 17th impression, 2008.

CWSV, vol.5, Kolkata: Advaita Ashrama, 21st impression, 2009.

Das, Manoj, *Sri Aurobindo: Life and Times of the Mahayogi*: *The Pre-Pondicherry Phase*, Pondicherry: Sri Aurobindo International Centre of Education, 2020.

——, *Sri Aurobindo in the First Decade of the Twentieth Century*, Pondicherry: Sri Aurobindo Ashram, 2nd edition, 2003.

Das, Sisir Kumar, *The English Writings of Rabindranath Tagore*, vol.2, New Delhi: Sahitya Akademi, rpt. 2008.

Dasgupta, R.K., Introduction to *Studies in the Bengal Renaissance*, Kolkata: National Council of Education, Bengal, 3rd edition, 2002.

——, 'National Education' in *Concept of National Education in India*, Kolkata: National Council of Education Bengal, 1967.

Dass, Banesvar edited, *The Social and Economic Ideas of Benoy Kumar Sarkar*, Calcutta: Chuckervertty Chatterjee & Co.

De, Amalendu, *Sri Aurobindo's Role in Indian Freedom Struggle*, Kolkata: Asiatic Society, 2003.

——, *Raja Subodh Chandra Mallik and His Times*, Kolkata: National Council of Education, Bengal, 1996.

Devi, Shanta, *Bharater Mukti-Sadhak: Ramananda Chattopadhyay O Ardha-Shatabdir Bangla* (Sadhaka of India's Freedom: Ramananda Chattopadhyaya & the Bengal of Five Decades), Kolkata: Dey's Publishing, 2005.

Dharampal, Gita edited, *Essential Writings of Dharampal*, New Delhi: Publications Division, Govt of India, 2015.

Dharampal, *The Beautiful Tree*, Collected Writings, vol.3, Goa & Mussorie: Other India Press & Society for Integrated Development of Himalayas (SIDH) reprint, 2007.

Dowsett, Norman C., 'The New Approach to Education' in *A New Approach to Education*, Pondicherry: Sri Aurobindo Society, 1974.

Dutt, Paramananda, *Memoirs of Motilal Ghose*, Calcutta: Amrita Bazar Patrika, 1935.

Dutta, Bhupendranath, *Swami Vivekananda: Patriot-Prophet – a study*, Kolkata: Nababharat Publisher, 1954.

Findlay, J.J. edited, *The School and the Child: Being Selections from the Educational Essays of John Dewey*, London: Blackie & Sons Ltd, 1906.

Fraser, Bashabi edited, *The Tagore-Geddes Correspondence*, Kolkata: Visva-Bharati, 2004.

Gaekwad, Fatehsinghrao, *Sayajirao of Baroda: The Prince and the Man*, Bombay: Popular Prakashan, 1989.

Gandhi, Rajmohan, *Patel: A Life*, Ahmedabad: Navajivan Publishing House, 1991.

Ganguly, Anirban & Avadesh Kumar Singh, *Syama Prasad Mookerjee: His Vision of Education*, New Delhi: Dr Syama Prasad Mookerjee Research Foundation & Wisdom Tree, 2017.

Ganguly, Anirban, Alternate Perceptions of India: Arguing for a Counter Narrative, Occasional Paper: New Delhi; Vivekananda International Foundation, May 2013.

——, *Debating Culture*, New Delhi: D.K. Printworld, 2013.

Ghosh, Hemendra Prasad, *Congress O Bangla: Sataborsher Rajnitik Itihas* (Bengali), (Congress and Bengal: a Hundred Years of Political History), Kolkata: Samhati Karyalaya, Date not stated.

Ghosh, Sisir Kumar edited, *Four Indian Critical Essays*, Kolkata: Jijnasa, 1977

Ghosh, Yatindrakumar, *Bengal Provincial Conference 1905 & 1906*, Kolkata: Dey's Publishing, combined edition, 2007.

Gordon, Leonard A., *Bengal: the Nationalist Movement (1876-1940)*, New Delhi: Manohar, (1974), rpt 1979.

Guha, Arun Chandra, compiled & edited, *The Story of Indian Revolution*, Kolkata: Prajnananda Jana Seva Sangh, 1972.

Guha, Ramachandra, *The Independent Journal of Opinion*, Seminar – 481, New Delhi, 1999.

Guha-Thakurta, Tapati, 'Recovering the Nation's Art' in Partha Chatterjee edited. *Texts of Power: Emerging Disciplines in Colonial Bengal*, Minneapolis: University of Minnesota Press, 1995.

Gupta, Nolini Kanta, *Shikkha O Dikkha* (1926) (translated as *Education and Initiation*), Pondicherry: Sri Aurobindo Centre for Advanced Research, 2003.

——, 'The Standpoint of Indian Art' in *Collected Works of Nolini Kanta Gupta* (*CWNKG vol.1*, Kolkata: Nolini Kanta Gupta Birth Centenary edition, 1989.

Havell, E.B., *The Ideals of Indian Art*, London: John Murray, 1920.

——, 'Art and Education in India' (1901) in *Indian Art, Industry an Education*, Madras: G.A. Natesan & Co., 1901.

Heehs, Peter, *Sri Aurobindo: A Brief Biography*, New Delhi: Oxford University Press, 5th impression, 2005.

——, *The Bomb in Bengal*, New Delhi: Oxford University Press, reprint 2004.

Hozumi, Nobushige, *Ancestor Worship & Japanese Law*, Tokyo: Z.P. Maruya & Co. Ltd., 1901.

Iyengar, K.R. Srinivas, *Sri Aurobindo – A Biography & a History*, Pondicherry: Sri Aurobindo International Centre of Education, 5th ed., 2006.

James, H.R., *Education and Statesmanship in India (1797 to 1910)*, London: Longmans, Green & Co., 2nd ed. 1917.

Jordens, J.T.F., *Dayananda Sarasvati: His Life and Ideas*, Delhi: Oxford University Press, 1960.

Joshi, Kireet & Artaud Yvonne, *Exploration in Education – Two Essays*, Auroville, 1974.

Joshi, Kireet, *Education at Crossroads*, New Delhi: The Mother's Institute of Research, 2nd edition, 2007.

K.M. Munshi: His Art & Work, Vol.1: Early Life & Career as Lawyer, (1956) Mumbai: Bharatiya Vidya Bhavan, 2nd ed. 2015.

Keer, Dhananjay, *Dr Babasaheb Ambedkar: Life & Mission*, (1954), Mumbai: Popular Prakashan, 5th edition, 2016.

Keer, Dhananjay, *Lokmanya Tilak – Father of Our Freedom Struggle*, Publisher: V.D. Limaye, Bombay, 1959.

Kelkar, N.C., *Landmarks in Lokmanya's Life*, Madras: S. Ganesan & Co, 1924.

Ker, J.C., *Political Trouble in India: 1907-1917* (1917), Delhi: Oriental Publishers, 1973.

Kopf, David, *British Orientalism and the Bengal Renaissance: the Dynamics of Indian Modernisation: 1773-1835*, Kolkata: Firma K.L. Mukhopadhyay, 1969.

Kumar, Krishna, 'Origins of the Textbook Culture' in *What is Worth Teaching*, New Delhi: Orient Longman, 3rd edition, 2004.

——, 'The Problem' – in '*Neglected Teacher – A Symposium on the Need to Reform Teacher Training & Education*' papers published in Seminar Magazine, no. 592, December, 2008, New Delhi.

——, *Political Agenda of Education – A Study of Colonialist and Nationalist Ideas*, New Delhi: Sage Publications, 2nd edition, 2005.

Lala, Lajpat Rai, *The Problem of National Education in India*, London: Allen & Unwin, 1920.

Lipner, Julius J., *Brahmabandhab Upadhyay: The Life & Thought of a Revolutionary*, New Delhi: Oxford University Press, 1999.

Majumdar, Biman Behari, 'Reaction Against Derozians & Young Bengal' in *Concept of National Education in India*, Kolkata: National Council of Education, Bengal, 1967.

Majumdar, Biman Behari, *History of Indian Social and Political Ideas: From Rammohan to Dayananda,* Kolkata: Firma KLM, (1934), reprint, 1996.

Majumdar, Biman Behari, *Militant Nationalism in India and Socio-Religious Background (1897-1917),* Kolkata: General Printers & Publishers, 1966, p.1.

Majumdar, R.C., *History of the Freedom Movement in India,* Vol.1, Kolkata: Firma K.L. Mukhopadhyay, (1962, 1971) Rpt. 1997.

——, *History of the Freedom Movement* vol.2, Kolkata: Firma KLM Ltd, reprint, 1997.

——, *Glimpses of Bengal in the Nineteenth Century,* Kolkata: Firma K.L. Mukhopadhyay, 1960.

Malaviya, Madan Mohan, *Speeches and Writings,* Madras: G.A. Natesan & Co, 1919.

Mitra, Krishna Kumar, *Atmacharit,* (1937) edited by Supriya Bhattacharya, Kolkata: Patralekha, 2017.

Mitra, Sisir Kumar, *The Liberator: Sri Aurobindo, India & The World,* Bombay: Jaico, 1954.

Mitter, Partha, *Art and Nationalism in Colonial India: 1850-1922,* Cambridge: Cambridge University, 1994.

Mookerjee, Radha Kumud, *Ancient Indian Education,* New Delhi: Motilal Banarsidass, reprint, 1998.

Mookerjee, Syama Prasad, *Sir Asutosh Mookerjee: Creator of the Modern Calcutta University,* Kolkata: Sutradhar, 2021.

——, Debate on the Visva Bharati Bill, 1st May 1951, Parliament of India.

Mukherjee, Dr. Amitabha, *Fifty Years of National Education – The Story of an Experiment 1906-1956,* Kolkata: National Council of Education, Bengal, 1992.

Mukherjee, Haridas and Uma, 'Jatiya Shiksha Andalone Rabindranath' in *Swadeshi Andolone O Banglar Nabajug* [Beng], Kolkata: Dey's Publication, reprint, 2004.

Mukherjee, Haridas and Uma, *Bipin Chandra Pal and India's Struggle for Swaraj,* Kolkata: Dey's Publishing, reprint, 2007.

——, *The Origins of the National Education Movement,* Kolkata: National Council of Education, Bengal, 2nd revised edition, 2000.

——, *Sri Aurobindo and the New Thought in Indian Politics,* Kolkata: Firma K.L.M, 2nd revised edition, 1997.

Mukherjee, Jugal Kishore, *Principles and Goals of Integral Education*, Pondicherry: Sri Aurobindo Ashram, 2005.

Mukherjee, Prithwindra, *The Intellectual Roots of India's Freedom Struggle (1893-1918)*, New Delhi: Manohar, 2017.

——, '*Les Racines Intellectuelles du Mouvement de d'Independence de L'Inde (1893-1918)*, (The Intellectual Origins of the Indian Fight for Freedom – 1893-1918), Paris: Éditions Codex, 2010.

——, *Sadhak Biplabi Jatindranath* [Beng] Kolkata: West Bengal Govt. Book Board, 1990.

Mukherjee, Radhakamal, *India: the Dawn of a New Era*, New Delhi: Radha Publications, 1997.

Mukhopadhyay, Prabhat Kumar, *Rabindra Jibani* [Beng], vol.2, Kolkata: Visva Bharati Publication Dept, 1423 [Beng era].

Mukhopadhyay, S.C. edited, *The Light of the East*, Vol.1 No.1, September 1892, Printed & Published by: L.M. Das.

Munshi, K.M., *Pilgrimage to Freedom*, Vol.1 Mumbai: Bharatiya Vidya Bhavan, (1967), 2nd ed. 2012.

Naik, J.P. & Nurullah Syed, *A Student's History of Education in India-(1800-1973)*, New Delhi: Macmillan, 6th revised 1974.

Narain, S., *Examinations in Ancient India*, Delhi: Arya Book Depot, 1993.

Nevinson, Henry W., *The New Spirit in India*, London & New York: Harper & Brothers, 1908.

Nitobe, Inazo, *Bushido: The Soul of Japan – An Exposition of Japanese Thought*, New York: G.P. Putnam's Sons, 10th revised edition, 1905.

O'Connell, Kathleen M., *Rabindranath Tagore: The Poet as Educator*, Kolkata: Visva-Bharati, 2002.

O'Donnell, J.C., *The Failure of Lord Curzon: A Study in "Imperialism"*, London: T. Fisher Unwin, 1903.

Pal, Bipin Chandra, *Memories of My Life and Times*, Kolkata: Modern Book Agency, 1932.

——, *Indian Nationalism: Its Principles and Personalities*, Madras: S.R. Murthy & Co., 1918.

Palit, R., *Life of Aravind Ghose*, Howrah: self published, 1911.

Pandit, M.P. edited, *Glossary of Sanskrit Terms in Sri Aurobindo's Works*, Pondicherry: Sri Aurobindo Ashram, reprint, 2002.

Pannikar, K.M., *Essays on Education Reconstruction in India*, Madras: Ganesh & Co, 1920.

——, *Indian Nationalism: Its Origin, History and Ideals*, London: The Faith Press, 1920.

Parameswaran, P., *Marx and Vivekananda: a Comparative Study*, (1987), Chennai: Vivekananda Kendra Prakashan Trust, 2007.

Pavitra (P.B. Saint-Hilaire), *Education and the Aim of Human Life*, Pondicherry: Sri Aurobindo Ashram, reprint, 1999.

Purani, A.B., *The Life of Sri Aurobindo*, Pondicherry: Sri Aurobindo Ashram, 5th impression, 2006.

——, *Evening Talks with Sri Aurobindo,* Pondicherry: Sri Aurobindo Society, 2nd imp, 1995.

Rai, Lajpat, *Young India: an Interpretation & a History of the Nationalist Movement from Within*, New York: B.W. Huebsch, 1916.

Rai, Lala Lajpat, The *Arya Samaj: an account of its origin, doctrines and activities, with a biographical sketch of its founder*, London: Longman Greens & Co, 1915.

Rao, Ragunatha C.S. edited, *Notable Speeches of Lord Curzon*, Madras: Arya Press, 1905.

Ray, Dr Prafulla Chandra, *Essays & Discourses*, Madras: G.A. Natesan & Co, 1918.

Raychaudhuri, Tapan, *Europe Reconsidered: Perceptions of the West in Nineteenth Century Bengal*, New Delhi: Oxford University Press, 2nd edition, 2002.

Rishabchand, *Sri Aurobindo: His Life Unique*, Pondicherry: Sri Aurobindo Ashram, 3rd impression, 2007.

Roshan and Apurva, *Sri Aurobindo in Baroda*, Pondicherry: Sri Aurobindo Ashram, 1993.

Roy, Dinendra Kumar, *With Aurobindo in Baroda*, (trans. Maurice Shukla), Pondicherry: Sri Aurobindo Ashram, 2006.

Samanta, Amiya K., *Terrorism in Bengal, vol.1-6,* Kolkata: Government of West Bengal, 1995.

Sanyal, Indrani & Anirban Ganguly edited, *Education: Philosophy & Practice*, Kolkata/New Delhi: Centre for Sri Aurobindo Studies, Jadavpur University & Decent Books, 2011.

Sanyal, Indrani, 'History as Applied Metaphysics' in Indrani Sanyal & Krishna Roy edited, *Sri Aurobindo and His Contemporary Thinkers*,

Kolkata: Centre for Sri Aurobindo Studies, Jadavpur University & D.K. Printworld, 2007.

——, 'What it is to be Educated? In the Light of Sri Aurobindo's Philosophy' in Sanyal Indrani & Roy Krishna edited *Understanding Thoughts of Sri Aurobindo,* Kolkata: Centre for Sri Aurobindo Studies, Jadavpur University, 2007.

Sarkar, Hemchandra edited, Sophia Dobson Collet's *The Life and Letters of Raja Rammohun Roy*, Calcutta, 1914.

Sarkar, Sumit, *The Swadeshi Movement in Bengal (1903-1908),* New Delhi: People's Publishing House, 1973.

Sarkar, Susobhan, 'The National Council of Education' in *On the Bengal Renaissance*, Kolkata: Papyrus, 3rd edition, 2003.

Satabarsher Aloy Syama Prasad (Bengali) (Syamaprasad in the Light of his Centenary), Kolkata: Sristi Prakashan, with Dr Syama Prasad Mookerjee Smarak Samiti, 2002.

Selected Chapters of the Report of the Calcutta University Commission, Calcutta: Superintendent Government Printing, 1919.

Sen, S.P. edited, *Dictionary of National Biography, vols. 1/4,* Calcutta: Institute of Historical Studies, 1972/1974.

Sen, Sukumar, 'Essays and Essay writers (1850-1914)' in *Studies in Bengal Renaissance*, Kolkata: National Council of Education, Bengal, 3rd revised edition, 2002.

Sengupta, Subodh Chandra & Anjali Basu edited, *Samsad Bangali Charitabidhan*, vols. 1 & 2, Kolkata: Sahitya Samsad, 2nd imp. 2002.

Sengupta, Subodh Chandra & Anjali Bose edited, *Samsad Bangali Charitabidhan*, vol.1, 2nd ed. Kolkata: Sahitya Samsad, 2002.

Shannon, Richard, *Gladstone-II: 1865-1898,* California: University of North Carolina Press, 1999.

Singh, Karan, *Prophet of Indian Nationalism: A Study of the Political Thought of Sri Aurobindo Ghosh: 1893-1910*, Bombay: Bharatiya Vidya Bhavan, 3rd edition, 1991.

Sinha, Narendra Krishna, *Asutosh Mookerjee: a Biographical Study*, Calcutta: Asutosh Mookerjee Centenary Committee, 1966.

Sinha, Probodh Chandra, *Sir Asutosh Mookerjee: a Study,* Calcutta: The Book Company, 1928.

Smith, George, *The Life of Alexander Duff*, vol.2, New York: A.C. Armstrong & Sons, 1879.

Speeches and Addresses of His Highness Sayaji Rao III, Maharaja of Baroda, Vol.1 (1877-1910) Cambridge: University Press, 1927.

Stanley, Rice, *Life of Sayaji Rao III, Maharaja of Baroda*, Vol.1, London: Humphrey Milford, 1931.

Swami, Ramakrishnananda, *Role and Responsibility of Teachers in Building up Modern India*, Mumbai: Bharatiya Vidya Bhavan, 2006.

——, *For Thinkers on Education*, Madras: Sri Ramakrishna Math, 1949.

Swarup, Devendra edited, *Deendayal Upadhyaya's Integral Humanism: Documents, Interpretations, Comparisons*, New Delhi: Deendayal Research Institute, 1992.

Syed, Nurullah & J.P. Naik, *History of Education in India: During the British Period*, Bombay: Macmillan & Co, 1943.

The Mother, *Education-Part III: Physical Education*, Pondicherry: Sri Aurobindo Ashram, 2nd impression, 1997.

The Report of the University Education Commission (December 1948 – August 1949), Simla: Govt of India Press, 1949.

Tilak, Bal Gangadhar, *His Writings and Speeches*, Madras: Ganesh & Co., 3rd edition, 1919.

Varma, V.P., *The Political Philosophy of Sri Aurobindo*, Mumbai: Asia Publishing House, 1960.

Williams, Monier, *Indian Wisdom or Examples of the Religious Philosophical & Ethical Doctrines of the Hindus*, Read Books, reprint, 2006.

Woodroffe, John, *The Seed of Race: An Essay in Indian Education*, Madras: Ganesh & Co., 1919.

JOURNALS

Madhabendra Nath Mitra edited reprint of *The Dawn volumes*, Kolkata: Jadavpur University & National Council of Education, Bengal.

Annie Besant, 'The Foundations of Education' in *The Dawn*, September, 1899, vol.3.

The Dawn, January, 1900, vol.3

The Dawn, September 1900, vol.4

The Dawn, January, 1901, vol.4

The Dawn and Dawn Society's Magazine, January 1906, vol.9.

The Dawn and Dawn Society's Magazine, September, 1907, vol.11.

De Abhik Kumar, 'Rabindranath O Charu Chandra Dutt: Kayekti Prasanger Prekhite' [Beng] in *Chaturanga Vol.67 No.1.*

Carey A. Watt, 'Education for National Efficiency: Constructive Nationalism in North India, 1909-1916' in *Modern Asian Studies*, May, 1997, Vol. 31, No. 2 (May, 1997), pp. 339-74, published by Cambridge University Press.

Bengal Provincial Conference at Barisal, 14th & 15th April, 1906 Author(s): K.L. Chattopadhyay Source: *Proceedings of the Indian History Congress*, 1979, Vol. 40 (1979), pp. 581-586

The Modern Review, January, 1908, vol.III, No.1

Sumitra Gupta, 'The Arya Samaj and Indian National Movement', in *Proceedings of the Indian History Congress*, 2002, Vol. 63 (2002), pp. 722-32, published by Indian History Congress.

OTHERS

Kamat, A.R., *PROSPECTS: the quarterly review of education*, vol. XXIV, no.1/2, 1994, page 203-16, UNESCO, International Bureau of Education, Paris.

Position Paper 3.7. National Focus Group on Work and Education, National Council for Education Research and Training (NCERT), New Delhi, 2007.

Position Paper, National Focus Group on Health and Physical Education, National Council of Education Research and Training (NCERT), New Delhi, 2006

ARCHIVAL SOURCES

New India Files, Microfilm Copies, National Library of India, Kolkata.

Report of the Indian Universities Commission, Simla: Government Central Printing Press, 1902.

Sri Aurobindo Archives and Research, vol.3, no.1, April 1979, Pondicherry: Sri Aurobindo Ashram Trust, 1979.

Sri Aurobindo Archives and Research, vol.14, no.1, April 1990, Pondicherry: Sri Aurobindo Ashram Trust, 1990.

Complete Works of Sri Aurobindo (*CWSA*)

CWSA vol.1, Early Cultural Writings, Pondicherry: Sri Aurobindo Ashram, 2003.

CWSA vol.6, Bande Mataram – I, Pondicherry: Sri Aurobindo Ashram, 2002.

CWSA vol.7, Bande Mataram – II, Pondicherry: Sri Aurobindo Ashram, 2002.

CWSA, vol.8, Karmayogin, Pondicherry: Sri Aurobindo Ashram, 1997.

Collected Works of The Mother (CWM)

Collected Works of the Mother (CWM) vol. 12, Centenary Edition, Pondicherry: Sri Aurobindo Ashram, 1978.

Index

"

We recognise no political object of worship except the divinity in our Motherland, no present object of political endeavour except liberty, and no method of action as politically good or evil except as it truly helps or hinders our progress towards national emancipation.

– **The Doctrine of Passive Resistance, *Bande Mataram*, 1907**